2011

D0558652

Mozambique

Mary Fitzpatrick

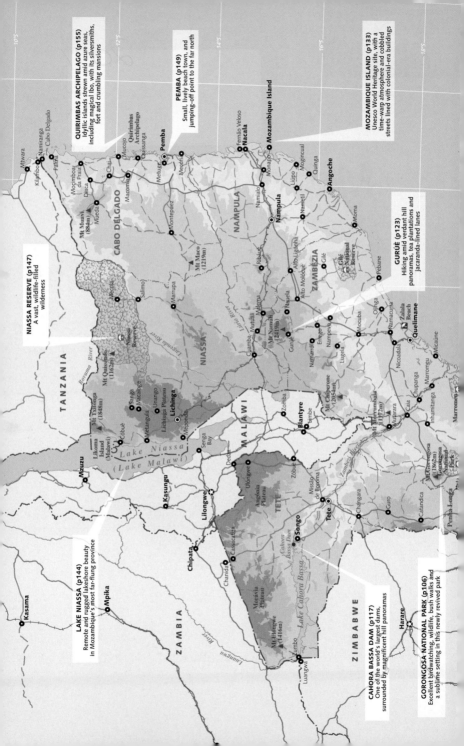

QUIRIMBAS ARCHIPELAGO (p155)
Idyllic islands strewn amid azure seas, including magical Ibo, with its silversmiths, fort and crumbling mansions

PEMBA (p149)
Small, lively beach town, and jumping-off point to the far north

MOZAMBIQUE ISLAND (p133)
Unesco World Heritage site, with a time-warp atmosphere and cobbled streets lined with colonial-era buildings

NIASSA RESERVE (p147)
A vast, wildlife-filled wilderness

GURUÉ (p123)
Hiking amid verdant hill panoramas, tea plantations and jacaranda-lined lanes

LAKE NIASSA (p144)
Remote and rugged lakeshore beauty in Mozambique's most far-flung province

CAHORA BASSA DAM (p117)
One of the world's largest dams, surrounded by magnificent hill panoramas

GORONGOSA NATIONAL PARK (p106)
Excellent birdwatching, wildlife, bush walks and a sublime setting in this newly revived park

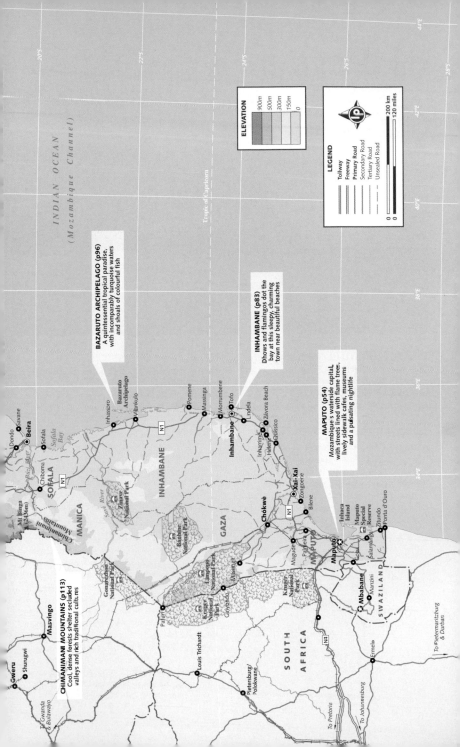

BAZARUTO ARCHIPELAGO (p96)
A quintessential tropical paradise, with incomparably turquoise waters and shoals of colourful fish

INHAMBANE (p83)
Dhows and flamingos dot the bay at this sleepy, charming town near beautiful beaches

MAPUTO (p54)
Mozambique's waterside capital, with streets lined with flame trees, lively sidewalk cafes, museums and a pulsating nightlife

CHIMANIMANI MOUNTAINS (p113)
Cool, dense forests shelter secluded valleys and rich traditional cultures

INDIAN OCEAN
(Mozambique Channel)

ELEVATION
900m
500m
300m
150m
0

LEGEND
Tollway
Freeway
Primary Road
Secondary Road
Tertiary Road
Unsealed Road

200 km
120 miles

Tropic of Capricorn

Beira
Dondo
Savane
Chiboma
Sofala
Sofala Bay
Búzi River
Mt Binga (2436m)
Chimanimani Mountains
Manica
MANICA
Gweru
Shurugwi
Masvingo
To Gwanda & Bulawayo

Inhassoro
Bazaruto Archipelago
Vilankulo
Pomene
Massinga
Morrumbene
Tofo
Inhambane
Indela
Závora Beach
Inharrime
Quissico
Helene

SOFALA
N1
Save River
Zinave National Park

INHAMBANE
Banhine National Park
Mapinhane

GAZA
Massingir
Gilé
Gigingire

Gonarezhou National Park
Limpopo National Park
Kruger National Park
Pafúri
Massingir
Giyani

Xai-Xai
Zongoene
Chókwè
Bilene

MAPUTO
N1
Magude
Padilela
Maguda

Maputo
Inhaca Island
Maputo Special Reserve
Catembe
Salamanga
Ponta d'Ouro
Ntundo

SOUTH AFRICA
Louis Trichardt
Pietersburg/ Polokwane
Mbabane
Manzini
SWAZILAND
Ermelo
N4
To Pretoria
To Johannesburg
To Pietermaritzburg & Durban

On the Road

MARY FITZPATRICK Coordinating Author

This photo was taken on the shores of Lake Niassa (p144), Mozambique's 'other' coastline. Getting there is half the fun, involving either a boat ride or an adventurous overland journey. It's the type of place where it's easy to stay for days, surrounded by the rhythms of traditional life, and mesmerised by star-filled night skies and waves lapping softly on the shoreline.

MY FAVOURITE TRIP

I'd start out with as much time as possible in northern Cabo Delgado province (p152) between Pemba and Palma, especially island hopping in the Quirimbas Archipelago (p155) and time on Ibo Island (p156). Niassa province would be next on the list, exploring the Lake Niassa coastline (p144) and visiting the Niassa Reserve (p147).

Heading southwards, essential stops would include Mozambique Island (p133), the islands near Angoche (p131), lovely Gorongosa National Park (p106), Pomene (p92), charming Inhambane (p83), the long beaches around Chidenguele (p82) and windswept Ponta Malongane (p75), before finishing up in and around Maputo (p54).

ABOUT THE AUTHOR

Mary is from the USA, where she spent her early years in Washington, DC, dreaming, more often than not, of how to get across an ocean or two to more exotic locales. After finishing graduate studies, she set off for several years in Europe. Her fascination with languages and cultures soon led her further south to Africa, where she has spent much of the past two decades living and working all around the continent, including almost four years in Mozambique. She has authored and co-authored numerous other guidebooks to various African destinations, and heads off to Mozambique's beaches at every opportunity.

Mozambique Highlights

Magical, mysterious, sublime, seductive... Mozambique beckons with its beaches and swaying palms, its traditions and its cultures, and offers travellers a wealth of choices. In this enigmatic southeast African country you'll find long, deserted stretches of soft, white sand; azure waters with abundant fish and corals; graceful dhows with billowing white sails; remote archipelagos and luxurious island getaways; moss-covered ruins; colonial-style architecture; pulsating nightlife; vast tracts of remote bush populated with elephants, lions and birds galore; and an endlessly fascinating cultural mix. Bring along some patience and a sense of adventure and jump in for the journey of a lifetime.

MATT FLETCHER

❶ IBO ISLAND

We arrived on sleepy, sunbaked Ibo Island (p156) on a holiday, and were treated to a morning of dancing and singing under the shade of a huge, spreading mango tree. Afterwards, a young boy led us through the sandy lanes to a tiny house with a hand painted 'café' sign tacked outside. Inside were a group of laughing women who offered us plates of piping hot rice and sauce.

Mary Fitzpatrick

MOZAMBIQUE ISLAND

There are no crowds and few vehicles, but Mozambique Island (p133) is hardly silent. Echoes of its past mix with the squawking of chickens, the sound of children playing and the call of the muezzin to remind you that the island is still very much alive.

Mary Fitzpatrick

2

NAMPULA–CUAMBA TRAIN RIDE

The Nampula train station was a hive of activity in the predawn darkness. By the time the sky began to lighten, the conductor was insistently sounding the whistle, and at 5.15am we rolled off into the lush surrounding countryside. One stop melted into the next – each with its own personality, and each with plenty of bustle, as vendors hawked their wares on long sticks held up to the train windows. When we arrived in Cuamba 12 hours later, the nearby mountains were bathed in the light of the setting sun.

Mary Fitzpatrick

3

4

DHOW TRIP ACROSS INHAMBANE BAY

The Arabic boat was old, chapped, worn out like its captain. A man and his boat, their stories etched in the faded wood. As I embarked the dhow, I was surprised at how hot the water in the bay was. No relief from the scorching sun here! The dhow had holes where water leaked in, but not so fast that the rest of the young crew couldn't send it back over in their plastic tubs. Wind was scarce. We spent a while trying to get across Inhambane Bay – the route was not direct, but who cares? Life goes slow in Mozambique and you learn to appreciate it. Finally, in Maxixe the icy Laurentinas went down well and after a bit of shopping we headed back to our leaky dhow and our charming old captain with the toothless smile.

Meruschka Govender, Traveller, South Africa

MAPUTO NIGHTLIFE

Maputo's heart begins to beat in the early evening. Start with a meal of *piri-piri* chicken, followed by a few caipirinhas on the waterfront, the breeze of the Indian Ocean so beautiful and calm. At around 10pm or 11pm, the amazing local music venues start to pulsate with life. Everyone is welcome, young and old, a collage of cultures, and all are jammed inside dancing and heaving with the joy of being alive.

Robin Mason, Traveller, Maputo, Mozambique

ARIADNE VAN ZANDBERGEN

5

6 MAPUTO

One of my favourite ways to spend a Saturday afternoon in Maputo (p54) is down at Costa do Sol, either sitting on the terrace at Restaurante Costa do Sol (p66), or stopping by at the fish market, negotiating with the vendors and then waiting at one of the small tables watching the passing scene while my shrimp are grilled and seasoned to perfection.

OLIVER STREWE

Mary Fitzpatrick

TOM COC.

7 BUS TRAVEL

There's something strangely addictive about getting up in the 3am darkness to catch a 4am bus departure, with the slight hint of adventure as you rattle down the empty road in the still-cool air, watching the day break over the countryside. It's easy to think that if all goes well, you might just be at your destination by noon – easy to think, at least until the first breakdown.

Mary Fitzpatrick

TOFO

Tofo (p87) is a little gem tucked away along the seemingly endless Mozambican coastline. In the same day you can walk down to the artsy little enclave of Tofinho (p88), do yoga at the Turtle Cove surf camp (p88), snorkel with whale sharks, dive with humpbacks and select from wonderful cuisine options, including fantastic salads – a vegetarian's heaven! Finish the day off with a great Brazilian jazz band up on the bluff before strolling back to your bungalow under a full moon.

Riley & Pamela Ganz, Travellers, Zambézia province, Mozambique

ROBBERT KOEN

8

TIM ROCK

9
WHALE SHARK SNORKELLING IN VILANKULO

Sliding off the boat into the warm water you suddenly find yourself face to face with the most massive creature you have *ever* seen. Your only thought looking into that gigantic mouth, aiming straight for you: 'Oh my god!' Beautiful, wondrous and amazing.

Traveller, Canada

ALEX BRAMWEL

10 ## BAZARUTO ARCHIPELAGO

Play pirates through the clear waters of the Bazaruto Archipelago (p96) on a dhow. You can do a day trip and have a seafood feast on Magaruque Island (p98) in between snorkelling among the most beautiful sea life while drifting along with the gentle tidal current. You can easily walk around the island and have a wild time running down the vast sand dunes that make up the island. When the tide is low and you're back on dry land, just look out and see the sand and pools of water going on for ever. You may also see a mermaid if you are very lucky – otherwise known as a dugong!

Edwina Jessel, Traveller

Contents

Getting Started

Unless you have plenty of time, Mozambique is too large a country to cover in one visit, so it's worth giving some advance thought as to which areas you'd most like to include in your itinerary. Very roughly summarised: the south is optimal for a relatively easy beach holiday, while the centre and the north are ideal destinations for adventure travel or for pampered island and bush getaways.

In major cities and coastal tourist areas, all budgets and travel styles are catered for. Here you'll find a decent selection of sleeping and eating options, and good flight and bus connections. In much of the interior and in the far north, travel is more rugged. At the budget level, plan on at least several long bus rides. For top-end travel, charter flights are readily arranged.

WHEN TO GO

See Climate Charts (p169) for more information

Mozambique is best visited during the cooler dry season from May to October/November, although travel is enjoyable at any time of year. In the early part of the rainy season (November to January), temperatures are warmer. At the height of the rainy season during February and March – which is also the travel low season – be prepared for washed-out roads in more remote areas, and flooding in parts of the south and centre.

Apart from weather, another consideration – primarily in the south – is South African school-holiday period. During the travel high season – Christmas–New Year holidays, around Easter and again in August – the southern coastal resorts fill up with holidaying South Africans, and advance bookings are recommended.

COSTS & MONEY

Mozambique has a well-deserved reputation for being expensive in comparison with its neighbours. Accommodation and internal flights will be your highest-cost items; fruit, produce and seafood bought at local markets, together with local road transport, are among the least costly items.

DON'T LEAVE HOME WITHOUT...

You can get most things you'll need in Maputo and other major cities, except for specialised camping and sporting equipment, and certain toiletries (eg contact lens solution). Some essentials to bring from home:

- mosquito repellent, net and prophylaxes
- torch (flashlight)
- shore-shoes for beach walking
- sunscreen and sunglasses
- travel alarm (to help you wake up in time to catch those early morning buses)
- Visa card for accessing cash at ATMs
- sturdy water bottle
- travel insurance, including cover for medical air evacuation to Johannesburg
- Portuguese phrasebook
- jerry cans for carrying extra fuel (if driving)
- passport and a notarised copy of front and visa pages

COST-CUTTING TIPS

Some tips for saving money, whatever your budget:

- Focus on one area of the country to minimise long-haul transportation costs
- Use public transport
- Eat local food
- Always ask about children's, midweek and low-season discounts
- Keep your schedule flexible to take advantage of last-minute deals
- Avoid peak-season travel (eg Christmas and New Year, Easter), when prices are highest
- Watch for flight/accommodation packages from Johannesburg, especially for the southern resorts and Pemba, and for special-offer fares on Linhas Aéreas de Moçambique

---

For accommodation, especially at the budget and midrange levels, you'll need to hunt for value for money (and you should expect to pay more than in South Africa), although there are an increasing number of places catering to backpackers in the south and the far north, as well as a good network of midrange options. Staying in basic lodging, eating local food and travelling with public transport will cost from US$30 per day.

Midrange travel with some comforts will cost between US$50 and US$150 per day, excluding airfares. At the top end, plan on between US$150 and US$500 (or more) per day at some of the exclusive island lodges, excluding hire cars and flights.

TRAVELLING RESPONSIBLY

Tourism is rapidly increasing in Mozambique, and making environmentally and culturally sensitive choices can have a significant impact. This is especially true along the coast, where quad biking and beach driving often go unchecked. For some guidelines, see p46. Also check out the GreenDex (p215) for community oriented and environmentally friendly organisations.

ResponsibleTravel.com (www.responsibletravel.com) has several volunteer holiday opportunities in Mozambique.

TRAVEL LITERATURE

Kalashnikovs and Zombie Cucumbers: Travels in Mozambique (1995) by Nick Middleton – part travelogue and part historical overview – is a highly entertaining read, covering everything from colonial times and the war, to aid and development.

With Both Hands Waving: A Journey Through Mozambique (2003) by Justin Fox is another insightful and often humorous look at Mozambique in the early 1990s.

Lisa St Aubin de Terán's *Mozambique Mysteries* (2007) is as much about the author as it is about Mozambique, but it offers insight into a little-visited corner of the country.

Empires of the Monsoon (1998) by Richard Seymour Hall is a scholarly yet easy-to-read book, which covers a broad historical and geographical sweep, including Mozambique, and gives an excellent overview of the influences shaping coastal cultures.

A Complicated War: The Harrowing of Mozambique (1993) by William Finnegan examines the roots of Mozambique's civil war through a series of vivid close-ups on various areas of the country, and is essential reading for anyone interested in gaining a deeper understanding of the country's post-colonial era.

HOW MUCH?

Plate of grilled prawns Mtc300

Single dive (day) US$50

Short taxi ride Mtc100

Dhow safari (day) Mtc1500

Maputo–Inhambane bus fare Mtc350

TOP 10

THINGS TO DO IN MOZAMBIQUE

...If You Have Plenty of Money

1 Treat yourself to several days in the Bazaruto Archipelago (p96)

2 Enjoy your own tropical paradise at one of the private island getaways in the Quirimbas Archipelago (p53)

3 Base yourself at Nkwichi Lodge on the shores of Lake Niassa (p144) and explore the surrounding Mozambican bush

4 Do a multinight walking safari in Gorongosa National Park (p106)

5 Visit the Niassa Reserve (p147)

...If You're on a Shoestring Budget

6 Sail on a dhow around the Quirimbas Archipelago (p157)

7 Visit Mozambique Island (p133) – also add this to the list if you have plenty of money

8 Spend a week chilling out at Tofo Beach (p87), a long arc of white sand near Inhambane

9 Take the train between Cuamba and Nampula (p141), and enjoy the passing glimpses of rural life

10 Go sailing and snorkelling around the islands of the Bazaruto Archipelago (p93)

MOZAMBICAN MUSIC

For an introduction to Mozambique's music scene, dip into some of the following:

1 *Bumping* – Massukos

2 *Karimbo* – Mabulu

3 *King Marracuene* – Fany Mpfumo

4 *Timbila Ta Venáncio* – Venáncio Mbande

5 *Vana Va Ndota* – Ghorwane

6 *Timbila* – Eduardo Durão

7 *Katchume* – Kapa Dêch

8 *Dilon* – Dilon Djindji

9 *Afrikiti* – Stewart Sukuma

10 *Automy Dzi Txintxile* – Léman

CULTURAL EXPERIENCES

Whatever your budget, there's nothing better than immersion for getting to know local life. Give the following a try:

1 Spend an early morning or late afternoon sitting at a dhow port, watching the boats arrive with their catch

2 Watch *mapiko* dancing (p160)

3 Listen to church singing

4 Browse a small-town market

5 Sail in a dhow (p167)

6 Share a plate of *xima* or *matapa* with locals

7 Watch the sun rise over the Indian Ocean

8 Walk around Mozambique Island (p133) or Ibo Island (p156) at dawn

9 Spend an afternoon in a small village without a camera

10 Observe Makonde woodcarvers at work in the villages around Mueda (p161)

Peter Stark's *At the Mercy of the River* (2005) is an adventurous read before visiting the Niassa Reserve.

Although not travel literature as such, any of the novels of Mia Couto, Mozambique's foremost author, make an excellent introduction to the country. Two to start with are *The Last Flight of the Flamingo* (2004) and *Sleepwalking Land* (2006).

INTERNET RESOURCES

African Studies Centre Mozambique Page (www.africa.upenn.edu) Follow the 'Countries' link.

Club of Mozambique (www.clubofmozambique.com) A Mozambique business portal with free tourism-related newsletters, events listings and more.

Images du Mozambique (www.imagesdumozambique.com) Check the 'Gallery' section of this site when planning your trip for a preview of what to expect.

Lonely Planet (www.lonelyplanet.com) Travel tips, the Thorn Tree bulletin board and other links.

Mozambique Guide (www.mozguide.com) Helpful if you'll be visiting Mozambique with your own vehicle, with a chat site and information on routes and road conditions.

Moçambique (www.visitmozambique.net) The Ministry of Tourism's official site.

Mozambique News Agency (www.poptel.org.uk/mozambique-news/) Mozambique news in English.

Itineraries
CLASSIC ROUTES

THE SOUTHERN COAST
10 to 14 days / Maputo to Vilankulo

For an introduction to Mozambique's wonderful beaches, spend a few days in **Maputo** (p54) getting oriented. Take the bus north to **Inhambane** (p83), with its flamingos and dhows, before heading to the beaches at **Tofo** (p87) or **Barra** (p89). Divers should add two or three extra days to the itinerary (more for a certification course). Continue north to **Vilankulo** (p92) for snorkelling or a dhow safari around the **Bazaruto Archipelago** (p96) before returning to Maputo by bus, or flying from Vilankulo directly out to Johannesburg.

Recommended detours along the way include **Inhaca Island** (p71) and the **Maputo Special Reserve** (p78) – allow two to three extra nights from Maputo for either – or one of the beaches around **Xai-Xai** (p82).

If driving (4WD), consider entering Mozambique through South Africa's Kruger National Park and **Limpopo National Park** (p80) en route to the coast. Alternatively, travel via the Kosi Bay border crossing with time at **Ponta d'Ouro** (p75) and **Ponta Malongane** (p75). Another possible coastal stop for self-drivers is **Pomene** (p92), with its beautiful beach and estuary.

This 1000km journey combines Maputo with some of Mozambique's best beaches in an easy route that can be done by driving, flying or a bit of both in an air–road circuit in/out of Johannesburg. It's also easy to do in reverse, from north to south.

ROADS LESS TRAVELLED

GRAND TOUR   Two to three months / Maputo to Pemba

Except for the southern beaches, most of Mozambique is a 'road less travelled'. For a grand overland tour, start in the south, following the itinerary outlined under the Southern Coast (opposite), with stops in Maputo, Inhambane, Tofo or Barra, Vilankulo and the Bazaruto Archipelago. From Vilankulo, continue by bus north to **Beira** (p102), with a day or two in this old port city before detouring inland for a couple of nights in **Gorongosa National Park** (p106) followed by a visit to the **Chimanimani Mountains** (p113).

The overland route continues north via **Quelimane** (p119) and **Nampula** (p127) to **Mozambique Island** (p133), where it's easy to spend two or three days taking in the sights. Possible detours include **Gurúè** (p123) for some walking, or **Nacala** (p139) for relaxing and diving. Continue northwards by bus to **Pemba** (p149). Spend a few days enjoying this sunny, low-key beach town and the surrounding area before heading to the **Quirimbas Archipelago** (p155). **Pangane** (p160) is the next stop – it can be reached by road, after returning to Pemba, or by dhow from the Quirimbas Archipelago. Then it's on to **Moçimboa da Praia** (p162) and then over the Rovuma River into Tanzania. Alternative routes include returning from the Quirimbas Archipelago to Pemba, and flying directly to Maputo or South Africa from there, or taking the **Nampula–Cuamba train** (p141) west from Nampula (after visiting Mozambique Island) through to **Cuamba** (p140) and then continuing on to **Lichinga** (p142), **Lake Niassa** (p144) and into Malawi, or – from Lichinga – north into Tanzania.

Allow as much time as possible for this 3700km-long adventure along the coast, including inland detours. It's possible to use public transport (perhaps with a flight or two to break up the longer stretches) or as self-drive, and is just as good done from north to south.

TAILORED TRIPS

'BEST OF MOZAMBIQUE' SAMPLER

Mozambique's highlights are its beaches and islands, its people and cultures, and the adventure of it all. Here's a small sampling of some of the best the country has to offer in each area. For beaches and islands, there are too many to name all of them, but among the highlights are **Ponta d'Ouro** (p75), **Tofo** (p87), **Chidenguele** (p82), **Pomene** (p92), the **Bazaruto Archipelago** (p96), **Angoche** (p131) and the **Quirimbas Archipelago** (p155). The two archipelagos, together with **Mozambique Island** (p133) – a Unesco World Heritage site – easily crown the list of island getaways.

Cultural highlights include **tufo dancing** (p33) on Mozambique Island, masked **mapiko dancing** (p160) in the far north, **Chopi timbila orchestras** (p83) around Quissico and a sampling of Maputo's **art museums** (p61) and its **nightlife** (p68). For pure adventure, it's hard to beat Cabo Delgado and Niassa provinces, especially the coastal stretch from **Pangane** (p160) north to the Rovuma River; the **Niassa Reserve** (p147); and the beautiful **Lake Niassa** (p144) shoreline between Cóbuè and Metangula. All are ideal destinations for getting an authentic taste of the African bush.

INLAND IDYLLS

Many of Mozambique's attractions are along the coast, but there are some inland gems as well. If you're after greenery and something offbeat, don't miss the **Chimanimani Mountains** (p113), with cool forests, hiking and community-based tourism. The wilderness, birds and animals at **Gorongosa National Park** (p106) are another highlight for nature lovers, and both vehicle and walking safaris are possible.

For anglers, or anyone after something different, a few days at **Lake Cahora Bassa** (p117) makes a lovely respite, with attractive hill scenery, a cool, refreshing climate and the massive dam. **Gurúè** (p123), with its tea plantations, and the sacred **Mt Namúli** (p124) nearby, is another worthwhile stop.

Limpopo National Park (p80) is a convenient place to visit if you're arriving with your own vehicle from South Africa, and anyone interested in birdwatching should consider the area south and east of **Caia** (p118), perhaps with a detour to **Mt Gorongosa** (p107) en route.

The train ride between **Nampula** (p127) and **Cuamba** (p140) is one of southern Africa's classic journeys, cutting through striking, inselberg-studded landscapes and past remote villages, and offers a great slice of Mozambican life. At the top of the list of inland idylls are **Lake Niassa** (p144), with its unspoiled coastline and crystal clear waters, and the wild and remote **Niassa Reserve** (p147).

History

From Bantu-speaking farmers and fishers to Arabic traders, Goan merchants and adventuring Europeans, Mozambique has long been a crossroads of cultures.

IN THE BEGINNING

The first people to see Mozambique's Indian Ocean sunrises were small, scattered clans of nomads who were likely trekking through the bush as early as 10,000 years ago. They may have been distant cousins of the San – skilled hunter-gatherers who left rock paintings throughout southern Africa and who still live in the region today. However, Mozambique's early nomads left few traces and little is known about this era.

The real story begins about 3000 years ago, when Bantu-speaking peoples from the faraway Niger Delta in West Africa began moving through the Congo basin in one of the greatest population migrations on the African continent. Over a period of centuries they journeyed into East and southern Africa, reaching present-day Mozambique sometime around the 1st century AD, where they made their living farming, fishing and raising livestock.

See www.pbs.org/wgbh /evolution/humans /humankind/d.html for an overview of human evolution in southern Africa.

EARLY KINGDOMS

Most of these early Mozambicans set themselves up in small chiefdoms, some of which gradually coalesced into larger states or kingdoms. In central Mozambique, the most organised of these states were those of the Karanga (Shona), who by the 11th century AD were grouped into a loose confederation with its centre at Great Zimbabwe, in present-day Zimbabwe. Sometime around 1450, Great Zimbabwe was mysteriously abandoned. However, the related Manyikeni chieftaincy (located inland from Vilankulo) prospered as a trading centre until the 17th century (you can visit the remains, see p81). Other Karanga kingdoms – most notably Manica, along the current Mozambique–Zimbabwe border – continued to thrive as late as the 19th century.

At about the same time that Great Zimbabwe began to decline, the renowned kingdom of Monomotapa emerged. This kingdom, named after the *mwene mutapa* (the title of the ruler), was based south and west of present-day Tete. From this pivotal point it controlled the lucrative gold trade between the Zambezi and Save Rivers. It was the tales of these legendary goldfields that first attracted European interest in Mozambique. However – perhaps ironically – both the goldfields and Monomotapa's kingdom were smaller and less cohesive in reality than the Europeans believed.

TIMELINE

c 100 AD	9th century	late 15th century
The first Bantu-speakers begin arriving in present-day Mozambique, part of a series of great population migrations that shape the face of southern and East Africa as it is today.	The trading settlement of Sofala is established along the coast. By the 15th century it has become one of East Africa's most influential centres, with ties to Madagascar, India and beyond.	Tales of the kingdom of Monomotapa and its legendary goldfields pique European interest in Mozambique. Ironically, both the goldfields and Monomotapa's kingdom are smaller than the Europeans believed.

MOZAMBIQUE

No one is quite sure where the name Mozambique (Moçambique in Portuguese) originated. According to some sources it's derived from the name and title of the sultan on Mozambique Island when the Portuguese arrived there in the late 15th century – Musa Mbiki (Musa bin Mbiki), or possibly Musa Malik.

In northern Mozambique, one of the most powerful groups was the Maravi (also known as the Malâwi), who exercised dominion over a large area extending from the Zambezi River into what is now southern Malawi and Zambia. Maravi rule was based on control of the ivory trade. At the height of its power in the late 17th century AD, it reached as far as Mogincual and Angoche on the coast, although the kingdom was plagued by weak central structure and infighting. In the far north, near Lake Niassa and in present-day Niassa province, were various Yao chiefdoms. Their power gradually increased, until by the 17th and 18th centuries Yao commercial networks extended across Mozambique to the Indian Ocean, where they were the main trading partners with Arab ivory and slave merchants. Yet, like the Maravi, the Yao remained only loosely organised and decentralised.

In the northeast, in what are now Nampula and Zambézia provinces, were groupings of Makua-Lomwe peoples. Their largest political unit was the village, although some loosely confederated chiefdoms began to form around the 16th century.

Southern Mozambique, which was settled by the Nguni and various other groups, remained decentralised until the 19th century when consolidation under the powerful kingdom of Gaza gave it at least nominal political cohesion.

Malyn Newitt's *A History of Mozambique* (1995) is a detailed analysis of Mozambican history from about 1500, and the definitive work on the country.

THE ARRIVAL OF THE ARABS

From around the 8th century AD sailors from Arabia began to arrive along the East African coast. Trade flourished and intermarriage with the indigenous Bantu-speakers gave birth to the Swahili language and culture. By the 9th century several settlements had been established – most notably Kilwa island, in present-day Tanzania, which soon became the hub of Arab trade networks throughout southeastern Africa.

Along the Mozambican coast, the most important trading post was at Sofala (p108), near present-day Beira, which by the 15th century was the main link connecting Kilwa with the old Shona kingdoms and the inland goldfields. Other early coastal ports and settlements included those at Mozambique Island, Angoche, Quelimane and Ibo Island, all ruled by local sultans. Today the traces of this long history of eastward trade, carried out

1498	early 16th century	17th century
Vasco da Gama lands on Mozambique Island. A Portuguese settlement is soon established, and the island becomes the capital of Portuguese East Africa.	The coastal settlement of Angoche enjoys a period of trading prominence as a counterweight to the Portuguese monopoly of the Sofala gold trade.	The Portuguese divide large areas of central Mozambique into *prazos* (vast agricultural estates). Before long, some are effectively functioning as independent feudal states.

over the centuries on the winds of the monsoon, are still evident in the rich cultural melange found in Mozambique's coastal towns.

PORTUGUESE ADVENTURERS

In 1498 Vasco da Gama landed at Mozambique Island en route to India. It is likely that another Portuguese explorer, the intrepid Pêro da Covilhã, had reached Sofala even earlier via an overland route, disguised as a Muslim merchant. Within a decade after da Gama's arrival, the Portuguese had established themselves on the island and gained control of numerous other Swahili-Arab trading posts – lured in part by their need for supply points on the sea route to the east and in part by their desire to control the gold trade with the interior.

Over the next 200 years the Portuguese busily set up trading enclaves and forts along the coast, making Mozambique Island the capital of what they called Portuguese East Africa. By the mid-16th century, ivory had replaced gold as the main trading commodity and by the late 18th century, slaves had been added to the list, with close to one million Africans sold into slavery through Mozambique's ports.

The first major journey inland was made around 1511 by António Fernandes, who got as far as the kingdom of Monomotapa and returned with extensive information about river routes and trade conditions in the interior. Following Fernandes' trip, several other expeditions went inland. By the 1530s the Portuguese had occupied settlements that had been established earlier by Arab traders in the Zambezi River Valley at Tete and Sena, and over the next century they became increasingly involved at the *feiras* (trading fairs), although the coast continued to be the focus of activity. Yet, both on the coast and inland, there was little cohesion to the Portuguese ventures, and their influence in Mozambique remained weak and fragmented.

PORTUGAL'S POWER STRUGGLE

In the 17th century the Portuguese attempted to strengthen their control by setting up *prazos* (vast agricultural estates) on land granted by the Portuguese crown or by wresting control of it from local chiefs. This, however, did little more than consolidate power in the hands of individual *prazeiros* (holders of the land grants).

The next major effort by the Portuguese to consolidate their control came in the late 19th century with the establishment of charter companies, operated by private firms who were supposed to develop the land and natural resources within their boundaries. Major companies included the Zambezia Company (with a concession in present-day Tete and Zambézia provinces); the Mozambique Company (in Manica and Sofala provinces, and also under British control); and the Niassa Company (in present-day Cabo Delgado and Niassa provinces). In reality these charter companies

Pounders of Grain – A History of Women, Work & Politics in Mozambique (2002) by Kathleen Sheldon offers insightful portrayals of the role of women in Mozambican history and society.

1791	1850s	1898
The star-shaped Fort of São João is built on Ibo Island. It becomes notorious for its dark, cramped holding cells and its role in the slave trade.	The kingdom of Gaza reaches its height under Soshangane. Its influence stretches from south of the Limpopo River, north to the Zambezi and west into present-day Zimbabwe, Swaziland and South Africa.	The government of Portuguese East Africa is transferred from Mozambique Island to Lourenço Marques (now Maputo).

operated as independent fiefdoms, and did little to consolidate Portuguese control. They were also economic failures (only the Zambezia Company was profitable), and soon became notorious for labour abuses and for the cruel and appalling conditions under which the local populations within their boundaries were forced to live.

With the onset of the 'Scramble for Africa' in the 1880s, Portugal faced growing competition from Britain and the other colonial powers and was forced to strengthen its claims in the region. In 1891 a British-Portuguese treaty was signed, which set the boundaries of Portuguese East Africa and formalised Portuguese control in the area. Despite this, the country continued without cohesion. The Portuguese were only able to directly administer the area south of the Save River (which had attained some degree of political unity under the rulers of the Gaza kingdom) and Mozambique Island. The rest of the centre and north remained under the control of *prazeiros*.

THE EARLY 20TH CENTURY

One of the most significant events in early-20th-century Mozambique was the large-scale labour migration from the southern provinces to South Africa and Rhodesia (present-day Zimbabwe). This exodus was spurred by expansion of the Witwatersrand goldmines, and by passage of a new labour law in 1899 which formally divided the Mozambican population into non-indigenous (*não indígenas* or *assimilados*), who had full Portuguese citizenship rights, and indigenous (*indígenas*), who were subject to the provisions of colonial law and forced to work, to pay a poll tax and to adhere to passed laws. For an African to acquire non-indigenous status, it was necessary to demonstrate Portuguese 'culture' and a certain level of education. For indigenous Mozambicans who were unable to get employment on European-run plantations in their home regions, the options were limited to accepting six months of annual labour at minimal pay on public works projects, leaving Mozambique to seek a better life in the surrounding colonies or accepting employment as a contract labourer in South Africa.

Every Man is a Race (1994) by Mia Couto is a literary look at the legacies of colonialism and war in Mozambique, told through a series of personal profiles.

The other major development defining early-20th-century Mozambique was the growing economic importance of the southern part of the country. As ties with South Africa strengthened, Lourenço Marques (as Maputo was then known) took on increasing importance as a major port and export channel and in the late 19th century the Portuguese transferred the capital here from Mozambique Island.

In the late 1920s António Salazar came to power in Portugal. To maximise the benefits that Portugal could realise from its colonies, he sealed them off from non-Portuguese investment, terminated the leases of the

early 20th century	**1962**	**1964**
A large-scale labour migration begins from southern Mozambique to South Africa, spurred by expansion of the Witwatersrand goldmines. The impact of this ongoing labour migration pattern is still evident.	On 25 June the Mozambican Liberation Front (Frelimo) is founded in Dar es Salaam, Tanzania, under the leadership of the charismatic Eduardo Mondlane.	Frelimo's military campaign against colonial rule is launched in the northern village of Chai on 25 September. Eduardo Mondlane declares the beginning of the independence war.

various concession companies in the north, abolished the remaining *prazos* and consolidated Portuguese control over Mozambique. While some of his policies, including the introduction of agricultural schemes, resulted in economic growth, overall conditions for Mozambicans worsened considerably. There was not even a pretence of social investment in the African population and of the few schools and hospitals that did exist, most were in the cities and reserved for Portuguese, other whites and privileged African *assimilados*.

THE MUEDA MASSACRE

Discontent with the situation grew and a nationalist consciousness gradually developed. This was nurtured by Mozambican exile groups and by the country's small group of educated elite, including nationalist intellectuals such as the poets Marcelino dos Santos, José Craveirinha and Noémia de Sousa.

In June 1960, at Mueda in northern Mozambique, an official meeting was held by villagers protesting peacefully about taxes. Portuguese troops opened fire on the crowd, killing a large number of demonstrators. Resentment at the 'massacre of Mueda' helped to politicise the local Makonde people and became one of the sparks kindling the independence struggle. From this point onwards, the Mozambican liberation movement began to grow. External support came from several sources, but most notably from the government of Julius Nyerere in neighbouring Tanganyika (now Tanzania). In 1962, following a meeting of various political organisations working in exile for Mozambique independence, the Frente pela Libertação de Moçambique (Mozambique Liberation Front; Frelimo) was formed in Dar es Salaam, Tanzania. The first president of the organisation was Eduardo Chivambu Mondlane, a southern Mozambican educated in the USA, Portugal and South Africa who had spent several years working with the UN.

THE INDEPENDENCE STRUGGLE

Frelimo was plagued from the outset by internal divisions. However, under the leadership of the charismatic Mondlane and operating from bases in Tanzania, it succeeded in giving the liberation movement a structure and in defining a program of political and military action to support its aim of complete independence for Mozambique. On 25 September 1964 Mondlane proclaimed the beginning of the armed struggle for national independence, which Frelimo initiated by attacking a Portuguese base at Chai, in Cabo Delgado province.

By 1966 large areas of Cabo Delgado and Niassa provinces were liberated, but progress was slow. A setback for Frelimo came in 1969 when Mondlane was assassinated by a letter bomb delivered to him at his office in Dar es Salaam. He was succeeded as president by Frelimo's military commander and another southerner, Samora Moises Machel. Under Machel, Frelimo

In addition to being one of Mozambique's most prominent literary figures, Marcelino dos Santos was also a founding member of Frelimo, and, later, its vice president.

Eduardo Mondlane's *The Struggle for Mozambique* (1969) offers historical insights into the colonial era and the roots of Mozambique's independence struggle from one of its main architects.

1974	1975	1980s
The construction of Cahora Bassa Dam – one of the largest dams in the world – is completed, although it will be at least three more decades before it begins to reach its potential.	Mozambique gains independence, with Samora Machel as president. Machel leads the country with his wartime motto, '*A luta continua*' ('The struggle continues').	Externally supported Renamo destabilisation tactics ravage the country, as roads, bridges, railways, schools and health clinics are destroyed.

WHAT'S IN A NAME?

Spend enough time in Mozambique and you'll soon notice that many street names are the same. Here's a quick guide to some of the figures and events behind them.

25 de Junho Mozambican independence day (1975).

25 de Setembro Start of the independence war in 1964.

Amilcar Cabral Freedom fighter and revolutionary leader in Guinea-Bissau.

Eduardo Mondlane Founding president of Frelimo, and leader of the independence movement.

Josina Machel A prominent freedom fighter, married to Samora Machel; Mozambican Women's Day (7 April) was inaugurated in her honour, on the anniversary of her death.

Julius Nyerere First president of Tanzania (then Tanganyika) and major supporter of the Mozambican independence movement.

Kwame Nkrumah Ghanaian president, founding member of the Organisation for African Unity and leader of the Pan-African movement.

Samora Machel Successor of Mondlane as Frelimo president, and first president of independent Mozambique.

sought to extend its area of operations to the south. The Portuguese meanwhile attempted to eliminate rural support for Frelimo by implementing a scorched earth campaign and by resettling people in a series of *aldeamentos* (fortified village complexes) where they would be isolated from contact with Frelimo forces, and where they could receive social services (provided by the Portuguese in an effort to win support for the Portuguese cause). However, struggles within Portugal's colonial empire and increasing international criticism sapped the government's resources. The final blow for Portugal came in 1974 with the overthrow of the Salazar regime. In 1974, at a ceremony in Lusaka (Zambia), the Portuguese government agreed to hand over power to Frelimo and a transitional government was established. On 25 June 1975 the independent People's Republic of Mozambique was proclaimed with the wartime commander Samora Machel as president and Joaquim Chissano, a founding member of Frelimo's intellectual elite, as prime minister.

Mozambique History Net (www.mozambique history.net) – still a work in progress – has various original documents, useful for those taking an academic approach to learning about the country.

INDEPENDENCE – THE EARLY YEARS

The Portuguese pulled out virtually overnight, leaving the country in a state of chaos with few skilled professionals and virtually no infrastructure. Frelimo, which found itself suddenly faced with the task of running the country, threw itself headlong into a policy of radical social change. Ties were established with the USSR and East Germany and private land ownership was replaced with state farms and peasant cooperatives. Meanwhile, schools, banks and insurance companies were nationalised and private practice in medicine and law was abolished in an attempt to disperse skilled labour. Education

1983	**1984**	**1986**
Mozambique is crippled by drought and famine, forcing Frelimo to open the country up to the West in return for Western aid.	Mozambique and South Africa sign the Nkomati Accord, under which Mozambique agrees to expel the ANC and open up the country to South African investment.	Samora Machel dies in a plane crash under questionable circumstances; Joaquim Chissano takes the reins as president.

assumed a high priority and literacy programs were launched with the aim of teaching 100,000 people each year to read and write. Much assistance was received from foreign volunteers, notably from Sweden. Maoist-style 'barefoot doctors' provided basic health services such as vaccinations and taught hygiene and sanitation.

However, Frelimo's socialist program proved unrealistic and by 1983 the country was almost bankrupt. Money was valueless and shops were empty. While collectivisation of agriculture had worked in some areas, in many others it was a disaster. The crisis was compounded by a three-year drought and by South African and Rhodesian efforts to destabilise Mozambique – largely because the oppositional African National Congress (ANC) and Zimbabwe African People's Union (ZAPU), both of which were fighting for majority rule, had bases there.

Onto this scene came the Resistência Nacional de Moçambique (Mozambique National Resistance; Renamo). This ragtag group had been established in the mid-1970s by Rhodesia (now Zimbabwe) as part of its destabilisation policy. It was kept alive in later years with backing from the South African military and some sectors in the West.

RAVAGES OF WAR

Renamo, which had been created by external forces rather than by internal political motives, had no ideology of its own beyond the wholesale destruction of social and communications infrastructure within Mozambique, and the destabilisation of the government. Many commentators have pointed out that the war which went on to ravage the country for the next 17 years was thus not a 'civil' war, but one between Mozambique's Frelimo government and Renamo's external backers.

For a well-researched look at the roots of civil war in Mozambique and Angola, including the role of apartheid-era South Africa in continuing the conflicts, read William Minter's *Apartheid's Contras: An Inquiry Into the Roots of War in Angola and Mozambique* (1994).

Recruitment by Renamo was sometimes voluntary but frequently by force. Roads, bridges, railways, schools and clinics were destroyed. Villagers were rounded up and anyone with skills – teachers, medical workers etc – was shot. Atrocities were committed on a massive and horrific scale.

Ironically, the Frelimo re-education camps that were established after independence contributed to Renamo's growth. Inmates of the camps included political opponents as well as common criminals notorious for their human rights abuses. Rather than establishing respect for state authority, the camps provided a fertile recruitment ground for Renamo.

The drought and famine of 1983 crippled the country. Faced with this dire situation and the reality of a failed socialist experiment, Frelimo opened Mozambique to the West in return for Western aid.

In 1984 South Africa and Mozambique signed the Nkomati Accord, under which South Africa undertook to withdraw its support of Renamo, and Mozambique agreed to expel the ANC and open the country to South African investment. While Mozambique abided by the agreement,

Since 1995 Mozambique has been part of the Commonwealth of Nations, to which all of its neighbours also belong. It is the first member not to have been ruled by Great Britain at some point.

1992	1994	1995
After protracted negotiations brokered by the Sant'Egidio Community, a peace accord is finally signed in Rome between Frelimo and Renamo on 4 October.	In October Mozambique holds its first multiparty elections. Close to 90% of the electorate participates, with many waiting in line for hours in the hot sun for a chance to vote.	Mozambique becomes a member of the British Commonwealth. It is the first member not to have ever been ruled by Britain.

CHIEFS & PROVINCES

Before independence, most villages were led by *régulos* (traditional leaders, often inherited positions). Beginning in the late 1970s, the Frelimo government displaced these leaders, installing *secretários* (local government administrators) in their place. Population displacement during the war further weakened traditional authority structures. More recently, many traditional leaders have been reinstated and both structures often coexist, with power divided between the chief and the government-appointed administrator, and many communities organised around a council of elders, headed by a chief.

Mozambique's 10 provinces (each with a governor and some autonomy) and their capitals: Maputo (Maputo), Gaza (Xai-Xai), Inhambane (Inhambane), Sofala (Beira), Manica (Chimoio), Tete (Tete), Zambézia (Quelimane), Nampula (Nampula), Niassa (Lichinga) and Cabo Delgado (Pemba). Maputo city is sometimes considered an 11th province.

South Africa exploited the situation to the full and Renamo's activity did not diminish.

Samora Machel died in a plane crash in 1986 under questionable circumstances, and his leadership role was assumed by the more moderate Joaquim Chissano. The war between the Frelimo government and the Renamo rebels continued but by the late 1980s political change was sweeping through the region. The collapse of the USSR altered the political balance, and the new president of South Africa, FW de Klerk, made it more difficult for right-wing factions to supply Renamo.

PEACE AT LAST

By the early 1990s, Frelimo had disavowed its Marxist ideology, announcing that Mozambique would switch to a market economy, with privatisation of state enterprises and multiparty elections. After protracted negotiations in Rome, a ceasefire was arranged, followed by a formal peace agreement in October 1992 and a successful UN-monitored disarmament and demobilisation campaign.

Moçambique para todos (http://macua.blogs.com) has a comprehensive survey of current events in Mozambique, in Portuguese, with English translations available.

Since the signing of the peace accords, Mozambique has been remarkably successful in moving beyond war and transforming military conflict into political competition. In October 1994 the country held its first multiparty elections. With close to 90% of the electorate participating, Renamo won 38% of the vote, compared with 44% for Frelimo, and majorities in five provinces. The results were attributable in part to ethnic considerations and in part to Frelimo's inability to overcome widespread grassroots antipathy. In the second national elections, held in December 1999, Renamo made an even stronger showing, winning in six out of 11 provinces. However, unlike the first elections, which earned Mozambique widespread acclaim as an African model of democracy and reconciliation, the 1999 balloting sparked

1999	2000	2004
Renamo make an even stronger showing in the country's second national election, winning six out of 11 provinces.	Maria de Lurdes Mutola wins Mozambique's first Olympic gold medal (in the 800m run) in Sydney, Australia.	Long-time Frelimo insider, Armando Guebuza, is elected to succeed Joaquim Chissano as president.

protracted discord. Renamo accused Frelimo of irregularities in counting the votes and boycotted the presidential inauguration, sparking a wave of rioting and violence.

MOZAMBIQUE TODAY

In December 2004 prominent businessman and long-time Frelimo insider Armando Guebuza was elected with a solid majority to succeed Chissano, who had earlier announced his intent to step down. Since taking the reins, Guebuza has pursued a more hardline approach than Chissano, and tensions between Frelimo and Renamo have sharpened. Frelimo has also increased its dominance of political life, and gained re-election in October 2009, polling a majority landslide 75% of the votes.

Although Mozambique still wins acclaim (and donor funding) as a successful example of postwar reconciliation and democracy-building in Africa, it has a long list of challenges, including widespread corruption and Renamo's ongoing struggles to prove itself as a viable political party. Natural calamities also take their toll, with frequent severe flooding and destructive cyclones. Yet Mozambique has shown a remarkable ability to rebound in the face of adversity, and most observers still count the country among the continent's bright spots.

There are many small political parties, but none with parliamentary seats. Political allegiance tends to be regional – Renamo is strong in the centre, Frelimo in the north and south.

2005

The cornerstone is laid for the 'Unity Bridge' linking Mozambique and Tanzania across the Rovuma River.

2007

Joaquim Chissano is awarded the Mo Ibrahim prize, which gives US$5 million and international recognition to a retired African head of state for excellence in leadership.

2009

The Armando Emílio Guebuza Bridge, crossing the Zambezi River, is officially inaugurated on 1 August, providing the first proper road link between southern and northern Mozambique in the country's history.

The Culture

THE NATIONAL PSYCHE

You don't need to travel for long in Mozambique before hearing the word *paciência* (patience). It's the great Mozambican virtue and most Mozambicans have it in abundance, with each other and with outsiders. You'll be expected to display some in return, especially in dealings with officialdom, and impatience is always counterproductive. While at times frustrating, it is this same low-key, warm Mozambican way that soon gets hold of most visitors to the country and keeps them here much longer than they had originally planned. But don't let the languid, tropical pace sway you completely: underlying it is a rock-hard determination that has carried Mozambique from complete devastation following two decades of war to near the top of the list of the continent's success stories.

Another feature of modern-day Mozambique is its cultural diversity. To casual observers, the country may look like one long beach backed by faceless bush, yet it is remarkably decentralised when compared with many of its neighbours, with each province boasting its own unique history, culture and tradition. There has long been an undercurrent of north–south difference, with geographically remote northerners often feeling neglected by powerhouse Maputo, where proximity to South Africa and good road links have pushed economic development along at a rapid pace. Yet this tension has remained low-level, and tribal rivalries don't play a major role in contemporary Mozambican life. Religious frictions are also minimal, with Christians and Muslims living side by side in a relatively easy coexistence.

HIV/AIDS continues to cut its dark swathe through Mozambican society. Infection rates are highest in the south and centre, where they exceed 20% in some areas. Public discussion has opened up dramatically in recent years, spurred in part by former first lady Graça Machel, who was one of the first to break the taboo with her announcement a decade ago that her brother-in-law (the former president Samora Machel's brother) had died of HIV/AIDS-related complications. There are prominent public advertising campaigns in major towns and lots of work being done at the local level – especially through theatre groups and peer chat sessions at schools – to break down the stigmas. Yet discussion still remains muted in many areas and deaths are commonly explained away as 'tuberculosis' or with silence.

LIFESTYLE

Much of Mozambique moves to the rhythms of the harvest and the monsoon. About 80% of Mozambicans are involved at least part-time in subsistence agriculture, tending small plots with cassava, maize and other crops. You'll see these *machambas* (farm plots) wherever you travel, along with large stands of cashew trees (especially in the north), mangoes and, in the central highlands around Gurúè, tea plantations. Along the coast, fishing is a major source of livelihood. The small ports are fascinating to watch at dawn and in the late afternoon when the boats come in with their catch. At the national level, commercial fishing – especially the prawns for which Mozambique is famous – accounts for about 25% of merchandise exports.

Tourism has become an increasingly important source of income, as the world discovers the country's charms. This is particularly evident in Maputo, where top-end hotels are rapidly multiplying, and in the far north, where there has been extensive investment in the luxury travel market.

Cultures and Customs of Mozambique by George Ndege gives an overview of Mozambique's ethnic and cultural composition and many of its traditions.

Samora Machel's famous rallying cry, '*A luta continua*' ('The struggle continues'), inspired Mozambicans in the early independence years, and still stirs up national pride.

SOCIAL ETIQUETTE

Most Mozambicans are fairly easygoing towards foreigners. However, keeping a few basics in mind will help to smooth your interactions.

- Always greet others and enquire about their well-being prior to launching into questions or conversation. It's also usual to greet people when entering or leaving a room.
- When shaking someone's hand, the custom in many areas is to touch your left hand to your right elbow.
- Ask permission before photographing anyone, especially in remote areas, and follow through if you promise to send a copy of the photo.
- In traditional Mozambican culture, elders and those in positions of authority are treated with deference and respect. It smoothes things considerably to follow suit.
- When visiting villages, ask to see the chief to announce your presence. Always request permission before setting up camp or wandering around – you will rarely be refused.
- When receiving a gift, it's polite in many areas to accept it with both hands, sometimes with a slight bow or, alternately, with the right hand while touching the left hand to the right elbow. When only one hand is used to give or receive, make it the right hand.
- Spoken thanks are not as common as in the West, so don't be upset if you are not verbally thanked for a gift.
- Shorts and sleeveless tops are fine at beach resorts. In traditional communities, you'll have an easier time with more conservative garb. Long trousers or a skirt, and a top with some sort of sleeve are appropriate anywhere.

Despite the tourism boom and encouraging economic news, much of daily life is shaped by the struggle to make ends meet. Gross national income per capita is about US$320 (compared with about US$42,000 in the UK), and most Mozambicans strive to earn a living in the expansive and lively informal sector as traders, street vendors and subsistence farmers.

Mozambique's main social security system and welfare net is the community and extended family, and family obligations are taken seriously. If one family member is lucky enough to have a good job, it is expected that their good fortune will filter down to even distant relatives. Another example is seen with funerals, which are always attended by all those concerned, even if this necessitates long journeys and time away from work. It is expected that friends, acquaintances and other family members will make a small donation – either monetary or in-kind (such as a bag of rice) – to the family of the deceased to help them cover expenses and get by in the months ahead.

Funerals themselves are generally lengthy affairs and are preceded by a period of mourning at the family homestead, where friends and acquaintances go to pay their last respects and offer condolences. It's common for widows and other members of the immediate family to wear black for up to a year after the death in remembrance.

Customs surrounding engagements and weddings are similarly oriented to encompass the entire family, and payment of *lobola* (bride price) by the family of the husband to the family of the wife is common.

EDUCATION

The Mozambican educational scene shows a mixed picture. On the one side, there is an ever-increasing number of university graduates and, thanks to a major government campaign, primary school enrolment levels have increased to a nationwide average of more than 70%. On the other side, drop-out rates are high, and just over 5% of the population goes on to complete secondary

---

THE GENDER GAP

The gender gap in Mozambican education has been narrowing at the primary level over the past decade, thanks to the strong government priority placed on increasing enrolment levels across the board. However, at the secondary level, the gap has widened. Only about one-third of students at the upper secondary school level, and about a quarter of tertiary level students, are girls. Maputo city is the only place in the country where there is a negligible gender gap at all levels.

Comparatively lower enrolment rates and higher drop-out rates countrywide among girls are due in part to cultural attitudes. There is a traditional preference for sons to be educated and a pervasive expectation that girls will take on chores at home. Early marriages and early pregnancies are another factor. HIV/AIDS is also a major contributor. As the number of AIDS orphans rises – there are currently an estimated 400,000 in Mozambique – girls are required to stay home to take care of ill family members or younger siblings.

---

school. One factor is the financial constraint, with annual fees (about US$80 per year) a formidable sum for many rural families. Uneven school distribution is another factor, as many zones are still without adequate facilities, despite a massive postwar school rebuilding program.

Other issues include low levels of teacher training and low staff morale. Close to 40% of teachers at the primary level are inadequately trained and salaries are often low, missed or delayed. High teacher-to-pupil ratios (sometimes as high as one primary-level teacher for 60 or more pupils) mean that in many classrooms little learning is occurring. AIDS is also an increasingly serious problem. The Ministry of Education predicts that within the next decade, about 17% of teachers in the country will die of AIDS across all educational levels.

POPULATION

With about 21.6 million inhabitants, Mozambique has a population density averaging about 27 people per sq km – well below all of its neighbours, with the exception of Zambia. About half of the population is concentrated in the centre and north, especially in Zambézia and Nampula provinces, which – with about 40% of the total – are the most densely populated provinces in the country. More than 60% of the total population lives in rural areas. Settlement in the south of the country is primarily along the coastal belt, with only scattered villages in the dry interior. Niassa province – the Siberia of the southern hemisphere – is the least densely populated province, with about seven inhabitants per sq km. Mozambique's population-growth rate is estimated at about 1.8%, tempered by an HIV/AIDS infection rate that is officially estimated at about 12.5% countrywide, but exceeds 20% in some areas such as the Tete and Beira corridors. Average life expectancy in Mozambique is about 41 years.

There are 16 main ethnic groups. The largest is the Makua, who inhabit the provinces of Cabo Delgado, Niassa, Nampula and parts of Zambézia, and comprise about 25% of the total population (although the designation 'Makua' was externally determined and actually includes many distinct subgroups). Other major groups include the Makonde in Cabo Delgado; the Sena in Sofala, Manica and Tete; and the Ronga and Shangaan, who dominate the southern provinces of Gaza and Maputo. You'll likely also encounter Lomwe and Chuabo (Zambézia); Yao and Nyanja (Niassa); Mwani (Cabo Delgado); Nyungwe (Tete); and Tswa and Chopi (Inhambane).

Patrilineal systems predominate in southern Mozambique and in the Islamic coastal areas of the far north (among the Mwani, for example), while in the centre and in northern inland areas many groups, including the Lomwe, Makonde, Makua and Nyanja, are matrilineal. Some groups in the

Zambezi River valley, such as the Chuabo, Sena and Nyungwe, incorporate elements of both systems in their traditions.

About 1% of Mozambique's population is of Portuguese extraction, most of whom are at least second generation and consider themselves Mozambicans first. There is also a small number of other European and Asian residents. As expected with such ethnic diversity, there is also a rich array of languages. For more, see p201, which includes an introduction to Portuguese pronunciation and a glossary of words and phrases.

Among many matrilineal peoples, clan members are believed to descend from a common female ancestor. Family name and important decisions are determined through the mother or through her brother or other male relatives.

SPORT

Football (soccer) is the main spectator sport. Local games always draw large and enthusiastic crowds – the whole village may turn out in rural areas – and the nationally known teams, including Maxaquene, Costa do Sol and Ferroviário de Maputo, inspire fierce loyalty on the part of their fans.

Second to football is basketball, which also draws crowds – especially women's basketball.

The track and field scene is still dominated by the internationally acclaimed 800m runner, Maria de Lurdes Mutola (the 'Maputo Express'), who won numerous international titles and in 2000 became Mozambique's first Olympic gold medallist.

MEDIA

Mozambique has a lively media sector, which includes the government-aligned *Notícias* (the most widely circulated daily) and a number of independent publications. Its growth since state press controls were loosened in the early 1990s was spearheaded largely by Carlos Cardoso. Cardoso, one-time head of the state news agency, *Agência de Informação de Moçambique* (AIM), was Mozambique's leading investigative journalist and founder of the independent *Mediafax,* a publication once described by the *New York Times* as the vanguard of free press in Africa. Cardoso's murder in November 2000, in connection with his investigation into a massive banking scandal in which high-ranking government circles were implicated, sent shock waves through the press world both in Mozambique and abroad. Stories about his convicted assassin, Anibal Antonio dos Santos Junior ('Anibalzinho') – currently serving a 30-year term from which he has escaped and been re-imprisoned several times – continue to garner headlines, and shadows still linger over open reporting in Mozambique.

RELIGION

About 35% of Mozambicans are Christians, about 25% to 30% are Muslims, and the remainder are adherents of traditional religions. Among Christians, the major denomination is Roman Catholicism. However, membership in evangelical Protestant churches is growing rapidly, particularly in the south. One church you're also likely to come in contact with is the local Zionist church, whose members are often seen on the beach along Maputo's Avenida Marginal in the early morning carrying out initiation rituals. Muslims are found primarily in the northern provinces of Nampula, Cabo Delgado and Niassa, with the highest concentrations on the coast and along old trading routes.

Traditional religions based on animist beliefs remain widespread, and traditional beliefs are often incorporated into the practice of Christianity. In most areas there are strong beliefs concerning the powers that the spirits of ancestors have over the destiny of living persons. There is also often identification of different levels of deities. In the south for example most groups identify an all-powerful God as well as various lesser spirits who

TRADITIONAL HEALERS

Traditional medicine is widely practised in Mozambique – often as the only remedy, but sometimes in combination with Western medical treatment. As a result, *curandeiros* (traditional healers) are respected and highly sought-after. They are also often relatively well paid, frequently in kind rather than in cash. In some rural areas far from health clinics or a hospital, the *curandeiro* may be the only provider of medical assistance.

Individual *curandeiros* have various powers, so selection of the proper one is important. After clamping down on *curandeiros* following independence, the government now permits them to practise, although it attempts to regulate the system. A national association has been formed (Associação dos Médicos Tradicionais de Moçambique; Ametramo), with centres in each of the provincial capitals. Officially, each *curandeiro* must be registered at the provincial level, although unlicensed practice remains widespread.

The practice of traditional medicine is closely intertwined with traditional religions, and in addition to *curandeiros,* you may encounter *profetas* (spirit mediums or diviners) and *feticeiros* (witch doctors). All three power areas can be vested in one person, or they can be different individuals. While *curandeiros* and *profetas* are commonly recognised, the identity of a *feticeiro* is usually not known.

Most larger markets have a traditional-remedies section selling bird claws, dried leaves and plants, and the like. Diviners often carry a small sack of bones (generally matching male and female parts of the same species) which facilitate communication with the ancestors.

receive prayers and influence events. In connection with these beliefs, there are many sacred sites, such as forests, rivers, lakes and mountains, that play important roles in the lives of local communities.

WOMEN IN MOZAMBIQUE

To understand the reception that you're likely to receive as a woman travelling in Mozambique, it's worth taking a look at the status of local women. The country is notable for holding a place among the top 20 countries worldwide for its percentage of female parliamentarians. Currently, about 35% of deputies in Mozambique's parliament are women. The prime minister is also a woman, and there are several female cabinet ministers (including the Minister of Foreign Affairs) and vice-ministers, and a small but influential group of highly educated Mozambican women in the private sector. The national women's organisation, Organização das Mulheres Moçambicanas (OMM), although politicised, is well established and enjoys a high profile throughout the country. In the heady post-independence days of the early 1970s, Frelimo declared women's emancipation to be an integral aspect of Mozambique's revolutionary struggle.

In contrast with this encouraging picture is the fact that in many areas, especially among the country's large rural population, women are frequently marginalised. The difference in male and female literacy rates (about 33% for women versus 64% for men), and the education gender gap at the secondary and tertiary levels, are just two indicators. And the realities can be seen simply by looking around: one of your most lasting impressions of travel in Mozambique is likely to be how hard the women work.

Despite a progressive land law, women still struggle for land rights. Polygamy, which is common in many areas, is another factor influencing land rights, as is migrant labour. Thanks to the high percentage of men (especially in southern Mozambique) who are migrant workers in South African mines, many women are left to raise their families alone. When their husbands return home, they bring back better salaries from the mines, and potentially AIDS. Economic realities and limited job opportunities also force many women to turn to sex for survival. About 55% of Mozambican AIDS sufferers are women.

ARTS

During the colonial era, indigenous artistic expression in Mozambique was generally suppressed, especially if it was deemed to display overly strong nationalist leanings. Those traditions that were permitted to continue were often trivialised by the colonial administration and relegated to the realm of folklore.

With independence, the situation changed. The new Frelimo government made promotion of indigenous culture one of its priorities, and actively supported international artistic exchanges. The start of the civil war brought this heady period for the arts to an abrupt halt. Fortunately things are again on the upswing. Since the signing of the peace accords, Mozambique's rich artistic traditions have been at the forefront, and today – despite an influx of Western influences – are thriving.

Dance

Mozambicans are superb dancers, and experiencing their rhythm and movement, whether in a Maputo nightclub or at a traditional dance performance in the provinces, is a chance not to be missed.

Dance, music and singing accompany almost every major occasion. Many dances tell a story, and often also offer political and social commentary. Others are specific to particular events. Most dances involve some sort of costume, which frequently includes rattles tied to the legs. Masked dancing is not as common in Mozambique as in some areas of Africa and is done primarily by the Makonde in northern Mozambique (see p160) and the Chewa-Nyanja in Tete province, who are known for their Nyau masks.

On Mozambique Island and along the northern coast, you're likely to see *tufo*, a dance of Arabic origin. It is generally performed by women, wearing matching *capulanas* (sarongs) and scarves, and accompanied by special drums (some more like tambourines) known as *taware*. *Tufo* was traditionally danced to celebrate Islamic feast days and other special events. A similar dance, usually performed to celebrate the Islamic feast of Maulidi, is also found in Zanzibar and around Kilwa, in Tanzania.

Other dances found in the north, particularly around Moçimboa da Praia, include *muáli,* a dance of initiation; *batuque,* sometimes performed at circumcision ceremonies; and *rumba.*

In the south, one of the best known dances, particularly in Maputo, is *makwaela,* characterised by a cappella singing accompanied by foot percussion. It developed in South Africa among mineworkers who were often forced to practise their dance steps without disturbing their white guards. The lyrics focused traditionally on the hardships and dreams of daily life. It was Mozambique's Grupo Makwaela dos TPM that, together with South Africa's Ladysmith Black Mambazo, helped internationalise *makwaela.*

In Tete and Manica provinces, a common dance is *nyanga,* which involves a dancer who simultaneously sings and plays the panpipes (which are also known as *nyanga*).

A good place to get information on traditional dance performances are the *casas de cultura* (cultural centres), found in every provincial capital. These exist primarily to promote traditional culture among young Mozambicans by offering music and dance lessons and similar training. You can often see rehearsals and performances of local song and dance groups at these centres, and staff can be a good source of information on cultural events in the province.

'Along the northern coast and on Mozambique Island you're likely to see *tufo,* a dance of Arabic origin'

Literature

Mozambique has a rich body of literature, written almost exclusively in Portuguese. However, a number of major works (including all titles in this section cited in English) have been translated. Despite the harshness of the colonial era, the Portuguese language is not viewed with animosity, but rather as playing a unifying role for Mozambique's various ethnic groups. It takes on a unique richness in the context of Mozambican literature, where it has given voice to the country's aspirations for independence and expression to its national identity.

During the colonial era, local literature generally focused on nationalist themes. Two of the most famous poets of this period were Rui de Noronha and Noémia de Sousa. De Sousa in particular focused on affirmation of Mozambican nationalism through definition of racial identity.

In the late 1940s José Craveirinha (1922–2003) began to write poetry focusing on the social reality of the Mozambican people and calling for resistance and rebellion – which eventually led to his arrest. Today, he is honoured as Mozambique's greatest poet, and his work, including 'Poem of the Future Citizen', is recognised worldwide. A contemporary of Craveirinha's was another nationalist called Luis Bernardo Honwana, famous for short stories such as 'We Killed Mangey Dog' and 'Dina'.

As the armed struggle for independence gained strength, Frelimo freedom fighters began to write poems reflecting their life in the forest, their marches and the ambushes. One of the finest of these guerrilla poets was Marcelino dos Santos. Others included Sergio Vieira and Jorge Rebelo.

With Mozambican independence in 1975, writers and poets felt able to produce literature without interference. This new-found freedom was soon shattered by Frelimo's war against the Renamo rebels, but new writers emerged, including the internationally acclaimed Mia Couto, whose works include *Voices Made Night, Every Man is a Race, Under the Frangipani* and *The Last Flight of the Flamingo*. Other writers from this period include Ungulani Ba Ka Khossa, Heliodoro Baptista and Eduardo White. More recent is Farida Karodia, whose *A Shattering of Silence* describes a young girl's journey through Mozambique following the death of her family.

Lilia Momple, born on Mozambique Island in 1935, has long been a major voice in contemporary literary circles. Her works include *Neighbours – The Story of a Murder* and *The Eyes of the Green Cobra*. Other contemporary female writers include journalist and activist Lina Magaia, who is known for her *Dumba-Nengue – Run for Your Life: Peasant Tales of Tragedy in Mozambique,* and Paulina Chiziane, who authored *Niketche – A Story of Polygamy,* and whose *Balada de Amor ao Vento* (Love Dance for the Wind, 1990) was the first novel to be published by a Mozambican woman.

A significant development was the establishment of the Mozambique Writers' Association in 1982, which has been active both in publishing new material and in advancing the spread of indigenous literature throughout the country. Its prestigious José Craveirinha prize was recently awarded to Mia Couto and Paulina Chiziane.

Music

TRADITIONAL

Traditional music is alive and well in Mozambique, particularly in villages and rural areas. The *timbila* orchestras of the Chopi people in southern Mozambique are one of the best-known musical traditions in the country; for more information, see p83.

Some musical instruments you are likely to see around the country include the following:

The Last Flight of the Flamingo speaks of…an extreme theft of hope committed by the ruthlessness of the powerful. The advance of these consumers of nations forces us…writers, to a growing moral obligation. Against the indecency of those who enrich themselves at the expense of everything and everyone…against the lies and crime and fear, against all of this the words of writers should be constructed…' (Mia Couto)

Poet and political activist José Craveirinha is credited with discovering and encouraging Olympian Maria de Lurdes Mutola to become a runner when she was still an unknown football player.

- *mbila* (plural *timbila*): a marimba or xylophone common in central and southern Mozambique, that can range from less than 1m to several metres in length. The keys are made of wood, under which are resonance chambers made from gourds and covered by animal membrane.
- *nyanga* (panpipe): the *nyanga* is found around Tete city and in southern Tete province. It is made from hollow cane tubes joined together by cord. *Nyanga* is also the name given to the dance which is traditionally done to the accompaniment of panpipes.
- *pankwe*: a small guitarlike instrument made from a hollow gourd and wooden stem with six or seven strings. It is found primarily in Nampula, as well as in parts of Niassa and Cabo Delgado provinces.
- *tchakare*: this is another stringed instrument found in northern Mozambique. It has only one string, which is played with a bow similar to a hunting bow.
- *xikitsi*: this flat, hollow instrument is made with reeds and filled with stones or grain kernels, and is found throughout southern Mozambique. The *xikitsi* is played by shaking it back and forth with the hands while simultaneously using the thumbs to beat a rhythm, and is commonly used as accompaniment for vocal groups.

MODERN

Modern music flourishes in the cities and the live music scene in Maputo is excellent. *Marrabenta* is considered Mozambique's national music. It developed in the 1950s in the suburbs of Maputo (then Lourenço Marques) and has a light, upbeat style and distinctive beat inspired by the traditional rural *majika* rhythms of Gaza and Maputo provinces. It is often accompanied by a dance of the same name. Initially, *marrabenta* was played with acoustic guitars, traditional drums and other percussion instruments, with a lead singer and a female chorus. Later, electric guitars and other modern instruments were introduced. One of *marrabenta*'s best known proponents was Orchestra Marrabenta, formed in the 1980s by members of another popular band, Grupo RM, together with dancers from Mozambique's National Company of Song and Dance. When Orchestra Marrabenta split in 1989, several members formed Ghorwane, and still perform frequently in Maputo.

There are numerous new generation bands. One of the best known is Kapa Dêch (pronounced 'kapa dezh'), a group of musicians who have taken traditional beats and built popular melodies around them using a keyboard and other modern instruments. Another is Mabulu, a band that combines classic *marrabenta* rhythms (in the venerable persons of the late Lisboa Matavel together with Dilon Djindji) with hip-hop. They recorded their top-selling first release, *Karimbo*, in 2000 when much of the southern part of the country was severely flooded, followed by *Soul Marrabenta*.

Other acclaimed musicians include Chico António, who plays sophisticated, traditionally based melodies with conga drums and flute, and bass, electric and acoustic guitars; José Mucavele, an acoustic guitarist who plays a mixture of traditional and contemporary rhythms; Roberto Chidsondso; and Elvira Viegas. Fany Mpfumo, now deceased, was one of Mozambique's best known *marrabenta* musicians and still features on some recordings.

For a list of CDs to get you introduced to the Mozambican music scene, see p14.

MozHits (www.mozhits
.com) is a music portal
dedicated to Mozambican
musicians and music,
created by students
at Maputo's Eduardo
Mondlane university.

Sculpture & Painting

Mozambique is well known for its woodcarvings, particularly for the sandalwood carvings found in the south and the ebony carvings of the Makonde.

MALANGATANA

Malangatana Valente Ngwenya – known universally as 'Malangatana' – is one of Mozambique's and Africa's greatest artists. Although best known for his paintings, Malangatana has also worked in various other media, including murals, sculptures and ceramics. His style is characterised by its dramatic figures and flamboyant yet restrained use of colour, and by its highly symbolic social and political commentary on everything from colonialism and war to peacetime rebuilding and the universality of the human experience.

In addition to his artwork, which is displayed in galleries worldwide, Malangatana has left his mark across a broad swathe of Mozambican cultural life. This has included playing founding roles in the establishment of the National Art Museum (p61) and the Núcleo de Arte (p61) and setting up the Matalana Cultural Centre (Centro Cultural de Matalana; p73).

Ricardo Rangel's photographs – many of which were banned – served as a moving documentary of injustice and cruelty during Mozambique's colonial era.

The country's most famous sculptor is the late Alberto Chissano, whose work received wide international acclaim and inspired many younger artists. The main centre of Makonde carving is in Cabo Delgado province, particularly around Mueda on the Makonde Plateau, with carving communities also located around Pemba, and in Nampula province. While some pieces have traditional themes, many Makonde artists have developed contemporary styles. One of the leading members of the new generation of Makonde sculptors is Nkatunga, whose work portrays different aspects of rural life. Others carvers include Miguel Valíngue, and Makamo, who is known for his sandalwood carvings that combine Makonde influences with southern stylistic elements from his native Gaza.

The most famous painter in the country is Malangatana (see boxed text, above). Other internationally famous artists include Bertina Lopes, whose work reflects her research into African images, colours, designs and themes; Roberto Chichorro, known for his paintings dealing with childhood memories; and Samate, one of Mozambique's earliest painters. Naguib, Victor Sousa and Idasse are among the best-known artists in the newer generation. All of these painters and sculptors have exhibits in the National Art Museum (p61) in Maputo.

The late Ricardo Rangel, known for his black-and-white stills, is widely regarded as Mozambique's most famous and influential photographer.

Cinema

Mozambique's tiny film industry is distinguished primarily by its short but powerful documentaries on current social issues. One of the most esteemed directors is Licínio Azevedo, whose films *Disobedience* (2001), which tells the tale of a woman accused of causing her husband's suicide, and *Hóspedes da Noite* (2007), set in Beira, have both received critical acclaim. His *Time of the Leopards* is another classic, based on stories from Mozambique's independence war.

Isabel Noronha's *Ngwenya, O Crocodilo* (2007) documents the life of internationally acclaimed artist Malangatana.

Another prominent director is Gabriel Mondlane. His credits include co-directing *A Miner's Tale* (2001), the story of a Mozambican migrant worker in the South African gold mines and the scourge of AIDS that he brings back to his rural community. His more recent *Voz Nocturna* (2007), set in Beira, also deals with AIDS.

For a historical perspective, watch for Margarida Cardoso's *Kuxa Kanema – The Birth of Cinema* (2003), a chronicle of the birth and rise of Mozambican cinema in the heady post-independence days under the direction of Samora Machel, and then its downfall a decade later with Machel's death.

Food & Drink

Mozambique's cuisine blends African, Indian and Portuguese influences, and is especially noted for its seafood, including *camarões* (prawns), *lagosta* (crayfish) and the ubiquitous *peixe grelhada* (grilled catch of the day). Even local dishes, especially along the coast, have a pizazz that sets them apart from those in neighbouring countries, with liberal use of coconut milk and *piri-piri* (chilli pepper) to liven up what might otherwise be bland. Meat lovers are catered for too, with a good selection of high-quality meats from nearby South Africa.

Whatever the meal may be, it's hard to beat the coastal backdrop and the warm and lively local hospitality.

STAPLES & SPECIALITIES

Local dishes generally consist of a maize- or cassava-based staple (called *xima* or *upshwa*) or rice, served with a sauce of beans, vegetables or fish. In rural areas, this type of food – together with grilled chicken and chips, which is found almost everywhere – is the main option. Specialities to watch for include *matapa* (cassava leaves cooked in a peanut sauce, often with prawns or other additions, and rumoured to be one of President Armando Guebuza's favourite dishes) in the south, and *galinha á Zambeziana* (chicken with a sauce of lime juice, garlic, pepper and *piri-piri*) in Quelimane and Zambézia provinces. *Caril* (curry) dishes are also common, as are *chamusas* (samosas – triangular wedges of fried pastry, filled with meat or vegetables). Avocado salads – often with tomatoes – are another treat. Grilled chicken is either plain with salt or liberally seasoned with *piri-piri*.

Hoje Temos… Receitas de Moçambique (2004), edited by Marielle Rowan, and available in Maputo bookshops, has recipes for Mozambican dishes in English and Portuguese.

Along the coast and at most restaurants, the highlight is the excellent and reasonably priced seafood. In addition to grilled prawns, lobster and crayfish, *lulas* (calamari) is also popular, usually served grilled or fried. Inland, around Lake Niassa, the most popular fish is *chambo*.

Throughout the country, bakeries sell fresh bread rolls every morning.

DRINKS

Mozambicans enjoy their drinks, and *cerveja* (beer) is available almost everywhere, though outside major cities you'll be lucky to find it cold. Local brands include Manica and Laurentina, and are sold by the *garafa* (bottle) or *lata* (can). Dois M (2M) – the national lager – is produced jointly by Mozambique and

---

IS THERE FISH ON THE MENU?

Long gone are the old war days when dining out in Mozambique meant bringing your own food to the restaurant. But eating out can still be something of an experience, especially when it comes to figuring out the rationale behind menu cards. These cards are often grand affairs – with long listings of *entradas* (entrées), *pratos principais* (main courses) and *sobremesas* (desserts). They get your mouth watering and hold out the promise of a fancy three-course meal with all the trimmings. Yet when it gets down to placing your order, what's actually available is often much more limited – although it can take a while to find this out. You'll ask the waiter for cordon bleu, as advertised on the menu. He will duly write down the order, head to the kitchen and then reappear several minutes later to tell you that cordon bleu *'acabou'* (is 'finished'). Perhaps the process will be repeated again and then again until finally *you* get the hang of it and ask what *is* available. The answer will almost always be *peixe grelhada* (grilled fish) – most likely not the barracuda or other speciality described in glowing terms on the menu but (usually) just as good.

South African Breweries. South African beers are also easy to find, including Castle, Black Label, Lion and Amstel, as are Namibian beers, such as Windhoek Lager. Portuguese *vinho* (wine) is sold in hotels and in supermarkets in larger towns, and South African wines are easy to find in Maputo and other cities.

The most common local brews (called *nipa* in some areas of the north) are made from the fruit of the cashew as well as *mandioca* (cassava), mango and sugarcane. They're generally quite lethal and best avoided, at least in larger quantities. *Sura* (palm wine), which is slightly tamer, is common in southern Mozambique, particularly in the area south and west of Maputo, where it's manufactured and then sold over the border in South Africa. The best places for trying local brew are at weddings or other local celebrations, where they're almost always served.

> According to tradition, *ukanhi*, a southern Mozambique traditional brew made from the fruit of the *canhoeiro* tree, should never be sold.

Água mineral (bottled water) is available in all larger towns. In villages and rural areas, it can be harder to find, so it's worth carrying a filter if you'll be travelling extensively away from main towns.

Soft drinks (*refrescos* or 'sodas') are available almost everywhere. In cities and larger towns, you usually have the choice of local-brand soft drinks (for example, *cola nacional)* or the more expensive international brand. Good imported nonsweetened fruit juices from South Africa, sold in long-life cartons, are available in all larger towns.

WHERE TO EAT & DRINK

Most towns have a *café, pastelaria* or *salão de chá* where you can get coffee or a pastry, and inexpensive snacks and light meals such as omelettes, *pregos* (thin steak sandwiches) or burgers. Many of these places also offer more substantial meals (averaging less than Mtc150), such as chicken and chips and similar fare. Bread is often served, though you may be charged extra for this.

Larger towns and provincial capitals will have at least one fancier restaurant and generally several. Prices and menu offerings at these places are remarkably uniform throughout the country, ranging from about Mtc200 to Mtc300 for meals such as grilled fish or chicken with rice, or with potatoes – either fried (*batatas fritas),* or boiled (*batatas cozidas).* Most of these midrange restaurants also offer Portuguese-style soups, such as *caldão verde* (made with greens and often flavoured with sausage), with bread, and sometimes will have a small dessert menu that will include *salada de fruta* (fruit salad – made almost everywhere with banana, papaya and mango in season) and perhaps a few other choices. In addition, Maputo, Beira and larger towns have an array of restaurants offering a good selection of other cuisines. In villages and rural areas, sometimes the only choice are *barracas* (small food stalls).

> Larger towns have street-side cafes where you can enjoy *bolos* (cakes) or light meals, plus *café espresso* or *chá* (tea), while watching the passing scene.

If a hotel or restaurant tells you meals or particular dishes are available *por encomenda,* it means that you'll need to make a special order. The best thing to do is to call or stop by in the morning and order a meal for that evening.

Most restaurants are open daily for lunch and dinner. Some stay open straight through, but more standard are lunch hours from about 11am or noon to about 3pm, and dinner from about 6.30pm until 10pm. The smaller the town, the earlier its eating establishments will close. Bookings are almost never necessary and are generally not possible anyway. Mozambique's restaurants are not known for their speedy service and waits of up to an hour (or more, especially when away from major centres) are common. If you're in a rush, stop by the restaurant several hours before you want to eat and put in an order. For information on tipping, see p175.

Quick Eats

Everywhere in Mozambique – from cities to the smallest villages – you'll find *barracas,* often along the roadside or at markets, where you can get a plate of local food such as *xima* and sauce for about US$3 or less. If the *barraca* seems to do a good business (with high food turnover), the surroundings are reasonably clean and the food is well-heated and freshly prepared, you should have no trouble eating at these places, and they offer a fine insight into local life.

For self-caterers, it's easy anywhere along the coast or around Lake Niassa to make arrangements with local fishermen for a fresh catch, which you can then have cooked at your hotel. The best times to look are early morning and late afternoon when the boats come in with their catch. If you plan on shopping frequently at fish markets, it's a good idea to carry your own pocket-sized weighing scale and a plastic bag for the fish.

Markets in all larger towns sell an abundance of fresh tropical fruits – papayas, mangoes, bananas, pineapples, tangerines, oranges and lychees are among the highlights – along with a reasonably good selection of vegetables, plus rice and other grains.

Maputo, Beira and larger towns have well-stocked supermarkets selling imported goods at high prices. South African products are widely available through Shoprite, a South African supermarket chain, which has stores in Maputo, Beira, Chimoio and Nampula.

VEGETARIANS & VEGANS

Vegetarians who eat seafood will have no problems in Mozambique. Otherwise, you will need to be more creative, as many sauces contain meat or seafood. *Feijão* (bean dishes) are available, although not as widely as in other parts of the region, and those served at Brazilian and Portuguese restaurants often include pork or other meat. Nuts – especially *amendoins* (peanuts) and *castanhas de caju* (cashews) – are easy to find on the streets and in markets. For lacto-ovo vegetarians, boiled eggs are available everywhere. Supermarkets in the larger towns usually stock long-life cheese. Yogurt is available in most provincial capitals, though it is often the sweetened, long-life variety.

There is a large Indian population along the coast and Indian shop owners can often point you in the direction of a good vegetarian meal.

HABITS & CUSTOMS

Meals connected with any sort of social occasion are usually drawn-out affairs for which the women of the household will have spent several days preparing. Local style is to eat with the hand from communal dishes in the centre of the table. Soft drinks are the usual meal accompaniment. If water is on the table, it will generally be unpurified.

Piping-hot roasted maize cobs are a popular street snack – watch for vendors and their small charcoal burners along the roadsides.

Flavours of Moçambique by Gill MacInnes and Jenny Flint is a good place to start learning how to cook using Mozambican ingredients. It's available in Maputo, or order it online at www .qualcocc.com.

DOS & DON'TS

- If you receive an invitation to eat and aren't hungry, it's OK to explain that you have just eaten, but still try to share a few bites of the meal in recognition of the bond with your hosts.

- Try to leave a small amount on your plate at the end of the meal to show your hosts that you have been satisfied.

- For the same reason, don't take the last bit of food from the communal bowl or serving plate – your hosts may end the evening worrying that they haven't provided enough.

- Don't handle or eat food with the left hand; it's also generally considered impolite to give someone something with the left hand.

- If everyone else is eating with their hands, try to do the same, even if cutlery is provided.

- Defer to your host for any customs that you are not sure about.

DINING MOZAMBICAN STYLE

An invitation to share a family meal in Mozambique is a real treat. Before eating, a bowl of water is passed around for washing hands. The usual procedure is to hold your hands over the bowl while your hostess pours water over them. Sometimes soap is provided, as is a towel for drying off.

A maize- or cassava-based staple or rice will be the centre of most meals. You'll often be offered utensils, but if everyone else is eating with their hands, it's good to do the same. It's a bit of an art and it may seem awkward at first but will start to feel more natural after a few tries. The usual procedure is to take a bit of the staple with the right hand, roll it into a small ball with the fingers, dip it into the sauce and eat it, trying to avoid letting the sauce drip down your arm.

While containers of water or home brew may be passed around from person to person, it is not customary to share coffee, tea or bottled soft drinks. Following the meal, the water and wash basin are brought around again for the hands.

Three meals a day is the norm, although breakfast is frequently nothing more than tea or coffee and a piece of bread. Coffee is often made with a heavily sweetened mixture of Nescafé or an unappealing chicory blend and Nido milk powder, except in cafes and restaurants where the real thing is available. The main meal is usually eaten at midday.

Street snacks and meals-on-the-run are common. European-style restaurant dining – while readily available in major cities – is not really a part of local Mozambican culture, except among the small elite class, although street-side cafes are popular across a broad spectrum. Also common are gatherings at home, or perhaps at a rented hall, to celebrate special occasions, with the meal being the focal point.

EAT YOUR WORDS

Want to know your *lagosta* from your *legumes*? Get behind the cuisine scene by getting to know the language. For pronunciation guidelines, see p201.

Food & Drink Glossary

FOOD

arroz	a·*rrosh*	rice
batatas	ba·*taa*·tash	potatoes
batatas fritas	ba·*taa*·tash *free*·tash	chips/fries
bife	*bee*·fe	steak
camarão	ka·ma·*rowng*	prawn
caril	ka·*reel*	curry
carne	*kaar*·ne	meat
chamusa	sha·*moo*·sa	meat- or vegetable-filled fried dough triangle; also samosa
feijão	fay·*zhowng*	beans
frango/galinha	*frang*·goo/ga·*lee*·nya	chicken
fruta	*froo*·ta	fruit
lagosta	la·*gosh*·ta	crayfish/lobster
legumes	le·*goo*·mesh	vegetables
lulas	*loo*·lash	squid (calamari)
mandioca	man·dee·o·ka	cassava/manioc
ovos	o·voosh	eggs
ovos mexidos	o·voosh me·*shee*·doosh	scrambled eggs
pão	powng	bread
peixe	*pay*·she	fish
prego no pão	*pre*·goo noo powng	steak sandwich
sopa	*so*·pa	soup

DRINKS

agua ...	*aa*·gwa ...	... water
fervida	fer·*vee*·da	boiled (OK to drink)
mineral	mee·ne·*raal*	mineral
quente	*keng*·te	hot
(chávena de) chá ...	(*shaa*·ve·na de) shaa ...	(cup of) tea ...
(chávena de) café ...	(*shaa*·ve·na de) ka·*fe* ...	(cup of) coffee ...
com (leite)	kong (*lay*·te)	with (milk)
sem (açúcar)	seng (a·*soo*·kar)	without (sugar)
um copo de ...	oong *ko*·poo de ...	a glass of ...
cerveja	ser·*ve*·zha	beer
leite	*lay*·te	milk
refresco	rre·*fresh*·ko	soft drink
sumo de laranja	*soo*·moo de la·*rang*·zha	orange juice

CONDIMENTS

açucar	a·*soo*·kar	sugar
piri-piri	*pee*·ree *pee*·ree	chilli pepper
sal	saal	salt

OTHER

almoço	aal·*mo*·soo	lunch
barraca	ba·*rra*·ka	street food stall
conta	*kong*·ta	bill
cozido/a (m/f)	koo·*zee*·doo/a	boiled
grelhado/a (m/f)	gre·*lyaa*·doo/a	grilled
jantar	zhang·*taar*	supper
mata bicho	*ma*·ta *bee*·shoo	breakfast (slang, literally, 'kill the beast')
menu	me·*noo*	menu (a set meal)
mercado	mer·*kaa*·doo	market
pequeno almoço	pe·*ke*·noo aal·*mo*·soo	breakfast
quiosque	kee·*osh*·ke	snack bar
recibo	rre·*see*·boo	receipt
restaurante	res·tow·*rang*·te	restaurant

Environment

THE LAND

Mozambique's size is impressive: about 800,000 sq km in area (or more than three times the size of the UK), with a 2500km coastline, and shares borders with six other countries, including Malawi, which almost slices it in half.

Unlike most other southern African coastal countries, Mozambique has extensive coastal lowlands, which form a broad plain 100km to 200km wide in the south and leave it vulnerable to seasonal flooding. In the north, this plain narrows and the terrain rises to mountains and plateaus on the borders with Zimbabwe, Zambia and Malawi. Also in the south is a chain of shallow, coastal barrier lakes strung between Ponta d'Ouro and the Bazaruto Archipelago. In central Mozambique, the predominant geographical feature is the Zambezi River valley and its wide delta plains. In many areas of the north, particularly in Nampula and Niassa provinces, towering granite outcrops or inselbergs dominate the landscape.

Two of southern Africa's largest rivers – the Zambezi and Limpopo – cut through Mozambique on their way to the sea. Other major rivers are the Save River, dividing southern and central Mozambique, and the Rovuma River to the north, which forms the border with Tanzania.

Mozambique's highest peak is Mt Binga (2436m) in the Chimanimani range on the Zimbabwe border.

WILDLIFE

Animals

Niassa Reserve is Mozambique's largest protected area. The Niassa-Selous corridor, spanning the Mozambique–Tanzania border, is the world's largest elephant range.

Mozambique doesn't have the animal herds you'll see in neighbouring Tanzania, Zambia or South Africa, as most of its large animal populations were decimated during the war. Yet wildlife is on the rebound and there's plenty to see, with more than 200 types of mammals wandering the interior. Challenging access, dense vegetation and skittishness on the part of the animals can make spotting difficult, and the country shouldn't be viewed as a 'Big Five' destination. However, if you're seeking something wildlife-related that's different and adventurous, Mozambique is the place to come. Work is proceeding in reviving several parks and reserves, especially Gorongosa National Park, Limpopo National Park and the Niassa Reserve, and the wildness and relatively low visitor numbers of these destinations ensure a rewarding safari experience.

The largest wildlife numbers are found in the Niassa Reserve in Mozambique's far north, which is home to large herds of elephants, buffaloes and zebras. Modest but increasing populations of elephants, hippos and a variety of other large mammals can also be found in Gorongosa National

MOZAMBIQUE'S COASTAL LAKES

Mozambique is one of two countries in East Africa with major coastal barrier lakes or lagoons (the other being Madagascar). The lakes are separated from the sea by well-developed longshore dune systems, and most are no more than 5m deep. They include Uembje Lagoon at Bilene, Lake Inhampavala north of Xai-Xai, Lake Quissico, just east of Quissico town, and Lake Poelela, about 30km north of Quissico and traversed by the N1.

With the exception of Uembje, none of the lakes have links with the sea and their brackish waters are rich with marine and birdlife. These include numerous freshwater fish species, and white storks, little egrets and pink flamingos. At Lake Quissico alone, between 50 and 60 bird species have been recorded.

ELEPHANTS OF THE SEA

The dugong, whose closest terrestrial relative is believed to be the elephant, is a lumbering marine mammal that favours the tropical coastal waters of the Indian and western Pacific oceans. They may live up to 70 years, can reach up to 3m in length and tip the scales at 170kg. To maintain their rotund figures, dugongs spend their days lazing in the shallows and feeding on sea grasses and algae.

Dugongs are prized for their meat and fat, and their large size and gentle manner make them easy prey for hunters. They also frequently become trapped in fishing nets and are then killed for their meat. Today they are classified as endangered.

Dugongs have been sighted in many areas along the Mozambican coastline, including around Inhambane Bay, Angoche, Mozambique Island, Nacala and the Quirimbas Archipelago. However, the largest population – which is also considered to be the largest population in East Africa – is found in the waters of the Bazaruto Archipelago. Dugong numbers here plummeted to fewer than 100 but seem to be stabilising, thanks to the sanctuary provided to them by Bazaruto National Park.

Park. With the reopening of Limpopo National Park as part of the Great Limpopo Transfrontier Park (Parque Internacional do Grande Limpopo; www.greatlimpopopark.com), and the establishment of open borders with South Africa's Kruger National Park, work is underway to encourage wildlife populations in the south to rebound.

Mozambique is officially home to about 170 reptile and 40 amphibian species, although the actual numbers are almost certainly much higher. In the Chimanimani area alone, about 60 reptile species (including the endemic flat rock lizard and about 34 species of snake) have been identified. More visible are the crocodiles, which you'll likely either see or hear about if you spend time near any of the country's rivers.

Mozambique's rich insect biodiversity includes an endemic dragonfly (*Ceriagrion mourae*) and the malaria-carrying *anopheles* mosquito. Endemic mammal subspecies include the blue Niassa wildebeest and a subspecies of Burchell's zebra, both of which are found only in northern Mozambique.

BIRDS

Mozambique is a prime birdwatching destination for those with an adventurous bent.

Of the approximately 900 bird species that have been identified in the southern Africa region, close to 600 have been recorded in Mozambique. Among these are numerous aquatic species found primarily in the southern wetlands. On Inhaca Island alone, 300 bird species, including seven species of albatross, have been recorded. Rare and unique species (most of which are found in isolated montane habitats such as the Chimanimani Mountains, Mt Gorongosa and Mt Namúli) include the dappled mountain robin, the chirinda apalis, Swynnerton's forest robin, the oliveheaded weaver and the greenheaded oriole. Other rare species include the Cape vulture, the east coast akalat and the longbilled apalis.

MARINE LIFE

Among the highest profile wildlife attractions in Mozambique are those swimming around under the sea. The country's coastal waters host populations of dolphins, including spinner, bottlenose, humpback and striped dolphins, and Ponta d'Ouro is one of the best places in the region for swimming with these graceful creatures. Mozambique's waters are also renowned as the home of the elusive dugong (see the boxed text, above), as well as loggerhead, leatherback, green, hawksbill and olive ridley marine turtles.

The recently discovered forest on Mt Mabu is believed to be home to at least 10 new animal and bird species.

Books for ornithologists: *Birds of the Niassa Reserve* (2005) by Vincent Parker; *Birds of the Maputo Special Reserve* (2000) by Vincent Parker & Fred de Boer; Vincent Parker's *Atlas of the Birds of Sul do Save, Southern Mozambique* (1999).

The waters around the Primeiras and Segundas Islands are notable for their abundant and diverse coral reefs, and for hosting breeding sites for five of the world's seven marine turtle species.

The Mozambican coast serves as a winter breeding ground for the humpback whale, which occurs primarily in the country's southern waters between Ponta d'Ouro and Inhambane. Between July and October, it's also common to see whales in the north, offshore from Pemba.

For more on the best times and places for spotting some of this marine life, see the boxed text, p53.

ENDANGERED SPECIES

Mozambique's once abundant wildlife herds have been exploited since at least the 16th century, when there are records of a thriving trade in ivory and tortoise shell. In more recent times, the war and poaching have taken their toll. Today, large mammals believed to be extinct or on the verge of extinction in the country include the black rhino, white rhino, giraffe, tsessebe, roan antelope and the African wild dog. The blue Niassa wildebeest is found in the Niassa Reserve but is thought to be endangered. One snake species, the African rock python, is also believed to be endangered.

The dugong is probably the best known among endangered marine species, while marine turtles are considered threatened. Endangered birds include thyolo alethes and wattled cranes.

Plants

Mozambique is bursting at the seams with colourful and varied flora. This is most obvious in the array of lavender jacarandas, brilliant red flamboyants, and other flowering trees that you'll see lining the streets of Maputo and other provincial capitals. Along the coast are vast stands of coconut palms, especially in Inhambane and Zambézia provinces, while in drier inland areas, such as around Tete, the landscape is dotted with enormous baobabs.

See www.mozambique flora.com for the latest news on Mozambique's flowering plants.

Large tracts of central and north-central Mozambique are covered by miombo or light woodland, characterised by broadleaf deciduous *brachystegia* trees. Mopane woodland derives its name from the tall, multistemmed mopane tree, which grows well in soils with a high clay content. It is predominant in southern inland areas between the Limpopo and Save Rivers, and in the upper Zambezi River Valley.

New plant species are being discovered in Mozambique all the time, with close to 6000 recorded thus far. Of these, an estimated 250 are thought to be found nowhere else in the world. The Maputaland Centre of Plant Diversity, straddling the border with South Africa south of Maputo, is considered one of the most important areas of the country in terms of plant diversity and has been classified as a site of global botanical significance. The Chimanimani Mountains along the Zimbabwe border are also notable for their diversity of plants, with at least 45 endemic species. Other important highland areas include Mt Namúli, the Gorongosa Massif, Mt Chiperone in western Zambézia province and Mt Mabu.

SACRED FORESTS

A good example of the contributions that local traditions can make to biodiversity conservation is seen in western Manica province around the foothills of the Chimanimani Mountains. Communities here recognise various types of sacred areas. One is the *dzimbahwe* (chief's compound), where each chiefdom has its own spot, generally in a densely forested area, and access is strictly limited. Another is the *gwasha*, a forest area used by chiefs, elders and spirit mediums for rainmaking and other ceremonies. Both the *dzimbahwe* and the *gwasha* are treated with great respect and no development, wood cutting or harvesting are permitted. Hunting is under the control of the chiefs, as is the gathering of medicinal and other plants.

MAJOR NATIONAL PARKS & RESERVES

Park	Features	Activities	Best time to visit
Bazaruto National Park (p96)	islands, sea; corals, dolphins, dugongs, marine turtles, flamingos	diving, snorkelling, birdwatching	year-round
Chimanimani National Reserve (p113)	montane forests; birds, small reptiles	hiking, birdwatching, community tourism	May-Nov
Gorongosa National Park (p106)	grasslands, coastal plain, rainforest, lakeshore; birds, waterbucks, impalas, elephants, sable antelopes, hippos, lions	birdwatching, hiking, vehicle & walking safaris, community tourism	Apr & May-Nov
Limpopo National Park (p80)	rivers, bush, farmland; elephants, hippos, crocodiles, plus smaller wildlife & birds	short vehicle & walking safaris, birdwatching, multinight canoe trips, wilderness 4WD drives	May-Dec
Maputo Special Reserve (p78)	woodlands, grasslands, dry forest, coast; elephants, birds	camping, limited vehicle safaris	May-Dec
Niassa Reserve (p147)	miombo woodland, savannahs, wetlands, rivers, riparian forests; elephants, antelopes, buffaloes, zebras	walking, vehicle & canoe safaris	May-Dec
Quirimbas National Park (p155)	islands, sea, mangroves, coastal forest; corals, marine turtles, coconut crabs, dugongs & more	diving, snorkelling, community tourism	year-round

NATIONAL PARKS & RESERVES

Mozambique has six national parks: Gorongosa (p106), Zinave, Banhine and Limpopo (p80) in the interior; Bazaruto National Park (p96) offshore; and Quirimbas National Park (p155), encompassing both coastal and inland areas in Cabo Delgado province.

Bazaruto is known for its quintessential tropical island setting, its offshore coral reefs and fish, and the fact that it hosts the largest remaining dugong population in the region. Various islands within Quirimbas National Park can also be easily visited, and diving can be arranged with lodges both in Quirimbas National Park and on Bazaruto.

Gorongosa, which has received a major boost thanks to the involvement of the US-based Carr Foundation, is easy to visit, and a prime destination for birdwatchers, or for those wanting to experience the bush. Wildlife is also making a strong comeback.

Limpopo National Park, which shares a border with South Africa's Kruger National Park, is straightforward to visit. Zinave and Banhine do not yet have any visitor infrastructure. Both will ultimately be incorporated into a 'transfrontier conservation area' surrounding the Great Limpopo Transfrontier Park, which links Mozambique's Limpopo National Park with South Africa's Kruger National Park and Gonarezhou National Park in Zimbabwe. For all parks, children under 12 years of age are admitted free and those aged between 13 and 20 are eligible for the child rate.

In addition to Niassa Reserve (p147), Mozambique's wildlife reserves include Marromeu (p119), Pomene (p92), Maputo (p78) and Gilé (p123) – now being rehabilitated with assistance from the French government plus numerous controlled hunting areas and forest reserves. The Chimanimani National Reserve has a network of rustic camps for hikers.

The government has also approved development of several 'transboundary natural resources management areas', including one which is to form part of the Great Limpopo Transfrontier Park. The goal is to try to create

Drawn from the Plains – Life in the Wilds of Namibia & Moçambique (2007) by Lynne Tinley has alluring descriptions of Gorongosa National Park.

The website of Gorongosa National Park (www .gorongosa.net) has extensive information on the park and its ecosystems, and frequent updates on work being done in the surrounding communities.

an environment favourable for both local residents and the local wildlife, without regard to national boundaries.

A new protected area is in the process of being declared around the Primeiras and Segundas Islands, offshore between Angoche and Pebane. It will protect one of Mozambique's largest green turtle nesting sites. The area is also known for its whales, coral reefs and prolific birdlife, and is a major breeding ground for sooty terns. Another projected park, though still in the early planning stages, is the Zimoza Transfrontier Park at the confluence of the Zambezi and Luangwa Rivers, and joining areas in Zimbabwe and Zambia with Mozambique's Zumbo district in the far west of Tete province.

For more on what's happening environmentally in Mozambique, check out WWF-Mozambique at www.wwf.org.mz and www.panda.org.

ENVIRONMENTAL ISSUES

From rampaging elephants destroying farmers' crops to massive flooding to the plundering of natural resources by unscrupulous timber harvesters and commercial fishing operators, Mozambique's challenges in preserving its exceptional ecosystems read like a high-adventure novel. Fortunately the country and its natural resources have come increasingly into the international spotlight over the past decade, and WWF (Worldwide Fund for Nature) and other organisations partnering with the Mozambican government have made large strides in protecting the country's wealth.

Some of the most exciting progress is the protection of Mozambique's marine resources. Highlights include the creation of Quirimbas National Park, the creation and recent extension of Bazaruto National Park, and ongoing efforts to declare a new protected marine area around the Primeiras

---

RESPONSIBLE TOURISM

With the increase in tourism in Mozambique, popular coastal resorts are beginning to show the effects of degradation. Some things you can do to prevent the situation from worsening:

■ Don't drive on the beaches – it's bad for the environment, and illegal in Mozambique.

■ Support the local economy whenever possible – shop at local markets, patronise local establishments and buy local crafts, preferably directly from those who make them.

■ Pack up your litter from beaches and campsites.

■ Save natural resources. Water especially is a precious resource throughout much of the country. Try not to waste it in hotels, and in rural areas try to avoid spilling or wasting water from communal pumps. Ask permission before drawing water from a community well.

■ Look for opportunities to interact with local communities. Take advantage of culturally oriented programs where they are available, and try to choose itineraries that are well-integrated with the communities in the areas where you will be travelling.

■ Choose tour operators and tourist establishments that treat local communities as equal partners, and that are committed to protecting local ecosystems.

■ Always ask permission before photographing anyone.

■ Reciprocation of kindness is fine, but indiscriminate distribution of gifts from outside is never appropriate. Donations to recognised projects are more sustainable and have a better chance of reaching those who need them most.

■ Don't buy items made from ivory, skin, shells, turtles, coral etc.

■ Respect local culture and customs.

GOING GREEN

Here's a sampling of what's happening in Mozambique:

- **Ibo Eco School** (www.iboecoschool.be; p156) gives Ibo Island children a good start in their crucial early years. It also takes volunteers
- **Feliciano dos Santos**, cofounder and director of the NGO Estamos, and his renowned band, the Niassa province–based **Massukos** (www.massukos.org), have received international acclaim for their work promoting social change and sanitation awareness.
- **Teatro dos Oprimidos** spreads social awareness messages on HIV/AIDS and malaria.
- Community tourism initiatives in **Quirimbas National Park** (p155) train locals to be bird guides, and establish community-run campsites, home-stay programs and a tourist information centre.
- **Eco-Micaia** (www.micaia.org) is working to establish community-based tourism in the Chimanimani Mountains.
- The **Carr Foundation** (p106) and staff at **Gorongosa National Park** (p106) are doing extensive and impressive work in collaboration with the communities surrounding the park, including in the areas of health, education and literacy.
- The **Manda Wilderness Community Trust** (p146) and **Nkwichi Lodge** (p146) are promoting sustainable tourism and community development along the shores of Lake Niassa.

and Segundas Islands. In the Quirimbas Archipelago, the area's protected status has already brought noticeable improvement to the previously rapidly declining fish populations at inshore fishing areas. On the Primeiras and Segundas islands, local fishermen are working with the WWF to protect sooty tern and green turtle breeding grounds, with a focus on minimising the sale and consumption of eggs and products.

On the terrestrial side, as conservation measures and antipoaching efforts have begun to show success, and populations of elephants and other wildlife increase, instances of human and elephant conflicts are increasing. This is particularly a problem in the far north, where elephants eat and destroy crops in large areas of Niassa province, as well as in coastal sections of Quirimbas National Park and elsewhere. Thus far, the main way of combating this has been to lay electric fencing in community areas. However, the fences are expensive and difficult to maintain and it is not possible to use them in all affected areas. More sustainable techniques are gradually being introduced to complement the fences, including encouraging the cultivation of Mozambique's famous *piri-piri* (chilli peppers), the clearing of small buffer zones between crop areas and the bush, and roping off crop areas with strings soaked in a mixture of oil and chilli peppers.

Illegal timber practices are more complicated to combat, with entrenched interests at every level. An illustration of the challenges is seen in northern and central Mozambique, where tropical hardwoods are felled with little or no regulation. The inspectors who are supposed to patrol forest areas and control logging activities are poorly paid, with little incentive and inadequate resources to do their job. Bribery is commonplace and controls are weak or nonexistent. Reports indicate that even if companies get a logging permit they often operate outside the areas assigned to them. In addition to environmental damage, the widespread practice of exporting unprocessed logs (rather than processing the timber in Mozambique, with the attendant local economic gain) means local communities receive little benefit from timber resources. There is often neither replanting nor sustainable harvesting (ie taking one tree in every 10 in a cyclical pattern)

The Mozambique- and UK-based Eco-Micaia (www.micaia.org) is working to support local sustainable economic and cultural initiatives. Check its website to see how to help.

MANGROVES

In addition to being famous for its beautiful beaches, the Mozambican coast is also notable for its extensive mangrove swamps, especially in the centre and the north of the country. These play an essential role in coastal ecosystems by curbing erosion, enriching surrounding waters with nutrients, and providing resources for local communities. The wood of mangroves is resistant to insects, and is prized for building houses, beds and fishing traps. Around Pemba, an infusion of the bark of one species of mangrove is used for dyeing fishing nets.

Despite their usefulness, Mozambique's mangroves have come under attack. Large stands have been cleared for the establishment of solar salt pans and shrimp aquaculture ponds, while others have been cut for charcoal production and firewood.

---

and the potential for farming on the cleared forest is limited, as soils are unsuitable or too thin.

While lasting improvements in the protection and management of Mozambique's timber and other natural resources will only be possible as the country's overall economic situation progresses, there are several bright spots in the picture, including a network of smaller-scale projects focused on sustainable development and community resource management in the Chimanimani Mountains, the Quirimbas Archipelago, the area surrounding Gorongosa National Park and various other parts of the country.

Diving

Mozambique remains a largely unknown and underrated diving destination, yet it offers many unique attractions. In addition to the length of its coastline, there's the chance to sight dolphins, whale sharks, manta rays and dugongs, plus opportunities to do exploratory diving and discover new sites. Other draws include an almost complete lack of overdevelopment and commercialism, the natural beauty of the Mozambican coast, seasonal humpback whale sightings, excellent fish diversity and a generally untouched array of hard and soft corals, especially in the north. You'll also have most spots almost to yourself – a treat if you've been fighting for space in more popular dive destinations.

For stunning underwater photos plus information on dive sites, look for a copy of Jean-Paul Vermeulen's *Gone Diving Mozambique* (also available through www .imagesdumozambique .com).

Equipment, instruction and certification are available in most main coastal areas, including Ponta d'Ouro, Inhaca, Závora, Tofo, Vilankulo, the Bazaruto Archipelago, Nacala, Pemba and the Quirimbas Archipelago. Prices are comparable to elsewhere in East Africa, although somewhat higher than in South Africa.

INFORMATION
Conditions & Seasons

While Mozambique is considered a year-round diving destination, conditions and visibility vary significantly. The best months are generally April/May to July and again in November/December (August to October can get quite windy). The worst months tend to be February and March, when rains are heavy, and some resorts only operate with skeleton staff, though all this varies as you move up the coast. Visibility is usually best in late autumn and winter (April through to October), when water temperatures are between 22° and 25°C. In summer the water temperature rises to 28°or 29°C.

Lonely Planet's *South Africa: Diving & Snorkeling* includes a section on southern Mozambique, and is well worth hunting up for general background information on diving in the region.

All ability levels are catered for, with dive sites ranging from shallow snorkelling reefs close to shore, to deeper dives, with depths varying from about 7m to more than 35m. Most dives are done from rubber inflatable boats powered by two 85HP motors, or a similar configuration, although there are also operators who use refitted dhows or yachts.

Depending on the location and season, most divers are comfortable with a full 3mm wetsuit, though some operators use 5mm suits as standard.

DIVING SAFETY

Some things to keep in mind before diving:

- Possess a current diving certification card from a recognised scuba-diving instructional agency (and don't forget to bring it with you, together with your log book).
- Be sure you are healthy and feel comfortable diving.
- Obtain reliable information about physical and environmental conditions at the dive site (eg from a reputable local dive operation).
- Dive only at sites within your realm of experience; if available, engage the services of a competent, professionally trained dive instructor or dive master.
- Be aware that underwater conditions vary significantly from one region, or even site, to another and that seasonal changes can significantly alter any site and dive conditions.
- Ask about local laws, regulation and etiquette regarding local marine life and the environment.

RESPONSIBLE DIVING

As Mozambique's popularity as a tourist and diving destination grows, pressure on dive sites is increasing. Following are some tips for helping preserve the ecology and beauty of the reefs:

- Don't use anchors on reefs and take care not to ground boats on coral.

- Avoid touching living marine organisms or dragging equipment across the reef. If you must hold on to the reef, only touch exposed rock or dead coral.

- Be conscious of your fins. Even without contact, the surge from heavy fin-strokes near the reef can damage delicate organisms. Take care not to kick up clouds of sand, which can smother delicate reef organisms.

- Practise and maintain proper buoyancy control. Major damage can be done by divers descending too fast and colliding with the reef.

- Take care in underwater caves. Spend as little time in them as possible as your air bubbles may get caught within the roof, leaving previously submerged organisms high and dry. Take turns to inspect the interior of a small cave.

- Resist the temptation to collect or buy corals or shells (which is not only ecologically damaging, but also illegal).

- Take home all rubbish. Plastics in particular are a serious threat to marine life.

- Don't feed fish, as this disturbs their normal eating habits and encourages aggressive behaviour.

- Minimise your disturbance of marine animals, including dolphins and turtles.

Dive Training & Certification

Many travellers get their dive certification in South Africa and then come to Mozambique to actually dive, although quality dive instruction and certification (generally PADI) is available at most of the coastal dive resorts listed opposite. For local dive operator listings, see the regional chapters.

Prices for dives and instruction are fairly uniform, with some of the best deals available up north. Throughout, there are often low-season discounts. Rates average about US$50 per single dive, including equipment and boat travel. With your own equipment, expect to pay from about US$30 per dive. Four-day open-water certification courses cost from about US$350 to US$450 and should generally be booked in advance, especially during peak seasons, and in the south. Depending on where you are in the country, and who is running the dive shop, dive prices may be quoted in dollars, rand or meticais, although payment can usually be made in any of the three.

It's also worth considering booking a dive-accommodation package. Most of the resort-based operators listed in the regional chapters offer these.

Contacts for live-aboard arrangements include Fim do Mundo Safaris (p157), and several other of the Ibo Island–based operators (p157). Pemba Beach Hotel (p153) arranges live-aboards in the Quirimbas Archipelago or its luxury yacht.

Dive Operators & Dive Tours

Most operators are resort-based, with reliable rental equipment, secure washing and drying facilities, and South African staff who are familiar with the local terrain and conditions. When choosing an operator, quality should be the main consideration. Take into account the operator's experience and qualifications, knowledgeability and competence of staff, and the condition of equipment and frequency of maintenance. Try to assess whether the overall attitude is serious and professional, and ask about safety precautions – radios, oxygen, emergency evacuation procedures, boat reliability and back-up engines, first-aid kits, safety flares and life jackets. On longer dives, do you get an energising meal, or just tea and biscuits?

PRINCIPAL DIVE SITES
Southern Mozambique
Most dive sites are in the south, where there is a wide choice of operators.

PONTA D'OURO & PONTA MALONGANE
This stretch of coast (p75) is a popular destination for divers from South Africa, and gets crowded during the April and December South African school holidays, when it is recommended that certification courses be booked in advance. Visibility is generally better than at sites just over the border, coral growth is prolific at some sites and, with luck, it's possible to dive among sharks (primarily hammerheads and Zambezis), plus potato bass and dolphins. There's also an on-site dolphin tour operator, see p75. Many sites are within a short boat ride from shore and there's a good reef wall at the southern end of the point for snorkelling. Most diving operates out of informal dive camps catering to budget travellers, and dive-accommodation deals are available. For more upmarket diving, contact Ponta Mamoli (p77).

INHACA ISLAND
Diving from Inhaca Island (p71) is tide-dependent and conditions are variable, with poor visibility often an issue, although on good days you can expect to see a variety of sharks, manta rays, potato bass and more. Bottlenose and humpback dolphins are also sometimes seen, and occasionally dugongs. August and September should be avoided, as it's often too windy to go out.

The best snorkelling is in the sheltered waters around Cape Santa Maria, off Inhaca's southernmost tip. There's one island-based dive operator next to Pestana Inhaca Lodge (p72).

ZÁVORA
Závora Beach (p83), off the N1 near Inharrime, is a relatively new addition to southern Mozambique's diving scene, with a long beach, untouched reefs, sharks, manta rays and even a wreck – all beginning close to shore, and extending about 10km to the outer reefs. Exploratory diving is still ongoing. For site descriptions, check out www mozdivers.com. There's no instruction here – qualified divers only.

MOZAMBIQUE'S CORALS
Corals are found only between the latitudes of 30° north and 30° south, and although scattered coral communities extend along the Mozambican coast into South Africa, the reefs near Mozambique's Inhaca Island are considered to be the southernmost of the African mainland.

In addition to being fascinating to explore, coral reefs are among the most productive and diverse of the earth's ecosystems. About 25% of the world's fish species depend on reefs during at least some stage of their life cycle. Reefs also protect the coast from damaging wave action and erosion, and contribute to the formation of islands and sandy beaches.

Despite some areas of damage, Mozambique's reefs – including extensive fringing reef systems in the north, and the southern reefs dotting the southern coast at intervals between the Bazaruto Archipelago and Inhaca Island – are considered to be in generally very good condition and are mostly unexplored; a notable exception are those off Inhaca Island, which have been extensively studied. Studies are also underway of the northern reefs around the Quirimbas Archipelago, with early reports indicating that these may be some of the richest reefs along this side of the continent.

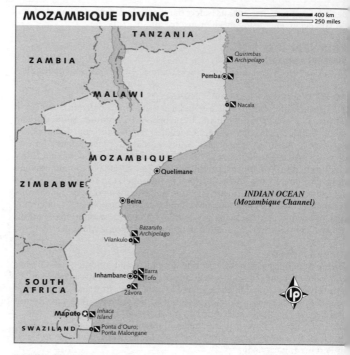

MOZAMBIQUE DIVING

TANZANIA

ZAMBIA

Quirimbas Archipelago

Pemba

MALAWI

Nacala

MOZAMBIQUE

Quelimane

ZIMBABWE

INDIAN OCEAN
(Mozambique Channel)

Beira

Bazaruto Archipelago

Vilankulo

Inhambane — Barra
Tofo

SOUTH AFRICA

Závora

Maputo — Inhaca Island

SWAZILAND — Ponta d'Ouro;
Ponta Malongane

TOFO & BARRA

It was diving that put Tofo (p87) on the map, and it's is still one of the most popular places in Mozambique to dive and get certified. There's a selection of operators and a lively dive subculture. Corals aren't as plentiful as to the south or north but this is compensated for by the likelihood of manta and whale shark sightings, and the relative proximity to the world-class Manta Reef, along with Amazon and other choice sites.

Dive facilities at Barra (p89) are similar, although Barra has somewhat more midrange accommodation offerings and you'll need to travel a bit further to get to many of the better sites.

Several of the resorts south of Tofo in the Inhambane area (see p86) have in-house dive operators and this is another possible base for diving in this area. While the area is convenient to Manta Reef (and to snorkelling at Pandane Reef just offshore), you'll have to travel a bit to the other main sites.

BBC's 'Andrea – Queen of the Mantas' focuses on marine ecologist Andrea Marshall's pioneering work with manta rays in the waters near Tofo in southern Mozambique.

VILANKULO & BAZARUTO ARCHIPELAGO

There is fine diving and snorkelling around the islands of the Bazaruto Archipelago (p96), although it tends to be slightly pricier than further south and most sites are well offshore. Among the draws are Two Mile Reef, two miles (3.2km) northeast of Benguera Island (and about an hour in a speedboat from Vilankulo), which is considered the best in the area and has a variety of sites. On the inside of the reef is the sheltered Aquarium, which is also ideal for snorkelling. Dolphins and dugongs are a highlight, as are seasonal humpback whales. Santa Carolina Island, which is the only rock island of the archipelago, offers excellent snorkelling. Magaruque Island is also a rewarding snorkelling destination, with plenty of fish on the reef just

---

WATCHING WHALES & MORE

The likelihood of seeing whale sharks, humpback whales, dolphins, manta rays and dugongs is one of the highlights of diving off the Mozambican coast. Whale sharks – the world's largest fish – are most prolific in the south during the summer months from about November to March/April, although they are occasionally seen at other times of the year.

Humpback whales migrate up the southeast African coastline from Antarctica to mate and calve, reaching Mozambican waters around June. Between July and September/October, it's common to see them offshore along the length of the country.

Dolphins can be seen year-round, although the winter months of June through to August tend to be particularly good. Mantas can also be seen year-round, and are almost guaranteed around Tofo and Barra and the nearby Manta Reef. Green and other sea turtles are a highlight of the north. Dugongs are usually sighted around the Bazaruto Archipelago – see p43.

---

off its western shore. The main drawback of the islands is the relatively long boat ride to most sites, especially if you're based in Vilankulo (p92). Budget and midrange travellers should arrange things in Vilankulo, while top-end travellers are catered for by dive operators affiliated with the top-end resorts on the islands.

Northern Mozambique

The north is Mozambique's adventurous frontier, not only for travel, but also for diving. Pemba has long had a low-key but quality dive scene that's now beginning to gain more attention. The newest developments are in the Quirimbas Archipelago and surrounding areas which are considered to have some of the best unexplored diving to be found anywhere.

NACALA

Nacala's only, but recommended, dive operator (Libélula, see p140) will guide you into the depths of enormous, blue Nacala Bay – an ideal destination for anyone seeking something different and well away from standard tourist loops. There's an array of sites within relatively close reach, fine visibility, and night dives can be organised from shore. Whales are an attraction from about September to November, the hard corals are beautiful, dolphins may grace you with their presence, and there are many smaller, fascinating sea creatures.

PEMBA

Pemba (p149) has good-value diving with a range of rewarding dive sites, a relaxed, beachside ambience and personalised operators catering to all sections of the market. There are a range of sites, suitable for all levels and diveable year-round.

The diving begins about 500m offshore from Wimbi Beach, where the coastal shelf drops off steeply, offering a spectacular wall dive. Once you've had your fill here, there are other sites nearby and the Quirimbas Archipelago is within easy reach.

QUIRIMBAS ARCHIPELAGO

Much of this long archipelago (p155) is still largely unexplored. It's possible to arrange diving at any of the island-based resorts, and also through dive operators on Ibo Island (p156). Highlights include the protected marine sanctuary around Quilaluia Island and the famed St Lazarus Bank. Vamizi and Rongui Islands both have lovely coral gardens close to shore, and snorkelling sites abound.

A Field Guide to the Seashores of Eastern Africa & the Western Indian Ocean Islands by Matthew Richmond, *Coral Reefs of the Indian Ocean – Their Ecology and Conservation* by TR McClanahan et al and *Marine Life of the Pacific & Indian Oceans* by Gerald Allen all have detailed info on regional reefs and marine life.

Check out the website of the Manta & Whale Shark Research Centre (www .giantfish.org) for more on Mozambique's (and the world's) largest fish, and what you can do to help with their conservation.

Maputo

Maputo

With its Mediterranean-style architecture, waterside setting and wide avenues lined with jacaranda and flame trees, Maputo is easily one of Africa's most attractive capitals. It's also the most developed place in Mozambique by far, with a wide selection of hotels and restaurants, well-stocked supermarkets, shady sidewalk cafes and a lively cultural scene.

The heart of the city is the bustling, low-lying baixa. Here, Portuguese-era buildings with their graceful balconies and wrought-iron balustrades jostle for space with ungainly Marxist-style apartment blocks. *Galabiyya*-garbed men gather in doorways for a chat, Indian traders carry on brisk business in the narrow side streets and women wrapped in colourful *capulanas* (sarongs) sell everything from seafood to spices at the massive Municipal Market.

A few kilometres away, along the seaside Avenida Marginal, life takes a more leisurely pace. Fishermen stand along the roadside with the day's catch, hoping to lure customers from the constant parade of passing vehicles; banana vendors loll on their carts in the shade, with Radio Moçambique piping out eternally upbeat rhythms in the background; and local football teams vie for victory in impromptu matches in the sand.

Maputo is pricier than elsewhere in the country, especially for imported goods brought in on the toll road linking Johannesburg and the South African economy with Maputo's port and the sea. Yet there's enough selection to make it a good destination no matter what your budget. Getting to know the city is a highlight of visiting Mozambique and essential to understanding the country. Don't miss spending time here before heading north.

HIGHLIGHTS

- Catch some culture at one of Maputo's many **museums** (p61)
- Dine out in style, sample a different **restaurant** (p66) every night
- Shop for souvenirs and browse for bargains at the city's colourful **markets and craft shops** (p68)
- Experience the pulsating pace of the capital's thriving **nightlife** (p68)
- Enjoy the laid-back ambience of **Inhaca Island** (p71)

HISTORY

Long before Europeans discovered Maputo's charms, the local Ronga people were living here, fishing, whale hunting, farming and trading. In 1545 Portuguese navigator Lourenço Marques happened upon Delagoa Bay (now Maputo Bay), in his journey up the southern African coastline. His reports attracted other traders who established temporary settlements offshore on Inhaca and Xefina Grande islands as bases for ivory trading forays to the mainland. Yet the Portuguese attention to the area was only fleeting. They soon turned their sights northwards, all but abandoning their activities in the south.

Lourenço Marques – as the area later became known – took on a new importance in the mid-19th century, with the discovery of diamonds and gold in the nearby Transvaal Republic. Around 1898 it replaced Mozambique Island as the capital of Portuguese East Africa. A new rail link with the Transvaal in 1894 and expansion of the port fuelled the city's growth. In the 1950s and 1960s, 'LM' became a favoured playground for Portuguese holiday makers, and for apartheid-era South Africans who came over the border in droves seeking prawns, prostitutes and beaches. With Mozambican independence in 1975, the city's original residents reasserted themselves and in 1976 President Samora Machel changed the name to Maputo, honouring an early chief who had resisted Portuguese colonialism.

ORIENTATION

Maputo sits on a low escarpment overlooking Maputo Bay, with the long avenues of its upper-lying residential sections spilling down into the baixa.

Some budget accommodation and many businesses, the train station, banks, post and telephone offices are in the baixa, on or near Avenida 25 de Setembro, while embassies and most better hotels are in the city's upper section, especially in and around the Sommerschield diplomatic and residential quarter. Maputo's tallest building and a good landmark is known as 'trinta e trés andares' (33 Storey Building), in the baixa at Avenida 25 de Setembro and Rua da Imprensa. At the northernmost end of the Marginal and about 7km from the centre is Bairro Triunfo and the Costa do Sol area, with a small beach and several places to stay and eat.

About 10km west of Maputo is the large suburb of Matola, home to many industries and new developments.

Maps

The Planta de Endereçamento do Centro da Cidade de Maputo (1997), put out by Conselho Municipal in collaboration with Coopération Française, is dated and difficult to find, but still the best city map. There's a larger version of the same map in book form (Guia das Vias 1997) which includes the city's outskirts. Other city maps, including the Páginas Amarelas Maputo Guide, are widely

---

MAPUTO IN...

Two Days

After breakfast at your hotel or a street-side cafe, head to Praça 25 de Junho and get an early start on some of the nearby sights, including the **Municipal Market** (p61), the **Money Museum** (p62) and the **train station** (p61). Once finished, hire a tuk-tuk to take you along Avenida Marginal to **Restaurante Costa do Sol** (p66) for lunch. The **National Art Museum** (p61) is an ideal afternoon stop, before heading to **Rua d'Arte** (p68) or another venue for an evening sampling Maputo's **nightlife** (p68).

Spend day two taking in some more sights, including the **old fort** (p62), the **Chissano Gallery** (p61) and **Praça da Independência** (p61). While you're here, don't miss shopping for crafts at the **Bazar de Arte** (p68). In the late afternoon head down to the **Fish Market** (p61) to take in the ambience and enjoy an informal meal, before heading out for another night on the town (or getting to bed early to catch an early bus north).

Four Days

Follow the two-day itinerary. On day three, take an excursion to the **Maputo Special Reserve** (p78). Consider spending the night there. Alternatively, spend days three and four on **Inhaca Island** (p71), relaxing and snorkelling.

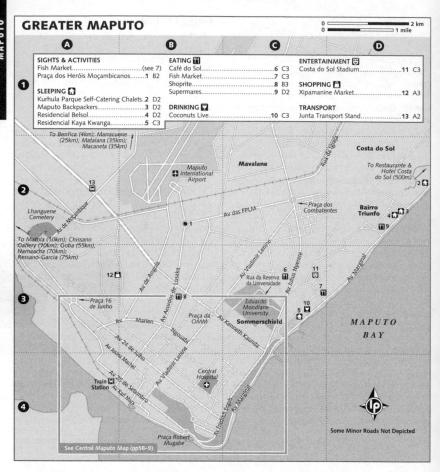

GREATER MAPUTO

SIGHTS & ACTIVITIES	**EATING** 🍴	**ENTERTAINMENT** 🎭
Fish Market.....................(see 7)	Café do Sol.................................6 C3	Costa do Sol Stadium...............11 C3
Praça dos Heróis Moçambicanos.......1 B2	Fish Market.................................7 C3	
	Shoprite......................................8 B3	**SHOPPING** 🛍
SLEEPING 🛏	Supermares.................................9 D2	Xipamanine Market....................12 A3
Kurhula Parque Self-Catering Chalets.2 D2		
Maputo Backpackers.....................3 D2	**DRINKING** 🍸	**TRANSPORT**
Residencial Belsol.........................4 D2	Coconuts Live.............................10 C3	Junta Transport Stand................13 A2
Residencial Kaya Kwanga...............5 C3		

available at bookshops. Most backpackers hostels and some hotels also have free photocopied city maps.

INFORMATION
Bookshops
Livraria Europa-América (Map pp58–9; ☎ 21-494692; peamoz@tdm.co.mz; 377 Avenida 24 de Julho) Next to the Geology Museum, with maps and a good selection of English-language books and magazines.
Sensações (Map pp58–9; cnr Avenidas Julius Nyerere & Eduardo Mondlane) A small selection of CDs; next to Mundo's restaurant.

Cultural Centres
Centro Cultural Franco-Moçambicano (Map pp58–9; ☎ 21-314590; www.ccfmoz.com; Praça da Independência) An excellent place, with art exhibitions, music and dance performances, films, theatre and more.
Centro Cultural Português (Map pp58–9; Instituto Camões; ☎ 21-493892; ccp-maputo@instituto-camoes .pt; 720 Avenida Julius Nyerere) Art and photography exhibits; opposite the South African High Commission.
Centro de Estudos Brasileiros (Map pp58–9; ☎ 21-306840; ceb.eventos@tvcabo.co.mz; cnr Avenidas Karl Marx & 25 de Setembro) Exhibitions by Lusophone artists and Portuguese language courses.

Emergency
Official emergency numbers are listed here, but they rarely work. It's better to seek help from your hotel or embassy. For emergency medical treatment, see opposite.

MAPUTO

Central Hospital (Map pp58–9; ☎ 21-320011/8, 21-325000; cnr Avenidas Eduardo Mondlane & Augustinho Neto)
Fire (☎ 21-322222, 800-198198)
Police station (☎ 21-325031, 21-322002)

If you are the victim of a crime and need to get a police report for your insurance company, these can be obtained with time and patience at the police station nearest the site of the crime. Useful stations include those on Avenida Kim Il Sung, 1½ blocks south of Avenida Kenneth Kaunda; near the corner of Avenidas Mao Tse Tung and Amilcar Cabral; and on Avenida Julius Nyerere, three blocks south of Avenida 24 de Julho. Some insurance companies will accept a report from your embassy instead.

Internet Access
Wi-fi spots are noted in the Sleeping (p64) and Eating (p66) listings.
Mundo's Internet Cafe (Map pp58-9; Avenida Julius Nyerere; per hr Mtc50; ☺ 8.30am-9pm Mon-Sat, 10am-4pm Sun) Next to Mundo's restaurant.
Pizza House Internet Cafe (Map pp58-9; Avenida Mao Tse Tung; per hr Mtc40; ☺ 8am-10pm) Upstairs at Pizza House.
Teledata (Map pp58-9; Avenida 24 de Julho; per hr Mtc30; ☺ 7.30am-8pm Mon-Fri, 9am-7pm Sat) One block west of Avenida Vladimir Lenine at the corner of Rua das Malotas, and diagonally opposite África Bar.

Medical Services
Clínica de Sommerschield (Map pp58-9; ☎ 82-305 6240, 21-493924/5/6; 52 Rua Pereira do Lago; ☺ 24hr) Just off Avenida Kim Il Sung, with a lab, and a doctor on call. Advance payment required (meticais, rand, dollars or Visa card).
Farmácia Capital Franca Centro Comercial (Map pp58-9; ☎ 82-301 4055; ground fl, Franca Centro Comercial, cnr Avenidas 24 de Julho & Amilcar Cabral; ☺ 24hr); Avenida Mao Tse Tung (Map pp58-9; ☎ 82-301 4056; Avenida Mao Tse Tung; ☺ 24hr) The Mao Tse Tung branch is just up from Pizza House.
Swedish Clinic (Map pp58-9; ☎ 21-492922, emergencies only 82-300 2610; www.indevelop.se/maputo.asp; 1128 Avenida Julius Nyerere) A private membership-only clinic with Western standards and prices.

Money
There are 24-hour ATMs all over town, including at the airport and Shoprite.

For changing cash, in addition to the banks there are foreign exchange bureaus (casas de câmbio) along Avenida Julius Nyerere south-east of the Hotel Polana, at Hotel Pestana Rovuma on Rua de Sé and on Avenida Mao Tse Tung around Avenida Tomás Nduda. Out of hours, try Cotacambios airport (open for all international flights), which changes cash only, although its rates aren't much better than those offered by many hotels.
Standard Bank Praça 25 de Junho (Map pp58-9; Praça 25 de Junho); Avenida Julius Nyerere (Map pp58-9; Avenida Julius Nyerere, opposite Hotel Avenida) Has 24-hour ATMs; dispenses up to Mtc10,000 per transaction.

Post
Main post office (CTT; Map pp58-9; Avenida 25 de Setembro; ☺ 8am-6pm Mon-Sat, 9am-noon Sun)

Telephone
Talk-and-pay service is available at the main post office (Mtc1 per impulse, available 8am to 5pm Monday to Friday). You can see the amount you'll owe as you speak. Mcel and Vodacom have representatives everywhere for buying starter packs and recharge cards.

Travel Agencies
Dana Agency (Map pp58-9; ☎ 21-484300; travel@dana .co.mz; 1170 Avenida Kenneth Kaunda) Sister agency to Dana Tours and in the same compound; does domestic and international flight bookings.
Dana Tours (Map pp58-9; ☎ 21-495514; info@danatours .net; 1170 Avenida Kenneth Kaunda) A top-notch agency that specialises in travel to the coast, and can also sort you out for destinations throughout Mozambique (plus in Swaziland and South Africa). Midrange and up, with occasional budget offerings.
Mozaic Travel (Map pp58-9; ☎ 21-451376; www .mozaictravel.com; 240 Rua da Massala, Bairro Triunfo) This long-standing, reliable outfit is a good contact for organising excursions to Limpopo National Park. It can also help with arrangements for the Bazaruto Archipelago, and elsewhere in the country.

DANGERS & ANNOYANCES
Although most tourists visit Maputo without mishap, be vigilant when out and about both during the day and at night, and take the precautions discussed on p170. In particular, avoid carrying a bag, wearing expensive jewellery or otherwise giving a potential thief reason to think that you might have something of value. Don't put yourself in isolating situations, and at night, always take a taxi. Areas to avoid during the day include the isolated stretches of the Marginal between Praça Robert Mugabe and the Southern Sun

MAPUTO

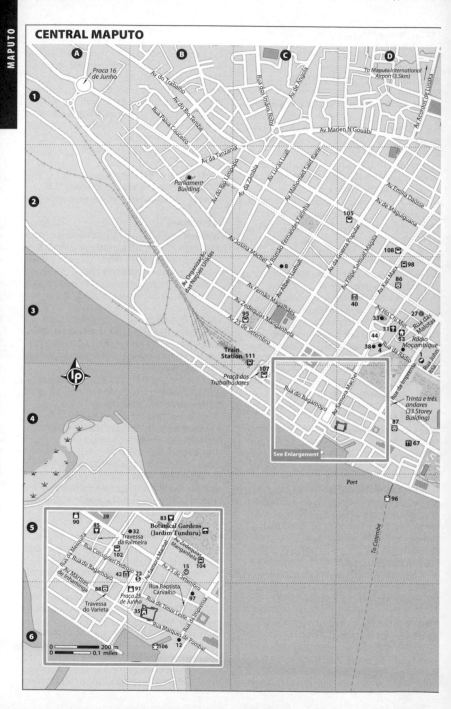

CENTRAL MAPUTO

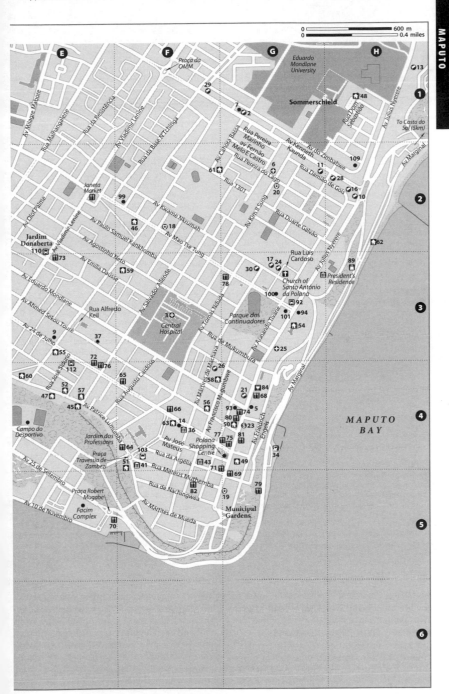

hotel, and the access roads leading down to the Marginal from Avenida Friedrich Engels. Also avoid the area below the escarpment just south of Avenida Patrice Lumumba.

Carry a notarised copy of your passport (photo and Mozambique visa pages) when out and about (see the boxed text, p179). It's rarely checked, but when it is, it's usu-

ally by underpaid policemen looking to top up their meagre salaries with bribes. Keep the notarised copy handy (and away from your other valuables). If you do get stopped, always insist on going to the nearest police station *(esquadrão)*, and try to avoid handing over your actual passport. Ask at your hotel where the nearest notary is. Many embassies also provide notary service. The more you can do to minimise the impression that you're a newly arrived tourist, the lower your chances of getting stopped for a document check.

There are several restricted areas that are off-limits to pedestrians (no photos). These include the eastern footpath on Avenida Julius Nyerere in front of the president's residence and the Ponta Vermelha zone in the city's southeastern corner.

On a more prosaic note, Maputo has traffic lights, but they don't always work, and when they work, they're not always heeded, so be careful when cruising through an intersection on green.

SIGHTS

The heart of old Maputo is in the baixa, which is where most of the sights are.

National Art Museum

Half a block west of Avenida Karl Marx, the **National Art Museum** (Museu Nacional de Arte; Map pp58-9; ☎ 21-320264; artemus@tvcabo.co.mz; 1233 Avenida Ho Chi Min; admission Mtc20; ☒ 11am-6pm Tue-Fri, 2-6pm Sat, Sun & holidays) has an excellent collection of paintings and sculptures by Mozambique's finest contemporary artists, including Malangatana and Chissano.

Núcleo de Arte

This long-standing **artists' cooperative** (Map pp58-9; ☎ 21-492523; www.africaserver.nl/nucleo; 194 Rua da Argélia; ☒ 10am-5pm Mon-Sat) has frequent exhibitions featuring the work of up-and-coming artists (some of which is for sale), including pieces made in the 'Guns into Art' project. Check its website for more information. There's also a pottery area, and a garden where you can talk with the artists and watch them at work (afternoons are best for this). Adjoining is a small cafe.

House & Studio of Malangatana

It is occasionally possible to visit the **house and studio of Malangatana** (☎ 21-465286, 21-465681; Rua de Camões, Bairro do Aeroporto; ☒ by appointment only), Mozambique's most renowned painter. It's filled with dozens of his own paintings as well as sculptures by Alberto Chissano. Bookings are best arranged through Kulungwana Espaço Artístico (right). The house is located several kilometres outside the city centre; ask for directions when arranging the visit.

Chissano Gallery

Works of renowned sculptor Alberto Chissano are on display in his family's residence at the **Chissano Gallery** (Galeria Chissano; off Map p56; Rua Torre de Vale, Bairro Sial, Matola; admission Mtc50; ☒ 9am-noon & 3-5pm Tue-Sun), together with the works of other sculptors and painters. Taxis charge from Mtc600 return, including waiting time.

Train Station

Maputo's landmark **train station** (Caminho dos Ferros de Moçambique or CFM; Map pp58-9; Praça dos Trabalhadores) – recently voted by *Newsweek* as one of the 10 most beautiful train stations in the world – is one of the city's most imposing buildings. The dome was designed by an associate of Alexandre Gustav Eiffel (of Eiffel Tower fame), although Eiffel himself never set foot in Mozambique. Also impressive are the wrought-iron lattice work, pillars and verandahs gracing the pistachio-green exterior. Inside (to the left, at the end of the platform, at 'Sala de Espera'), is the **Kulungwana Espaço Artístico** (Map pp58-9; ☎ 21-333048; kulungwana@clubnet .co.mz; ☒ 10am-5pm Tue-Fri, to 3pm Sat & Sun), with a small exhibition of works by local and visiting artists, and sculptures and paintings for sale.

Praça de Independência

This wide plaza is rimmed on one side by the white, spired **Cathedral of Nossa Senhora da Conceição** (Map pp58-9) and on the other by the hulking, neoclassical **City Hall** (Conselho Municipal; Map pp58-9). Just off the square is the **Iron House** (Casa de Ferro; Map pp58-9), which was designed by Eiffel in the late-19th century as the governor's residence, though its metal-plated exterior proved unsuitable for tropical conditions.

Markets

The **Municipal Market** (Mercado Municipal; Map pp58-9; Avenida 25 de Setembro), with its long rows of vendors, tables piled high with produce, fresh fish and colourful spices, and stalls overflowing with everything from brooms to plastic buckets, is Maputo's main market, and well worth a stroll. Get there early in the morning when everything is still fresh, and before the crowds. The smaller and lively **Fish Market** (Mercado de Peixe; Map p56), just off Avenida Marginal, sells a good sample of what lies underneath the nearby waters; choose what you'd like and get it grilled at one of the small restaurants nearby (see p67).

Fort

The old **fort** (Fortaleza; Map pp58-9; Praça 25 de Junho; admission free; ☺ 8am-5pm) was built by the Portuguese in the mid-19th century near the site of an earlier fort. Inside is a garden and a small museum with remnants from the era of early Portuguese forays to the area.

Natural History Museum

The **Natural History Museum** (Museu de História Natural; Map pp58-9; ☎ 21-490879; Praça Travessa de Zambezi; adult/child Mtc50/10, free Sun; ☺ 9am-3.30pm Tue-Fri, 10am-5pm Sat & Sun), near Hotel Cardoso, is worth a stop to see its Manueline architecture and its garden with a mural by Malangatana. Inside are some moderately interesting taxidermy specimens, and what is probably the region's only collection of elephant foetuses.

Geology Museum

The recently renovated **Geology Museum** (Museu da Geologia; Map pp58–9; ☎ 21-498053; museugeologia@tvcabo.co.mz; cnr Avenidas 24 de Julho & Mártires de Machava; admission Mtc50; ☺ 9am-5pm Tue-Fri, 9am-2pm Sat, 2-5pm Sun) has mineral exhibits and a geological relief map of the country.

National Money Museum

Housed in a restored yellow building on the corner of Rua Consiglieri Pedroso, the **National Money Museum** (Museu Nacional da Moeda; Map pp58-9; Praça 25 de Junho; admission Mtc20; ☺ 9am-noon & 2-5pm Tue-Thu & Sat, 9am-noon Fri, 2-5pm Sun) dates from 1860. Inside are exhibits of local currency, ranging from early barter tokens to modernday bills.

Praça dos Heróis Moçambicanos

The large Praça dos Heróis Moçambicanos (Map p56), along Avenida Acordos de Lusaka near the airport, is notable for its 95m-long mural commemorating the revolution. The star-shaped white marble structure in its centre holds the remains of Mozambique's revolutionary and post-independence heroes, including Eduardo Mondlane and Samora Machel, as well as those of national poet José Craveirinha. Photography is prohibited. The public is only permitted to visit (including walking across the praça) on 3 February.

ACTIVITIES

For lap swimming, try the 25m pool at **Clube Naval** (Map pp58-9; ☎ 21-492690; www.clubenaval.intra.co.mz; Avenida Marginal; per month Mtc720). There's also a 15m pool at **Girassol Indy Village** (p65; adult/child Mtc300/125). The pool at Hotel Polana (p66) is 25m at its widest, but only open to hotel guests. Swimming at the beach along Avenida Marginal is possible though inadvisable due to considerations of cleanliness, currents and occasional rumours of sharks.

The best contacts for boat rentals and fishing charters is **Mozambique Charters** (☎ 84-323 6420; www.mozambiquecharters.com) and Clube Naval.

There are frequent tennis tournaments at the courts at the botanical gardens (Jardim Tunduru, corner Rua da Imprensa and Rua da Rádio), where short- and long-term memberships can be arranged. Clube Naval has courts open to its members, and several of the top-end hotels have courts for their guests.

WALKING TOUR

> **WALK FACTS**
>
> **Start** Praça 25 de Junho
> **Finish** Praça 25 de Junho
> **Distance** about 3km
> **Duration** Two hours, plus time for visiting the market, museums and other sights

Central Maputo is easily explored on foot. Many of these sights are also stops on the Mozambique City Tours train (p64).

A good place to start is at Praça 25 de Junho, with the old **fort** (1; left) on its eastern side. Diagonally opposite is the **National Money Museum** (2; left). Leave Praça 25 de Junho to the west via Rua Consiglieri Pedroso which, together with Rua de Bagamoyo one block south, forms the heart of the oldest area of the city. The second cross street you'll reach is Rua da Mesquita, where the **Jumma Masjid (3)** stands on the site of what was once Maputo's oldest mosque.

Continue south along Rua da Mesquita to the building housing the **National Archives** (4; Archivo do Patrimónío Cultural), to your left on Rua de Bagamoyo. Turning west (right) on Rua de Bagamoyo brings you soon to Praça dos Trabalhadores, with its large WWI monument and Maputo's impressive **train station** (5; p61).

Head north one block to Avenida 25 de Setembro, then east to the **Municipal Market** (6; p61). Continue east along Avenida 25 de Setembro for 1½ blocks, and then north along Avenida Samora Machel for three blocks to **Praça da Independência** (7; p61) and the large,

MAPUTO WALKING TOUR

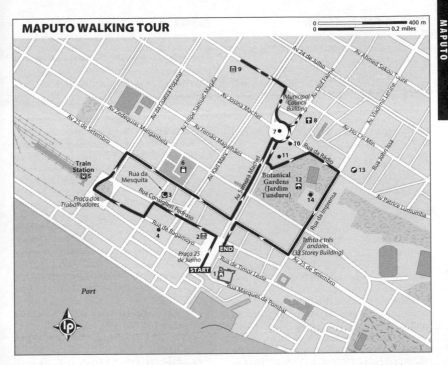

white **Cathedral of Nossa Senhora da Conceição** (8; p61). Next to the cathedral to the west is the Municipal Council (City Hall) building, which was completed around 1945. One block north of Praça da Independência and 1½ blocks west of City Hall is the **National Art Museum** (9; p61) – well worth a detour.

From the museum, return to Praça da Independência. On the praça's southeastern edge is the beautifully restored building housing the **Centro Cultural Franco-Moçambicano** (10; p56) and the Bazar de Arte (p68). On the small street just southwest of the cultural centre is the **Iron House** (11; p61). Opposite are Maputo's overgrown **botanical gardens** (12), known as Jardim Tunduru, which were laid out in 1885 by the English landscaper Thomas Honney. The tennis courts on the garden grounds serve as headquarters of the Mozambican Tennis Federation, and you can often see some of the country's best players practising. At the main entrance to the botanical gardens on Avenida Samora Machel is a large statue of Machel, Mozambique's first president. Exit the gardens to the north on Rua da Rádio, where Rádio Moçambique is located, and then head one block east to Avenida

Vladimir Lenine. The attractive building on the opposite corner houses the **British High Commission** (13). Go south on Avenida Vladimir Lenine (which turns into Rua da Imprensa here), passing the **Supreme Court** (14) building on your right. The second cross street you reach is Avenida 25 de Setembro. Go right one long block to Avenida Samora Machel, and then left one block, bringing you back to your start at Praça 25 de Junho.

COURSES

The main African languages spoken in Maputo are Shangana and the closely related Ronga. There's no formal instruction, but tutors can be easily arranged; ask around for reliable teachers at the language schools listed here, at your embassy, or at local businesses and offices.

The following offer Portuguese-language classes:

Centro de Estudos Brasileiros (Map pp58-9; ☎ 21-306840, 21-306774; ceb.eventos@tvcabo.co.mz; cnr Avenidas Karl Marx & 25 de Setembro)

Instituto das Línguas (Map pp58-9; ☎ 21-325684, 21-305473; marketing.il@tvcabo.co.mz; 1260 Avenida Ahmed Sekou Touré)

MAPUTO FOR CHILDREN

There's a large lawn, a playground and several eateries at **Jardim dos Namorados** (Map pp58-9; Avenida Friedrich Engels). Just next door are the municipal gardens, overlooking the bay. There's also a tiny playground attached to Mundo's restaurant (p66).

Good bets are also the swimming pools listed on p62, especially the pool at the Girassol Indy Village, which has an attached play area and large surrounding gardens. In the same compound, in the central gymnasium building, is an indoor playroom, where you can also leave your child with a nanny while working out.

TOURS

Dana Tours (p57) organises half-day city tours, and 'A Day in the Life' tours, both recommended. The latter takes in a visit to a local school and village, traditional dancing and a local meal, and offers glimpses into local life and culture. Dana Tours also organises 'Maputo by Night' tours, and excursions to various sites around Maputo, including Inhaca Island, Maputo Special Reserve and South Africa's Kruger National Park.

Mozambique City Tours (Map pp58-9; www.mozambique citytours.com), with a kiosk at the train station entrance, has a hop-on-hop-off 'train' that runs in a two-hour loop to all the city's main sites, with 10 scheduled stops, and four circuits daily. A ticket costs US$36/18 per adult/child, and is valid all day.

FESTIVALS & EVENTS

There's almost always an art or music festival going in Maputo. The best contacts for information include Centro-Cultural Franco-Moçambicano (p56), Rua d'Arte (p68), Kulungwana Espaço Artístico (p61), and posters around town.

SLEEPING

Maputo has a wide accommodation selection, with something for all tastes. If you want to be in the thick of things, choose somewhere in or near the baixa or in the central area just above the baixa. For sea breezes and more tranquillity, head to the upper part of town in and around Sommerschield, or to Avenida Marginal and Costa do Sol. Except as noted, continental breakfast is included in all budget and midrange listings, and full breakfast buffet in the top-end listings.

Budget

You can pitch a tent in the small, enclosed grounds at Fatima's Place (below), Base Backpackers (above) and across the bay in Catembe at Kingston House (p70). The closest camping grounds are well north of town, at Macaneta.

None of these backpacker hostels have signs – just house numbers.

Base Backpackers (Map pp58-9; ☎ 21-302723, 82-452 6860; thebasebp@tvcabo.co.mz; 545 Avenida Patrice Lumumba; dm/d Mtc220/600) Small but popular and often full, with a convenient, quiet location on the edge of the baixa. It has a kitchen, backyard bar, terrace and braai (barbecue) area with views to the port in the distance. Via public transport from Junta, take a 'Museu' chapa (minivan or pickup truck) to the final Museu stop, from where it's a short walk.

Fatima's Place (Map pp58-9; ☎ 82-414 5730; www .mozambiquebackpackers.com; 1317 Avenida Mao Tse Tung; campsite per person Mtc200, dm Mtc300, d Mtc750-1100) In the upper part of town, with an outdoor kitchen-bar, a tiny area for camping and a mix of rooms. The same management runs a backpackers in Tofo (p87), although its shuttle service between the two comes with lots of complaints.

Maputo Backpackers (Map p56; ☎ 21-451213, 82-467 2230; 95 Quarta Avenida, Bairro Triunfo; dm Mtc300, d with shared bathroom Mtc1000, d Mtc1500, tr Mtc1500) A small, quiet place near Costa do Sol, with a handful of rooms – including eight- and 10-bed dorms – with fans but no nets. Cooking is permitted if the house isn't too crowded. Chapas to/from town (Mtc7.50) stop nearby, though getting an early one to catch a bus north can be difficult – arrange a taxi the day before.

Other than the backpackers, good, safe shoestring accommodation in Maputo is scarce, and most people opt to pay a bit more for one of the places hovering between budget and midrange. These include:

Hotel África II (Map pp58-9; ☎ 21-488729; safilaher@ tvcabo.co.mz; 322 Avenida Julius Nyerere; s/d without bathroom Mtc1300/1700, s/d Mtc1600/2200; ⚡ 🖥) Straightforward but soulless rooms – the ones with bathrooms are nicer – in a central location.

Hotel Costa do Sol (off Map p56; ☎ 21-450115; rcs@ teledata.mz; Avenida Marginal; s/d US$37/70; 🅿) Above Restaurante Costa do Sol, with pretty standard rooms with fan, and the beach across the road.

Hotel-Escola Andalucia (Map pp58-9; ☎ 21-323051/4; 508 Avenida Patrice Lumumba; s/d Mtc1000/1625; 🔊) Just up from Base Backpackers, this hotel training school has a large wood staircase, mostly spacious rooms with clean linen but sagging mattresses, and a restaurant.

Hotel Santa Cruz (Map pp58-9; ☎ 21-303004/6; www .teledata.mz/hotelsantacruz; 1417 Avenida 24 de Julho; s/d with shared bathroom Mtc700/1000, d/ste Mtc1250/1375; ✖) The most basic of the bunch, with clean, reasonable rooms in a nondescript high-rise near the corner of Avenida Amilcar Cabral. Not optimal for solo women travellers.

Residencial Belsol (Map p56; ☎ 82-860 7960; belsol@ intra.co.mz; 65 Segunda Avenida, Bairro Triunfo; r 1500) Clean, simple rooms, all with bathroom, above a restaurant featuring Portuguese specialities. It's just in from Avenida Marginal near Costa do Sol.

Midrange

Hoyo-Hoyo Residencial (Map pp58-9; ☎ 21-490701; www .hoyohoyo.odline.com; 837 Avenida Francisco Magumbwe; s/d US$40/55; P ✖) This solid, no-frills hotel lacks pizzazz, but its 36 rooms are comfortable, serviceable and fairly priced. The in-house restaurant, O Petisco, is known for its Goan cuisine.

Mundo's (Map pp58-9; ☎ 21-494080, 84-468 6367; www.mundosmaputo.com; cnr Avenidas Julius Nyerere & Eduardo Mondlane; s/d US$40/70; ✖) Four large rooms next to Mundo's restaurant, all with TV. Breakfast isn't included in the rates.

our pick **Residencial Palmeiras** (Map pp58-9; ☎ 21-300199, 82-306 9200; www.palmeiras-guesthouse.com; 948 Avenida Patrice Lumumba; s/d US$55/70; P ✖ �🛈) A popular place with bright decor, comfortable, good-value rooms – all but one with private bathroom, and all with TV – and a small garden. It's near the British High Commission, and about 10 minutes on foot from the Panthera Azul office if you're coming from Johannesburg. If it's full, there are several other hotels further uphill on the same street.

Residencial Kaya Kwanga (Map p56; ☎ 21-492706/7; www.kayakwanga.co.mz; Avenida Marginal; s/d US$60/75; P ✖ ⌨ 🛈) This sprawling place has slightly faded chalet-style rooms with TV set around a large, grassy compound en route to Costa do Sol. There's a restaurant and conference facilities (often in use). The pool area, which is also open to the public, attracts large crowds on weekends and holidays.

Kurhula Parque Self-Catering Chalets (Map p56; ☎ 21-450115; rcs@teledata.mz; Avenida Marginal; 4-person chalets US$119; P) Under the same management as Hotel Costa do Sol and just next door, with serviced self-catering chalets each with a double bed and a loft with two twin beds. It's

set behind a fence on the inland side of the beach road.

Residencial Sundown (Map pp58-9; ☎ 21-497543; www.hotelmaputo.com; 107 Rua 1301; s/d from Mtc1820/2340; ✖ 🛈) A popular place with good-value, well-appointed rooms in a small apartment block on a quiet street in the Sommerschield residential area. Meals are available on order, and staff can help arranging excursions. Full breakfast is included in the price.

Hotel Monte Carlo (Map pp58-9; ☎ 21-304048; www .montecarlo.co.mz; 620 Avenida Patrice Lumumba; r/ste Mtc2000/2500; P ✖ ⌨ 🛈) Convenient central location, dark but tidy rooms and a restaurant. Favoured by local business travellers.

Mozaika (Map pp58-9; ☎ 21-303939, 21-303965; www .mozaika.co.mz; 769 Avenida Agostinho Neto; s/d Mtc2000/2250, executive d Mtc2750, apt Mtc4800; P ✖ ⌨ 🛈 🛈) This boutique hotel – in a convenient central location one block west of the Central Hospital – is justifiably popular, with eight small rooms, each decorated with its own theme and set around a small garden courtyard with a small pool. Note that there's just one non-executive room. There's also a self-catering apartment and a bar, though no restaurant. Breakfast is included in room rates. Advance bookings are recommended.

Villa das Mangas (Map pp58-9; ☎ 21-497078; villa dasmangas@tvcabo.co.mz; 401 Avenida 24 de Julho; s/d from Mtc2350/2850; ✖ 🛈 🛈) Villa das Mangas has a busy, albeit convenient, location, and tiny, overpriced rooms around a small garden. Rooms come with TV, lots of mosquitoes and a rather mediocre breakfast, and there's an adjoining restaurant and bar. Check 'extras' such as the air-conditioner before settling on a room to be sure everything is working.

Hotel Terminus (Map pp58-9; ☎ 21-491333; www.terminus .co.mz; cnr Avenidas Francisco Magumbwe & Ahmed Sekou Touré; s/d from Mtc2000/2900; P ✖ ⌨ 🛈 🛈) This three-star establishment in the upper part of town has small but well-appointed rooms with TV, plus good service and facilities, a business centre, a small garden, a tiny pool and a restaurant. It's popular with business travellers and often fully booked.

Top End

Girassol Indy Village (Map pp58-9; ☎ 21-498765; www .girassolhoteis.co.mz; 99 Rua Dom Sebastião; r from Mtc2895; P ✖ ⌨ 🛈) This place, in a quiet corner of Sommerschield, has well-appointed rooms and apartments set in expansive, manicured, enclosed gardens. There's a pool with an adjoining children's play area, plus a gym and a restaurant. It's ideal for families and for long-term rentals.

Hotel Cardoso (Map pp58-9; ☎ 21-491071; www.hotel cardoso.co.mz; 707 Avenida Mártires de Mueda; s/d US$140/155, with sea view from US$160/175; ⓟ ▯ ⚡ ▮) Opposite the Natural History Museum, and on the cliff top overlooking the bay, this 130-room hotel is a Maputo classic, with good service, well-appointed rooms (most have been recently renovated), a business centre and a bar with views over the water and port area.

Hotel Pestana Rovuma (Map pp58-9; ☎ 21-305000; www.pestana.com; 114 Rua da Sé; s/d from US$141/156; ▮ ▯ ▮) Centrally located just off Praça da Independência and opposite the cathedral, the 200-room Pestana Rovuma is another venerable Maputo establishment, with a long history, well-appointed rooms, a small gym, a business centre and a selection of shops and boutiques downstairs. It's run by the Pestana Group, and offers package excursions from Johannesburg that include its sister hotels on Inhaca Island and in the Bazaruto Archipelago.

Hotel Polana (Map pp58-9; ☎ 21-491001; www.serena hotels.com/mozambique/polana/home.asp; 1380 Avenida Julius Nyerere; s/d from US$265/290; ⓟ ▮ ▯ ⚡ ▮) In a prime location on the cliff top with uninterrupted views over the sea, the Polana is Maputo's classiest hotel. It has rooms in the elegant main building or in the 'Polana Mar' section closer to the water – all were undergoing refurbishment when we visited. There's a large pool set amid lush gardens, a business centre, and a restaurant with daily breakfast and weekend dinner buffets.

Other recommendations:

Girassol Bahia Hotel (Map pp58-9; ☎ 21-360360, 21-360350; www.girassolhoteis.co.mz; 737 Avenida Patrice Lumumba; s/d Mtc4000/4400; ▮ ▯ ▮) The Girassol Bahia offers reliable rooms and service, and stunning views over the bay from the dining room, although all this comes at a steep price.

Hotel Avenida (Map pp58-9; ☎ 21-484400; www .tdhotels.pt; 627 Avenida Julius Nyerere; s/d US$267/309; ⓟ ▮ ▯ ⚡ ▮) A high-rise in a busy location in the upper part of town with efficient service, a business centre and sleek rooms with all amenities, plus a restaurant. Price includes use of the health club and sauna.

Southern Sun (Map pp58-9; ☎ 21-495050; www .southernsun.com; Avenida Marginal; s/d from US$215/245; ⓟ ▮ ▯ ▮) An attractive setting directly on the water (though there's no swimming), with rooms and services on a par with those of other regional Southern Sun hotels, plus a small gym and a waterside restaurant.

EATING
Restaurants

Mimmo's Flôr de Avenida (Map pp58-9; ☎ 21-309491; cnr Avenidas 24 de Julho & Salvador Allende; meals Mtc150-250) This bustling street-side pizzeria also has pastas, and seafood and meat grills. It has a newer, slicker sister restaurant – Mimmo's Flôr d'Avenida at the corner of Avenidas Vladimir Lenin and Maguiguana – with air-con. At both, check your bill and your change carefully.

Café Milano (Map pp58-9; Avenida 24 de Julho; meals from Mtc150) Just off Rua Augusto Cardoso, this place has a large street-side eating area and tasty felafel, shawarma, freshly baked pita bread and other Lebanese snacks and light meals, plus the usual array of standards. It also does takeaway.

our pick **Restaurante Costa do Sol** (Map p56; ☎ 21-450038, 21-450115; Avenida Marginal; meals from Mtc200; ⏱ 11am-10.30pm Sun-Thu, to midnight Fri & Sat; ⓟ) A Maputo classic, this beachside place draws the crowds on weekend afternoons. There's seating on the large sea-facing porch or indoors, and an array of delicious seafood dishes and grills. It's about 5km from the centre at the northern end of Avenida Marginal.

Vintage India (Map pp58-9; ☎ 21-486430; 450 Avenida Julius Nyerere; meals from Mtc200; ⏱ lunch & dinner) The rather drab interior of this place is compensated for by tasty curries and Mughlai cuisine, plus a lunchtime buffet (Mtc170).

Dock's (Map pp58-9; ☎ 21-493204; Avenida Marginal; meals from Mtc200; ⏱ 9am-2am) At Clube Naval, with good seafood grills and burgers, and breezy, waterside seating. There's live music on most Thursday (jazz, advance reservations required) and Friday evenings, and a late-night bar. The Mtc20 Clube Naval compound entry is deducted from your meal bill.

Mundo's (Map pp58-9; ☎ 21-494080; www.mundos maputo.com; cnr Avenidas Julius Nyerere & Eduardo Mondlane; meals Mtc200-350; ⏱ 8am-midnight; ⚡) Burritos, burgers, great pizzas and other hearty fare – all served up in large portions on wooden tables set around a street-side verandah and cooled by a misting system in the summer months. There's also all-day breakfast and a small play area for children.

Manjar Os Deuses (Map pp58-9; ☎ 21-496834; Avenida Julius Nyerere; meals from Mtc250; ⏱ lunch & dinner Sun-Fri, diiner Sat) Not quite 'food of the gods', but nevertheless quite nice, with tasty cuisine (featuring dishes from Portugal's

Alentejo and Algarve regions) served in a pleasant, wood-toned ambience.

Xhova's InterThai Restaurant (Map pp58-9; Rua Mateus Sansão Muthemba; meals from Mtc250; 🕑 lunch & dinner Tue-Sat, lunch Sun) Delicious Thai food in garden surroundings, complete with a fish pond. It's between Avenida Julius Nyerere and Hotel Cardoso.

Maputo Waterfront Restaurante & Bar (Map pp58-9; ☎ 21-301408; Praça Robert Mugabe; meals from Mtc250; 🕑 closed Sun dinner; 🍺) This popular place has well-prepared seafood dishes (some meat dishes as well), indoor and outdoor seating, plus views over the water, a pool (adult/child Mtc150/80) and live music some evenings.

Feira Popular (Map pp58-9; Avenida 25 de Setembro; admission Mtc20; 🕑 lunch & dinner; 🅿) is another Maputo institution, where you can mix and mingle with the crowds as you wander amid dozens of small bars and restaurants set inside a large, walled compound. **O Escorpião** (☎ 21-302180; meals from Mtc200), with hearty Portuguese fare, and **Palma d'Ouro** (meals from Mtc200), with *galinha zambéziana* (chicken Zambézia) and other traditional dishes, are two of the most popular. Taxis wait outside until the early hours.

Other recommendations:

Micasa (Map pp58-9; cnr Avenida Julius Nyerere & Rua da Argélia; meals around Mtc250; 🕑 9.30am-3pm & 6-10pm Mon-Fri, 6-10pm Sat) A classy, subdued ambience, with candles, water goblets and linen cloths on the closely spaced tables, and nicely prepared seafood, meat and pasta dishes.

O Dragão (Map pp58-9; ☎ 21-305850; 313 Avenida Salvador Allende; meals from Mtc180; 🕑 10am-10pm) A tiny place lacking ambience, but service – for Chinese meals and takeaways – is relatively efficient and the food is tasty.

Taverna (Map pp58-9; ☎ 84-445550; 995 Avenida Julius Nyerere; meals Mtc250-400; 🕑 lunch & dinner Tue-Sat, dinner Sun) Delicious Portuguese cuisine served in rather dark surroundings; it's just up from Mundo's restaurant.

Cafes

The cafe tradition is one of the nicer things left behind in Maputo by the Portuguese, and the city's cafes have become somewhat of an institution. Most of the older ones have a staid feel to them, and the faded ambience and worn furnishings that you'd expect from places that have been around for decades, while the newer ones tend to be young and lively. All serve a selection of tasty *bolos* (cakes) and light meals, plus *café espresso* and *chá* (tea), and make good spots for a break.

Café Acacia (Map pp58-9; Jardim dos Professores, Avenida Patrice Lumumba; snacks from Mtc50) Garden setting, children's play area and bay views, and pastries and coffees supplied by the nearby Hotel Cardoso.

Café do Sol (Map p56; 98 Rua Beijo da Mulata; snacks from Mtc75; 🕑 6.30am-7.30pm Mon-Fri, 7.30am-7.30pm Sat & Sun; 🖥 🛜) A very Western place just off the extension of Avenida Julius Nyerere, with connoisseur-quality coffees (including bags of its own blend for sale), pastries and sandwiches.

Cristál (Map pp58-9; 554 Avenida 24 de Julho; snacks from Mtc50, meals from Mtc230) This long-standing place has vintage 1960s decor, a good restaurant with indoor or street-side terrace seats and a delicious *pastelaria* (shop selling pastries, cakes and often light meals).

Náutilus Pastelaria (Map pp58-9; cnr Avenidas Julius Nyerere & 24 de Julho; light meals Mtc150; 🕑 6am-9pm; 🖥) Crêpes, sandwiches and light meals in a glassed-in dining area from where you can watch the passing street scene.

Surf (Map pp58-9; Jardim dos Namorados, Avenida Friedrich Engels; snacks from Mtc50) A large, amenable place with indoor and garden seating, a children's play area and fast service.

Quick Eats

Gelati (Map pp58-9; Avenida Julius Nyerere) Delicious Italian gelato next to Xenon cinema.

our pick Fish Market (Mercado da Peixe; Map p56; off Avenida Marginal) En route to Costa do Sol (the turnoff is opposite Clube Marítimo), you buy your fish fresh here, then choose an adjoining stall to cook it. Waits can be long on weekends, but there are tables where you can sit and enjoy the scene. The best time to visit is late afternoon.

Pizza House (Map pp58-9; ☎ 21-485257; 601/607 Avenida Mao Tse Tung; pizzas & light meals Mtc100-200; 🕑 6.30am-10.30pm) Popular with locals and expats, this place has outdoor seating, plus reasonably priced pastries, sandwiches, burgers, grilled chicken and other meals. There's also a small convenience store, and upstairs is an internet cafe.

Piri-Piri Chicken (Map pp58-9; Avenida 24 de Julho; meals from Mtc200; 🕑 11am-midnight, later on Fri & Sat) A Maputo classic, with grilled chicken – with or without *piri-piri* (spicy chilli sauce) – plus spicy shrimp curry, cold beers and a good local vibe. It also does takeaway.

Self-Catering

Supermarkets in Maputo are on the pricey side, but well-stocked, with a wide selection of imports from South Africa. Papayas, mangoes and other excellent tropical fruits and vegetables are available at Maputo's markets and from street-side vendors.

Shoprite (Map p56; Avenida Acordos de Lusaka; ☉ 9am-8pm Mon-Sat, to 1pm Sun) Just outside the city centre, with an ATM next door, in the same shopping complex.

Supermares (Map p56; Avenida Marginal, Costa do Sol; ☉ 9am-7pm Mon-Sat, to 1pm Sun) Pricey but well-stocked, with ATMs inside and outside the store.

DRINKING & ENTERTAINMENT
Pubs & Clubs

Maputo's thriving nightlife scene includes a large and frequently changing selection of cafes, pubs, bars and clubs. Thursday through Saturday are the main nights, with things only getting going after 11pm. Cover charges at most places range from Mtc50 to Mtc250.

La Dolce Vita Café-Bar (Map pp58-9; 822 Julius Nyerere; ☉ 10am-late Tue-Sun) This sleek tapas and late-night place near Xenon cinema has live music on Thursday evening. By day, try the juices and smoothies.

Rua d'Arte (Map pp58-9; ruadarte@gmail.com; Travessa de Palmeira; ☉ 7pm-late Wed-Sat) One of Maputo's main evening venues, with live music (mostly jazz, but also other styles) plus dancing, poetry readings, photography exhibitions, food and drinks and a constantly changing program of artists. It's in the small street opposite the Central Market.

Café-Bar Gil Vicente (Map pp58-9; 43 Avenida Samora Machel) Another place with a constantly changing array of groups; check www.mozhits.com for announcements of upcoming performances.

África Bar (Map pp58-9; ☎ 21-322217; www.africabar .blogspot.com; 2182 Avenida 24 de Julho; admission Mtc50; ☉ from 5pm Wed-Sun) Next to Ciné Africa, this hip spot is a good place to start or finish the evening. It draws the crowds on Thursday (jazz night, admission free).

Kapfumo (Map pp58-9; ☉ Thu-Sat, evenings only) This unsignposted jazz cafe – formerly Chez Rangel – is at the train station. It has a dusty, old world ambience and a mix of live music and CDs.

Coconuts Live (Map p56; ☎ 21-322217; Complexo Mini-Golfe, Avenida Marginal; disco Mtc200, lounge free; ☉ disco Fri & Sat, lounge Wed-Sun) A weekend disco catering to a younger, less formal crowd, plus a popular chill-out lounge.

Dock's (Map pp58-9; ☎ 21-493204; Avenida Marginal; ☉ 9am-2am) The late-night waterside bar here is especially popular on Friday (happy hour from 11pm), and when the weather is warm.

Also recommended:

Complexo Sheik (Map pp58-9; cnr Avenidas Julius Nyerere & Mao Tse Tung; admission Mtc200; ☉ 10pm-5am Thu-Sat) Dance with the elite set until dawn; upstairs is a restaurant.

Hotel Terminus Pool Bar (Map pp58-9; ☎ 21-491333; cnr Avenidas Francisco Magumbwe & Ahmed Sekou Touré) Good for a quiet drink, or if you want to stay local.

Traditional Music & Dance

Check with the Centro Cultural Franco-Moçambicano (p56) for upcoming music and dance performances.

The **National Company of Song & Dance** (Companhia Nacional de Canto e Dança; Map pp58-9; http://myspace .com/cncdmoz; Cine Teatro África, 2182 Avenida 24 de Julho), Mozambique's renowned national dance company, has regular rehearsals, usually between 8am and 3pm Monday to Friday, that are open to the public, and you can get schedules of upcoming performances.

Theatre

Teatro Avenida (Map pp58-9; ☎ 21-326501; teatro avenida@tvcabo.co.mz; 1179 Avenida 25 de Setembro) is home to one of Maputo's best-known theatre groups, Mutumbela Gogo. Plays are in Portuguese. M'Beu is a theatre group for high-school students formed under the auspices of Mutumbela Gogo. Another well-known group is **Teatro Gungu** (Map pp58-9; Travessa do Varietá), which is based at Cinema Matchedje, and has performances most weekends at 6pm.

Sport

Football (soccer) is the national passion. You can watch or join informal weekend matches along the northern end of Avenida Marginal, or on any empty field. To see a game, head to Costa do Sol stadium (Map p56) on weekend afternoons.

SHOPPING

Maputo has a wide selection of reasonably priced crafts.

Craft market (Map pp58-9; Praça 25 do Junho; ☉ about 8am-1pm Sat) A good place to start is the Saturday morning craft market, with an array of woodcarvings and other items, some of which are of quite decent quality. In the upper part of town, try the craft vendors (Avenida Julius Nyerere) who spread their woodcarvings and other wares daily in front of Hotel Polana; hard bargaining is required.

Bazar de Arte (Bazart; Map pp58-9; Centro Cultural Franco-Moçambicano, Praça da Independência; ☉ 10am-7pm

---

STOLEN GOODS & BIRD CLAWS

Not exactly a tourist attraction, but a Maputo institution nonetheless, is the enormous and chaotic **Xipamanine Market** (Mercado de Xipamanine, Map p56). The market, which sprawls over the length of several football fields beyond the termination of Avenida Eduardo Mondlane, is the place to go to buy everything from used appliance parts to mattresses and sofas. More interesting is the enormous selection of traditional medicines and remedies, including an array of animal pelts, bird claws and more. Xipamanine is also notorious as the hub of the local underworld, with an impressive assortment of stolen items for resale.

Mon-Fri, to 3pm Sat) This relatively new place has an excellent selection of crafts, textiles, artwork, traditional instruments and more from Mozambique and elsewhere in southern Africa, with a focus on promoting Mozambican and African cultural identity through art.

Artedif (Map pp58-9; ☎ 21-495510; Avenida Marginal; ☺ 9am-2.30pm Tue, 9am-3.30pm Wed-Mon) This co-operative for disabled people is about 400m south of Southern Sun hotel. Crafts sold here are slightly more expensive than those at the street markets, but tend to be of higher quality. Prices are fixed.

Casa Elefante (Map pp58-9; Avenida 25 de Setembro; ☺ closed Sun) A good place to buy *capulanas* (sarongs); opposite the Municipal Market. This is also a good place to look for a tailor (*alfaiataria*).

GETTING THERE & AWAY
Air
For domestic and international flights to/from Maputo, see p180.

Airline offices in Maputo include:

Kenya Airways (Map pp58-9; ☎ 21-483144/5, 82-303 5931; sales@kenya-airways.co.mz; 252 Avenida Mao Tse Tung) At Aquarium Travel.

LAM Central Reservations (Map pp58-9; ☎ 800 147 000, 82-147, 84-147, 21-468000, 21-326001, 21-465074; www .lam.co.mz; cnr Avenidas 25 de Setembro & Karl Marx); Sales Office (Map pp58-9; ☎ 21-490590; cnr Avenidas Julius Nyerere & Mao Tse Tung)

South African Airways (Map pp58-9; ☎ 21-488970/3, 84-389 9287; www.flysaa.com; Avenida do Zimbabwe,

Sommerschield) Near the South African High Commissioner's residence.

TAP Air Portugal (Map pp58-9; ☎ 21-303927/8; www .flytap.com) At Hotel Pestana Rovuma.

TransAirways (☎ 21-465108; Maputo airport)

Bus
Most of the main bus depots (listed following) are outside the city centre, so time your travels to avoid arriving at night. For upcountry fares and journey times, see individual town listings.

Benfica (Map p56; Avenida de Moçambique) Chapas to Marracuene.

Fábrica de Cerveja Laurentina ('Ferroviario'; Map pp58-9; cnr Avenidas 25 de Setembro & Albert Luthuli) Chapas to Swaziland (Mtc250), South Africa, Namaacha, Boane and Goba depart from behind the beer factory from about 6am.

Junta (Map p56; Avenida de Moçambique) Maputo's chaotic long-distance bus depot – the main departure point for all up-country travel – is about 7km (Mtc300 in a taxi) from the centre. Nothing is organised – you'll need to ask where to find your bus. Most departures are about 5am. Coming into Maputo, some buses finish at Junta while others continue into the city to Ponto Final (corner Avenidas Eduardo Mondlane and Guerra Popular), from where it's about Mtc100 in a taxi to the central area.

There are also several other bus transport options:

TCO Turismo (Map pp58-9; ☎ 82-768 4410; Avenida Vladimir Lenine, just down from Avenida Emília Dausse) runs an air-con bus to Beira, departing from its office at Jardim Donaberta (Jardim Nangade). Book direct or through **Golden Travel** (Map pp58-9; ☎ 82-305 1741, 21-309421/2; Rua Baptista Carvalho, just off Avenida 25 de Setembro).

Private, reasonably priced minivan transport for individuals or groups to Inhambane (about Mtc500) and Massinga can be arranged through Residencial Palmeiras (p65).

Cheetah Express (Map pp58-9) to Nelspruit (p184) departs from Avenida Eduardo Mondlane next to Mundo's restaurant.

Departure and ticketing points for express buses to Johannesburg include the following (see p184 for times and prices):

Greyhound (Map pp58-9; ☎ 21-355700; www.greyhound .co.za; 1242 Avenida Karl Marx) At Cotur Travel & Tours.

Panthera Azul (Map pp58-9; ☎ 21-302077/83; panthera@tvcabo.co.mz; 273 Avenida Zedequias Manganhela) Behind the main post office.

Translux (Map pp58-9; ☎ 21-303825, 21-303829; www .translux.co.za; 1249 Avenida 24 de Julho) At Simara Travel & Tours.

Train

Slow trains (most economy class only) connect Maputo with the following destinations. Rehabilitation plans are underway on several of these routes, so it's likely that fares and journey times will change. With luck, the changes might be posted on www.cfmnet.co.mz.

Chicualacuala (on the Zimbabwe border) Departing at 1pm on Wednesday from Maputo and at 1pm on Thursday from Chicualacuala (Mtc110, 17hr).

Chokwé Departing Maputo at 9.55am on Saturday, and from Chokwé about 4pm on Sunday (Mtc40, 10 hours).

Marracuene Departing Maputo daily at 3.15am and 5.45pm, and from Marracuene at 4.45am and 7.30pm (Mtc5, 1½ hours).

Matola Departing morning and evenings in each direction (Mtc5, 1½ hours).

Ressano-Garcia Departing Maputo at 7.45am, and Ressano Garcia at 12.10pm (Mtc15, four to five hours).

GETTING AROUND
To/From the Airport

Maputo International Airport is 6km northwest of the city centre (Mtc300 in a taxi, more at night).

Boat

For boat charters to Inhaca, Cape Santa Maria (just south of Inhaca) or Xefina Grande, and for fishing charters, see the companies listed on p72.

Bus & Chapa

Buses have name boards with their destination. City rides cost about Mtc3.

Chapas go everywhere, with the average price for town trips from Mtc5. Most are marked with route start and end points, but also listen for the destination called out by the conductor. To get to Junta, look for a chapa going to 'Jardim'; coming from Junta into town, look for a chapa heading to 'Museu'. Useful transport stands:

Museu (Natural History Museum; Map pp58-9) Chapas to the airport and Junta (Mtc5 from Museu to Junta).

Ponto Final (Map pp58-9; cnr Avenidas Eduardo Mondlane & Guerra Popular) Terminus for some upcountry buses, and for chapas running along Avenida Eduardo Mondlane.

Praça dos Trabalhadores Chapas to Costa do Sol; these also depart from the corner of Avenidas Mao Tse Tung and Julius Nyerere.

Ronil (Map pp58-9; cnr Avenidas Eduardo Mondlane & Karl Marx) Chapas to Junta, Benfica and Matola.

Car

For general information on car rentals, see p189. As in other major cities in the region, car crime happens in Maputo, and it's advisable to park in guarded lots when possible, or tip the young boys on the street to watch your vehicle. Rental agencies include the following:

Avis (☎ 21-465497/8, 21-494473; maputo.airport@avis .co.za; airport)

Europcar (Map pp58-9; ☎ 82-300 2410, 21-497338; www.europcar.co.mz; 1418 Avenida Julius Nyerere) Next to Hotel Polana and at the airport. The only company offering unlimited kilometres at the time of writing.

Hertz (Map pp58-9; ☎ 21-303172/3, 82-327 6220; http://hertz-moz.info) At the airport and at Hotel Polana.

Imperial (Map pp58-9; ☎ 21-465250, 82-300 5180; imperialmaputo@hotmail.com; 1516 Avenida Mao Tse Tung) Diagonally opposite Janeta Market (Mercado Janeta) and at the airport.

Taxi & Tuk-Tuk

There are taxi ranks at Hotel Polana, at most other top-end hotels, at the Municipal Market and on Avenida Julius Nyerere in front of Mundo's restaurant. Town trips start at Mtc100. From central Maputo to Costa do Sol costs about Mtc250. From Junta to anywhere in the city centre costs about Mtc300.

Maputo also has several fleets of tuk-tuks – three-wheelers that can be chartered for daytime sightseeing or rides along Avenida Marginal. Most have meters, with prices roughly equivalent to city taxi prices, or about Mtc50 per kilometre, though this is negotiable for longer distances. You can find them at Hotel Cardoso, Southern Sun, Hotel Polana and other major hotels, or call the tuk-tuk central booking number (☎ 84-410 0001).

AROUND MAPUTO

CATEMBE

Catembe, a bucolic town on the south side of Baía de Maputo, offers a taste of upcountry for those who won't have a chance to leave the capital. Head here for a day or overnight, munch on prawns, enjoy the views of Maputo's skyline from across the bay and get into local rhythms.

Sleeping & Eating

Kingston House (☎ 82-817 9918; ineedatent@hotmail .com; campsite Mtc200; s/d Mtc300/400) A small local

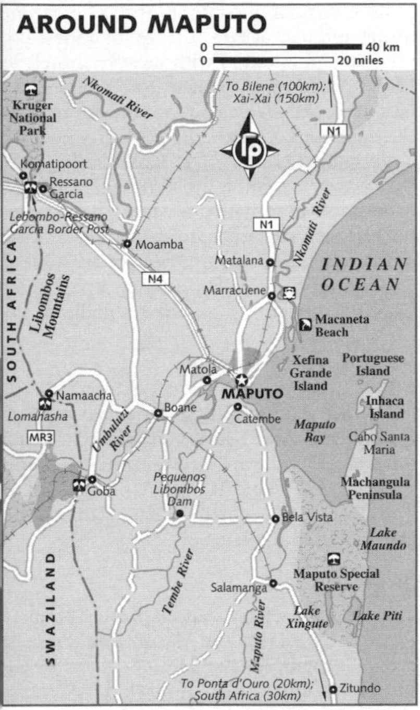

B&B-type place with a couple of rooms sharing bathroom, space to pitch a tent and meals on request. It's about 30 minutes on foot from the ferry (go left when exiting the ferry). Shortly after the bakery, and before reaching Pensão Catembe, look for the yellow house on the beach side of the road.

Pensão Catembe (☎ 21-380050; www.catembe.net; d without bathroom US$60) has a waterside setting and reasonable rooms, but erratic service and standards. It's 4km north of the ferry dock.

Other places to try for a meal include **Esplanada-Bar Retiro de Catembe** (meals from Mtc170), about 400m down to the right on the beach when leaving the ferry pier, and the long-standing local hangout, **Diogo's** (meals from Mtc150), about 300m down the beach to the left of the ferry pier, serving grilled prawns.

Getting There & Away

At the time of writing, a new ferry, the *Mpfumo*, was about to start service between Maputo and Catembe, so expect changes both in the timing and price of the journey across the bay. Meanwhile, the dilapidated *Bagamoyo* ferry runs daily from the dock near the Ministry of Finances (per person Mtc5, per large vehicle weekday/weekend Mtc150/200, 20 minutes). The first boat from Maputo departs at 5am, then 6am, 7am, 8.30am and thereafter every few hours or so until 10pm. From Catembe, the first departure is at 5.30am; evening departures are at 5pm, 6pm, 7.30pm, 9.30pm, 10.45pm and 11.30pm (final boat sometimes leaves early). Smaller, passenger-only boats (Mtc5) also run throughout the day between about 7am and 7pm, although they are often unsafe, especially in bad weather.

INHACA ISLAND

Just 7000 years ago – almost like yesterday in geological terms – Inhaca (Ilha de Inhaca) was part of the Mozambican mainland. Today, this wayward chunk of Mozambican coastline lies about 40km offshore from Maputo, and is a popular weekend getaway. It's also an important marine research centre, known in particular for its offshore coral reefs. The reefs are among the most southerly in the world and, since 1976, parts of the island and surrounding waters have been designated a reserve (per person per visit US$10) to protect them and local marine life. About 3km northwest of Inhaca is the tiny, uninhabited **Portuguese Island** (Ilha dos Portuguêses), a beautiful white patch of sand surrounded by clear waters. It was formerly a leper colony and is now part of the Inhaca marine reserve system.

The majority of Inhaca's residents belong to a subgroup of the Tembe-Tsonga and speak a dialect of Ronga distinct from (but mutually intelligible with) that found on the mainland.

Sights & Activities

The best **beaches** are on the island's northeastern edge past the lighthouse, and on Portuguese Island. The closest good beach to the ferry pier is about 2km south, along the bay. On Inhaca's southwestern edge is a marine biology research station and a small **museum** (☎ 21-760009; admission Mtc75; 🕑 8.30-11.30am & 2-3.30pm Mon-Fri, from 9.30am Sat, Sun & holidays) with specimens of local fauna. Transport can be arranged through Pestana Inhaca Lodge or Restaurante Lucas. Otherwise, it's a 50-minute walk to the marine research station, and double that to the lighthouse.

Birdwatching opportunities abound, with about 300 bird species recorded on Inhaca.

This is a remarkable figure considering that the island measures only about 72 sq km in area. Among others, watch for great-winged and white-chinned petrels, mangrove kingfishers, crab plovers and greater frigate birds.

The **woodcarvers** based at Pestana Inhaca Lodge work with light-coloured wood, which is then painted, or darkened with a mixture of finely powdered charcoal and water, followed by a layer of shoe polish.

Just south of Inhaca, across a narrow channel at the tip of Machangula Peninsula, is beautiful **Cape Santa Maria**, with quiet beaches and crystal-clear waters ideal for snorkelling. The area, which is also known for its pelicans and flamingos, is usually visited by boat from Inhaca or direct from Maputo, although there's also an overland route through the Maputo Special Reserve and two self-catering camps; see p78.

Dive Africa Watersports (www.diveafrica.com) operates out of Pestana Inhaca Lodge, and offers diving instruction and equipment rental, plus snorkelling, windsurfing and sea kayaking.

Sleeping & Eating

Marine Biology Research Station (☎ 21-760009, 21-760013; fax 21-492176; r per person Mtc450) Just in from the water on the island's southwestern edge, these no-frills rooms have shared facilities and cold-water showers. It's primarily for students and researchers but is open to the public on a space-available basis. There is a kitchen, and a cook can be arranged, but you will need to bring your own food. Book rooms at least five days in advance.

Inhacazul (www.inhacazullodge.itgo.com; 6-/8-person chalets US$180/240) Just in from the beach north of Pestana Inhaca Lodge and an easy walk from the ferry pier, with self-catering chalets. Discounted midweek rates are available. Bring your own nets and towels.

Pestana Inhaca Lodge (☎ 21-760003; www.pestana .com; s/d/f with half board US$245/372/392; ⌘ ⌘) Set in expansive, shaded gardens just north of the ferry pier on the island's western side, this four-star establishment is Inhaca's main hotel. Rooms are bright and cheery, with mosquito nets, fan and air-con. The family rooms (most of which are wheelchair-friendly) have one double bed, a sofa bed that can take two children, and a small verandah. Once you move past the hustle at the pier, it makes for a relaxing retreat (go midweek or in the off-season when it's even quieter). There's a saltwater

swimming pool, a restaurant with a lunchtime buffet and package deals from Johannesburg (also in combination with its sister hotels in Maputo and on the Bazaruto Archipelago). Note that there's a two-night minimum stay during peak periods.

Restaurante Lucas (☎ 21-760007; meals Mtc250-450; ⌚ from 7am) This long-standing local-style restaurant is the main place to eat. It's pricey, but the seafood grills are delicious, and the ambience is laid back. Order in advance if you're in a rush or if you fancy a particular dish. It's next to Pestana Inhaca Lodge.

Getting There & Away

AIR

There are daily flights to/from Maputo on **TransAirways** (☎ 21-465108, 21-465011; return per person Mtc2000), departing Maputo at 3.45pm Monday to Friday, at 8am Saturday and at 4pm Sunday. Departures from Inhaca are about 30 minutes later.

BOAT

The Vodacom ferry departs from Maputo's Porto da Pesca (off Rua Marques de Pombal) at 8am on Saturday and Sunday (Mtc750/1250 one way/return, two hours). Departures from Inhaca are at about 3pm. A new ferry is planned for this route, so expect changes to the price and timing information given here.

For speedboat charters to Inhaca or to Cape Santa Maria, contact **Mozambique Charters** (☎ 84-323 6420; www.mozambiquecharters.com). The ride takes about one hour, and can be rough during the windy months of August and September. All boats drop you at the beach in front of Pestana Inhaca Lodge, and usually stop at Portuguese Island en route. Transport to Portuguese Island is also easy to arrange with local fishermen on the beach in front of Pestana Inhaca Lodge, and at low tide it's sometimes possible to walk from Inhaca. Dana Tours (p57) also organises Inhaca excursions.

Getting Around

Car hire with a driver can be arranged at Restaurante Lucas (above) or Pestana Inhaca Lodge (left) from about US$80 per day.

MARRACUENE & MACANETA BEACH

Macaneta is the closest open-ocean beach to Maputo, with stiff sea breezes and long stretches of dune-fringed coast. It's on a narrow peninsula divided from the mainland by the Nkomati River, and is reached via Marracuene, 35km north of Maputo along the N1. Marracuene was a getaway for wealthy Maputo residents during colonial days and the scene of some heavy fighting in the 1980s during the war. Today, it's a small riverside town with a sleepy, faded charm, its main street lined with bougainvilleas and old Portuguese villas in various states of repair.

Sights & Activities

Just north of Marracuene is Matalana village, birthplace of renowned artist Malangatana, and site of his **Matalana Cultural Centre** (Centro Cultural de Matalana). When finished, it is intended to be a local cultural hub, with an arts and crafts centre, arts training for children, an open-air theatre. All are now in varying stages of completion, although it's possible to visit and look around.

At Macaneta, the main activity is swimming. Currents can be strong, so take care when plunging in, and when swimming with children.

Sleeping & Eating

Macaneta Lodge (Complexo Turistico de Macaneta; ☎ 82-715 2813; macanetalodge@tdm.co.mz; Macaneta Beach; 2-/4-person bungalows US$75/150; 🍴) Popular with day visitors, with a good beachside restaurant, straightforward but rather soulless rondavels and a weekend disco.

Tan n' Biki (☎ 82-388 5142; www.tanbiki.co.za; Macaneta Beach; campsite per person US$12; 4-/6-person chalet US$87/119; 🍴) Just back from the beach near Macaneta Lodge, with campsites, self-catering chalets and a restaurant.

Incomati Estuary Lodge (☎ in South Africa 015-793 816; info@transfrontiers.com; 8-person self-catering lodge S$435) This tranquil place on the Nkomati River has four double self-catering bungalows. With advance notice, there's also a restaurant-bar and fully catered accommodation available with a two-person, three-night minimum). Transport to Macaneta beach can be arranged, as can birdwatching and canoe trips along the river. Advance bookings are essential, and there are no day-visitor facilities – it's for overnight visitors only.

Getting There & Away

Take any northbound chapa from Benfica (Mtc50, one hour) to Marracuene, from

GWAZA MUTHINI

Each year in February, Marracuene fills up with visitors commemorating those who died resisting colonial rule in the 1895 Battle of Marracuene, known locally as Gwaza Muthini. At the heart of the festivities is the killing of a hippo from the Nkomati River and the *kuphalha* ceremony (invocation of the ancestors), although the hippo hasn't been very forthcoming in recent times and a goat is usually roasted instead. Gwaza Muthini also marks the beginning of the season for *ukanhi* – a traditional brew made from *canhu*, the fruit of the *canhoeiro* tree found throughout Maputo and Gaza provinces, and considered sacred in much of the region.

where it's a 10-minute walk through town to the Nkomati River ferry (return per person/vehicle Mtc4/180, five minutes, 6am to 6pm). On the other side, follow the rutted road for about 5km to a junction of sorts, from where you'll find most of the Macaneta places about 5km to 8km further, and signposted. There's no public transport; hitching is slow except at weekends. For drivers, a 4WD is essential, except to get to Macaneta Lodge.

For Matalana, continue north on the N1 past Marracuene for about 7km to the Matalana junction, following signs first for the police training centre, and then for Centro Cultural de Matalana.

NORTH OF MARRACUENE

About 20km north of Marracuene and signposted just off the N1 are several useful places for breaking up your travel if you're doing a self-drive visit from South Africa, including the family-run **Blue Anchor Inn** (☎ 82-308 4290; www.blueanchorinn.com; adult/child Mtc600/300), with pleasant rooms and cottages in large grounds, and a restaurant, and **Casa Lisa** (☎ 82-304 1990; buckland@teledata.mz; campsite per person Mtc210, chalets per person Mtc480-660), with a mix of dorm beds and straightforward chalets, plus camping with hot-water showers. Most accommodation has a private bathroom, and there's a restaurant (breakfast and dinner only, no self-catering).

Southern Mozambique

For more than 500 years, visitors have been marvelling at the beauty of the southern Mozambican coastline. For the early Portuguese explorers, its white sands and sheltered bays served as a gateway to the fabled goldfields of the interior, and as convenient staging points on the long sea journey to the Orient. In more recent times, a steady stream of holiday-makers have been lured by promises of plates heaped with giant prawns and grilled *lagosta* (crayfish); languid days cooled by gentle Indian Ocean breezes; sultry nights enlivened by pulsating *marrabenta* rhythms; and the best diving and game fishing to be found in the region.

Mozambique's southern coast is the most developed part of the country for tourism. And its popularity is well justified. From Ponta d'Ouro, with its pounding surf and windswept dunes, to the serene lagoons and shallow coastal lakes between Bilene and Závora, and the legendary beaches of Tofo and Barra, it boasts some of the most beautiful stretches of sand on the continent. In addition to the beaches, Southern Mozambique has a wealth of cultural highlights, if you have the time to seek them out. These include the famed *timbila* (marimba) orchestras of the Chopi people and a rich body of traditional lore, much of which focuses on the old kingdom of Gaza.

Tourism infrastructure is fast expanding and caters to all budgets. Transport links, especially with nearby South Africa, are good, with sealed major roads and a reliable bus network. If you want an easy introduction to Mozambique or a beach holiday, the south is a good place to start.

HIGHLIGHTS

- Plunge into the turquoise waters of **Bazaruto Archipelago** (p96), with its shoals of colourful fish
- Stroll along the waterfront promenade in **Inhambane** (p83), watching dhows silhouetted against the setting sun
- Drift off to sleep, lulled by the sounds of the sea at **Ponta d'Ouro** (opposite) and **Ponta Malongane** (opposite)
- Wander along the white, palm-fringed sands lining **Tofo** (p87)
- Enjoy time at **Chidenguele** (p82) and **Pomene** (p92), two of the south's lesser-known beaches

★ Bazaruto Archipelago

★ Pomene

Inhambane ★★ Tofo

★ Chidenguele

★ Ponta d'Ouro & Ponta Malongane

PONTA D'OURO & PONTA MALONGANE

The sleepy colonial-era town of Ponta d'Ouro has boomed in popularity in recent years and is the first Mozambique stop on many southern Africa overland itineraries. Its best asset is its excellent beach – long, wide and surf-pounded. Offshore waters host abundant sea life, including dolphins and whale sharks and – from July to October – whales. Thanks to Ponta d'Ouro's proximity to South Africa, it fills up completely on holiday weekends.

About 5km north is the quieter and even more beautiful Ponta Malongane, with a seemingly endless stretch of windswept coastline fringed by high, vegetated dunes and patches of coastal forest.

There are no internet cafes, banks or ATMs. South African rands are accepted everywhere. (Meticais and US dollars can also be used.)

Activities

DIVING

The Tandje Beach Resort compound (right) is the base for a number of dive-camp operators. All offer simple tented and/or reed or wooden hut accommodation sharing ablutions with the camping ground, catered or self-catering options, diving courses and equipment rental. Most offer low-season and midweek discounts. Dive camps include:

Scuba Adventures (☎ in South Africa 011-648 9648; www.scubatravel.co.za)

Simply Scuba (☎ in South Africa 011-678 0972; www.simplyscuba.co.za)

Whaler (☎ in South Africa 011-213 0213; www.thewhaler.co.za)

In addition to the operators based at Tandje Beach Resort, local dive bases include Devocean Diving (right) and Ponta Malongane (p77).

DOLPHIN TOURS

Dolphins frequent the waters offshore from Ponta d'Ouro, and catching a glimpse of these beautiful creatures can be a wonderful experience. However, they're wild, which means sightings can't be guaranteed – let them come to you, if they wish, and don't go off in wild pursuit or try to touch them.

The best tours are with **Dolphin Encountours** (☎ 84-330 3859, in South Africa 011-462 8103; www.dolphinencountours.co.za), which is based in the Tandje

Beach Resort compound, and which also offers simple, well-maintained accommodation. The tours are generally part of a three-night package from the Kosi Bay border post, priced from about US$450 per person. They include a short marine ecology course plus accommodation with half-board, transfers to/from the Kosi Bay border post and – weather permitting – daily dolphin excursions. Walk-ins are accommodated on a space-available basis. Between June and August it's chilly in the boats, so bring a windbreaker.

KITE SURFING

Kite surfing can be organised through Moya Kite/Surf, based at Dolphin Encountours (left).

Sleeping

PONTA D'OURO

Tandje Beach Resort (campsite per person Mtc350, per vehicle Mtc10) In addition to the facilities of the dive camps located on its grounds (see left), which all have budget accommodation, Tandje also has a shaded, seaside camping area with shared ablutions. It's at the southern end of town.

Kaya Kweru (☎ 21-758403; www.kaya-kweru.co.za; dm US$20; 2-person cottage US$105-115, 4-person cottage US$175-185; ☑) About 200m north of the town centre with rows of closely spaced stone-and-thatch cottages with bathrooms, all set in a rather featureless compound redeemed by its location just in from the beach. There's also a restaurant, an open-air bar facing the sea, a full range of activities, and transfers to/from South Africa and Maputo.

Devocean Diving (☎ in South Africa 083-657 4050, 9am-4pm Mon-Fri; www.devoceandiving.com; s/d tented accommodation from US$25/35, s/d r from US$30/40, 8-person self-catering house US$295) About 400m from the sea along the main road into town, this is basically a dive camp but more pampered, and with good meals. Accommodation is in rooms in the main house or in furnished safari-style tents set around a small garden, with two self-catering houses nearby.

Café del Mar (☎ 21-650048; cafedelmarponta@tropical.co.mz; r per person with half-board US$55) This restaurant also has rooms, in spiffy reed chalets closely spaced around a small garden. All have nets, fans and shared bathrooms with hot water. It's perched on a hilltop in the town centre about 200m in from the beach – look for the orange building. If you're after some

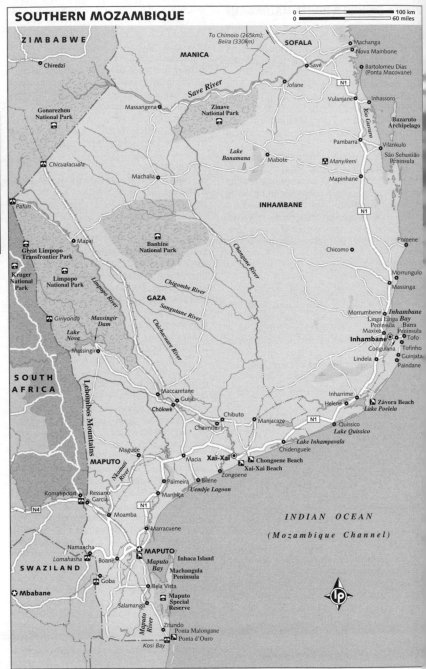

quiet, midweek is best; on weekends the bar has music until dawn.

Motel do Mar Beach Resort (☎ 21-650000; www .pontadoouro.co.za; 4-person chalets without/with sea view US$85/105) In a good seaside location (though not all rooms manage to have full sea views), this motel is a throwback to colonial days. It has a restaurant that does seafood grills, a 1960s ambience and blocks of faded two-storey self-catering chalets, each with two twin-bedded rooms.

BougainVilla Sol (☎ 82-310 4360, 82-306 9090; bougain villasol@gmail.com; d US$80, 5-person self-catering house US$200; ⊠) A cosy guesthouse with nicely decorated rooms set around a garden, braai (barbecue) facilities, and the beach just a five-minute walk away. It's near the police station, and signposted from the entrance to town. Breakfast costs US$10 extra (order in advance).

Praia de Ouro Sul (☎ in South Africa 012-348 2690; www.pontadoouro.co.za; d/q tent from US$150/170; ⊠) Well-appointed safari-style tents set on a forested hillside, and with a restaurant on-site. It's about 5km south of Ponta d'Ouro town, and signposted from town.

PONTA MALONGANE

Ponta Malongane is quieter and more spread out than Ponta d'Ouro, without a town, and with an excellent beach. You'll need your own transport here.

Ponta Malongane (☎ in South Africa 013-741 1975; www.malongane.co.za; campsite per person US$15, live-camp tents from US$30, log hut d US$45, self-catering chalets US$90) This long-running, laid-back place is based at the sprawling and shaded Parque de Malongane. It has various accommodation options, including camping, two-person ron-davels and small, rustic twin-bedded log cabins. There's also a restaurant, and a large self-catering area. Ask about dive-accommodation deals.

Tartaruga Marítima Luxury Camp (☎ in South Africa 083-309 3469, www.tartaruga.co.za; s/d US$100/155; ⊠) About 2km further north, Tartaruga is a lovely and tranquil retreat, with spacious, comfortable safari-style tents tucked away in the coastal forest behind the dunes and just a few minute's walk from a wonderful stretch of beach. There's no restaurant but there is a raised lounge-bar and self-catering braai area with views over the open ocean.

Ponta Mamoli (☎ in South Africa 083-444 6346; www .pontamamoli.com; sea-facing chalet with half-board s/d US$170/225; ⊠) Cosy and pleasant two- and four-person log-cabin-style chalets, a restaurant, a bar with good views, a braai area and a small pool surrounded by a large sun deck overlooking the sea. It's ideal for a pampered getaway, set on a quiet and deserted stretch of coastline 11km north of Ponta Malongane, and signposted. Diving, fishing and horseback riding can be arranged.

Eating

The following are all located in Ponta d'Ouro; the only dining options for Ponta Malongane are the restaurants at Ponta Mamoli (left) and Ponta Malongane (left).

Scandals (meals Mtc50-150; ☽ breakfast, lunch & dinner) This amenable divers' hang-out just outside Tandje Beach Resort has all-day breakfasts, omelettes and light meals.

A Florestinha do Índico (meals from Mtc150; ☽ lunch & dinner) Several doors south of Fishmonger Barracas, with seating under thatched umbrellas scattered around a shady lawn and a selection of grills and other standards.

Fishmonger Barracas (☎ 21-650026; meals from Mtc150; ☽ breakfast, lunch & dinner) A popular rooftop gathering spot in front of Café del Mar, with filling breakfasts, seafood platters and other hearty fare.

Café del Mar (☎ 21-650048; meals from Mtc200; ☽ lunch & dinner Wed-Mon) Café del Mar has the best food in town, featuring crêpes and other French fare, plus a bar with live music most weekends.

Getting There & Away

Ponta d'Ouro is 120km south of Maputo. The road is in decent shape for the first 60km, but it's slow going through soft, deep sand thereafter. Allow about 3½ hours in a private vehicle (4WD only).

Chapas depart Maputo's Catembe ferry pier at 8am on Tuesday and Friday (Mtc150, five hours). Departures from Ponta d'Ouro are at 8am Wednesday and Saturday. Otherwise, take the ferry (p71) to Catembe, where you can find transport to Salamanga (Mtc75, two hours) or Zitundo (Mtc120, four hours), two villages en route. From Zitundo, there's sporadic transport to Ponta d'Ouro (Mtc30, 30 minutes), which is 20km further south.

Kaya Kweru (p75) has a twice weekly shuttle from Maputo (US$33 per person, minimum two).

Kosi Bay border post is 11km south of Ponta d'Ouro along a sandy track (4WD), but there's no public transport. Coming from South Africa, there's a guarded lot at the border where you can leave your vehicle in the shade for about US$5 per day. All the hotels do pick-ups from the border from about US$10 to US$15 per person, minimum two. Allow about five hours for the drive to/from Durban (South Africa).

There's no public transport to Ponta Malongane, though chapas between Maputo and Ponta d'Ouro stop at the signposted turn-off, about 5km before Ponta Malongane. To get between Ponta d'Ouro and Ponta Malongane, you can walk along the beach at low tide or go via the road.

MAPUTO SPECIAL RESERVE

En route to Ponta d'Ouro and just two hours from the capital is the 90-sq-km **Maputo Special Reserve** (adult/child/vehicle Mtc200/100/200), which runs along a spectacularly beautiful and completely isolated stretch of coastline. It was gazetted in 1969 to protect the local elephant population (about 350 in the late 1970s), plus several turtle species. Until recently it was known as the Maputo Elephant Reserve. The elephants, who suffered from the effects of the war and poaching, are estimated to number only about 180 today – most quite skittish and seldom seen, but planned restocking should improve chances of sightings. There are also small populations of antelope, hippo and smaller animals. The main attractions are the pristine wilderness feel – it offers a true bush adventure close to the capital – and its birds. Over 300 different types of birds have been identified, including fish eagles and many wetland species. The coastline here is also an important nesting area for loggerhead and leatherback turtles; peak breeding season is November to January.

The heart of the reserve is Ponta Milibangalala, about 35km from the main gate along the sea. While there are few spots that can rival the beauty of the coastline here, the bush road in from the gate is also interesting, as it passes through the reserve's rich diversity of habitats, including woodlands, grasslands and dry forests.

Although rehabilitation is scheduled, in conjunction with the planned extension of the reserve, and its ultimate merger with South Africa's Tembe Elephant Park, there are currently no facilities, apart from a basic beachside **camping ground** (campsite adult/child

Mtc200/100) at Ponta Milibangalala. You'll need to be completely self-sufficient, including food and water (water suitable for washing is sometimes available at the main entrance). There's also an area at the main entrance next to the reserve office where you can pitch a tent, though almost everyone goes further in to camp along the beach.

Outside the reserve, and signposted along the road to Ponta d'Ouro, are a couple of community-run 'lodges' offering very basic accommodation and the chance to arrange cultural activities and local excursions. Advance bookings for accommodation and meals are recommended for both, although as neither has a fixed telephone number, this can be a challenge. The best thing to do is arrive prepared to self-cater, just in case. **Gala Ntiti** (campsite per person Mtc250, d tent Mtc500, tw/q Mtc850/1500), just south of the reserve in Gala village, can also arrange trips with a local fisherman on the nearby lake.

At **Tsakane ka Madjadjane** (campsite per person with own/hire tent Mtc50/150, d Mtc300), about 8km south of Salamanga town, you can also learn about honey harvesting and mat weaving.

Continuing north within the reserve, past its northern boundary and on to the tip of the Machangula Peninsula, brings you to **Ponta Torres Camp** (☎ 82-252 4670; www.africaafrica .co.za/Pontatorres.htm; 3-bed tent US$80), a self-catering place on Cape Santa Maria (p72) with safari-style tents. It's targeted at anglers and birdwatchers. Also on Cape Santa Maria, the same management runs **Nhonguane Lodge** (☎ 82-252 4670; www.nhonguanelodge.co.za; per person US$50), with well-equipped self-catering chalets. For both places, bring all food and drink. A 4WD is essential and you'll need to pay vehicle and entry fees for the reserve.

Getting There & Away

Dana Tours (p57) and Mozambique City Tours (p64) operate day and overnight trips to the reserve. Otherwise, you'll need your own transport (4WD). The main entrance, known as *campeamento principal,* is about 65km from Catembe along the Ponta d'Ouro road. From here, it's 3km to the park gate, and then about 35km further through the reserve to the coast and the camping ground. There's a second entrance further along the Ponta d'Ouro road, marked with a barely legible signpost, from where it's about 22km into the reserve.

NAMAACHA

Cool Namaacha lies on the border with Swaziland, about 70km west of Maputo. Its streets are lined with lavender, jacaranda and bright-orange flame trees, and thanks to its favourable climate, it is the source of many of the flowers for sale on Maputo's street corners. The ornate colonial-era church is the main building of interest. At Namaacha's eastern edge is a rusty sign marking the way down to a small *cascata* (waterfall), 3.6km north of the main road, and a good picnic spot.

Located on the main road in the town centre, **Hotel Libombos** (☎ 21-960102; d/ste Mtc2000/2500; 🍴) has comfortable rooms, some with views over the hills, plus a restaurant and a casino.

Behind the church, **Xisaka** (☎ 21-960330; s/d/ste Mon-Thu Mtc2210/2600/2750, Fri-Sun Mtc1950/2495/2600; 🍴 ▣ 🛜) has pleasant rooms with TV, a restaurant and conference facilities.

Chapas run throughout the day to/from Maputo (Mtc50, 1½ hours), departing Namaacha from the border, and stopping in front of the market on the main road.

BILENE

This small resort town sits on the large Uembje Lagoon, which is separated from the open sea by a narrow, sandy spit. Thanks to its sheltered waters and its position as the first resort area north of Maputo, it's a popular destination with vacationing South African families, and on holiday weekends you'll be tripping over motorboats, windsurfing boards and quad bikes. If you're based in Maputo with a car at your disposal, it makes an enjoyable getaway but if you're touring and want some sand, head further north to the beaches around Inhambane or south to Ponta d'Ouro.

Unlike most of Mozambique's other coastal lakes and lagoons, Uembje gets influxes of fresh water via a narrow channel to the sea, so conditions vary with the seasons. In general the winter months are best, with breezes and waves.

In the 19th century, the area around Bilene served as capital for the Gaza chief, Soshangane. During colonial days, Bilene was known as São Martinho and the saint's feast on 4 November is still celebrated, often with processions, singing and dancing in the upper part of town away from the beach.

Sleeping

Complexo Palmeiras (☎ 282-59019; http://complexo palmeiras.blogspot.com; campsite Mtc170, plus per person Mtc150, 2-/4-person chalets Mtc2200/2550) At the northern edge of town on the beach, with camping, no-frills chalets with fridge, braai facilities and a restaurant. Bring your own towels, linens, pans and cutlery. It's about 500m past the market and transport stand: follow the main road into town to the final T-junction, then go left for 1km.

Praia do Sol (☎ 82-319 3040; www.pdsol.co.za; chalets & r with half-board per person Mtc750) About 4km south of town along the beach, this place has a collection of spacious two-, four- and five-person A-frame chalets overlooking the lagoon, plus some double rooms; all come with bathroom and nets. There's a restaurant (no self-catering) and bar, and diving, canoeing, snorkelling and quad-bikes, plus boat trips across the lagoon to the ocean. Turn right onto the beachfront road and continue for about 3km, staying right at the fork.

Complexo Aquarius (☎ 282-59000; www.aquarius bilene.co.mz; r Mtc2000; 🍴) Just to the right (south) of the main T-junction on a nice, semi-shaded section of beach, with red-roofed stone chalets and a restaurant. It's worth checking out.

Eating

Most of Bilene's eateries are clustered along or just off the beachfront road. All are open daily for lunch and dinner. Some recommended eateries:

Café O Bilas (pizzas from Mtc120) Next to the petrol station.

Complexo Aquarius (see above) A large menu of seafood grills and Portuguese cuisine.

Estrela do Mar (meals from Mtc75) With seafood grills.

Tchin-Tchin (meals Mtc75) Grilled chicken and chips.

Getting There & Away

Bilene is 140km north of Maputo and 35km off the main road. A direct chapa departs Maputo's Xipamanine Market (Map p56) at about 7am (Mtc100, five hours). Otherwise, go to Junta and have any northbound transport drop you at the Macia junction, from where pick-ups run throughout the day to/from Bilene (Mtc25, 30 minutes).

Leaving Bilene, a direct 30-seater bus to Maputo departs daily at 6am (and sometimes again at 1pm) from the town centre near the market (Mtc100, four to five hours). Otherwise take a chapa (from either the market or the roundabout at the entrance to Bilene, about 1.5km from the beach) to Macia and get onward transport from there.

If you're driving, the road to Bilene is tarmac throughout. With a 4WD (or by chartering a boat – possible at most hotels), it's possible to reach the other side of the lagoon and beach on the open sea. Boats can also be arranged with local fishermen from about Mtc250 return.

LIMPOPO NATIONAL PARK

Together with South Africa's Kruger National Park and Zimbabwe's Gonarezhou National Park, **Limpopo National Park** (Parque Nacional do Limpopo; ☎ 21-713000; www.limpopopn.gov.mz; adult/child/vehicle Mtc200/100/200, payable in meticais, South African rand or US dollars) forms part of the Great Limpopo Transfrontier Park (p43). Gonarezhou connections are still in the future, but Kruger and Limpopo are now linked via two fully functioning border posts.

Wildlife on the Mozambique side can't compare with that in South Africa's Kruger, and sightings are still very hit and miss: it's quite possible to spend time in the park without seeing large animals. Yet, Limpopo's bush ambience is alluring, and the park area also offers the chance for cultural and adventure tourism. There are people living within the park boundaries so it's likely that you'll see some of these communities on the park's eastern fringes.

Most visitors use Limpopo as a transit corridor between Kruger and the coast. There's also a five-day 4WD Shingwedzi Trail, starting at Kruger's Punda Maria camp and continuing south through Limpopo park to the Lebombo/Ressano Garcia border post (book through www.dolimpopo.com or www.sanparks.org).

Additional offerings include a four-day hiking trail from Massingir Dam west along the Machampane River, and (best) a four-day canoe expedition along the Elefantes (Olifants) River from its confluence with the Shingwedzi River to its confluence with the Limpopo River. Both of the latter can be booked through Machampane Wilderness Camp (see right).

Sleeping & Eating

Campismo Aguia Pesqueira (campsite per person Mtc100; tent hire per day Mtc100) This good park-run camping ground is along the edge of the escarpment overlooking Massingir Dam, about 50km from Giriyondo border post. All campsites have views over the dam, plus braai facilities, and there's a communal kitchen and ablutions.

Campismo Albufeira (☎ 82-654 7968; campsite per person Mtc100, s & d chalets Mtc1900) Just inside Massingir gate and near the dam wall, with four simple, clean en suite self-catering reed chalets with braai facilities, plus a camping ground with communal ablutions and kitchen.

Covane Community Lodge (☎ 82-760 7830; www .covanelodge.com; campsite Mtc250, d in traditional house Mtc900, 5-person self-catering chalet Mtc1900) This community-run place is about 13km outside Limpopo's Massingir gate on a rise overlooking the dam. For camping, it's better to stay at the nicer park campsites, but for cultural activities, this is a good bet, with simple, clean local-style bungalows, including one with self-catering facilities. Staff can help you organise boat trips on the lake, traditional dancing performances, village walks and visits to the park. Local-style meals are available with notice. Advance accommodation bookings are recommended. Chapas run daily from Maputo's Junta (p69) to Massingir town (Mtc175), where staff will come and collect you.

Machampane Wilderness Camp (www.dolimpopo .com; s & d tent with full-board per person US$315) The upmarket Machampane has five spacious, well-appointed safari tents in a tranquil setting directly overlooking a section of the Machampane River where you're likely to see (or at least hear) hippos plus a variety of smaller wildlife and many birds. Activities are the highlight here and include guided walks, a multinight hiking trail and a four-day canoe expedition along the Elefantes River. Machampane Camp is about 20km from Giriyondo border post, and pick-ups can be arranged from Massingir village or from Kruger park's Letaba camp (where you can leave your car). Bookings can also be made through Mozaic Travel (p57) in Maputo.

Getting There & Away

The main park entrance on the Mozambique side is **Massingir Gate** (☽ 6am-6pm), about 5km from Massingir town. It's reached via a signposted turn-off from the N1 at Macia junction that continues through Chokwé town (where there's an ATM and a petrol station) on to Massingir.

To enter Limpopo from South Africa's Kruger park, you'll also need to pay Kruger park entry fees, and Kruger's gate quota system (see www.sanparks.org for information) applies. For border crossing information, see p185.

If you transit between the Pafuri border post (see p185), at Limpopo's northern tip, and Vilankulo, it's worth detouring about 30km before reaching Mapinhane to visit the overgrown ruins of **Manyikeni** (signposted to the north of the Mapinhane road). Manyikeni was once the seat of a major trading centre and chieftaincy which was occupied between the 13th and 17th centuries, and which had links to Great Zimbabwe. At the moment the site is neglected, although it has been proposed for inclusion as a Unesco World Heritage site.

The closest tanking up stations on the Mozambique side are in Xai-Xai and Chókwe (where there is also an ATM) and, less reliably, in Massingir itself. Travelling via Mapai, there is no fuel until Mapinhane.

XAI-XAI

Xai-Xai (pronounced 'shy-shy', and known during colonial times as João Belo) is a long town, stretching for several kilometres along the N1. It's of little interest to travellers, but the nearby **Xai-Xai Beach** (Praia do Xai-Xai), about 10km from the town centre, has invigorating sea breezes, and is an agreeable overnight stop if you're driving to/from points further north.

The capital of Gaza province, Xai-Xai was developed in the early 20th century as a satellite port to Maputo, although its economic significance never approached that of the national capital. Running just south of Xai-Xai is the 'great, grey-green greasy' Limpopo River of Rudyard Kipling fame. It's Mozambique's second largest waterway, with a catchment area of more than 390,000 sq km, and drains parts of Botswana, South Africa and Zimbabwe as it makes its way to the sea. Despite its size, water levels vary dramatically throughout the year, leaving some sections as just small streams during the dry winter months. The wetlands around the Limpopo's lower reaches are rewarding birdwatching areas, and are most accessible near Zongoene.

Information

There are ATMs at **Millennium BIM** (N1, near Kaya Ka Hina); at **Standard Bank** (1 block behind Kaya Ka Hina); and at **Barclays** (N1, opposite the church). For internet access try **Telecomunicações de Moçambique** (per min Mtc1; ⏰ 7.30am-7pm), diagonally opposite Standard Bank and just behind the central market.

Sleeping & Eating

Kaya Ka Hina (☎ 282-22391; N1; s/d with shared bathroom Mtc400/500, tw/d with air-con from Mtc700/800) The centrally located Kaya Ka Hina is convenient if you're trying to catch an early bus or if you don't want to drive down to the beach. It has no-frills but clean rooms upstairs, and an inexpensive restaurant below. It's on the main road about 100m north of the praça transport stand. The hotel entrance is around to the side of the restaurant.

Complexo Halley (☎ 282 35003; complexohalley1@ yahoo.com.br; Xai-Xai Beach; d Mtc1000-1750; ⊠) This long-standing beachfront hotel is the first place you reach coming down the beach access road from town, and is an amenable, recommended choice. It has stiff sea breezes, a seaside esplanade, a good restaurant and

---

THE GAZA KINGDOM

Gaza province is now famous for its beaches and coastal lakes, but as recently as the mid-19th century it was renowned as the seat of the kingdom of Gaza, one of the most influential in Mozambican history. At the height of its power around the 1850s, it stretched from south of the Limpopo River northward to the Zambezi and westward into present-day Zimbabwe, Swaziland and South Africa.

One of Gaza's most famous chiefs was Soshangane, who ruled most of southern Mozambique from his base at Chaimite. Soshangane died in 1858 and was succeeded by his son, Umzila, who in turn was succeeded by his son, Ngungunhane. Ngungunhane's first priority was to defend the Gaza kingdom from ever-increasing European encroachment. While outwardly acknowledging Portuguese sovereignty, he allowed raiding parties to attack Portuguese settlements and struck numerous deals with the British, playing off the two colonial powers against each other.

By the mid-1890s, the tides began to turn. In 1895 Ngungunhane was captured by the Portuguese, and spent the remainder of his life in exile in the Azores. He died in 1906, and the mighty Gaza kingdom came to an end.

pleasant, homey rooms (ask for one that's sea-facing). All rooms have bathroom and some have air-con and TV. On Friday evening there's a disco at the hotel; on Saturday it's across the road at the esplanade.

Restaurante Kapulana (meals from Mtc150) This small place near the market has a range of standard fare.

Restaurante-Bar M3 (just south of the N1; meals Mtc200) At the far northern end of town, M3 has the usual array of standards, plus pizzas. Coming from town, the turn-off is near the Vodacom-painted building shortly before reaching Motel Concha (on the left).

Getting There & Away

The main praça transport stand is near the old Pôr do Sol complex on the main road at the southern end of town. Buses to Maputo depart daily at about 6am (Mtc200, four hours). It's marginally faster to take one of the north-south through buses, although getting a seat can be a challenge. Wait by the Pôr do Sol complex on the main road at the southern end of town or, better, take a chapa to the *pontinha* (bridge control post), where all traffic needs to stop.

To Xai-Xai Beach (Mtc5), chapas depart from the praça transport stand, or catch them anywhere along the main road. They run at least to the roundabout about 700m uphill from the beach and sometimes further.

AROUND XAI-XAI

The lagoon-studded coast north and south of Xai-Xai has a string of attractive beaches – all quiet, except during South African school holidays. The area is particularly suited to travellers with their own vehicle, as many of the lodges are located well off the N1, although some offer transfers.

The beach is particularly lovely at **Chidenguele**, about 70km north of Xai-Xai and just 5km off the N1 down an easy access road. The coast here is fringed by high, vegetated dunes stretching into the horizon in each direction. There's also an old **lighthouse**, reached via an unsignposted sandy track off the Chidenguele access road, and climbable when the keeper is around. Chidenguele village is notable for its large **cathedral** (visible from the N1), its bakery and its small market. About 12km north along the beach is **King's Pool** – a sheltered tidal pool that is ideal for snorkelling, and for fishing from the outer reef.

Paraíso de Chidenguele (☎ 84-390 9999; www.chid beachresort.com; 'overnight' r per person Mtc925, 4-/6-/8-person chalets Mtc3895/4920/5710) is a lovely place with accommodation in simple, twin-bed 'overnight' rooms, or in spacious, well-equipped self-catering cottages – some with stunning views over the sea, others nestled in the coastal forest. There's a restaurant-bar and a large, sparkling clean swimming pool. It's ideal for families. It also rents snorkelling equipment for trips to King's Pool.

Sunset Beach Resort (☎ 82-890 4019; www.sunset beachlodge.com; campsite per person Mtc385; 4-/6-person chalets Mtc1175/5545, 2-/4-person cottages Mtc1630/2705) is about 1.5km south of Paraíso de Chidenguele and perched above the same stunning stretch of beach. It has stone-and-thatch self-catering chalets, some more basic 'semi-self catering cottages', a camping area (no sea views) and a restaurant.

Well south of here – south of Xai-Xai and about 7km north of Bilene – is another lovely stretch of beach, and the pleasant **Zongoene Lodge** (☎ 282-42003, in South Africa 015-295 9038; www.zongoene.com; campsite US$10, plus per person US$15, s/d US$135/220, 4-person self-catering house from US$210-335; 🏊). It's just south of the mouth of the Limpopo River with spacious 'pool chalets', or more rustic self-catering houses set back from the beach. There's also camping, a restaurant and an array of activities including fishing and sunset cruises on the Limpopo River. The turn-off is about 15km south of Xai-Xai at Chicumbane, from where it's about 35km further down a sandy track that can be negotiated by 2WD during the dry months.

QUISSICO

About 130km northeast of Xai-Xai on the N1 is Quissico, capital of Zavala district. It is noteworthy for being one of the main meal and bathroom stops on long-haul bus routes along the N1. If the bus stops for long enough, look down the escarpment eastward to a chain of shimmering, pale blue lagoons in the distance. Quissico's other claim to fame is that it's the centre of the famed Chopi *timbila* (marimba) orchestras, and the site of an annual *timbila* festival (usually held around July/August).

There's a backpackers bush camp with basic facilities getting underway, where you can pitch a tent. It's down near the main lagoon and the sea, about 11km from Quissico down a rough (4WD) track, signposted just north of Quissico's main junction along the

N1. In town at the junction itself, **Pousada de Zavala 'Quissico'** (☎ 293-65007; N1; r Mtc500-600) has undistinguished, noisy rooms with shared bathrooms, and a restaurant, and is a possible option if you're stuck for accommodation. Just behind is a viewpoint over the lagoons.

ZÁVORA BEACH

About 55km north of Quissico and about 80km south of Inhambane is Závora Beach, with a lighthouse that is possible to climb if you can find someone around to open it. It's also home to the rustic, slightly frayed but fairly priced and backpacker-friendly **Závora Lodge** (☎ 84-702 2660; www.zavoralodge.com; campsite per person US$15, 4-person bungalow US$115, 4-/8-person sea-view house US$140/285). Camping is possible, including a few sites on the breezy sea side of the visibly eroding dunes. There's also a restaurant overlooking the sea, and some self-catering bungalows and houses. For views and breezes, try to get a house up on the dune top, rather than in the compound on the backside of the dune. The bungalows and houses come with bedding and nets, but otherwise, bring everything with you.

Závora Lodge's main attraction is its good in-house **dive operator** (www.mozdivers.com) who will guide you to see the area's many underwater attractions – manta rays, sharks, a nearby shipwreck and even some unexplored sites – all at better prices than at most other places along the coast. Note that there's currently no instruction, so diving here is for qualified divers only.

Getting There & Away
Závora is 17km from the N1 (usually negotiable with 2WD); the turn-off is signposted 11km north of Inharrime town. Free pickups to/from Inharrime can be arranged with Závora Lodge. Otherwise, there's a daily chapa (Mtc30, 45 minutes), departing Inharrime at about noon and Závora (just up from Závora Lodge) at about 7am. Transfers can also be arranged from Inhambane and Tofo.

LINDELA
This junction village is where the road to Inhambane splits off the N1. **Quinta de Santo António** (☎ 82-489 2420, 84-490 5105; www .stayonthebeach.co.za; N1; campsite per person Mtc175, 1-/2-/4-/6-person chalet Mtc650/1300/2200/2700; ⓟ) has well-equipped, self-catering chalets with fans, nets and microwaves, a shop selling a few basics, a resident parrot, meals with advance notice, and among the cleanest bathrooms along this stretch of the coastal road.

INHAMBANE
With its serene waterside setting, tree-lined avenues, faded colonial-style architecture and mixture of Arabic, Indian and African influences, Inhambane is one of Mozambique's

CHOPI TIMBILA ORCHESTRAS
The intricate rhythms and pulsating beat of Chopi *timbila* music are among southern Africa's most impressive musical traditions. The music is played on *timbila* (singular: *mbila*) – a type of marimba or xylophone made of long rows of wooden slats carved from the slow-growing *mwenje* (sneezewood) tree. In age-old rites of passage, young Chopi boys would go into the bush to plant *mwenje* saplings, which would then be harvested for *timbila* construction years later when their grandsons came of age.

At the heart of *timbila* music is the *mgodo* (performance), which involves an orchestra of up to 20 or more instruments of varying sizes and ranges of pitch, singers and dancers, rattle or shaker players and a single composition with movements similar to those of a Western-style classical symphony. Rhythms are complex, often demanding that the players master different beats simultaneously with each hand, and the lyrics are full of humour and sarcasm, dealing with social issues and community events.

Following a decline during the immediate post-independence and war years, *timbila* music is now experiencing a renaissance, due in part to the efforts of Venâncio Mbande, a master composer, player and *timbila* craftsman par excellence. Like many other Chopi, Mbande left Mozambique at a young age to seek work in the South African mines but kept the art of *timbila* alive and ultimately formed his own orchestra. In the mid-1990s Mbande returned to his home near Quissico, where he began teaching *timbila* music and craftsmanship. His orchestra, Timbila ta Venâncio, has received international acclaim. Numerous other orchestras have since been formed around Zavala district and Quissico is a centre for training young players.

SOUTHERN MOZAMBIQUE

INHAMBANE

```
0          200 m
0          0.1 miles
```

Ⓐ   Ⓑ

INFORMATION
Barclays Bank & ATM......................1 A4
Centro Provincial de Recursos Digitais de
  Inhambane..................................2 B5
Litanga Agência de Viagems...........(see 5)
Millennium BIM & ATM...................3 A5
Telecomunicações de Moçambique....4 A5
Tourist Information Centre................5 B5
Verdinho's..................................(see 20)

SIGHTS & ACTIVITIES
Cathedral of Nossa Senhora de
  Conceição..................................6 A4
Market..7 B5
Museum......................................8 B4
New Mosque................................9 B4
Old Mosque...............................10 A4

SLEEPING 🏠
Escola Superior de Hotelaria e
  Turismo...................................11 B4
Hotel Inhambane.........................12 A4
Pensão Pachiça...........................13 A4
Sensasol....................................14 A5

EATING 🍴
Á Maçaroca................................15 A5
Bistro-Café Sem Cerimônias..........16 B5
Inhambane Bakery.......................17 B5
Restaurant Tic-Tic......................18 B5
Supermarket..............................19 B5
Verdinho's.................................20 A4

ENTERTAINMENT 🎭
Casa de Cultura..........................21 A5

TRANSPORT
Bus & Chapa Stand......................22 B5
Ferry & Dhows to Maxixe..............23 A4

Inhambane Bay

Josina
Machel
Park
Governor's
Mansion
Av da Independência
Train Station
(disused)
To Casa
Jensen (1.5km);
Airstrip (5km);
Barra (22km);
Tofo (22km)
Inhambane
Bay
To Lindela (35km);
N1 (35km)

History

As early as the 11th century, Inhambane served as a port of call for Arabic traders sailing along the East African coast. Textiles were an important commodity, and by the time the Portuguese arrived in the early-16th century, the area boasted a well-established cotton-spinning industry. In 1560 Inhambane was chosen as the site of the first Jesuit mission to the region. Development was also helped along by Inhambane's favourable location on a sheltered bay, and before long it had moved into the limelight as a bustling ivory trading port. By the early-18th century, the Portuguese had established themselves here, together with traders from India. This mixture of Indian, Christian and Muslim influences continued to characterise Inhambane's development in later years, and is still notable today.

In the coming decades, the focus of trade shifted from cloth and ivory to slaves. By the mid-18th century, an estimated 1500 slaves were passing through Inhambane's port each year, and this human trafficking had become the town's economic mainstay.

In 1834 Inhambane was ravaged by the army of the Gaza chief, Soshangane. However, it soon recovered to again become one of the largest towns in the country. The abolition of the slave trade in the late-19th century dealt Inhambane's economy a sharp blow. The situation worsened in the early-20th century as economic focus in the region shifted southwards to Lourenço Marques (now Maputo). Many businesses moved south or closed, and Inhambane began a gradual decline from which it still has not recovered.

Information

Barclays Bank (Avenida da Independência) ATM.
Centro Provincial de Recursos Digitais de Inhambane (Avenida de Moçambique; per min Mtc0.50; 🕙 8am-8pm Mon-Fri, 9am-4pm Sat) Internet access.
Millennium BIM (Avenida Acordos de Lusaka) ATM.

most charming towns and well worth a visit. It has a history that reaches back at least 10 centuries, making it one of the oldest settlements along the coast. Today Inhambane is the capital of Inhambane province, although it's completely lacking in any sort of bustle or pretence. It is also the gateway to a fine collection of beaches, including Tofo and Barra.

LAND OF THE GOOD PEOPLE

Upon his arrival in Inhambane, 15th-century Portuguese explorer Vasco da Gama was reportedly so charmed by the locals that he gave the area the name *terra da boa gente* (land of the good people).

TANGERINAS DE INHAMBANE

Mention Inhambane province to a Mozambican, and chances are they will say something about *tangerinas de Inhambane*. In season, you'll see bushel baskets of tangerines lining the roadsides, piled to overflowing. The fruit has even made it into local pop culture through the poem, *As saborosas tanjarinas d'Inhambane*, written by renowned Mozambican poet José Craveirinha.

Telecomunicações de Moçambique (Avenida Eduardo Mondlane; ☿ 7am-10pm) Domestic and international telephone calls; head right coming off the ferry jetty.

Tourist Information Centre (☎ 293-56149; info@ inhambane-info.net; Avenida da Revolução, at Litanga Agência de Viagens) At the entrance to the central market, with city info, walking tours, dhow trips and more.

Verdinho's (Avenida da Independência; per hr Mtc80; ☿ 8am-10pm Mon-Sat) Broadband internet.

Sights & Activities

Strolling around Inhambane's quiet traffic-free streets comes as a treat if you've been frequenting some of Mozambique's other urban areas. The stately **Cathedral of Nossa Senhora de Conceição**, dating from the late 18th century, is one of the main landmarks. It rises up behind the newer cathedral, just north of the jetty. North of here, reached by following the waterfront road, is the small **old mosque** (1840). The **new mosque** is several blocks further east. Don't miss strolling along the **waterfront** at sunset, and watching the sun sink into the flamingo-frequented Inhambane Bay.

Inhambane's colourful **market** is at its best in the early morning. Also recommended is the tiny **museum** (Avenida da Vigilância; admission free, donations welcome; ☿ 9am-5pm Tue-Fri, 2-5pm Sat & Sun) near the new mosque. Its displays include collections of traditional musical instruments, clothing and household items from the surrounding area, with some captions in English.

About 10km northeast of Inhambane in the bay are two islands, **Isle of Rats** (Ilha dos Ratos) and **Isle of Pigs** (Ilha dos Porcos). Boats can be arranged through the tourist information centre.

Sleeping

Pensão Pachiça (☎ 293-20565, 82-355 9590; www .barralighthouse.com; Rua 3 de Fevereiro; dm/s/d

US$15/25/40, meals Mtc140-240) This recommended backpackers on the waterfront has clean rooms and dorm beds, a restaurant-bar serving pizzas and local cuisine, and a rooftop terrace overlooking the bay. From the ferry, take a left coming off the jetty and continue about 300m. The same management runs campgrounds at Tofinho and Barra lighthouse, and can help with bus travel info between Mozambique and South Africa. For more information see its other website, www.inhambane.co.za.

Sensasol (África Tropical; ☒) A row of small rooms facing a tiny garden – all with double bed, fan and net, and some with TV and minifridge – were set to open just after we passed through. Room rates will be about Mtc500. It's just off Avenida da Independência.

Escola Superior de Hotelaria e Turismo (☎ 293-20781; www.eshti.uem.mz; Avenida de Moçambique; tw Mtc550) By the train station at the eastern edge of town, this place has functional attached twins (no nets), with each two-room (four-bed) unit sharing a bathroom. Unless they are full, you'll usually only be charged per occupied bed, rather than for the entire room. From the ferry jetty, continue straight through town to the end of the main road.

Hotel Inhambane (☎ 293-20855; Avenida da Independência; s/d Mon-Thu Mtc1345/1905, Fri-Sun Mtc975/1345; ☒) Simple, clean rooms with minifridge, TV and hot water. It's in the town centre.

Casa Jensen (☎ 293-20883, 82-859 6150; casajensen inhambane@gmail.com; r Mtc900-1800; P ☒ 🛜) A convenient stopover for business or midrange travellers. Rooms – attached to a private house – have internet, cable TV and minifridge, and breakfast (included) is large and good. Takeaway meals can be arranged for lunch and dinner. It's just off the airport road; the turn-off is opposite Mercado Gilo. The same management also has several clean, pleasant local-style budget rooms (per person Mtc400) in the nearby village where you can arrange cultural visits, try local food and learn about village life.

Eating

Inhambane Bakery (Avenida da Revolução) For hot, fresh rolls. It's next to the market, and close enough to dash over to from the bus stand. Delicious.

Restaurante Tic-Tic (Avenida da Revolução 227a; meals from Mtc80) Inexpensive local meals, diagonally opposite the market.

Bistro-Café Sem Cerimônias (Avenida da Independência; meals from Mtc180; ☻ 7am-10pm; ☞) Across from the post office, with indoor and outdoor seating, pizzas, chicken and fish dishes and salads.

Á Maçaroca (☎ 293-20489; Avenida Acordos de Lusaka; meals from Mtc200; ☻ 9am-11pm Mon-Sat) One block south of Avenida da Independência, this Swiss-Mozambican place has a selection of grilled fish, meat, curries and other dishes.

Verdinho's (Avenida da Independência; salads from Mtc100, meals from Mtc200; ☻ 8am-10pm Mon-Sat; ☞) Currently the 'in' place in Inhambane with a large menu, including meze, gourmet salads and burgers and continental dishes – all delicious – and seating indoors or at shaded tables outside on the patio where you can watch the passing scene.

Supermarket (Avenida da Revolução) Diagonally opposite the market, and reasonably well-stocked.

Shopping & Entertainment

Inhambarte (acudes1@yahoo.com.br; ☻ 9am-5pm last Sat of the month) hosts an arts and crafts fair near the ferry jetty.

The provincial Casa de Cultura (House of Culture), across from the cinema, is a good place to meet local musicians or arrange lessons.

Getting There & Away

AIR

LAM (airport; www.lam.com.mz) has four flights weekly connecting Inhambane with Maputo, Vilankulo and Johannesburg.

Air Travelmax (☎ in South Africa 011-701 3222; www.airtravelmax.com) flies between Inhambane and Johannesburg's Lanseria airport. Another option is flying from Johannesburg to Vilankulo and then taking a bus to Inhambane.

BOAT

Small motorised passenger boats operate from sunrise to sundown between Inhambane and Maxixe (Mtc12.50, 25 minutes). The pier on the Maxixe side is just across the N1 from the main bus stand. Sailing dhows do the trip more slowly for Mtc5, and one of Inhambane's great morning sights is sitting on the jetty and watching them load up. To charter a motorboat for yourself costs about Mtc200 for the boat; the journey takes about 10 minutes.

BUS

The bus station is behind the market. Chapas to Tofo run throughout the day (Mtc20, one hour). There are two direct buses to Maputo daily, departing at 5.30am and 11am (Mtc350, seven hours, 450km). For other southbound buses, and for all northbound transport, you'll need to head to Maxixe.

Coming from Maputo, direct buses depart Junta between 5am and 7am, or take any northbound bus to Maxixe.

AROUND INHAMBANE

The coast southeast of Inhambane is lined by a succession of attractive beaches, and a long line of lodges. Facilities are geared toward drive-in visitors looking for a self-catering holiday, although most lodges can also organise transfers to/from Inhambane. Most places have only limited facilities during the off-season (any time other than South African holidays), and during the holidays they're often fully booked. All are accessed by well-signposted, sandy access roads (4WD), branching off the main road between about 10km and 35km south of Inhambane.

Sleeping & Eating

Paindane Beach Resort (☎ 082-569 3436; www.pain dane.com; campsite US$10, plus per adult/child US$12/6, 4-/6-/8-person chalets from US$90/140/210) About 35km southeast of Inhambane by road, the Paindane has camping with *barracas* (thatched shelters), as well as various sizes and styles of reed-and-thatch chalets on the dunes overlooking the sea. All are self-catering (bedding is supplied, but bring your own towels), and there's a restaurant. Diving and instruction are available, and there's snorkelling equipment for rent and wonderful snorkelling at low tide just offshore.

Jeff's Palm Resort (☎ 293-56063, 84-690 1310, in South Africa 013-932 1263; www.jeffsmoz.com; 8-person camping barracas US$30, plus per person US$10, 4-/8-person houses US$130/285) Jeff's Palm Resort is nestled in the palm groves behind the dunes, north of Guinjata Bay Resort. It has a collection of self-catering houses, plus *barracas* for camping, each with its own ablutions block and cooking area. There's a restaurant and bar, and diving and fishing can be arranged. Bring your own towels and mosquito nets (and, for the *barracas*, all camping gear).

Guinjata Bay Resort (☎ in South Africa 013-741 2795; www.guinjata.com; campsite with barraca per person US$15,

plus per site US$58, 2-/3-/4-bedroom chalets US$240/255/345)
A large, sprawling place set among the dunes,
with a range of campsites and self-catering
chalets, plus a restaurant. Fishing charters can
be arranged with advance notice and there's
diving (including instruction).

TOFO

Thanks to its sheltered azure waters, white
sands, easy access and fine diving, the beach at
Tofo has long been legendary on the southern
Africa holiday circuit. The beach runs in a
long arc, at the centre of which is a small town
with a perpetual party atmosphere. Many people come to Tofo expecting to spend a few
days, and instead stay several weeks or more.
For something quieter, head around the point
to Barra, or further north or south.

The closest ATMs and banks are in
Inhambane. **Tofo On-Line** (upstairs at Dino's
Beach Bar; per hr Mtc100; ☻ 10am-6pm Thu-Tue) has
internet access.

Activities

Tofo is Mozambique's unofficial diving capital. Operators (both PADI Gold Palm) include
Diversity Scuba (☎ 293-29002; www.diversityscuba.com,
town centre) and **Tofo Scuba** (☎ 293-79030, 82-826 0140;
www.tofoscuba.com, about 1km down the beach). Further
on is **Liquid Adventures** (☎ 293-29046, 84-545 3094;
www.divingtofo.com, Bamboozi Beach Lodge). All also
organise whale-shark snorkelling safaris.

Waterworks Surf & Coffee Shop next to
Diversity Scuba rents kayaks and surfboards.

For horseback riding on the beach (catering to riders of all levels), contact Cavalheiros
do Tofo in person – it's set back from the
beach just before reaching Bamboozi Beach
Lodge– or through www.tofotravel.com.

Sleeping
BUDGET

Note that some of the lower-lying camping
areas behind the dunes can get extremely wet
during the rainy season.

Fatima's Nest (☎ 82-414 5730; www.mozambique
backpackers.com; campsite per person Mtc150, dm Mtc300,
s/d tent Mtc500/650; s/d/tr bungalows Mtc500/650/950, s/d
Mtc750/1150) A makeshift, crowded place about
1.5km south of Bamboozi's on low dunes
overlooking the beach, worth noting primarily
because it's one of Tofo's cheapest options.
On offer: camping, small safari-style tents,
no-frills reed bungalows, a kitchen, bar, pool
table and evening beach bonfires.

Bamboozi Beach Lodge (☎ 293-29040; www.bam
boozibeachlodge.com; dm Mtc300, per person in open/closed
hut Mtc300/350, 3-person chalets Mtc2000, d sea-view chalet
Mtc3000; ☻) Good dorm beds and basic reed
huts – some with floor mattresses and others
with beds – all behind the dunes. There are
also five stilted ensuite reed A-frame 'chalets'
(a couple of which are self-catering) and a
nicer sea-view chalet up on the dune with
views. All accommodation has mosquito nets,
and the dune-top bar-restaurant has magnificent views. It's 3km north of town along a
sandy road. Wednesday and Friday are party
nights, and there's an on-site dive operator.

Nordin's Lodge (☎ 293-29009, 82-868 5950;
2-/4-person chalets Mtc1250/2500) The unassuming
Nordin's is at the northern edge of town in a
shaded location directly on the beach. It has
rustic, slightly rundown thatched chalets that
come with hot water, fridge and self-catering
facilities, and the venerable Nordin himself
ensuring that everything is OK. There are
no meals.

Mango Beach (☎ 82-943 4660; www.mangobeach
.co.za; d hut Mtc690, d Mtc1400, 4-/6-person chalets
Mtc1500/3200) Tofo's northernmost lodge at the
moment, and about 4km from town via road.
There's a dune-top bar/eating area with impressive views over the long beach and good
meals, plus a large cluster of cabanas and chalets behind the dunes. Rooms are basic, with
shared bathrooms and you'll need your own
linens. Nicer are the houses (also with shared
bathroom), and the chalets, which come with
their own kitchenette and bathroom. For
swimming, it's best to head a bit south to
avoid the rocks just in front.

Mundo's (☎ 293-29020; mundostofo@gmail.com;
s/d from Mtc1200/1800; ☻) Formerly Restaurante
Ferroviário, this sister-restaurant to Mundo's
in Maputo (p66) has a row of small but clean
rooms next to the restaurant – opposite
the market and about 100m back from
the beach. All have nets and hot water.
Check that your air-con is working first,
as the rooms aren't well-ventilated otherwise. Transfers from Inhambane can be
arranged.

MIDRANGE

Annex of Aquático Lodge (☎ 82-857 2850; www.aqua
ticolodge.com; tr US$70) This place has five nice,
clean and spacious attached self-catering
rooms directly on the beach next to Tofo
Scuba. Each has one double and one twin

bed, a refrigerator and a mini-cooker. It's good value and a good location.

Hotel Tofo Mar (☎ 293-290443; www.hotel-tofomar .com; s/d Mtc1250/2500, with sea view Mtc1600/2600; ✖) Situated in a prime location directly on the beach in the town centre, Hotel Tofo Mar is the only 'proper' hotel (ie non bungalow-style place) in Tofo. Rooms are on the modest side, but spacious and recently renovated, and there's a restaurant-bar. The sea-view rooms are worth the price difference.

Albatroz Lodge (☎ 293-29005; www.albatrozlodge .com; 4-/6-person chalets US$100/150) Large, if rather cluttered, stone-and-thatch self-catering cottages up on the bluff overlooking the beach – all with verandahs and a charcoal-filled braai. There's also a restaurant with a Sunday buffet, and a pool (though the water is sometimes not the most sparkling). Most rooms have an exterior window and a semi-interior one covered with thatching that can block ventilation.

Casa Barry (☎ 293-29007; www.casabarry.com; d reed casita Mtc1800, 4-/6-person chalets Mtc4920/5800, 4-person cabanas Mtc5600) The efficient and long-standing Casa Barry is well-located on the beach at the southern end of town. It has a camping area; basic, small and poorly ventilated double casitas (bungalows) on the back of the property (without sea views); much nicer, spacious reed-and-thatch self-catering chalets; and newer 'cabanas' bordering the beach. There's also a popular beachfront restaurant-bar.

Eating

Waterworks Surf & Coffee Shop (breakfasts & light meals from Mtc100; ☺ 7am-5pm Tue-Sun) All-day breakfasts featuring muesli, waffles, porridge and more, plus sandwiches and other light meals. It's next to Diversity Scuba in the town centre.

Tofo Scuba (www.tofoscuba.com; light meals from Mtc150) Head here for salads and other fresh, crunchy food – a good bet for vegetarians.

Dino's Beach Bar (meals from Mtc200; ☺ 10am-late Thu-Tue; 💻) One of Tofo's main hangouts, Dino's is on a fast-eroding section of beach just past Fatima's Nest. It's struggling a bit these days, but still has good vibes, good music and pricey but tasty food – pizzas, seafood, toasted sandwiches, desserts and more.

Mundo's (☎ 293-29020; mundostofo@gmail.com; meals from Mtc200; ☺ 8am-10pm) Good pizzas from a pizza oven, and a range of other meals, including paninis and sandwiches. It's at the main junction opposite the market.

Restaurante Concha (meals Mtc200-300) Opposite the market in the town centre, with local flavour (although Western prices). There's a wide menu selection of Mozambican and continental standards, and a bar.

Casa de Comer (meals from Mtc240-300; ☺ 9am-10pm Wed-Mon) Tasty Mozambique-French fusion cuisine – including vegetarian dishes – and some local artwork on display in the small adjoining garden. It's in the town centre.

Getting There & Away

Chapas run throughout the day along the 22km sealed road between Tofo and Inhambane, departing Tofo from about 5am (Mtc15, one hour). To Maputo's Junta, there's usually one direct bus daily, departing Tofo by about 4.30am (Mtc400, 7½ hours). Otherwise, you'll need to go via Inhambane or Maxixe. If you do this and want to catch an early north/southbound bus, it's possible in theory to sleep in Tofo, but for a more sure connection, stay in Inhambane the night before.

Between Johannesburg and Tofo, **Jozibeartours** (www.jozibeartours.co.za) does group transfers (eight to 12 people minimum) for about US$125 per person.

If you leave early from Maputo, it's possible to get to Inhambane in time to continue straight on to Tofo that day, with time to spare.

TOFINHO

Just around the point (to the south) and easily accessed from Tofo (by walking or catching a lift) is Tofinho. It's set on a green hillside looking out over turquoise waters, and is Mozambique's unofficial surfing capital. Board rental can be arranged with Turtle Cove (below), or with Waterworks (p87) in Tofo.

Sleeping & Eating

Turtle Cove Surf & Yoga Lounge (☎ 82-719 4848; www. turtlecovetofo.com; campsite per person US$6, dm US$11, d chalet without/with hot water US$44/60) The spot to go if you're interested in surfing or chilling, with Moorish-style stone houses with bathrooms, a few very basic grass huts, camping, a yoga centre, surfboard rental, and a restaurant. Breakfast is extra.

Tofinho Back Door Campsite (www.barralighthouse .com; campsite per person US$10, d casita US$30) Under the same management as Inhambane's Pensão Pachiça, with campsites overlooking the sea – all with *barracas*, power point and water – and simple reed *casitas* (bungalows) with hammocks, mosquito nets and shared hot-water ablutions.

Casa de John (Casa Amarela; ☎ 082-451 7498; www .casajohn.co.za; 2-/3-bedroom house US$125/190; ☒) Just back from the cliff near the monument, this place has lovely, well-appointed two- and three-bedroom self-catering houses in a breezy setting on the cliff overlooking the sea.

Café no Mar (☎ 84-826 1953; www.cafenomar.com; d Mtc3600) Next door to Cas de John, Café no Mar has four small but well-appointed and classy rooms with nets, fan and mini-fridge, and meals. Rates include morning and after-noon transfers to/from the beach at Tofo.

Annastasea (bookings through www.halogaia.com/surf -anastasea.htm or through Turtle Cove; 12-person house US$265) is a spacious, beautiful house with ochre, tile and wood overtones and a vaguely Moorish ambience. It's set on a large lawn with full facilities – well-equipped kitchen, washing machine etc – in the main house. There are also four adjoining three-person cottages. All accommodation comes with mosquito netting. In high season it's only rented in its entirety but off-season is gener-ally available for about US$27 per person.

Tofo Travel (☎ 82-426 5840; www.tofotravel.com) can arrange rental of simple self-catering cottages in both Tofo and Tofinho; also see www.tofo.co.za.

For eating, Turtle Cove is the place to go, with its eclectic mix of dishes, sometimes fea-turing sushi, and a laid-back ambience. Bar closing time is at 11.30pm. Everywhere else in Tofinho is self-catering.

BARRA

Barra sits at the tip of the Barra Peninsula, where the waters of Inhambane Bay mix with those of the Indian Ocean. On the bay side are stands of mangrove and wet-land areas that are good for birdwatching. It's all beautiful, but unlike Tofo, there's no town, and everything's spread out. Many self-drivers prefer Barra's quieter scene and its range of midrange accommodation options, but Tofo is a better bet if you're backpacking or relying on public transport.

Barra Dive Resorts (www.barradiveresorts.com; Barra Lodge) offers diving and instruction.

Sleeping & Eating

Barra Lighthouse (Farol de Barra; ☎ 82-960 3550; www .barralighthouse.com; campsite adult/child US$10/5) Under

the same management as Pensão Pachiça in Inhambane, this place has rustic camping next to the lighthouse at Barra point, with hot and cold ablutions, plug points, good security and views. Boats can be launched (note that quad bikes aren't permitted). Take the signposted sandy right off the Barra road (4WD only), when coming from Bar Babalaza (below).

Areia Branca Lodge (www.areiabranca.co.za; campsite per person US$15, 4-bed bungalow US$125) A collection of rustic self-catering reed chalets on the beach almost at the northwesternmost edge of the Barra Peninsula – just continue along the increasingly sandy track past Flamingo Bay Water Lodge.

Barra Lodge (☎ 293-20561, 82-320 6070; www .barralodge.co.za; bunkhouse d US$60, casita s/d with half-board US$150/250, 6-person self-catering cottages US$215; ☒) One of Barra's largest, longest-running and most outfitted places, with a range of accommodation – from small twin-bedded reed *casitas* with bathroom, to larger, well-equipped self-catering cottages – plus a beach-side bar-restaurant, a full range of activities, and excursions to its sister lodge at Pomene, further up the coast. For backpackers, there's a divers' bunkhouse with hot showers and a cooking area.

Flamingo Bay Water Lodge (☎ 293-56001/5; www.barraresorts.com; s/d with half-board US$230/375; ☒ ☐ ☒) Well-appointed wood-and-thatch stilt houses lined up in a row directly over the bay, and containing a restaurant. No children under 12 years of age permitted. It's under the same management as the nearby Barra Lodge, and transfers to/from the Barra Lodge beach are provided.

Apart from the lodge restaurants, the main eating option is **Bar Babalaza** (meals from Mtc100), about 6km from Barra at Josina Machel junc-tion where the roads to Tofo and Barra di-verge. It's a local institution, with meals and drinks, air for your tyres and local informa-tion. In Barra itself, there are no shops or nonhotel restaurants but fish is available from local fishers.

Getting There & Away

AIR

Barra Lodge and Flamingo Bay offer fly-in packages from Johannesburg. For connections by air to/from Inhambane (from where all the Barra lodges do transfers), see p86.

BUS

There are daily chapas between Inhambane and Conguiana village along the Barra road. From here, you'll need to sort out a pick-up or walk (about 4km to Barra Lodge).

CAR & MOTORCYCLE

The turn-off for Barra is about 15km from Inhambane en route to Tofo – go left at the Bar Babalaza junction. You can easily make it in a 2WD most of the way, but you'll need a 4WD to reach Barra lighthouse and the self-catering anglers' places at the point. Hitching is easy (in high season) from Bar Babalaza.

MAXIXE

Maxixe (pronounced ma-sheesh) is about 450km northeast of Maputo on the N1, and has nothing to recommend it except its convenient location as a stopping point for traffic up and down the coast. It's also the place to get off the bus and onto the boat if you're heading to Inhambane, across the bay.

There are ATMs at Millennium BIM, just in from the main road near Pousada de Maxixe, and at Barclays Bank – about 600m further north and just off the N1.

Maxixe Camping (☎ 293-30351; N1; campsite per person Mtc150), next to the jetty has an enclosed, scruffy camping ground overlooking the bay with reasonable ablutions. You can leave your vehicle here while visiting Inhambane or the Linga Linga peninsula (Mtc75 per vehicle per day).

Stop (☎ 293-30025; N1; meals from Mtc125; ✆ 6am-10pm), on the other side of the jetty, has good meals. The same management also rents clean **rooms** (r/ste Mtc900/1500; ✆) with air-con and hot-water bathrooms. The rooms are just up the road next to Barclays Bank.

Getting There & Away

Buses to Maputo (Mtc300, 6½ hours, 450km) depart from the bus stand by the Tribunal (court) from 6am. There are no buses to Beira originating in Maxixe – you'll need to try to get space on one of those coming from Maputo that stop at Maxixe's main bus stand (Mtc850 from Maxixe to Beira). Thirty-seater buses to Vilankulo originating in Maputo depart Maxixe from about 10am from the main bus stand. Otherwise, chapas to Vilankulo (Mtc175, 3½ hours) depart throughout the day from Praça 25 de Setembro (Praça de Vilankulo), just a couple

of blocks north of the bus stand in front of the Conselho Municipal.

MORRUMBENE

Morrumbene – a nondescript town along the N1 – is of interest as a possible jumping off point to the Linga Linga Peninsula. If you're stuck for accommodation or meals, try the no-frills and decidedly grubby **Pousada do Litoral** (N1; r without bathroom & with fan Mtc300-350), in Morrumbene centre.

Chapas run throughout the day to/from Maxixe (Mtc20, 30 minutes) and in the mornings to/from Vilankulo (Mtc150, 3½ hours). Once in Morrumbene, to continue to Linga Linga, ask for the *ponta* – it's 1.8km off the N1 and reached via walking down the unpaved road heading east off the highway from diagonally opposite Pousada do Litoral. At the *ponta*, you'll need to wait for a dhow to take you through the mangrove channel and around the point to Linga Linga (Mtc10, about one hour). Sailings depend on the tides and winds (departing on the incoming tide), but there's usually a public boat departing about 10am daily, except Sunday. While waiting, the fish market on the tiny beach is intriguing to watch – shrimp are the main catch. It's also possible to hire your own dhow (about Mtc150), though after about 3pm it can be difficult to find willing captains. When approaching Linga Linga, ask the captain to take you all the way to the point.

PONTA LINGA LINGA

This old whaling station is about 15km from Inhambane at the tip of a small peninsula on the northern side of Inhambane Bay. The offshore waters are home to a population of dugongs. Onshore is a small, sleepy village nestled among the coconut palms.

The relaxing and lovely **Castelo do Mar** (☎ 82-027 8356; www.castelodomar.co.za; r per person with full-board US$200) is a large waterside villa with six well-appointed rooms, tasty meals and various activities. Boat transfers from Inhambane are included in the price.

Neighbouring is the less luxurious but pleasant **Linga Linga Leisure** (☎ in South Africa 082-809 1407; zrb@mweb.co.za; s/d US$100/165; ✆), under the same management as Ugezi Tiger Lodge (p117), with a dozen stone-and-thatch self-catering chalets. Boat transfers from Inhambane cost US$47 per person, minimum two people.

For backpackers, there's **Funky Monkey** (campsite per person Mtc100, dm Mtc150), a very basic option with no electricity, no running water, camping and simple hut accommodation in the owner's home compound. Local-style meals are available on request, and the owner can help arrange canoeing in the nearby mangroves.

Linga Linga can be reached by boat from Morrumbene (see opposite) or from Inhambane. There's nothing regular from Inhambane, but the Tourist Information Centre can help you organise a charter (dhow or motor).

With a 4WD, Linga Linga can also be reached overland, except at high spring tides, via an unsignposted turn-off just after the petrol station and about 500m north of town opposite the cement bus stand. From the turn-off, it's about 20km further.

MASSINGA

Massinga is a bustling district capital on the N1. It's free of tourist attractions, although there is an interesting mural on the main street. Its numerous shops, petrol station and garage also make it a convenient stocking up/tanking up point before heading into the wilds beyond.

Like many parts of coastal Inhambane province, the town is surrounded by landscapes lush with coconut palms. In contrast, much of northern Massinga district (which stretches north and west from Massinga town) and other inland areas are arid and browner, and dotted with enormous baobab trees. There are some particularly impressive baobab stands about 50km north of Massinga, just west of the N1 at the turn-off for Chicomo locality. Local residents use hollows in the trunks of the trees for storing water during the dry season. These same communities rely on hunting as an important food source. It's normally done with bow and arrow, mostly at night when the landscape is illuminated by a full moon.

> ### TROPIC OF CAPRICORN
>
> There are no signs marking the spot, but you cross the Tropic of Capricorn – the southernmost latitude (22.5°) at which the sun is directly overhead – about 15km south of Massinga town on the border between Massinga and Morrumbene districts.

There are several ATMs, including **Millennium BIM** (one block west of the N1) and **BCI** (N1), at the southern end of town.

For accommodation, try **Dalilo's Hotel** (☎ 293-71043, 82-816 8950; N1; tw with shared/private bathroom from Mtc500/750, air-con ste Mtc1500) at the northern end of town, and meals at **Dalilo's Restaurant** (N1; meals from Mtc150), just south of Dalilo's Hotel.

Getting There & Away

Most north–south buses stop at Massinga. The first departure to Maputo is about 6am. Going north, buses from Maputo begin to arrive in Massinga by about 2.30pm, en route to Vilankulo.

MORRUNGULO

Several kilometres north of Massinga is the signposted turn-off for the lovely Morrungulo Beach (Praia de Morrungulo) and the equally lovely **Ponta Morrungulo** (www.pontamorrungulo.co.za; campsite adult/child Mtc320/160, 4-person chalet Mtc3500-3800), with a mix of beachfront and garden self-catering chalets and camping – all on a large, manicured bougainvillea-dotted lawn. There's also a restaurant (closed Monday). About 1.5km north of here is **Sylvia Shoal** (www.mozambique1.com; campsite per person US$15, barracas US$15, 2-/4-person chalet US$70/105), with camping, a few self-catering chalets set in large palm-studded grounds behind the dunes and a restaurant (open during low season with advance bookings only).

In between Sylvia Shoal and Ponta Morrungulo is **Baobab Lodge** (☎ 82-865 6980; baobab _lodge@yahoo.co.uk; campsite/barraca per person Mtc120/150, dm Mtc150, cliff/beach d Mtc750/1000, 6-person cottage Mtc2500), a rather neglected place with camping, rooms (dark, poorly ventilated and grubby) and a run-down self-catering cottage at the top of the small escarpment (five minutes' walk from the sea), plus more camping and rooms down near the water. Meals can be arranged with advance notice.

Getting There & Away

Morrungulo is 13km from the main road down a good sand track that is negotiable with a 2WD. Sporadic chapas (Mtc25) run from the Massinga transport stand (on the N1) to Morrungulo village – close to Ponta Morrungulo, and within a few kilometres walk of Sylvia Shoal.

POMENE

Pomene, the site of a colonial-era beach resort, is known for its fishing and birdwatching, and its striking estuarine setting. The surrounding area is part of the Pomene Reserve, which was gazetted in 1972 with 20,000 hectares to protect the mangrove ecosystems, dune forests and marine life of the area, including dugongs and turtles. The reserve is neglected, but the beach here – one of our favourites – is beautiful, especially up near the point by the lighthouse and the now derelict Pomene Hotel.

Pomene View (☎ in South Africa 083-962 9818; www .pomeneview.co.za; 3-/5-person chalets US$60/95; ☒), on a rise amid the mangroves and coastal vegetation on the mainland side of the estuary, is small and tranquil, with its own special appeal and wide views. Accommodation is in self-catering brick-and-thatch chalets, and there's a bar and restaurant. Take the same signposted turn-off north of Massinga as for Pomene Lodge, and then follow the Pomene View signs. Transfers across the estuary to Pomene Lodge and the beach are easily arranged, as are mangrove excursions and fishing charters.

Pomene Lodge (☎ 82-369 8580, in South Africa 011-314 3355; www.pomene.co.za; campsite per person US$15, 4-/6-person self-catering bungalow US$120/160, s/d water chalet with half-board US$160/285; ☒), in a fine setting on a spit of land between the estuary and the sea, has no-frills self-catering reed bungalows just back from the beach, plus a row of newer, spacious and very lovely 'water chalets' directly over the estuary – a great splurge. There's also camping (hot and cold water), and a restaurant/bar. Diving, quad bike rental and estuary boat trips can be arranged, as can transfers to/from Barra Lodge (p89).

Getting There & Away

Pomene is on the coast about halfway between Inhambane and Vilankulo off the N1. The turn-off is about 11km north of Massinga – which is the best place to stock up – and signposted immediately after the Morrungulo turn-off. From the turn-off, which is also the end of the tarmac, it's about 58km (1½ to two hours) further along an unpaved road to Pomene Lodge, and about 54km to Pomene View (branch left at the small signpost). In the dry season, it's possible to reach Pomene View with a 2WD with clearance. For Pomene Lodge, you'll need a 4WD. There's an airstrip for charter flights from Inhambane and Vilankulo.

Via public transport, there are one or two chapas weekly from Massinga to Pomene village (Mtc100), which is a few kilometres before Pomene Lodge. Most locals prefer to take a chapa from Massinga to Mashungo village (Mtc105, daily) on the north shore, and then a boat across the estuary to Pomene Lodge and village. However, the chapa departs Massinga about 3pm, reaching Mashungo about 8pm or 9pm. There is nowhere in Mashungo village to sleep, although you could try your luck asking locally for permission to camp.

VILANKULO

Vilankulo is the finishing (or starting) point of Mozambique's southern tourist circuit, and an institution on the southern Africa backpackers' and overlanders' scenes. It's also the gateway for visiting the nearby Bazaruto Archipelago, separated from the mainland by a narrow channel of turquoise sea. During South African holidays, Vilankulo is overrun with pick-ups and 4WDs, but otherwise it's a quiet, slow-paced town.

Orientation

Vilankulo is spread over about 5km and chapas are few and far between, so you may spend a fair amount of time walking. The bus stand, market area and ATMs are at the southwestern end of town near the main junction. About 3km northeast of here following the tarmac Avenida Eduardo Mondlane is Bairro Mukoke, with another ATM, the old Dona Ana Hotel (now being refurbished) and a cluster of sleeping options within easy reach. The beachfront road, with more accommodation options, parallels Avenida Eduardo Mondlane to the east.

Information

Barclays Bank (Avenida Eduardo Mondlane) ATM – Visa only; near the town entrance.

BCI (Avenida Eduardo Mondlane) ATM –Visa only; near the town entrance, just down from Barclays.

Millennium BIM (Avenida Eduardo Mondlane; Bairro Mukoke) ATM (Visa & MasterCard).

Telecomunicações de Moçambique (TDM; per min Mtc1; ◷ 7am-5pm Mon-Fri) Internet access and telephone calls in the town centre.

Tourist Information (www.vilankulo.com; ◷ 9am-noon & 1-4pm Mon-Fri, 8am-noon Sat) A helpful stop, with town maps and general info. It's at the *município* in the town centre.

WWF Office (☎ 293-82383; ◷ 7.30am-noon & 2-4pm Mon-Fri) Near TDM.

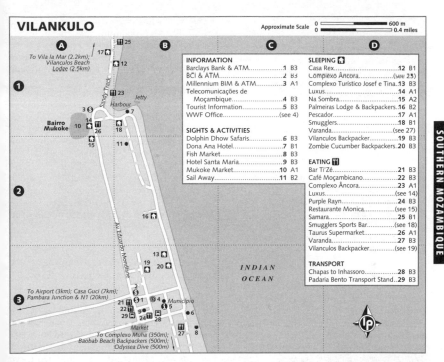

VILANKULO

Approximate Scale 0 — 600 m / 0 — 0.4 miles

INFORMATION
Barclays Bank & ATM..................1 B3
BCI & ATM...............................2 B3
Millennium BIM & ATM.............3 A1
Telecomunicações de
  Moçambique.........................4 B3
Tourist Information....................5 B3
WWF Office.............................(see 4)

SIGHTS & ACTIVITIES
Dolphin Dhow Safaris................6 B3
Dona Ana Hotel........................7 B1
Fish Market...............................8 B3
Hotel Santa Maria.....................9 B3
Mukoke Market.......................10 A1
Sail Away.................................11 B2

SLEEPING
Casa Rex................................12 B1
Complexo Âncora..................(see 23)
Complexo Turístico Josef e Tina.13 B3
Luxus......................................14 A1
Na Sombra..............................15 A2
Palmeiras Lodge & Backpackers.16 B2
Pescador.................................17 A1
Smugglers...............................18 B1
Varanda...............................(see 27)
Vilanculos Backpacker..............19 B3
Zombie Cucumber Backpackers.20 B3

EATING
Bar Ti'Zé................................21 B3
Café Moçambicano...................22 B3
Complexo Âncora....................23 A1
Luxus...................................(see 14)
Purple Rayn.............................24 B3
Restaurante Monica...............(see 15)
Samara.................................25 B3
Smugglers Sports Bar.............(see 18)
Taurus Supermarket.................26 A1
Varanda...............................(see 27)
Vilanculos Backpacker............(see 19)

TRANSPORT
Chapas to Inhassoro................28 B3
Padaria Bento Transport Stand..29 B3

To Vila la Mar (2.2km); Vilanculos Beach Lodge (2.5km)

Jetty
Harbour
Bairro Mukoke

INDIAN OCEAN

To Airport (3km); Casa Guci (7km); Pambara Junction & N1 (20km)

Município
Market

To Complexo Muha (350m); Baobab Beach Backpackers (500m); Odyssea Dive (500m)

Av. Eduardo Mondlane

SOUTHERN MOZAMBIQUE

Sights

It's worth taking a stroll through the bustling **market** area near the bus stand. Nearby is the now derelict **Hotel Santa Maria**, built by tycoon-entrepreneur Joaquim Alves. At the northern end of town on the beach is the rambling **Dona Ana Hotel**, also built by Alves and currently being refurbished. Just inland are the **Millennium BIM building**, which used to be Alves' residence, and the colourful **Mukoke market**.

The **fish-market beach**, below Varanda restaurant, is a hive of activity in the early mornings and late afternoons when the fishermen return with their catch.

Activities

Diving is very good, although the main sites are well offshore (about a 45-minute boat ride), around the Bazaruto Archipelago. The main operator is **Odyssea Dive** (www.odysseadive .com), based at Baobab Beach Backpackers.

For day or overnight dhow safaris around the Bazaruto Archipelago, there are several outfits, including the recommended **Sail Away** (☎ 293-82385, 82-387 6350; www.sailaway.co.za), on the road paralleling the beach road, about 400m

south of the old Dona Ana Hotel; Dolphin Dhow Safaris, just up from the beach near Varanda; and Mapapay Dhow Safaris (contact is through Tourist Information office). Prices average US$70 to USD$80 per person for a day snorkelling excursion to Magaruque, including park fees, lunch, snorkelling equipment, protective footwear (important, as the rock ledge can be sharp), lunch, and usually motoring there and sailing back; and from US$220 for a two-day safari. Day trips to Bazaruto are possible to arrange, but not usually done, given the comparatively long travel distance from Vilanculo. There's officially no camping on the islands in the park – most operators camp along the mainland coast.

There are many independent dhow operators in Vilankulo. If you go with a freelancer, remember that while some are reliable, others may quote tempting prices, and then ask you to 'renegotiate' things once you're well away from shore. Check with the tourist information office or with your hotel for recommendations and don't pay until you're safely back on land. For nonmotorised dhows, allow plenty of extra time to account for wind

---

CHIEF VILANKULO

Like many towns in Mozambique, Vilankulo takes its name from an early local chief (*régulo*), Gamala Vilankulo Mukoke. The name was rendered as 'Vilanculos' during colonial times, but was then changed back to Vilankulo after independence. Bairro Mukoke (Mucoque), west of Millennium BIM, is named after Gamala Vilankulo's son, who lived there.

---

and water conditions; it can take two to three hours (sometimes longer) under sail from Vilankulo to Magaruque, and much longer to the other islands.

For horseback riding on the beach, contact **Mozambique Horse Safari** (www.mozambique horsesafari.com).

Sleeping

Advance bookings are essential if you'll be travelling around the Christmas–New Year's or Easter holidays.

BUDGET

Baobab Beach Backpackers (campsite per person Mtc150, dm Mtc200, bungalow without/with bathroom Mtc500/1000) Rather scruffy these days, and still showing the effects of the severe cyclone that hit this part of the country in 2007, Baobab Beach has a waterside setting and remains nevertheless a decent spot to pitch a tent. If you're not into the party scene, head elsewhere.

Complexo Turístico Josef e Tina (☎ 82-965 2130, 82-406 3904; www.joseftina.com; campsite per person Mtc150, chalet r Mtc800, r Mtc1200, guesthouse Mtc3900) Just up from Zombie Cucumbers is this locally run place with camping, rooms in reed chalets sharing bathrooms, and simple rooms in a small self-catering guesthouse – all in a garden just back from the sea. All rooms have nets, there's a small self-catering kitchen area and meals are available on order.

Vilanculos Backpacker (Complexo Alemanha; www.vilanculosbackpacker.com; dm Mtc170, d bungalow with shared bathroom Mtc600) On the escarpment in the central part of town, and an easy walk from the market/bus stand area, with dorm beds, plus small stone-and-thatch double cottages – all clean and good value, and all sharing bathrooms. There's a small self-catering area and a good restaurant. The turn-off is signposted near Barclays, and the compound is unmiss-

able, with a huge German flag painted on the wall. There's no camping.

Zombie Cucumber Backpackers (www.zombie cucumber.com; dm Mtc280, chalet d Mtc850; ☒) Lots of space, hammocks, a bar, circular dorm, small chalets and meals on order. Very nice, very relaxing. It's just back from the beach road, south of Palmeiras Lodge.

Na Sombra (☎ 293-82429; Bairro Mukoke; s/tw/d/q with shared bathroom Mtc280/350/380/530) Tiny but fairly priced rooms with fans, and the good Restaurante Monica (opposite).

Complexo Muha (☎ 82-858 0170; complexomuha@ gmail.com; r per person with fan Mtc500) This small locally-run place in a private home has just one room at the moment, and meals with advance notice. It's just up from Baobab Beach Backpackers.

MIDRANGE

Smugglers (☎ 293-82253; www.smugglers.co.za; r without/ with bathroom US$50/70, cottage US$145; P ☐ ☒ ☒) Just southwest of the Dona Ana Hotel on the inland side of the road, this well-run place has clean, pleasant rooms around large, lush gardens with two small pools. Most of the rooms are twin-bedded with shared hot-water bathrooms, fans and nets. There are also larger rooms with bathrooms, a spacious two-room family cottage and a popular restaurant and sports bar. It's ideal for families.

Varanda (☎ 293-82412; varanda.barko@yahoo.com; r with fan/air-con Mtc1500/2000) Primarily an eating venue, Varanda also has two spotless rooms – one small, and one considerably larger – downhill behind the restaurant. From the compound, it's an easy walk down the dune to the fish market on the beach.

Luxus (☎ 82-851 1301; s/d Mtc1500/2000; ☒) This place has spacious, functional rooms with window screens located in a small shopping mall at the end of the main street and just opposite Taurus Supermarket.

Palmeiras Lodge & Backpackers (☎ 293-82257; www.smugglers.co.za; dm US$15; cottage d US$105; ☒) Just in from the beachfront road, and under the same management as Smugglers, this place is light, bright, airy and clean, with well-appointed whitewashed stone-and-thatch cottages set in lush, green grounds. Continental breakfast is included; there's no restaurant. The three rooms closest to the front of the property (and the sea) are breezier, and have fan only; the two rooms behind have air-con. There's also a large, self-catering backpackers house with braai area, fridge and small kitchen.

TOP END

Complexo Ancora (☎ 293-82444; www.ancorasuites.com; s/d Mtc2680/4155; ※ ☎) This is a block of spacious, well-appointed rooms – all with one double bed and one couch bed plus cable TV and minifridge, and all overlooking a small garden, the beach and the harbour. Next door is a restaurant.

Casa Guci (☎ 82-868 6540; www.casaguci.com; per person US$100; ☒) This small place is about 7km south of town overlooking the water, and signposted from the main road into town. It has a few modern, well-equipped two- and four-person self-catering chalets set around large grounds and a good restaurant with great pizzas. Each chalet has its own little patio, garden and fully-equipped kitchen. Self-catering rates are also available.

Pescador (☎ 293-82312; www.pescadormoz.com; s/d US$140/230; ☐ ☒) This boutique place is just up from and diagonally opposite Casa Rex, without a beachfront, although the rooms have views of the sea. It has six well-appointed rooms, classical music piping through the lobby and a poolside restaurant.

Vilanculos Beach Lodge (☎ 21-301618, in South Africa 011-658 0633; www.vilanculos.co.za) This place, about 3km north of the Dona Ana hotel along the water, has been acquired by Rani Resorts (which also runs lodges in the Bazaruto and Quirimbas archipelagos and in Pemba), and was being refurbished as this book was researched. It's scheduled to open soon.

Vila la Mar (☎ 293-82302; vilalamar@yahoo.com; 6-/10-person houses US$250/280; ☒) Spacious, well-equipped self-catering chalets, some overlooking the water, in manicured grounds just up from the old Aguia Negra Lodge. It's often fully booked, so check in advance.

Casa Rex (☎ 293-82048; www.casa-rex.com; s/d from US$140/220, acacia r US$180/300, ste US$210/360; ☐ ※ ☎ ☒) This lovely, midsized boutique hotel is the place to go if you're after an upmarket getaway. It sits in peaceful, manicured grounds about 500m north of the old Dona Ana Hotel, and has a range of rooms and suites, all with sea views. Meals are homemade and excellent, and the hotel is known for its personalised style.

Eating

Café Moçambicano (Avenida Eduardo Mondlane; pastries from Mtc15) Pastries, bread, yoghurt and juice; opposite Barclays Bank.

Purple Rayn (snacks & light meals Mtc15-100; ⏰ 8am-5pm-ish Mon-Fri, 8am-1pm Sat) This small place at the southern end of town has light meals and pastries, breakfast, burgers, samosas and, sometimes, smoothies. The colour gives the building away.

Bar Ti'Zé (Avenida Eduardo Mondlane; meals from Mtc75) A small local eatery on the main road near the bus stand, with inexpensive grilled chicken and fish and other local dishes. It's diagonally opposite Barclays Bank.

Vilanculos Backpacker (Complexo Alemanha; meals Mtc100) This German-run place does a good job of bringing in the locals, with tasty Mozambican cuisine and bargain prices.

Luxus (☎ 82-851 1301; meals from Mtc150; ☒) Burgers, fish and chips and other South African–style fast food, and a bar. It's in the small shopping mall opposite Taurus supermarket.

Smugglers Sports Bar (meals from Mtc200; ☎) Good breakfasts, hearty pub fare and ice cream, sports TV inside and a volleyball pitch out front. It's at Smugglers (opposite).

Complexo Âncora (☎ 293-82444; pizzas & meals Mtc150-250; ⏰ 7am-10pm Wed-Mon; ☎) This place on the waterfront by the port has pizzas, plus a wide selection of continental dishes. Portions are generally large, and there's an eating area overlooking the water. It also rents upmarket rooms next door. Everything is halal (no alcohol) and there's a takeaway service.

Restaurante Monica (Na Sombra; meals about Mtc250) This long-standing and unassuming place is renowned for its delicious local curries and seafood dishes. It's along the tarmac road near Millennium BIM, and seating is under a large, thatched roof.

Samara (☎ 82-380 6865; samara@tdm.co.mz; meals from Mtc250; ⏰ lunch & dinner in season) Samara's – just back from the beach – features Portuguese-style cuisine, and is known for its prawns and other seafood as well as for the long waits for meals. Management also rents out some rooms in stone-and-thatched chalets in the gardens behind the restaurant. Follow the main road to where the tarmac ends, take the small, signposted right-hand fork and continue down about 200m further.

Varanda (☎ 293-82412; varanda.barko@yahoo.com; meals from Mtc250; ⏰ 7am-9pm Tue-Sun) This small bar-restaurant set on the low escarpment directly above the fish market has Portuguese and local cuisine, and seating inside in the panelled bar area or at a few tables outside overlooking the beach below. It also rents a few rooms.

Casa Guci (☎ 82-868 6540; www.casaguci.com; meals from Mtc250) The restaurant at this lodge is known for its delicious pizzas and relaxing garden setting. It's 7km south of town – you'll need either your own vehicle or a taxi.

Taurus supermarket (Avenida Eduardo Mondlane) For self-catering; near the end of the tarmac road and diagonally opposite Millennium BIM.

Getting There & Away

AIR
If your budget permits, it's worth flying at least one way into Vilankulo to see the panorama of the Bazaruto Archipelago from the air (assuming your pilot does a flyover route, and the weather is clear). The seas are brilliant hues of turquoise and jade laced with shimmering white sand banks.

Offices for all airlines are at the airport. **LAM** (www.lam.com.mz) flies four times weekly to/from Maputo (about US$160 one way), with connections to Inhambane and Johannesburg. **Pelican Air** (☎ 293-82483, 293-84050, in South Africa 011-973 3649; www.pelicanair.co.za) flies daily between Johannesburg and Vilankulo (from US$280 one way), sometimes via Nelspruit. **Air Travelmax** (www.airtravelmax.com) flies several times weekly between Vilankulo and Johannesburg's Lanseria airport.

The airport is 3km from town, and just off the road running to Pambara junction and the N1.

BUS
Vilankulo is 20km east of the N1 down a tarmac access road, with the turn-off at Pambara junction. Chapas run between the two throughout the day (Mtc15). Except as noted, all transport departs from Vilankulo's main road just down from Padaria Bento and just up from the market.

To Maputo (Mtc500, nine to 10 hours), there are two to three buses daily, departing from in front of Bar Ti'Zé by 4.30am, and sometimes as early as 3am – check with the bus drivers the afternoon before. Coming from Maputo, get to Junta by about 4am.

To Beira (Mtc550, 10 hours), buses depart Vilankulo at 4.30am; book the afternoon before.

There's no direct bus to Chimoio. You'll need to take a Beira bus as far as Inchope junction (Mtc500 from Vilankulo), and then get a minibus from there.

To Maxixe (for Inhambane and Tofo), several minibuses depart each morning (Mtc175, three hours).

To Inhassoro, minibuses depart from just east of the market (Mtc65, 1½ hours).

Getting Around
Vilankulo is very spread out. For a taxi, try contacting **Junior** (☎ 82-462 4700) directly, or through your hotel. For car rental, try **Merkin 4x4** (☎ 82-012 9430; amiesmael@tdm.co.mz). Occasional chapas run along the main road, but not out to the beach places on the northeastern edge of town, and not to the airport.

BAZARUTO ARCHIPELAGO
The Bazaruto Archipelago has clear, turquoise waters filled with colourful fish, and offers diving, snorkelling and birdwatching. It makes a fine upmarket holiday if you're looking for the quintessential Indian Ocean getaway.

The archipelago consists of five main islands: Bazaruto, Benguera (also spelled Benguerra, and formerly known as Santo António), Magaruque (Santa Isabel), Santa Carolina (Paradise Island or Ilha do Paraíso) and tiny Bangué. Until about 10,000 years ago – relatively recent in geological terms – the larger islands were connected to the mainland at the tip of São Sebastião peninsula. The small population of Nile crocodiles that laze in the sun in remote corners of both Bazaruto and Benguera islands is evidence of this earlier link.

Since 1971 much of the archipelago has been protected as **Bazaruto National Park** (adult/child Mtc200/100). In late 2002 the park boundaries were extended southwards to encompass

---

THIEVES' ISLAND

Between Vilankulo and Benguera Island is a large sandbar, visible only at low tide. According to local lore, it used to be known as 'Ilha dos Ladrões' (Thieves' Island), and lawbreakers were brought here and left to drown when the tide came in. Now it's called Massoso by sailors, who know it as a place of refuge if their dhow starts to sink.

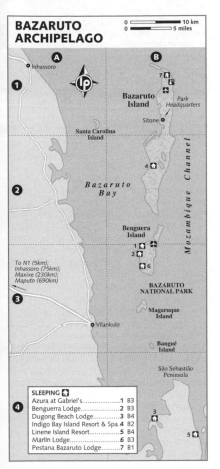

BAZARUTO ARCHIPELAGO

0 — 10 km
0 — 5 miles

Inhassoro

Bazaruto Island

Park Headquarters

Sitone

Santa Carolina Island

Mozambique Channel

Bazaruto Bay

Benguera Island

To N1 (5km);
Inhassoro (75km);
Maxixe (230km);
Maputo (690km)

BAZARUTO NATIONAL PARK

Magaruque Island

Vilankulo

Bangué Island

São Sebastião Peninsula

all of the islands, bringing the area under protection to about 1400 sq km. Thanks to this protected status, and to the archipelago's relative isolation from the ravages of war on the mainland, nature bursts forth here in full force. You'll see dozens of bird species, including fish eagles and pink flamingos. There are also red duikers, bushbucks, and, especially on Benguera, the Nile crocodiles. Dolphins swim through the clear waters, along with 2000 other types of fish, plus loggerhead, leatherback and green turtles. Most intriguing are the elusive dugongs (see p43), who spend their days foraging among seagrass meadows around the archipelago. As a backdrop to all this are excellently preserved coral formations, with up to 100 species of

hard coral and over two dozen soft coral species identified so far.

Living amid all the natural beauty are about 3500 Mozambicans who call the archipelago home.

History

Although many of the island residents are relatively recent arrivals who sought haven during the war years, the archipelago's history reaches well back. The islands (previously were known as the Hucicas or Vacicas) were long famed for their pearls and ambergris. By at least the 15th century, they were the site of a thriving maritime community sustained by the coastal dhow trade. The earliest Portuguese trading settlements dated from the mid-16th century, while the first permanent Portuguese settlement was established on Santa Carolina in the mid-19th century. Today, all of the islands except Bangué are inhabited .

At various times leading up to the colonial period, several of the islands – most notably Santa Carolina – served as penal colonies not only for Vilankulo, but for the entire region, including places as distant as present-day Beira. According to local lore, the variety of ethnic groups necessitated development of a common language, which led to the growth of a unique dialect now considered indigenous to the southern part of the archipelago. Although this dialect has largely been replaced by Xitswa (one of the major languages of Inhambane province) and Portuguese, it's still spoken by some older inhabitants.

Information

Entry fees should be paid in advance at the WWF office (p92) in Vilankulo, unless your hotel has done this for you (all the island-based hotels do so, as do most Vilankulo-based dhow safari operators). Park headquarters is located at Sitone, on the western side of Bazaruto Island. While fees for diving, walking and other activities within the archipelago have been approved in principle, they aren't currently being enforced.

If you're with your own boat, you'll also need to arrange the necessary licences and boat permits at the WWF office.

Activities

Dives, equipment rental and certification courses can be organised at any of the lodges, or in Vilankulo (see p93).

SOUTHERN MOZAMBIQUE

Game fishing – including for sailfish, tuna, barracuda and black, blue and striped marlin – is also excellent (and is all tag-and-release), and can be arranged at all of the lodges.

Sailing trips around the archipelago can be arranged with island hotels, and with the Vilankulo-based dhow safari operators (p93). Magaruque – the closest island to Vilankulo and the main destination for day sailing/snorkelling safaris from the mainland – has a rock shelf with lots of fish, although only isolated coral patches, on its western side. Surf shoes or other protective footwear are essential, as there are many sharp edges; most operators provide these.

Sleeping & Eating

There is no budget accommodation on the islands. The best options if you have limited purse strings are arranging an island dhow cruise from Vilankulo (see p93), or visiting in the off-season, when some of the lodges offer special deals.

BAZARUTO ISLAND

Pestana Bazaruto Lodge (☎ 84-308 3120; www.pestana.com; s/d with full-board from US$425/570; 🛇 🔲 🖳) This unpretentious four-star getaway is at the northwestern end of the island overlooking a small, tranquil bay. Accommodation is in two dozen A-frame chalets amid lush gardens beneath the sand dunes. There is also a honeymoon suite and some family style chalets. There's a two night minimum stay.

Indigo Bay Island Resort & Spa (☎ in South Africa 011-467 1277; www.indigobayonline.com; r per person with full-board from US$555; 🛇 🔲 🖳) Under the same ownership as Pemba Beach Resort Hotel in Pemba and the soon-to-reopen Vilanculos Beach Lodge in Vilankulo, Indigo Bay is the largest and most outfitted lodge in the archipelago. It offers a mix of villas and beachfront chalets, and a range of activities. While it lacks the laid-back island touch of some of the other places, for some visitors this will be compensated for by the high level of comfort and amenities.

BENGUERA ISLAND

Benguerra Lodge (☎ in South Africa 011-452 0641; www.benguerra.co.za; r per person with full-board from US$590; 🔲 🖳) Generally considered to be one of the most intimate of the island lodges, with well-spaced and spacious luxury chalets and villa near the beach. It's at the centre of the island's western coastline, and offers the usual activities.

Marlin Lodge (☎ in South Africa 012-460 9410; www.marlinlodge.co.za; s/d with full-board from US$710/960) Several kilometres south of Benguerra Lodge, Marlin Lodge has 17 sea-view chalets and a full range of activities.

Azura at Gabriel's (☎ in South Africa 011-258 0180; www.azura-retreats.com; r per person with full-board from US$775; 🛇 🔲 🖳) Offers accommodation in villas of varying degrees of luxury.

MAGARUQUE ISLAND

The original hotel on Magaruque was founded by tycoon-entrepreneur Joaquim Alves in colonial days, and was long a favoured haunt of the rich and famous. Completely refurbished (and in part newly built) accommodation is underway, but was not yet open at the time of research. For now, the small island is ideal if you fancy relaxing on a patch of tropical sand. It can be circled in a few hours, but bring plenty of shade or sunscreen. There's also fine snorkelling in the crystal clear shallows just off the beach on the island's southwestern corner.

SANTA CAROLINA ISLAND

The prettiest of the islands, with stands of palm and other vegetation, Santa Carolina was formerly the site of another Joaquim Alves property. Today, the old hotel is closed and crumbling, although renovation is planned, and meanwhile you can visit the island as a day excursion. It's an easy walk around its perimeter, but snorkelling here – among the best in the archipelago – is the highlight, and it is possible just offshore.

Getting There & Away

AIR

Pelican Air flies between Johannesburg, Nelspruit and Vilankulo, from where you can arrange island transfers with the lodges; see p96. **CFA Charters** (☎ 293-82055; www.cfa.co.za; Vilankulo airport) has twice-weekly flights connecting Bazaruto Island with Gorongosa National Park (US$275 one way) and with Maputo (US$295).

BOAT

All the top-end lodges arrange speedboat transfers for their guests. Most day visitors reach the islands by dhow from Vilankulo, where there are a number of sailing safari operators; see p93.

SÃO SEBASTIÃO PENINSULA

This isolated promontory just south of the Bazaruto Archipelago is part of the **Vilanculos Coastal Wildlife Sanctuary** (www.thesanctuary.co.za) – a private conservation and tourism initiative combining wildlife safaris and beach into one package. The sanctuary is dotted with small lakes, lagoons and stands of mangrove, and edged by the same turquoise waters that lap the islands of the archipelago. It's worth visiting if you're interested in birdwatching or just breaking away from it all. While some larger wildlife have been reintroduced, the main attractions are the flamingos and other water birds.

There are various lodges and time-shares, including the exclusive **Dugong Beach Lodge** (Map p97; www.dugonglodge.co.za; chalet s/d with full-board US$630/900; 🐛), on the western side of the peninsula. Accommodation is in 12 tented chalets, some right on the beach, and all have shaded verandahs and large baths. Dhow cruises, sea kayaking and other water sports can be organised, as can excursions to nearby Bangué island.

Linene Island Resort (Map p97; www.linene-island .com; per person with full-board from US$180) is a rustic angler's hideaway on the eastern side of the peninsula, with small twin-bedded wooden chalets linked by a raised walkway and a full range of fishing.

The peninsula is reached via speedboat charter from Vilankulo, arranged with the lodges.

INHASSORO

Sleepy Inhassoro – the last of the 'main' coastal towns before the N1 turns inland – is a popular destination for South African anglers. Its sunbaked, white-sand shoreline is uncluttered and inviting, although there's no surf or breeze, except during storms when the wind stirs up the waves a bit. Boat transfers to Bazaruto and Santa Carolina islands, both visible off-shore, can be arranged at any of the hotels, often on-the-spot, but better with advance notice. Prices vary, but expect to pay at least Mtc5000 to Mtc6000 per day for a six-person boat to Santa Carolina/Bazaruto. There are no ATM or internet facilities in Inhassoro – Vilankulo has the nearest banking.

The no-frills **Inhassoro Beach Lodge** (☎ 84-215 9794; d Mtc1000, 4-person cottage Mtc2000), just opposite the bakery, has blue-and-white self-catering cottages on large, tranquil grounds bordering the sea, plus some basic attached rooms and a restaurant.

Complexo Turístico Seta (☎ 293-91000/1, 82-302 0990; hotelseta@hotmail.com; campsite adult/child Mtc250/125, tw chalet Mtc1000-2000, 6-person self-catering chalet Mtc4000; 🐛), a long-standing place at the end of the main road leading into town from the N1, has large, quiet grounds, a restaurant-bar overlooking the sea, campsites (towards the back of the property), and accommodation in small sea-facing chalets (several sizes available). There are also basic self-catering cottages in an unappealing setting behind the parking-lot reception area.

Pensão Inhassoro (www.inhassoro.co.za; d US$75; 🐛 🐛) is an upmarket angling-oriented place a few kilometres further south along the coast, and signposted (follow the main road as it curves around past the bakery). Accommodation is in a row of well-appointed rooms overlooking a manicured green lawn, a pool and the sea, and there are both self-catering and restaurant facilities. Fully-equipped fishing excursions can be arranged, as can excursions to Bartolomeu Dias point, 40km north, and transfers to/from Vilankulo. Advance bookings are recommended.

Getting There & Away

Inhassoro is 15km east of the main road. Chapas run daily to/from Vilankulo (Mtc65, 45 minutes). To Beira, go to Vulanjane (the junction with the N1, Mtc10 in a chapa) and wait for passing northbound buses from there – ask staff at your hotel to help with the timing so you're not sitting there all day. Driving northwards, there's a bridge across the Save River.

BARTOLOMEU DIAS (PONTA MACOVANE)

About 35km north along the coast from Inhassoro, and reached (low-tide only) via a sandy 4WD track branching north just before Inhassoro's Complexo Turístico Seta, is **Bartolomeu Dias** (Ponta Macovane), a lovely, tranquil spot with dunes, birdwatching and fishing.

At Bartolomeu Dias, there's **BD Lodge** (www .bdlodge.co.za; 2-/6-person self-catering bungalow from Mtc1900/4600), with reed-and-thatch stilt cottages between the lagoon and the sea.

Central Mozambique

In the annals of ancient Africa, central Mozambique – Sofala, Manica, Tete and Zambézia provinces – had a much higher profile than it does today. It was here, at the old port of Sofala, that 15th-century traders from as far away as India and Indonesia gathered in search of vast caches of gold. And it was here that some of the region's most powerful kingdoms arose, including the Karanga (Shona) confederations along the Zimbabwe border and the legendary kingdom of Monomotapa southwest of Tete. It was also in central Mozambique – along the course of the Zambezi River – that early explorers and traders first penetrated the vast Mozambican hinterlands. During the 17th and 18th centuries, they set up a series of *feiras* (trading fairs) that reached as far inland as Zumbo on the Zambian border.

Today, the tides have turned and central Mozambique is seldom given more than passing mention in the tourist brochures. Yet while it lacks the accessible beaches of the south, the region has many attractions. In addition to wildlife watching at Gorongosa National Park, there's hiking amid the misty mountain landscapes of the Chimanimani range and in the tea country around Gurúè; fishing and relaxing around Lake Cahora Bassa and its dam; and birdwatching.

Central Mozambique is also an important transit zone, flanked by the Beira corridor (connecting landlocked Zimbabwe with Beira and the sea) and the Tete corridor, which links Zimbabwe and Malawi. As such, it makes a convenient route for travellers combining Mozambique with neighbouring countries.

CENTRAL MOZAMBIQUE

HIGHLIGHTS

- Wander into the wilds at wonderful **Gorongosa National Park** (p106)
- Hike in the cool, rugged **Chimanimani Mountains** (p113)
- Dine out in the port city of **Beira** (p105), famous for its seafood
- Marvel at the massive **Cahora Bassa Dam** (p117) and go fishing on the lake
- Go birdwatching in the twittering, chirping, song-filled forests around **Caia** (p118)

CENTRAL MOZAMBIQUE

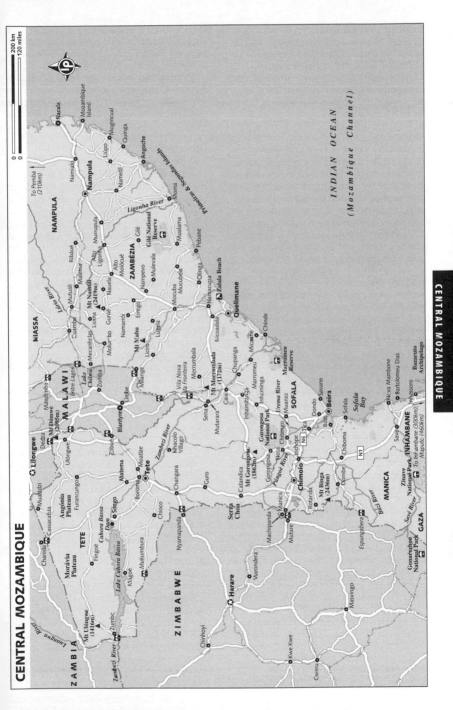

Getting There & Away

Central Mozambique is a transport crossroads. For more on land border crossings with Malawi, Zambia and Zimbabwe, see p183. For north–south travellers, there's a bridge across the Zambezi River at Caia (p119).

BEIRA

Beira, capital of Sofala province, is Mozambique's second-largest city. It's also the country's busiest port, and as famed for its seafood as for its tawdry nightlife. Yet, despite a somewhat tarnished image, Beira is a reasonably pleasant place with a compact central area, an addictive harbour-town energy, attractive colonial-era architecture and a short, breezy stretch of coastline.

Beira has a reputation as one of the easiest places in the country to catch malaria, so cover up well in the evenings, and travel with a net.

History

Settlement of the area around Beira dates to at least the 9th century AD, when small fishing and trading settlements dotted the nearby coastline. The most important of these was the fabled Sofala (see p108). Following Sofala's decline, trade continued well into the 19th century, although on a smaller scale.

In 1884 a Portuguese landholder and imperialist named Joaquim Carlos Paiva de Andrada established a base at the mouth of the Púngoè River (at the site of present-day Beira) as a supply point for his expeditions into the interior. He also wanted to promote development of the Mozambique Company – one of the many charter companies set up by the Portuguese in their attempts to solidify their control over the Mozambican hinterlands. Paiva de Andrada was not the only one enamoured of Beira's charms. The British also found the area enticing as an export channel from their landlocked inland territories to the sea. Over the next decade, it became a focus of dispute between the two colonial powers before ultimately going to Portugal in 1891.

Andrada, who meanwhile had made Beira the headquarters for his Mozambique Company, began to develop its harbour facilities. At the same time, a railway line to the interior was completed and Beira soon became a major port and export channel for Southern Rhodesia (Zimbabwe).

From the mid-20th century, Rhodesia's links with South Africa increased, cutting into Beira's transport monopoly. By this time, however, Beira's significance as a port was established and it continued to be one of Mozambique's hubs.

During the war years, Renamo leader Afonso Dhlakama had his headquarters at Marínguè, northwest of Beira near Gorongosa, and both Beira and Sofala province continue to be Renamo strongholds.

Orientation

The heart of the city is the area around the squares of Praça do Município and Praça do Metical (the latter marked by a large metical coin perched on a pedestal). Near here, you'll find shops, banks, telecom and internet facilities, plus an array of street-side cafes. North of the two squares is the old commercial area of the baixa, with the port and some impressive colonial-style architecture, while about 1km east is Maquinino, the main bus and transport hub. From Praça do Município, tree-lined streets lead south and east through the shady and charming Ponta Gêa residential area to Avenida das FPLM. This then runs for several kilometres along the ocean past the hospital to Makuti – another residential area fringing Beira's small stretch of beach. At the end is the old red-and-white Makuti lighthouse, dating to 1904.

MAPS

The excellent *Planta de Endereçamento da Cidade da Beira* and the companion map booklet, *Endereçamento da Cidade da Beira – Guia das Vias* are part of the series of maps put out by Coopération Française in cooperation with the Conselho Municipal. Copies are hard to come by these days, but you can try at the **Gabinete de Endereçamento da Cidade da Beira** (5 Praça do Município) at Conselho Municipal.

Information
EMERGENCY

Clínica Avicena (☎ 23-327990; Avenida Poder Popular; ⊙ 24hr) Try here for medical emergencies if Clínica Universitária is closed; just north of Praça do Metical.

Clínica Universitária (☎ 23-311823; just off Avenida das FLPM; ⊙ 8am-4pm Mon-Fri, paediatrics ⊙ 8am-noon Tue) The best bet for medical treatment. It's at the Catholic University Medical School in the pink multistorey building just across the canal from Clube de Sporting da Beira, and about 500m east of Praça da Independência.

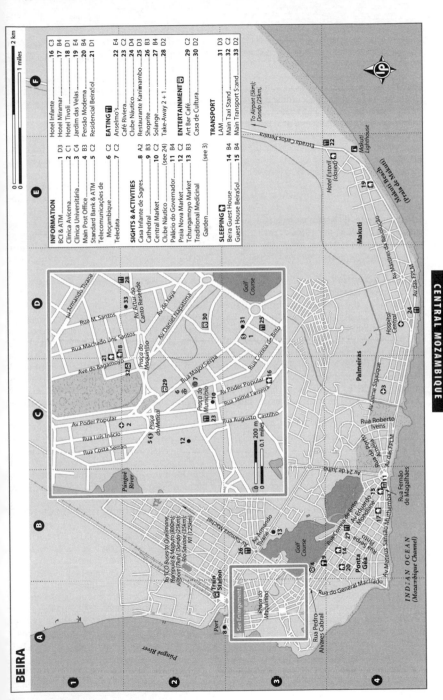

INTERNET ACCESS
Teledata (Rua Companhia de Moçambique; per hr Mtc60; ☾ 8am-6pm) Internet connection; diagonally opposite the telecom office.

MONEY
There are many ATMs, including at the airport; at **Shoprite** (Avenida Samora Machel); at **BCI** (Rua Major Serpa) opposite LAM; and at **Standard Bank** (Praça do Metical).

POST
Main post office (Rua Correia de Brito) Northwest of the cathedral.

TELEPHONE
Telecomunicações de Moçambique (Rua Companhia de Moçambique; ☾ 7am-10pm) Domestic and international telephone calls. In the green and white building just off Praça do Município, and just down from Teledata.

Sights & Activities
Beira's spired **cathedral** (Avenida Eduardo Mondlane), southeast of the centre, was built in the early-20th century with stones taken from the ruins of San Caetano fort in Sofala. Also worth a look are the surrounding **Ponta Gêa** area, with some charming old houses; **Praça do Metical**; and the area around the port, where the streets are lined with faded colonial-era buildings. One to watch for is the restored **Casa Infante de Sagres**, now the offices of Manica Shipping Company.

Makuti Beach (Praia de Makuti; Avenida das FPLM) is one of the better places in town to relax, though it can't compare with the coastline further south or north. The water is moderately clean, currents strong (ask locally where swimming is possible) and the breezes good. There's a **swimming pool** (Avenida das FPLM; admission Mon-Fri Mtc100, Sat & Sun Mtc150) at Clube Náutico and a **golf course** in the southern part of town.

The chaotic **Tchungamoyo Market** (Mercado de Tchungamoyo; Avenida Armando Tivane), known locally as 'Goto', is in the northeastern corner of town. It's full of imported goods, contraband and some unsavoury characters. The **Central Market** (Mercado Central; Rua Correia de Brito) in the town centre is quieter, and the best place to buy fruit and vegetables. If neither of these suit, try **Praia Nova Market**, west of Praça do Município, with piles of fresh seafood, and just about everything else.

A **traditional medicinal garden** at the Catholic University Medical School is open to the

public. It's in the multistorey pink building just off Avenida das FPLM near the Sporting Clube da Beira. Ask for '*jardim do projecto Medicina Verde*'.

With your own transport (or an arranged pick-up), Rio Savane (see below) makes a fine day or overnight trip.

Sleeping
While Beira doesn't distinguish itself with accommodation options, it has enough of a choice to satisfy most tastes and there are a few nice, new places.

BUDGET
Rio Savane (☎ 23-323555, 82-385 7660; campsite per person US$10, 4-person barracas US$15 plus per person US$8, self-catering bungalows d/q US$50/100) If you have your own vehicle (or even if you don't – pick-ups from Beira can be arranged) and want to escape for a day or two, it's well worth driving out to this rustic place, about 40km north of town in a serene setting on the Savane River, separated from the sea by a narrow peninsula. It has camping, *barracas* (thatched shelters) with mattresses and bedding, a couple of self-catering chalets, and meals. The surrounding wetlands are ideal for birdwatching. Follow the Dondo road past the airport to the right-hand turn-off for Savane. Continue 35km to the estuary, where there's secure parking and a small boat (until 5pm) to take you to the camp.

Hotel Miramar (☎ 23-322283; Rua Vilas Boas Truão; d without/with air-con Mtc400/450; ✷) A faded local-style hotel with rather dilapidated no-frills rooms – some with private bathroom – near the water (no beach), but inconvenient for the rest of town. There are no meals available.

Pensão Moderna (☎ 23-329901; Rua Alferes da Silva; d/tr with shared bathroom Mtc750/950, d Mtc980) One of the better budget bets, with adequate rooms – most with fan and shared bathroom. It's two blocks south of the cathedral.

Hotel Infante (☎ 23-326603; Rua Jaime Ferreira; s/d from Mtc900/1050; ✷) In a high-rise building in a congested section of town a few blocks from LAM, with small, clean rooms – some with fan and shared bathroom, others with air-con and private bathroom – and a restaurant.

MIDRANGE & TOP END
Residencial BeiraSol (☎ 23-236420; 168 Rua da Madeira; r Mtc1500; 🔀) Opposite Hotel Tivoli, with clean, modern rooms, although most have only interior windows – ask for a room to the front for more views. Despite this drawback, it is a clean, secure option in the baixa.

Jardim das Velas (☎ 23-312209; jardimdasvelas@ yahoo.com; 282 Avenida das FPLM, Makuti Beach; d/f US$75/85; 🔀) This quiet place, near the lighthouse, has spotless, well-equipped rooms with views to the sea upstairs, and a couple of four-person family rooms with bunk beds downstairs. All rooms have mosquito nets. There are no meals, but there's a small garden with braai facilities, and filtered water. The beach is just across the street. It's very popular and often full; advance bookings recommended.

Beira Guest House (☎ 23-324030, 82-315 0460; 1311 Avenida Eduardo Mondlane; s/tw Mtc2300/2550; 🔀 🖳 🛜) Another recommended place, this cosy residential-style B&B in the shady Ponta Gêa area has pleasant, well-appointed rooms with minifridge, TV and laundry service. Breakfast is included, although there's no other meals available. It's diagonally opposite the cathedral.

Hotel Tivoli (☎ 23-320300; h.tivoli-beira@teledata.mz; cnr Avenida de Bagamoyo & Rua da Madeira; s/d US$110/140; 🅿 🔀 🖳) Small and tidy albeit rather faded rooms with TV and amenities, in a high-rise in the baixa. Downstairs is a sleek restaurant/bar. Buffet breakfast is included in the price.

Guest House BeiraSol, (☎ 23-327202; Rua Fernão de Magalhæs; r Mtc2500-3500, ste Mtc3750; 🔀 🛜) Spacious, well-appointed rooms in a restored private villa with polished wood floors and lots of windows. It's just off Avenida Eduardo Mondlane, on the side street immediately next to the governor's residence (palácio do governador).

Eating
Beira's restaurants and cafes are full of faded charm, and the dining scene is where you can experience this old-fashioned port city at its best.

Café Riviera (Praça do Município; snacks & light meals from Mtc70; 🕑 7.30am-9pm) This classic, pink Old World street-side cafe is a good spot to sit with a cup of coffee and *bolo de mandioca* (almond cake) and watch the passing scene. There are soft, plump sofas inside and tables outdoors overlooking the beach.

Anselmo's (Avenida das FPLM; meals about Mtc200) This small, unsignposted local place past the lighthouse and opposite the old Hotel Estoril does tasty, local food. Stop by in the afternoon to place an order for dinner.

Take-Away 2 + 1 (Avenida Artur do Canto Resende; meals from Mtc100; 🔀) A small restaurant serving a selection of inexpensive local fare, just northeast of Praça do Município.

Restaurante Kanimambo (☎ 23-323132; Rua Pero de Alenquer; meals from Mtc150; 🕑 lunch & dinner Sun-Fri) Down a small side street opposite LAM, with tasty Chinese food and a friendly proprietor.

Solange (cnr Avenida Eduardo Mondlane & Rua Serpa Pinto; meals from Mtc220; 🕑 lunch & dinner; 🔀) Well-prepared meat and seafood grills in a dark, air-con interior.

Clube Náutico (☎ 23-311720; Avenida das FPLM; meals from Mtc200, plus per person entry Mtc20; 🕑 lunch & dinner) This colonial-era swimming and social club is another popular waterside hangout, with average food and slow service redeemed by the relaxing beachside setting. On Saturday afternoon, there are all-comers-welcome rugby matches on the sand in front. Out front are vendors with a modest array of woodcarvings and other crafts.

Shoprite (cnr Avenidas Armando Tivane & Samora Machel) For self-catering.

Entertainment
Art Bar Café (www.artbarcafe.co.cc; Cinema Novocine, 135 Rua Major Serpa; 🕑 5pm-late Wed-Sat) In the cinema building about five minutes' walk from Hotel Tivoli, Art Bar Café is the heart of Beira's cultural scene, with an ever-changing music, art and entertainment program. Check its website and posters around town.

Casa de Cultura (☎ 23-327858; off Rua Major Serpa) Opposite Hotel Embaixador, with theatre and dance performances. Information on upcoming programs is posted by the entrance.

Getting There & Away
AIR
There are flights on **LAM** (☎ 23-324141/2, 23-306000, 23-303112; 85 Rua Major Serpa) twice weekly to/from Johannesburg, daily to/from Maputo, and several times weekly to/from Tete, Nampula, Quelimane, Pemba, Vilankulo and Lichinga. **SAAirlink** (☎ 23-301569/70; www.saairlink.co.za; airport)

flies five times weekly between Beira and Johannesburg.

BUS & CHAPA

Beira's main transport hub is in the Praça do Maquinino area. There's no real order to things – ask locals where to go for buses to your destination.

TCO (☎ 82-509 2180, 82-775 0554) has an air-con bus departing at 4am daily except Saturday to Maputo (Mtc1300, 15 hours), and at 5am on Monday, Wednesday and Friday to Quelimane (Mtc690, nine hours). It has also just started a twice-weekly run between Beira and Nampula (Mtc1600, 16 hours), also departing at 4am, although the days vary. All departures are from the TCO office on Rua dos Irmãos Roby in Bairro dos Pioneiros, 1km north of the centre.

To Vilankulo (Mtc550, 10 hours), there's a direct bus daily departing by about 4.30am.

To Chimoio (Mtc150, three hours) and Machipanda (Mtc175, four hours), mini-buses go throughout the day from the main transport stand.

Another option for any northbound or southbound transport is to go to Inchope, a scruffy junction 130km west of Beira (Mtc100, two to three hours via chapa), where the EN6 joins the N1, and try your luck with passing buses there, although they are often full and waits are long.

Getting Around

The airport is 7km northwest of town (Mtc200 in a taxi).

Chapas to Makuti (Mtc5) depart from the main transport stand.

For vehicle rentals, head to **Imperial** (☎ 23-302650/1, 82-300 5190; imperialbeira@hotmail.com), which has an office at the airport.

The main taxi stand is at the western edge of Praça do Maquinino. Taxis don't cruise for business, and companies come and go, so ask your hotel for the updated numbers.

AROUND BEIRA
Gorongosa National Park

About 170km northwest of Beira is **Gorongosa National Park** (Parque Nacional de Gorongosa; www .gorongosa.net; adult/child/vehicle Mtc200/100/200, payable in meticais only; ☼ 6am-6pm Apr-Dec), which was gazetted in 1960 and soon made headlines as one of southern Africa's premier wildlife parks. It was renowned for its large prides of lions,

as well as for its elephants, hippos, buffaloes and rhinos. During the 1980s and early 1990s, hungry soldiers and poachers brought an end to this abundance. Because Renamo headquarters was nearby, the surrounding area was heavily mined and the park's infrastructure was destroyed. Rehabilitation work began in 1995, and in 1998 Gorongosa reopened to visitors. In recent years, the park has received a major boost thanks to assistance from the US-based Carr Foundation, which has joined with the Government of Mozambique to fund Gorongosa's long-term restoration and ecotourism development.

Animal numbers still pale in comparison with those of earlier times, and can't compare with those in other southern African safari destinations. However, wildlife is making a definite comeback and the park is highly recommended on any Mozambique itinerary. It's likely that you will see impalas, waterbucks, sable antelopes, warthogs, hippos, crocodiles and perhaps even elephants and lions.

A wildlife sanctuary has been created in the park, where restocking of zebras, buffaloes, wildebeests and other animals has begun. Another major attraction is the birdlife, with over 300 species, including many endemics and near-endemics, and an abundance of water birds in the wetland areas to the east around the Urema River.

Just as much a highlight as the wildlife is Gorongosa's unique and beautiful mixture of ecological zones, with a mix of jade-green floodplains, savannah, woodlands, forests of fever trees, stands of palm and hanging vines. Within its 5370 sq km it encompasses the southernmost part of the Great Rift system, the hulking Gorongosa massif, expanses of coastal plain and the Zambezi valley, and is considered to be the most biologically diverse of all Mozambique's conservation areas. The park's rehabilitation also involves a strong community development element, and the chance to see some of this work is another draw.

INFORMATION

Since Gorongosa's reopening, infrastructure has been upgraded, with more improvements ongoing. Check the excellent website for updates.

Park headquarters (☎ 23-535010, 82-302 0604; travel@gorongosa.net) are in Chitengo, about 15km east of the entry gate, from where rough tracks branch out to other park areas. Vehicle rental, guides for wildlife drives, and excursions to a nearby village can be arranged at park headquarters. Three-hour vehicle safaris cost Mtc780 per person. Highly recommended multinight bush walks and (in the wetter months) canoe trips can be arranged through Explore Gorongosa (see below).

SLEEPING & EATING

At Chitengo park headquarters, there's a shaded **camping ground** (campsite per person Mtc210) with ablution blocks and hot water, a good restaurant, a swimming pool and pleasant **rondavels** (s/d/f Mtc2500/2990/4680; ✷) scattered around an expansive, grassy fenced compound.

The highly recommended **Explore Gorongosa** (www.exploregorongosa.com; s/d with full-board US$500/800) runs walking safaris and canoe trips from its base in a semipermanent tented camp in one of the most scenic sections of the park. Its tents are spacious and comfortable, and for multinight bush walks, it operates a series of fly camps. Everything is custom-tailored, and it's an excellent bet for experiencing the bush. Rates include accommodation, meals, beverages, walks and other activities, and park entry fees.

If you're coming from the north and get stuck in Vila Gorongosa, **Pensão Azul** (r without/with bathroom Mtc400/800, with air-con Mtc1000), which is not blue at all, but white with yellow trim, has no-frills rooms and inexpensive meals. It's just east of the main road opposite the main junction.

GETTING THERE & AWAY
Air

At the time of writing, **CFA Charters** (☎ 21-466881, 293-82055; cfamoz@tdm.co.mz) was about to start twice weekly flights from Maputo to Gorongosa National Park via the Bazaruto Archipelago (US$570/275 one way from Maputo/Bazaruto to Gorongosa), making a fine, upmarket beach and bush option.

Road

The park turn-off is at Inchope, about 130km west of Beira, from where it's 43km north along good tarmac to Nota village and then 17km east along an all-weather gravel road to the park gate. You can easily reach the park entrance with a 2WD, but for exploring, you'll need a 4WD. Chapas heading north from Inchope to Gorongosa town (Vila

Gorongosa), about 25km beyond the park turn-off, will drop you at the turn-off, from where you can arrange a pick-up with staff (advance booking essential). Pick-ups are also possible from Beira, Chimoio and Inchope – see the park website for prices. Chapas cost Mtc160/50/20 from Beira/Inchope/Vila Gorongosa to the park turn-off.

Mt Gorongosa

Outside the park boundaries to the northwest is **Mt Gorongosa** (1862m), Mozambique's fourth-highest mountain. Steeped in local lore, it's known for its rich plant and birdlife and its abundance of lovely waterfalls. The mountain's slopes are the only place in southern Africa to see the green-headed oriole, and one of just a handful of places where you can see the dappled mountain robin and Swynnerton's forest robin.

Mt Gorongosa is considered sacred, but it's possible to climb to its upper slopes with a local guide. The Carr Foundation, which is financing the rehabilitation of Gorongosa National Park, is also supporting a community-based ecotourism and reforestation project on the mountain, centred around hiking trails and birdwatching, with a focus on conserving the mountain ecosystems that are essential for maintaining wildlife populations in the park. The project, which aims to give local communities alternative sources of livelihood other than slash-and-burn agriculture, is still in the early stages, but once going, it will encompass all tourism and hiking on the mountain. A base camp for hikers and birdwatchers has been set up near the beautiful Morumbodzi Falls, which are on the mountain's western side at about 950m. From the camp, there are paths to the falls (about one hour's easy walk away), birdwatching walks and overnight climbs to the summit (about six hours one way). To organise hikes, contact park headquarters (travel@gorongosa .net). All fees (to be determined soon – watch the park website for details) will go to the local communities.

According to tradition, no red can be worn when climbing the mountain and the climb must be undertaken barefoot, though this latter requirement seems to be conveniently waived these days. This is just as well: the mountain receives about 2000mm of rain a year, and the wet, humid conditions, combined with the steepness of the path on the upper reaches, make the going slippery approaching the summit. Good shoes and a reasonable degree of fitness are essential.

To get to the Morumbodzi base camp area, follow the N6 from Beira to the turn-off at Inchope. Continue north along the tarmac road, passing the turn-off for Gorongosa park and continuing another 25km or so further to Gorongosa town. About 10km beyond Gorongosa town, turn off the main highway to the right, and continue 10km along an unpaved track to the base camp. Transport from the park can be organised through park staff.

CHIMOIO

Chimoio is the capital of Manica province, and Mozambique's fifth-largest town. While its tourist attractions are decidedly modest, it's a pleasant place with an agreeable climate and worth a stop if you're in the area. It's also the jumping-off point for exploring the Chimanimani Mountains to the southwest.

Information

INTERNET

Internet Café (Rua Dr Araújo de la Cerda; per hr Mtc60) Next to Barclays Bank, and usually fast-ish.

Internet Café (Rua do Bárue; per hr about Mtc60) Next to Restaurante-Bar Jumbo; fast connections.

Teledata (cnr Avenida 25 de Setembro & Rua Mossurize; per min Mtc1; 🕑 8.30am-6pm Mon-Fri, 9am-noon Sat) Slow, but has wi-fi.

MONEY

There are many ATMs, including at **Standard Bank** (cnr Avenida 25 de Setembro & Rua Patrice Lumumba), at **Barclays Bank** (Rua Dr Araújo de la Cerda) and at Shoprite. The moneychangers loitering around the bus stand should be avoided.

TELEPHONE

Telecomunicações de Moçambique (cnr Ruas do Bárue & Patrice Lumumba) For international calls.

TOURIST INFORMATION

Mozambique Ecotours (www.mozecotours.com) – reachable through the **Eco-Micaia office** (☎ 251-23759; www.micaia.org; just off Rua Josina Machel, behind the Chimoio International School) is the best source of information on hiking in the Chimanimani Mountains. To get here, follow Avenida Liberdade north past the church. After crossing Rua Sussundenga, continue for three more blocks to Rua Josina Machel, where you take a left. Continue along Rua Josina Machel until the paved road turns right, and Eco-Micaia is immediately on your right.

Sights & Activities

About 5km northeast of town is **Cabeça do Velho**, a large rock that resembles the face of an old man at rest. To get here, take Rua do Bárue past Magarafa market and continue along the dirt road; you'll see the rock ahead of you in the distance. Once at the base, you can climb up in about 10 minutes to enjoy some views. As with all mountains and high

---

SOFALA

About 40km south of Beira and just south of the Búzi River is the site of the ancient gold-trading port of **Sofala**, dating from at least the 9th century AD. Sofala's importance lay in its role as the major link between the gold trade of the interior and the powerful sultanate at Kilwa in present-day Tanzania. By the 15th century, it had become one of East Africa's most influential centres, with ties as far away as Madagascar, India and Indonesia. San Caetano, the first Portuguese fort in Mozambique, was built at Sofala in 1505 with stones shipped from Portugal. However, soon after the Portuguese arrived, trade routes shifted northwards, Mozambique Island eclipsed Sofala as the main coastal base and Sofala and its fort rapidly sunk into oblivion. Today nothing remains of Sofala's former glory and the ruins of the fort have been overtaken by the sea. The area is, however, hauntingly beautiful and optimal for exploration by anyone wanting to get off the beaten track.

To get here from Beira by public transport, take any bus heading along the N6 towards Chimoio and get off at Tica, from where there is sporadic public transport south to Búzi, where there are several decent *pensões* (inexpensive hotels). If you are approaching by road from the N1, the turn-off is at Chiboma; ask locally about conditions from Chiboma to the coast. Alternatively, there's a daily ferry from Beira, which stops at various points along the coast, including Búzi and the small modern-day port of Nova Sofala.

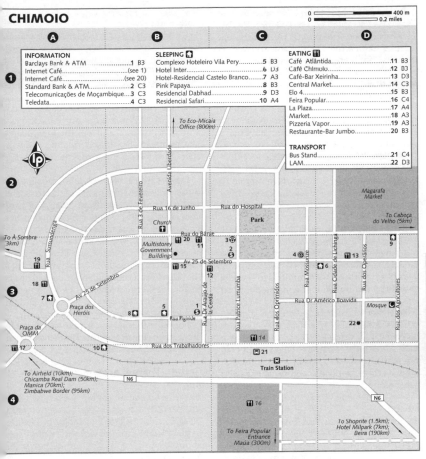

CHIMOIO

| 0 | 400 m |
| 0 | 0.2 miles |

INFORMATION
Barclays Bank & ATM 1 B3
Internet Café...........................(see 1)
Internet Café...........................(see 20)
Standard Bank & ATM..................2 C3
Telecomunicações de Moçambique...3 C3
Teledata...............................4 C3

SLEEPING 🏠
Complexo Hoteleiro Vila Pery............5 B3
Hotel Inter...................................6 D3
Hotel-Residencial Castelo Branco.......7 A3
Pink Papaya.................................8 B3
Residencial Dabhad.........................9 D3
Residencial Safari.........................10 A4

EATING 🍴
Café Atlântida................................11 B3
Café Chimolo..................................12 D3
Café-Bar Xeirinha............................13 D3
Central Market...............................14 C3
Elo 4...15 B3
Feira Popular.................................16 C4
La Plaza......................................17 A4
Market..18 A3
Pizzeria Vapor................................19 A3
Restaurante-Bar Jumbo.......................20 B3

TRANSPORT
Bus Stand.....................................21 C4
LAM...22 D3

To Eco-Micaia Office (800m)

To À Sombra (3km)

Rua 3 de Fevereiro
Avenida Liberdade
Rua Sussundenga

Rua 16 de Junho
Rua do Hospital
Church
Rua do Bárue
Multistorey Government Buildings
Av 25 de Setembro
Av 25 de Setembro
Praça dos Heróis
Rua Pigivide
Rua Dr Araújo de la Cerda
Praça da OMM
Rua dos Trabalhadores

Park

Rua Patrice Lumumba
Rua dos Oprimidos
Rua Mossurize
Rua Cidade de Lichinga
Rua dos Operários
Rua Cidade de Lichinga

Magarafa Market
To Cabeça do Velho (5km)

Rua Dr Américo Boavida
Mosque
Rua dos Agricultores

Train Station

To Airfield (10km); Chicamba Real Dam (50km); Manica (70km); Zimbabwe Border (95km)

N6

N6

To Shoprite (1.5km); Hotel Milpark (7km); Beira (190km)

To Feira Popular Entrance Maúa (300m)

CENTRAL MOZAMBIQUE

places in Mozambique, there are legends and traditions associated with this one and locals may still offer a prayer to the spirits once at the top.

There's a **swimming pool** (adult/child Mtc150/100) at Hotel Milpark.

Sleeping

BUDGET

Pink Papaya (☎ 82-555 7310; http://pinkpapaya.atspace .com; cnr Ruas Pigivide & 3 de Fevereiro; dm Mtc300, s/d Mtc550/700; **P**) Pink Papaya is the best budget option, with helpful management, a convenient central location, clean dorm beds and doubles, a well-equipped kitchen and braai area and breakfast available on request. Note that there is no camping. The owner can

also help with information on excursions to the Chimanimani Mountains, Gorongosa National Park and Penha Longa. It's about 10 minutes on foot from the bus stand: with the bus stand to your right and train station to your left, walk straight and take the fourth right into Rua 3 de Fevereiro. Go one block to Rua Pigivide. On request, staff will accompany you to the bus stop for early morning departures.

Residencial Safari (☎ 251-22894, 84-239 0234; Rua dos Trabalhadores; s/tw with shared bathroom Mtc700/1000, d Mtc1200) This place, targeted at local business clientele, is worth checking out if you're on a budget. There's internet connection if you have your own laptop. Breakfast is included, otherwise there are no meals.

Residencial Dabhad (☎ 251-23264, 82-385 5480; cnr Ruas do Bárue & dos Agricultores; s Mtc1150, d & tw Mtc1350) This friendly, no-frills place is worth checking if Pink Papaya is full. Continental breakfast is included, but there are no other meals.

MIDRANGE

Hotel Milpark (☎ 82-763 2313, 23-910021; milparkhotel@ hotmail.com; d Mtc1600-2100, ste Mtc2750; 🔲) About 7km outside town along the Beira road, with straightforward rooms around expansive grounds, a restaurant and a pool.

Complexo Hoteleiro Vila Pery (☎ 251-24391, 82-501 4520; vilapery@tdm.co.mz; Rua Pigivide; d/tw Mtc1800/1900) Bright paintings give a bit of ambience to this otherwise rather soulless hotel. Rooms – around a central cement courtyard – are clean and fine.

Hotel-Residencial Castelo Branco (☎ 251-23934, 82-522 5960; Rua Sussundenga; s/d Mtc1850/2000; 🅿 🔲) Catering to business travellers, this place has modern, comfortable twin-bed rooms around a small garden – all with minifridge – and a good breakfast buffet. It's signposted just off Praça dos Heróis and is often full.

Hotel Inter (☎ 251-24200, 84-242 0000; interchimoio@ gmail.com; Avenida 25 de Setembro, near Rua Cidade de Lichinga; r Mtc2200, ste from Mtc2750; 🔲) This newish multistorey place is trying to edge out Castelo Branco for the best rooms in town, although it's debatable whether it succeeds. There's also a restaurant.

Eating

At the southern edge of town, the Feira Popular, off the N6, has several good restaurants (most closed on Monday), including the longstanding and recommended Maúa (meals from Mtc150; open for lunch and dinner Tuesday to Sunday), with delicious grills and well-prepared Mozambican cuisine. It's mainly an option for those with their own transport, as taxis are difficult to find in the evenings.

Café Chimoio (Rua Dr Araújo de la Cerda; snacks & meals from Mtc150) and **Café Atlântida** (cnr Ruas do Bárue & Dr Araújo de la Cerda) offer inexpensive local meals.

La Plaza (Praça da OMM) The menu is unexciting – pizzas and standard fare – but the attached supermarket sells good bread.

Pizzeria Vapor (Rua do Mercado; pizza from Mtc120) Just down from Castelo Branco, this place has Chimoio's best pizzas. Go left when exiting Castelo Branco, past the market area; take the first left, and Pizzeria Vapor will be on your right-hand side.

Elo 4 (Avenida 25 de Setembro just before Avenida Liberdade; meals from Mtc150) Opposite the government building in the town centre, this place was closed for renovations when we passed through, but was scheduled to reopen with pizzas and Italian dishes.

Restaurante-Bar Jumbo (Rua do Bárue; meals from Mtc150) This is a basic but reliable place with tasty pizzas and continental dishes, and ice cream for dessert. Seating is downstairs in the bar or in a cosy wood-panelled room upstairs.

Café-Bar Xeirinha (Avenida 25 de Setembro; meals about Mtc220) An amenable ambience, a pool table and generally decent food – ranging from coffees and milkshakes to continental dishes. It's just before Rua Cidade de Lichinga.

À Sombra (☎ 82-953 6169; Bairro Tambara Dois; meals from Mtc250; 🕑 closed Mon) This German-Mozambican place, about 3km west of town, is the place to come for quality steaks and meats, including German specialities and international cuisine. The food is delicious and the ambience – with garden seating – relaxing.

For self-catering, try **Shoprite** (N6), 2km east of the town centre; the **central market** (near the bus station); and the **market** (near Castelo Branco).

Getting There & Around

AIR

There are several flights weekly on **LAM** (☎ 251-22531; mafuia@tdm.co.mz; Mafúia Comercial, Rua dos Operários) to Tete and Maputo. The airfield is 10km from town, and signposted about 5km west of Chimoio along the Manica road.

BUS & CHAPA

All transport leaves from near the train station.

Buses depart daily at 4am to Tete (Mtc350, seven hours) and between 2.30am and 4am to Maputo (Mtc900, 14 hours).

For Vilankulo, there's no direct bus – you'll need to take the Maputo bus and get dropped at Pambara junction. While the price should be pro-rated, it's difficult from Chimoio to get the drivers to come down from the full Mtc900. Chapas to Beira (Mtc150, three hours) and Manica (Mtc20, one hour) run throughout the day.

For Quelimane, you'll need to make your way in stages via Inchope and Caia. Watch for touts trying to sell you 'direct' tickets – you'll still need to get out at Inchope and wait for northbound transport. Another option is contacting TCO in Beira (see p106) and trying to book a seat with them from Inchope.

TAXI

Chimoio has a few taxis – look for them in front of the park on Avenida 25 de Setembro or by the market, or ask your hotel to ring one.

AROUND CHIMOIO

About halfway between Chimoio and Manica is the **Chicamba Real Dam** (Barragem de Chicamba Real), set among low hills, and popular with bass anglers. Head west from Chimoio for 32km to the Garuzo junction, and turn left (south) here towards the dam. Following this road for about 12km to 15km, past the village and down around the back side of the dam, you'll reach several small lakeside restaurant/accommodation places. The best of the bunch is **Mira Chicamba Lodge** (☎ 82-501 3190; r Mtc500) – the third one down – with a handful of simple twin rooms, tranquil views and delicious grilled fish.

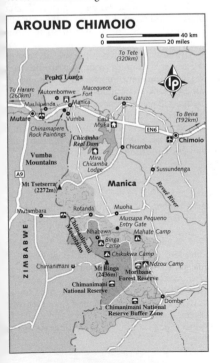

On the other side of the lake, reached via a signposted turn-off 45km west of Chimoio, is **Casa Msika** (☎ 82-440 4304; www.casamsika.com; campsite per person Mtc100, d Mtc920, 4-person rondavels Mtc1680;) with lakeside camping with hot-water ablutions, simple rooms and rondavels overlooking the lake and a restaurant. On weekends, it fills up completely with Zimbabwean anglers. It's about 4km from the turn-off; there's no public transport.

MANICA

Tiny Manica, 70km west of Chimoio, is situated in what was once the heart of the kingdom of Manica and an important gold-trading area.

There's an ATM at **Millennium BIM** (N6).

Sights

Near the town entrance, in a red-roofed colonial-era house, is a **Geology Museum**.

About 5km from town are the **Chinamapere rock paintings**. To get here, go west from Manica about 3km, and then south along a dirt road, following signs for 'pinturas rupestres'. The site of the paintings is considered sacred by local residents, and before your visit, an elderly lady will conduct a brief prayer ceremony. According to tradition, no pregnant or menstruating women can visit the site.

Several kilometres south of Manica is **Vumba** (which means 'mist' in the local Manika language) and the bottling plant for Mozambique's Água Vumba mineral water.

Northwest of town, off the Penha Longa road and signposted from Manica (4WD), are the ruins of **Macequece Fort** (Fortaleza de Macequece) – the location of an old gold-trading fair and site of an 1891 battle between Portuguese colonial forces and Cecil Rhode's British South Africa Company.

Sleeping & Eating

Pensão Flamingo (☎ 251-62385; EN6; r Mtc750) On the main road, a few blocks west of Millennium BIM, this spiffy place has simple rooms – all with bathroom and fan – plus a garden and a restaurant.

Manica Lodge (☎ 251 62452; d in small rondavel Mtc1200, s/d in large rondavel Mtc1500/1750) At the western end of town, and about 400m off the main road (watch for the signposted turn-off just after the immigration office), this amenable establishment has stone rondavels scattered around tranquil, manicured gardens. The

CENTRAL MOZAMBIQUE

larger ones are nice – all reasonably spacious, with TV and private bathrooms. In back are several less appealing rondavels that are tiny, and without TV. There's also a restaurant and a three-room self-catering house.

Also recommended:

Estalagem Selva (☎ 82-5702480; N6; r with fan & bathroom Mtc600, with air-con Mtc800; ☒) About 40km east of Manica, with straightforward rooms in large grounds with a restaurant, a children's playground and a pool (per person Mtc50). Mostly used as a day getaway from Chimoio.

Vumba Lodge (☎ 251-62452; r Mtc1750) This good restaurant will soon also have clean, simple rooms. Contact it through Manica Lodge.

Getting There & Away

All transport departs from the market, diagonally opposite Millennium BIM. Chapas run frequently to/from Chimoio (Mtc50, one hour) and to the Zimbabwe border (Mtc20, 30 minutes). Several times weekly there are direct chapas from Manica to Rotanda village in the Chimanimani Mountains.

PENHA LONGA

The mountainous Penha Longa area straddles the border with Zimbabwe, beginning about 20km north of Manica. It's cool and scenic and offers many walks, all of which can be easily undertaken from Casa Gaswa (below) or Quinta da Fronteira (right). The area is also home to the Shona people, and you'll see their traditional painted dwelling compounds dotting the hillsides. Although there is plenty of local cross-border activity, the only official border crossing is between Machipanda and Mutare (Zimbabwe) on the main road.

It's possible to arrange to sleep in the compound of a local family at **Casa Gaswa** (2-/3-person

rondavel Mtc500/700), a simple but nice rondavel in Penha Longa's Mutombomwe area. Local-style meals can be arranged, but it's a good idea to bring some food and drink with you from Manica. Guides for hiking can also be arranged. If Casa Gaswa is occupied, you can also pitch a tent on the grounds (campsite per person Mtc150).

Next door is **Casa Motombombwe** (☎ 82-659 0358, 82-380 2330; giftmashiri@yahoo.com.br; 4-person house Mtc1200), a simple but well-equipped self-catering house with electricity that sleeps up to four people. Hiking guides and a cook can be arranged.

There's also camping and a few basic rooms at **Quinta da Fronteira** (campsite Mtc150, r Mtc250), an old mansion about 3km from Casa Gaswa with a stream nearby and a once-lovely botanical garden. Bring all your own food and drink. Pink Papaya (p109) in Chimoio can help with arrangements for all of these places.

Getting There & Away

Chapas run several times daily between Manica and Penha Longa (Mtc40, one hour). From the chapa terminus in Penha Longa, it's a 20-minute walk to Mutombomwe and Casa Gaswa, and from there, about 3km further to Quinta da Fronteira. Ask locals to point out the way.

Driving, turn north at the intersection in the centre of Manica town towards the market. Continue past the market, staying left at the first fork, then right at the second. Penha Longa village is reached after about 20km. Mutombomwe *bairro* (neighbourhood), Casa Gaswa and Casa Mutombombwe are about 4km further. The road is unpaved, but in reasonable condition during the dry season.

A LEGEND OF PENHA LONGA

During the late-19th century, Penha Longa lay in the centre of a disputed area. To the west were the lands of the kingdom of Manica. To the southeast was the territory of the powerful Gaza chief Ngungunhane.

These two kingdoms had long been enemies, and Ngungunhane's troops staged frequent raids into Manica. To protect themselves from the invaders, the people of Penha Longa would send heralds up the mountain to Mudododo village (on what is now the Zimbabwe border), from where they had wide views down over the valleys. When these heralds saw Ngungunhane's forces coming, they would notify the villagers, who would set out roots from a certain plant for the invaders and then flee the village. Although this type of root closely resembled yam, a local staple, it was actually poisonous. The invaders were not able to tell the difference and would eat it and then fall ill. In this way, the residents of Penha Longa were able to protect themselves and resist the Gaza invaders.

THE MUTASA

Since long before colonial boundaries were drawn, the people of Penha Longa have been loyal to the *mutasa*, the dynastic title of the ruler of the kingdom of Manica, who controls the area from present-day Mutare (Zimbabwe). Despite a divisive 1891 Anglo-Portuguese treaty that put western Penha Longa under British control, and the eastern part under Portuguese control, cross-border ties remain strong and Mozambican residents of Penha Longa still profess loyalty to Nyakwanikwa (the present-day *mutasa*) in Mutare.

CHIMANIMANI MOUNTAINS

Silhouetted against the horizon on the Zimbabwe border southwest of Chimoio are the Chimanimani Mountains, with Mt Binga (2436m), Mozambique's highest peak, rising up on their eastern edge. The mountains are beautiful and exceptionally biodiverse, with vegetation ranging from lowland tropical forests and miombo woodland to evergreen forests and afro-alpine grasslands in the highest reaches. Much of the range is encompassed by the **Chimanimani National Reserve** (Reserva Nacional de Chimanimani; www.actf.gov.mz/reserva_chimanimani html; adult/child/vehicle Mtc200/100/200), which is part of the larger Chimanimani Transfrontier Conservation Area (ACTF), together with Chimanimani National Park in Zimbabwe.

Chimanimani is notable for its abundance of rare plants, with at least 90 species whose range is restricted to the Chimanimani area alone. Many are prized by traditional healers for their medicinal value. There is also a multitude of birds, including the rare southern banded snake eagle, Chirinda apalis and the barred cuckoo. Rounding out the picture are bushbuck, eland, sable, duiker, klipspringer and countless smaller animals.

Like the Penha Longa area to the north, the Chimanimani Mountains have a long history and rich traditional life. Rock paintings estimated to be 2000 years old, but possibly as much as 10,000 years old, and similar to those at Chinamapere (see p111), have been found at several locations. Many of the rivers and pools in this area are considered sacred by local communities, as are some of the forest areas in the foothills of the mountains, and some of the peaks themselves.

Hiking

It's possible to hike throughout the mountains, with plenty of suitable camping sites on the high plateaus close to mountain streams. Mt Binga can be climbed in two days, with one night spent on the mountain, but the highlands offer endless options for hikes of anything from a day to a week or more. Once up in the mountains you have to be entirely self-sufficient. Also, be prepared for sudden changes in weather, especially for mist, rain and cold, and keep in mind that the routes are physically demanding. Hikes begin at about 700m in altitude, while the highlands are at around 1800m and the highest peaks well above 2000m.

INFORMATION

The best contact for getting started exploring the mountains and the Chimanimani region in general is the highly recommended **Mozambique EcoTours** (www.mozecotours.com) which is working on establishing several community-run camps that should be open by the time this book is published. It can also be contacted through Eco-Micaia in Chimoio (p108).

The main reserve entrance, where you pay your entry fees, is at the Mussapa Pequeno River. For all hikes, you'll need to have a guide. These can be arranged at various points, including at the Mussapa Pequeno reserve entrance, at Nhabawa (shown as Mussimbiri on some maps), at Chikukwa camp (beyond Nhabawa) and at Mahate. Fees vary, depending on where you arrange your guide, but for a full day going up Mt Binga you should expect to pay at least Mtc450.

In addition to your own food supplies, bring along enough for your guides and porters, plus a sturdy water bottle for refilling at streams, and some water purifying tablets. Chimoio is the best place for stocking up for hikes, and an array of basics is also available in Sussundenga. Although there are rudimentary huts at several campsites (Mtc200 for a two-person hut within the reserve area), carrying a tent is recommended, as is bringing cool-weather gear; the mountains get cold, especially at night. Waterproofing your gear is essential, as is bringing along a bag to pack out your trash. As always, stick to beaten paths to avoid potential dangers from old landmines, especially in the forest areas.

There are many possible routes. For climbing Mt Binga, good starting points are Nhabawa or Chikukwa camp. By mid-2010, Eco-Micaia (the company behind Mozambique EcoTours) is planning to have **Binga Camp** open for visitors. The camp – at the junction of the Mussapa Grande and Nhamadze rivers – will have fixed tents, a campsite and self-catering facilities, and will make an ideal base for climbing Mt Binga and exploring the mountains. Meanwhile, the camp at Chikukwa village is scenically located in a valley surrounded by forest. Allow two to three days for climbing Mt Binga, including travel time between Chimoio and the base camps.

Another possible route in the area is Mahate, southwest of Sussundenga, where there's a basic rangers' camp overlooking the Mudzira River gorge. The lovely Moribane Forest – beautiful low- to mid-altitude tropical rain forest in the Chimanimani National Reserve buffer zone – is reached by taking the Sussungenga–Dombe road. Work is underway here on **Ndzou Camp** – a joint venture between Eco-Micaia and the local community that will have camping, rondavels and a small family lodge. Also on offer are guided forest walks, eco-learning activities and the chance to track the local population of forest elephants. Contact Mozambique EcoTours for more information.

For those with 4WD, Mt Tsetserra is another possible route. From its base, you can climb up a rough 4WD track through some beautiful, bird-filled montane rainforest to the top of the Tsetserra plateau (three to four hours return), or do various day or overnight walks. At the summit are the ruins of an old mansion (a hotel is planned), and camping.

Getting There & Away

The best access to the Chimanimani area on the Mozambique side is from Chimoio via Sussundenga and Rotanda. If you're driving, you'll need a 4WD to reach all of the sites highlighted in this section. To reach the main reserve entrance (*'portão'*) on the Mussapa Pequeno River via public transport, take a chapa from Chimoio to Sussundenga, where you'll need to wait for another vehicle going towards Rotanda. After passing Muoha, watch for the signposted Chimanimani turn-off. Ask the bus driver to drop you at the 'container', from where you'll have to walk about 5km along a track through lovely miombo woodland. Camping is possible at the entrance and you can get information from the reserve rangers. From there, it's about 15km further to Nhabawa, where you can arrange guides and porters for climbing Mt Binga. Chikukwa Camp is about 7km beyond this.

Moribane Forest Reserve can be reached via public transport from Sussundenga.

For Mt Tsetserra, take the signposted turn-off for Chicamba Real Dam for about 15km southwards to the dam administration buildings. From here, continue southwest (4WD) as the road winds scenically for about 60km up to the Tsetserra plateau.

TETE

Dry, dusty Tete doesn't have much in the way of tourist attractions and its reputation as one of the hottest places in Mozambique often discourages visitors. Yet the arid, brown landscape, dotted with baobab trees and cut by the wide swathe of the Zambezi River, gives it a unique charm and an atmosphere

EXPLORING MANICA PROVINCE

Although the Chimanimani National Reserve is the undisputed highlight, Manica province has many other attractions, including stunning terrain and a wealth of historical sites, including rock-art sites. Catandica town, en route to Tete, offers access to the beautiful Serra Choa plateau for self-drivers, while tiny Nhacolo, on the Zambezi River and with basic accommodation, holds the possibility for an interesting self-drive loop going via Sena, Caia, and the N1 south to Gorongosa park or north into Zambézia province. Once rehabilitation of the Dombe–Espungabera road is completed, other possibilities will also open, including combination itineraries with Zimbabwe. Work is well underway to open up tourism throughout the province, with an emphasis on ecotourism and community engagement, although as yet, there is little organised. Contact **Mozambique EcoTours** (www.mozecotours) for information on the latest developments, and for help with suggested routes and itineraries, as well as for information on combining exploration of Manica with visits to off-the-beaten track coastal destinations in Sofala province.

TETE PROVINCE

Tete province is an anomaly within Mozambique, lying inland and almost divided from the rest of the country by Malawi. While the south is hot and arid, northern Tete, much of which lies at altitude, enjoys a cooler climate, with beautiful hill panoramas. Tete province is also interesting as one of the few areas in Mozambique (in addition to Cabo Delgado) where you can see masked dancing, although it can be difficult to find. Try asking at the Casa de Cultura in the town centre.

---

quite unlike that of Mozambique's other provincial capitals.

History

Tete was an important Swahili Arab trading outpost well before the arrival of the Portuguese and today remains a major transport junction. It grew to significance during the 16th and 17th centuries when it served as a departure point for trade caravans to the goldfields further inland. At the end of the 17th century, it was all but abandoned when the Portuguese lost their foothold in the hinterlands. In the 18th century, it again began to prosper with the opening of the gold fair at Zumbo to the west and the expansion of goldmining north of the Zambezi. It became a regional administrative centre in 1767, and a hospital and a house for the governor were built. More recently, Tete received a boost with the building of the dam at Cahora Bassa, which opened in 1974. Today, with a population of roughly 50,000, it is one of the major towns in the Mozambican interior.

The main languages are Nyungwe, around Tete city; Chewa near the Malawi border; and Ngoni.

Information

mbondeiro Digital (Avenida Julius Nyerere; per hr Mtc60; 8.30am-6pm Mon-Fri, 9am-noon Sat) Just up from Univendas.

Immigration office (Rua Macombre) A few blocks up from Hotel Zambeze.

Standard Bank (cnr Avenidas Julius Nyerere & Eduardo Mondlane) ATM; next to Hotel Zambeze.

Sights & Activities

Tete's main sights are the impressive 538m-long **suspension bridge** that spans the Zambezi

River and the remains of an old Portuguese **fort** on the river near the bridge.

About 25km northwest of Tete, overlooking the river, is the **Missão de Boroma** (Boroma Mission). Founded in 1885 by Jesuit missionaries, it was known for its *colégio* (school), its carpentry-training centre and its attractive church. After being abandoned for many years, activities have recommenced on a small scale.

Northeast of Tete near the Malawi border is the district of **Angónia**, which is set on a plateau between 1000m and 1500m in altitude, and has a wonderfully cool and refreshing climate, especially if you've just come from Tete. It's also a scenic area and good for walks, although there are no tourist facilities. Ulóngwe, its pleasant capital, is just 20km west of the border and is closely tied into the Malawian economy; kwacha are accepted here as well as meticais.

Sleeping

There's camping at the very basic **Campismo Jesus é Bom** (campsite per person Mtc100), just over the bridge (on the north side), and 300m to your right.

Hotel Sundowner (r Mtc800-900) Just back from the river and just up from Motel Tete, with OK rooms – inspect a few, as they're not the cleanest – and meals.

Prédios Univendas (252-23198/9, 252-22670; Avenida Julius Nyerere; s/d with shared bathroom US$25/35, s/d from US$45/55;) The entrance to the rooms (most with fan, air-con and TV) is just around the corner from the Univendas shop on Avenida da Independência.

Smart Naira (82-686 4815; amadsatar@tdm.co.mz; Avenida da Independência just up from Avenida 24 de Julho; r Mtc1800-2750;) A small place catering to local business travellers. The clean, air-con rooms would be nothing special anywhere else, but they're a nice change of pace in Tete.

Motel Tete (252-22345; N103; r Mtc2000;) On the river, about 25 minutes on foot from the town centre along the main road to Changara, this unassuming place is a long standing Tete institution. Rooms are simple but pleasant. The older ones are low-ceilinged, and all are spacious with private bathroom and TV. There's also a riverside restaurant (no alcohol) serving large portions, and helpful management.

Hotel Zambeze (252-23101, 252-24000; Avenida Eduardo Mondlane; s/d Mtc2500/3500;) A large,

---

ZAMBEZI RIVER

The mighty Zambezi tumbles into Mozambique at Zumbo in western Tete province and flows about 1000km through the country before spilling into the sea near Chinde, south of Quelimane.

Up to 8km wide at points, it has long served as a highway between the coast and the interior. One of the notables it has carried is Livingstone, who took a paddle steamer up-river from the Zambezi delta to Tete before his progress was thwarted by the Cahora Bassa rapids. Earlier, Arab traders had made their way upriver at least as far as Sena and Tete, and the Portuguese had built settlements near the river delta in the hope of gaining access to western goldfields.

Apart from the bridge at Caia, the only links over the Mozambican portion of the river are the suspension bridge at Tete and the Dona Ana rail bridge between Mutarara and Sena.

---

multistorey place in the centre of town that's been recently renovated and is now trying to edge out Motel Tete for the honour of offering the best accommodation in town. Rooms have TV, some have minifridge, and there's a restaurant and snack bar. It's next to Standard Bank.

During the lifetime of this book, the **Park Inn Tete** (☎ in South Africa 011-245 8500; www.rezidorparkinn .com) is scheduled to open, targeting upmarket and business travellers.

Eating

Le Petit Café (cnr Avenidas Julius Nyerere & Liberdade; snacks & light meals from Mtc50; ⏲ 7.30am-8pm Mon-Sat; ✕) In Centro Comercial Fatima, with light meals, pastries, snacks and juices.

Pino's Restaurant (cnr Avenidas Julius Nyerere & Liberdade; pizzas & meals from Mtc180; ⏲ dinner) Just down from Le Petit Café at Clube de Chingale, with pizzas and Italian dishes.

Drinking & Entertainment

Good spots to enjoy a cool drink while watching the sun set over the Zambezi include the outdoor patio at Motel Tete, or (only go in a group) any of the small bars lining the river under the bridge.

Casa de Cultura (Avenida Eduardo Mondlane), near the Municipal Garden III Congresso at the lower end of town, provides information on upcoming cultural events.

Getting There & Away

AIR

LAM (☎ 252-22056; Avenida 24 de Julho) flies several times weekly to/from Maputo, Beira, Lichinga, Nampula, Quelimane and Chimoio. The airport is 6km from town on the Moatize road; take any chapa heading to Moatize.

BUS & CHAPA

For Chimoio (Mtc350, six to seven hours) transport leaves from opposite Prédio Emose on Avenida da Independência, just down from Smart Naira hotel and near Univendas. The first departures are between 4.30am and 5am.

To Songo (for Cahora Bassa Dam), several pick-ups daily depart from the old *correio* (post office) building in the lower part of town near the cathedral (Mtc120).

Chapas to Moatize (Mtc10) depart through out the day from the Moatize bus stand on Rua do Qua.

To Boroma, there are occasional direct cha pas leaving from Mercado da OUA. It's pos sible to hitch, although the going is slow. The best place to wait is at the Boroma road junc tion, about 1.5km west of Mercado da OUA

To Ulóngwe, there is at least one direc chapa departing daily from Mercado da OUA Otherwise, take any car heading to Zóbuè get out at the Angónia junction about 15km before Zóbuè and get onward transport from there.

For Malawi, chapas run to Zóbuè (Mtc70 two hours) and Dedza from Mercado da OUA on the western side of town. At the border you' need to change to Malawian transport.

For Harare (Zimbabwe), take a chapa to Changara (Mtc90, 1½ hours) from Mercado 1 de Maio, and get transport from there.

For Zambia, take a Moatize chapa over the bridge past the SOS compound to the petro station, where you'll find chapas to Matema and from there, infrequent transport t Cassacatiza on the border.

The efficient **Imperial Car Rental** (☎ 25 20261, 82-302 1344; imperialtete@hotmail.com) is a the airport.

CAHORA BASSA DAM & SONGO

About 150km northwest of Tete, near the town of Songo, is massive Cahora Bassa, the fifth-largest dam in the world. It was completed in 1974, and is set at the head of a magnificent gorge in the mountains and makes a good day or overnight trip from Tete. It's also a wonderful destination for anglers, and is renowned for its tiger fish.

History

Cahora Bassa Dam had its beginnings during the colonial era, when it was proposed as a means of flood control and for water storage to irrigate plantations downstream. The scheme was later enlarged to include a hydroelectric power station, with South Africa agreeing to buy most of the energy. Construction of the dam was highly politicised, with the Portuguese government intending it as a statement of its permanent presence in the region. Plans were made to place up to one million settlers, white and African, on the new farmland that the dam waters would irrigate. This was vigorously opposed by Frelimo. Party leadership viewed Cahora Bassa as a perpetuation of white minority rule in Southern Africa, and made blocking the dam's construction a major objective in the late 1960s. Opposition was organised on an international scale, as sympathetic groups in Western countries worked to discourage private investment.

Ultimately the contracts were signed and, despite repeated Frelimo attacks during construction, the massive undertaking was completed in 1974. To move all the equipment needed for the dam, existing roads and railways had to be modified, and a suspension bridge was built across the Zambezi at Tete. While resettlement of people living in the area was not as great a problem as it was with the construction of the nearby Kariba Dam on the Zambia–Zimbabwe border, more than 24,000 new homes had to be built.

Three decades after its construction, Cahora Bassa has not come close to fulfilling early expectations. One major reason was the destruction of power lines by Renamo rebels in the 1980s. Even after repairs were completed, power supplies remained grounded by contractual and pricing disputes between Mozambique, South Africa and Portugal. Silt is another impediment. Most of it is brought in via the Luangwa River, where overgrazing and poor farming practices lead to soil erosion and turn the waters muddy brown. In 2007 Portugal turned majority control of the dam over to Mozambique, finally opening the door for the dam to begin to reach its potential.

Information

The dam can be visited, including the impressive underground turbine rooms. To arrange a tour, contact the offices of **Hidroeléctrica de Cahora Bassa** (HCB; ☎ 252-82157, 252-82221/4) in Songo town and ask for Relações Públicas (Public Relations), which will help you organise things. There's no charge for a visit, and permits are no longer necessary to enter Songo. If you're already in Songo, ask locals to point you towards the HCB office in the *substação* (substation).

Sleeping & Eating

Centro Social do HCB (☎ 252-82454, 252-82508; r/ste Mtc1000/1250; 🖫) This pleasant place in the town centre has clean and comfortable twin-bedded rooms – all with fridge, window screens and private bathrooms with hot water – set in large, manicured grounds. Breakfast costs extra. Also here is Restaurante O Teles (meals from Mtc200).

Ugezi Tiger Lodge (☎ 82-599 8410, in South Africa 082-539 6411; www.ugezitigerlodge.com; campsite per person Mtc290, s/d Mtc1025/1580; 🖫 🖫) Anglers – or anyone wanting an escape to nature – will love this rustic fishing camp perched on a hill overlooking Lake Cahora Bassa. There's a choice of camping (tent rental possible), simple chalets on the densely vegetated hillside, or two eight- to 12-person self-catering houses. It's all very no-frills but the morning scenery on the lake at the base of the property (there's no beachfront) is beautiful. The restaurant serves delicious grilled fish, and boats are available

---

LAKE CAHORA BASSA

Lake Cahora Bassa, created by the dam, stretches for 270km westwards to the confluence of the Zambezi and Luangwa rivers on the Zambian border, and has the potential to generate more than 3500 megawatts of energy – enough to illuminate the entire region. En route, it partially covers the thundering Cahora Bassa rapids, which blocked David Livingstone's Zambezi River expedition in the late 1850s when he attempted to find a direct route into the interior.

for fishing charters and for lake tours up towards the dam. It's about 14km from Songo town and 6km beyond the dam.

Getting There & Away

There are frequent charter flights between Tete and Songo; check with the listed accommodation for details or ask at the airfield about seat availability.

Chapas run several times daily between Tete and Songo (Mtc120, three to four hours), departing Tete from the old *correios* building. Once in Songo, it's another 7km down to the dam, which you'll have to either walk or hitch. Ugezi Tiger Lodge does pickups from Tete.

ZÓBUÈ

Zóbuè, 115km northeast of Tete, is the main border town between Tete province and Malawi. There are a few basic *pensões,* and numerous moneychangers. Several vehicles go between here and Tete (Mtc60, two hours) daily. For more on getting to/from Malawi, see p184.

ZUMBO

Remote Zumbo's history dates back to at least 1715, when the Portuguese established a gold-trading fair at the eastern edge of the Luangwa River at its confluence with the Zambezi. The settlement grew rapidly and by the mid-18th century was one of the most prosperous European cities in Southern Africa, with numerous Portuguese trading houses. This boom was short-lived, and by 1765, Zumbo's wealth began to decline. The difficult overland journey along the Zambezi from Tete, shifting trade patterns, the town's fragile economic foundation and drought were all factors. By the mid-19th century, Zumbo had been all but abandoned and today it is little more than an oversized village.

Just downstream of Zumbo is **Chawalo Camp** (www.flycastaway.com), a rustic fishing lodge that needs to be booked as part of a multinight package based out of Luwangwa (Zambia).

The easiest access to Zumbo from Tete is via Zimbabwe or Zambia. On the Mozambican side, you can reliably get as far as Fingoé (north of the lake, and at the midway point between Songo and Zumbo) via public transport. From Fingoé to Zumbo, there's no public transport, but the road is passable with a 4WD. There is also an overcrowded boat, We have also heard of an overcrowded barge known as the *Kuza,* which sails roughly every two weeks between Zumbo and Songo, taking anywhere from four to eight days for the journey. Before taking it, it's worth keeping in mind that several previous boats plying this route have sunk.

SENA & MUTARARA

About 250km downstream from Tete along the Zambezi are the twin villages of Sena and Mutarara, known for the 3.6km Dona Ana railway bridge (built in 1934) which spans the river here. The bridge was being worked on when we passed through (no vehicles). There are a few basic *pensões* in both towns. The river here is known for its hippos, which you can sometimes see if you happen to be flying over in a charter flight, or by asking at your *pensão* for help to organise a local boat.

From Mutarara, you can continue north on an unpaved but reasonable road and a generally hassle-free border crossing into Malawi, or eastwards over the Shire River (bridged by a small, hand-cranked ferry, Mtc50) and then on to Morrumbala (where there's a good *pensão*) and the main road to Quelimane.

CAIA

About 60km further downstream from Sean and Mutarara is Caia, the main north–south crossing point. There's no decent accommodation in Caia itself, but in Catapu, 32km south of Caia along the main road, is the very good **M'phingwe Camp** (www.dalmann.com; s/d cabin with shared bathroom Mtc500/650, s/d cabin Mtc750/1000), with six rustic but spotless double cabins sharing facilities, plus one with its own bathroom. Note that there is no camping. Breakfast can be arranged with advance notice and there's a restaurant with tasty meals and cold drinks. Although most people just stop for an overnight, the surrounding forest is a fine birdwatching area and well worth longer exploration. The turn-off is signposted on the N1, from where M'phingwe is about 1.5km further.

North of Caia, signposted 1km north of the bridge and 800km off the N6, is the new **Cuácua Lodge** (☎ 82-312 0528; cuacualodge@gmail.com, s/tw Mtc1950/2400; ▨), with comfortable, well-appointed stone-and-thatch cottages, and a good restaurant with lovely views over the river. Birdwatching, river trips, forest walks and other excursions can be arranged.

The road from Inchope to Caia via Gorongosa village is good tarmac the entire way. From Caia northwards, it's being worked on, though it's in reasonable shape as far as Alto Molócuè. Chapas go daily between Caia and Sena.

The new Armando Emílio Guebuza toll bridge over the Zambezi River at Caia had just been inaugurated as this book was being researched. Tolls are Mtc80/800 for passenger vehicles/trucks.

MARROMEU

Marromeu is an old sugar-growing centre beside the Zambezi River, dating back to the late-19th century when the Portuguese Sugar Society of East Africa built a plantation and sugar factory here. After many years of neglect, the factory has been rehabilitated under Mauritian ownership, and is now Mozambique's largest sugar processing mill. There is no infrastructure to speak of other than that connected with the sugar company.

About 45km upriver from Marromeu, and easily accessed with 4WD from Caia, is **Chupanga Mission**, where Mary Moffat, wife of the missionary and explorer David Livingstone, is buried. She died here on 17 April 1862.

South of Marromeu begin the extensive wetlands of the Zambezi River delta, which is home to a wealth of water birds, including wattled crane, flamingo and pelican. On the coast is the **Marromeu Reserve** (Reserva de Marromeu) which was formerly known for its vast herds of buffalo – put by some estimates at

about 55,000 in the 1970s. Today only a fraction of that number remain, although plans are underway for restocking. The reserve is also home to populations of waterbuck, sable antelope, zebra and elephant, as well as rich birdlife. In 2004, it was proclaimed as a 'wetland of international importance' under the Ramsar convention.

In Marromeu town, there's accommodation at the basic but decent **Pensão Domino** (☎ 23-640420; r Mtc500). It's better, however, to base yourself at Catapu and explore from there.

Getting There & Away

There is an airstrip at Marromeu for charter planes. Chapas go daily to Marromeu from both Inhamitanga and Caia.

QUELIMANE

Bustling Quelimane is the capital of Mozambique's densely populated Zambézia province and heartland of the Chuabo people. While lacking the architectural charm of some other Mozambican towns – with the exception of the abandoned Portuguese cathedral near the waterfront, and the nearby mosque – its compact size and energetic atmosphere make it an agreeable place to break your travels.

Well outside town are several beaches that can't rival the coastal stretches further north or south, but make good getaways if you're based in Quelimane longer term. The riverfront is at its best at sunset.

CENTRAL MOZAMBIQUE

ZAMBEZI DONAS

Just as much a part of Quelimane history as the Bons Sinais River is the old Portuguese *prazo* system. As the Portuguese saw things, *prazos* were land-holdings granted to private individuals by the Portuguese government in an attempt to solidify control over the Mozambican hinterlands. The *prazeiro* (*prazo* holder) had to be a female Portuguese citizen who would then pass the *prazo* on to her female offspring when they married a white Portuguese. All sorts of rules and duties applied: the *prazeiro* was allowed to employ Africans, to raise a private army (generally made up of slaves) and to trade, and was responsible for maintaining law and order within the *prazo* area.

While some *prazos* were small, others were hundreds of square kilometres in extent. At the height of the system, the area encompassed by *prazos* was said to have been greater than the entire area of Portugal. By the 18th century, some *prazos* were effectively functioning as independent states, and the 'Zambezi *donas*' (as the *prazeiros* were known), enjoyed positions of prominence and power. Over time, the system became the basis for the rise of an Afro-Portuguese ruling elite, and formed a type of feudal aristocracy that dominated the affairs of the region.

However, the *prazo* system was inherently unstable and ultimately failed due in part to rivalries among the *prazeiros*, a scarcity of Portuguese women, African resistance, and poor economic performance. By the late-19th century, many of the *prazeiro* families had emigrated and the system lay in shambles. *Prazos* were finally abolished in the early 20th century when António Salazar came to power in Portugal.

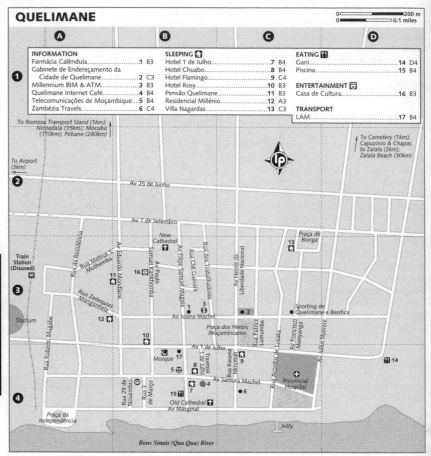

QUELIMANE

INFORMATION
Farmácia Calêndula............................1 B3
Gabinete de Endereçamento da
   Cidade de Quelimane.....................2 C3
Millennium BIM & ATM....................3 B3
Quelimane Internet Café..................4 B4
Telecomunicações de Moçambique..5 B4
Zambézia Travels.............................6 C4

SLEEPING
Hotel 1 de Julho..............................7 B4
Hotel Chuabo...................................8 B4
Hotel Flamingo.................................9 C4
Hotel Rosy.....................................10 B3
Pensão Quelimane..........................11 B3
Residencial Millénio........................12 A3
Villa Nagardas................................13 C3

EATING
Gani..14 D4
Piscina...15 B4

ENTERTAINMENT
Casa de Cultura...............................16 B3

TRANSPORT
LAM...17 B4

The excellent series of maps done by Coopération Française in collaboration with the local Conselho Municipal covers Quelimane – *Planta de Endereçamento da Cidade de Quelimane*. It's hard to find – try **Gabinete de Endereçamento da Cidade de Quelimane** (☎ 24-214912; 558 Avenida Josina Machel) in the Conselho Municipal building.

History
Quelimane stands on the site of an old Arab trading settlement dating to at least the 15th century and built on the banks of the Bons Sinais River in the days when this was still linked to the Zambezi River. Until the 19th century, when the river channel became clogged with silt, Quelimane served as the main entry

port to the interior. It was also an important export point for agricultural products, and a major slave-trading centre. Today few traces of this long history are evident and, apart from the cathedral, almost no old buildings remain.

Information
Farmácia Calêndula (☎ 24-213393; Avenida Josina Machel; ☻ 8am-8pm Mon-Sat, 9am-1pm Sun) For medical assistance.
Millennium BIM (Avenida Josina Machel) ATM.
Quelimane Internet Café (Avenida Samora Machel; per min Mtc1; ☻ 8am-6pm Mon-Fri, 9am-noon Sat) Diagonally opposite Hotel Chuabo. There's also wi-fi at Hotel Flamingo.
Telecomunicações de Moçambique (cnr Avenidas Samora Machel & Filipe Samuel Magaia) Near Hotel Chuabo.

Zambézia Travels (☎ 24-216174; travls@tdm.co.mz; Avenida Kwame Nkrumah) Helps with flight bookings and local travel arrangements. Diagonally opposite Hotel Chuabo.

Sleeping

Pensão Quelimane (☎ 24-212731; Avenida Eduardo Mondlane; s/d from Mtc450/900; ✷) Rather run-down, no-frills rooms, some with bathroom. There's no breakfast.

Hotel 1 de Julho (cnr Avenidas Samora Machel & Filipe Samuel Magaia; tw with shared bathroom Mtc500, with bathroom & air-con Mtc850; ✷) Near the old cathedral, this faded budget choice is a step up, with rooms containing fan, sink and bucket showers, a convenient location and meals available downstairs (breakfast is extra).

Hotel Rosy (☎ 24-214969; cnr Avenidas 1 de Julho & Paulo Samuel Kankhomba; s/d/tw Mtc1000/1150/1200; ✷) Centrally located near the central mosque, the Rosy has quite decent rooms – those on the ground floor have air-con, while those upstairs are marginally nicer, but with fan only. Breakfast is included in the price, and meals can be arranged.

Hotel Flamingo (☎ 24-215602; www.hflamingo .com; cnr Avenidas Kwame Nkrumah & 1 de Julho; s/d Mtc1550/1900; ✷ ☏ ☲) This recently reno-vated business and midrange travellers hotel has pleasant, good-value rooms, all with bathroom and air-con, plus a small pool, a tiny gym and a restaurant. Full breakfast is included in the price.

Residencial Millénio (☎ 21-213314; Rua Zedequias Manghanela; d/tw/ste Mtc1700/2200/2650) This con-verted villa has comfortable rooms but no meals. It's near Café Aguila and the cinema – head straight when exiting the cinema.

Villa Nagardas (☎ 24-212046; 79 Praça de Bonga; small/large r Mtc1900/2700; ✷) Villa Nagardas is a good choice, and one of Quelimane's nicest accommodation options, with African decor, pleasant, cosy rooms and a restaurant. It's near the municipal library.

Hotel Chuabo (☎ 24-213181/2; Avenida Samora Machel; s/d Mtc2100/2750; ✷) The Chuabo is a Quelimane institution – one of the few hotels anywhere in the country that managed to stay running throughout the war years. The spa-cious, faded rooms come with TV, fridge and air-con, and many have views over the river. The usually empty rooftop restaurant has rea-sonable meals, waiters in starched shirts and views over town.

Eating

Gani (Náutica; Avenida Marginal; meals from Mtc120; ☺ lunch & dinner) Quelimane's best dining, with riverside seating, good meals and good vibes, including music in the evenings. It's at the easternmost end of Avenida Marginal, near where it turns in to Avenida Maputo.

Piscina (Rua Filipe Samuel Magaia, just off Avenida Samora Machel; meals from Mtc150; ☲) This nicely refur-bished place has good meals and a pool, and is a popular spot for drinks in the evening.

Entertainment

The best place to find out about upcoming events is the **Casa de Cultura** (Avenida Paulo Samuel Kankhomba), near the 'new' cathedral. Montes Namúli, Zambézia province's excellent tradi-tional song and dance group, is based here, and it's often possible to watch its rehearsals.

Well-known local theatre groups include Falados da Zambézia, and Xenhê (pronounced wen-yay, the Chuabo word for 'scorpion'). As elsewhere in the country, theatre pieces here are frequently used to draw attention to social themes, or to carry out civic education on issues such as AIDS. For information on performances (all in Portuguese or Chuabo) ask at the Casa de Cultura.

Getting There & Away

AIR

LAM (☎ 24-212801; Avenida 1 de Julho) flies sev-eral times weekly to/from Maputo, Beira, Nampula and Tete. The airport is about 3km northwest of town at the end of Avenida 25 de Junho – start walking and you'll find a lift or ask your hotel to call one of Quelimane's handful of private taxis.

BUS & CHAPA

The transport stand (known locally as 'Romoza') is at the northern end of Avenida Eduardo Mondlane. Chapas run frequently to/from Nicoadala at the junction with the main road (Mtc30, 45 minutes).

To Nampula, a Grupo Mecula bus departs daily at 4.30am (Mtc350, 10 hours). Several ve hicles also run daily to Mocuba (Mtc120, two to three hours), from where you can get on-ward transport to Nampula via Alto Molócuè, or to the Malawi border at Milange.

To Gurúè (Mtc300, six to seven hours), there's a bus daily at 4.30am; buy your ticket the day before. Even with a ticket, it's best to show up early at the bus stand to be sure of a seat.

To Beira (Mtc690, nine hours), the best bet is TCO, which departs at 5am Tuesday, Thursday and Saturday from its office at Zambézia Travels.

Chapas to Zalala (Mtc25) depart Quelimane from the Capuchin mission *(capuzínio),* about 1km from the cemetery on the Zalala road.

AROUND QUELIMANE

The closest beach to Quelimane is **Zalala Beach**, about 30km northeast of town. It's long and wide, with sunrise views, a row of fringing palms, and a large village nearby. It's an ideal day excursion for getting a taste of local Zambézian life – at least until a planned large hotel project gets underway. The drive out from Quelimane is scenic, through extensive coconut plantations formerly owned by Companhia da Zambézia. As with other beach areas north of the Zambezi delta, the water here tends to be dark, lacking the turquoise hues of further north.

Zalala Beach Lodge (☎ 24-217055; www.zalalabeach .com; per person from US$75) was currently under construction when we visited, and scheduled to open around the time this book is published – contact it for an update. In addition to accommodation and a restaurant, it also plans to offer volunteering and cultural opportunities in the nearby village.

Chapas to Zalala (Mtc40, 45 minutes) depart Quelimane from the Capuchin mission, about 1km from the cemetery on the Zalala road.

PEBANE

About 280km northeast of Quelimane is Pebane – a fishing port and popular holiday destination during colonial times, and today a faded, quiet town not far from a long beach (though due to run-off from the Zambezi delta, don't expect the clear, turquoise waters that you'll find further north). There are inexpensive rooms with cold-water bucket baths and good meals at **Pensão Jamaima** (r Mtc300), near the administrator's house.

The South African–run **Pebane Fishing Charters** (☎ in South Africa 034-414 1058; mkuzesaf@ mweb.co.za; per person half-board US$80; ⚡) has well-maintained stone-and-thatch cottages facing the beach, and a restaurant.

About 6km north of town is **Macuacuane Lodge** (☎ 84-795 5925; www.macuacuane.com; s/d self-catering US$50/70), a rustic, Zimbabwean-run anglers camp with a few double chalets and fishing boat charters, and several more self-catering houses planned. It was temporarily closed when this book was researched – check for an update, and make a booking before showing up.

Pebane is reached in slow stages by public transport or with a 4WD, via Namacurra, Olinga (Maganja) and Mucubela. From Pebane northwards, it's best to go via Olinga to Mocuba and the main road northwards. Another option from Pebane heads north along a bush track (4WD) via the Gilé National Reserve to Gilé village and on to Alto Ligonha, from where it's straightforward to continue on to Nampula.

CULTURE ZAMBÉZIA STYLE

Zambézia province's rich culture is best discovered by getting out of Quelimane and into the surrounding districts. Namarrói, in the north of the province, is known for its snake dancers *(cobras de Namarrói).* After first performing a ritual to ensure success and safety, they go into the bush to capture snakes, dance with them and then return them alive to the bush.

In Morrumbala in southwestern Zambézia, and in bordering areas of Tete province's Mutarara district, you'll find marimba (known locally as *varimba* or *valimba)* players. Unlike the Chopi *timbila* (marimba) orchestras found in southern Mozambique, where each instrument is usually played by one person at a time, the large Morrumbala/Mutarara marimbas may be played by two or three people at once, often switching parts several times within the same song. The Morrumbala marimbas are also made using different materials and techniques, giving them a distinctive tone, although purists consider the tone quality of the *timbila* to be superior.

Gilé, northeast of Quelimane, is known for its dancers.

The best time to see local groups performing is on the *dia da cidade* (city/town day). Check with the Casa de Cultura or the local district administrator for information about upcoming events. None of these places have tourist facilities; you'll need your own vehicle or plenty of time to take public transport.

GILÉ NATIONAL RESERVE

Prior to the war, the 2100 sq km Gilé National Reserve (Reserva Nacional de Gilé) was home to elephants, buffaloes and other wildlife. It's currently being rehabilitated thanks to assistance from the French **Fondation IGF** (www.wildlife-conservation.org). According to a 2008 IGF survey, there are still populations – albeit small – of buffalo, elephants, sable antelope, leopard and other mammals.

The best road access is via Pebane or Alto Molócuè. There is no accommodation within the reserve, although camping is possible near Mualama (Mulela) on the reserve's southwestern corner, and there's a basic *pensão* in Gilé town, just north of the reserve.

MOCUBA

Mocuba – known for its dirty water and for being nobody's favourite Mozambican town – is the junction for travel between Quelimane and Nampula or Malawi. About 40km north, near Munhamade in Lugela district, are some **hot springs**. Also in Lugela district are the large **Mt Mulide caves** (cavernas do Monte Mulide), used during the war as a place of refuge by local populations. Both spots are considered sacred, and there are no facilities at either.

Do what you can to avoid staying overnight in Mocuba. If you do get stuck, **Pensão Cruzeiro** (☎ 24-810184; Avenida Eduardo Mondlane; r about Mtc400) on the main street has basic rooms and meals. **Muhamud's Take-Away** (snacks from Mtc50), near Millennium BIM, has samosas, burgers and, sometimes, yoghurt.

Transport to Quelimane (Mtc120, two to three hours) leaves from the market throughout the day. For Nampula, the best bet is to try to get a seat on the Mecula bus from Quelimane, which passes Mocuba from about 7am. There are several vehicles daily in the morning between Mocuba and Milange (Mtc200, four hours) departing from Mocuba's market, though you'll maximise your chances of a lift by walking west past the airstrip to the Milange road junction. Mocuba to Gurúè costs Mtc200.

MILANGE

Milange is a busy town on the border with southeastern Malawi with more than its share of hustlers. Millennium BIM has an ATM.

Pensão Reis (r Mtc500-1000), with hot running water, and the more basic **Pensão Fernandinho**

THE MAKUA

Although widely scattered today throughout large areas of central and northern Mozambique, most Makua people consider Mt Namúli as a common home. According to tradition, the Makua ancestors – all once living in the area around the mountain – split into several groups. Some followed the Malema River from its source on the mountain northwards into Nampula province, while others made their way southwards along the Licungo River (which also has its source on Namúli) into present-day Zambézia, thus resulting in the distinct Makua groupings of modern times.

(r Mtc500), with running water (although it's not always hot) are both centrally located and recommended as safe, with basic rooms, and meals with advance notice.

The road between Milange and Mocuba is fairly well travelled, and finding a lift usually isn't a problem. To Gurúè, there's sporadic public transport along a road to Molumbo, and from there to Lioma, from where you can get a chapa to Gurúè. Also see p184.

GURÚÈ

Gurúè sits picturesquely amid lush vegetation and tea plantations in one of the coolest, highest and rainiest parts of the country. Tea has long been one of the most important crops in Mozambique, and there are extensive holdings dating from colonial days. The surrounding area offers good walking and if you don't mind foregoing the comforts, it would be easy to spend up to a week here hiking in the hills.

Millennium BIM (Avenida da República) has an ATM, and nearby **Greenside Café** (per min Mtc1) has broadband internet access.

Sights & Activities

A good place to start is with a walk through the jacarandas on the northern edge of town. To get here, find the small church in the centre of Gurúè and head north along the road running in front of it. Continue for five to 10 minutes, following the edge of the hill and staying on the uphill side at the forks.

A popular destination for longer hikes is the **cascata** (waterfall) in the hills north of town. To get here, head first to the UP4 tea factory

MAKUA MARRIAGE CUSTOMS

Women contemplating marriage could take a tip from the matrilineal Lomwe-Makua people who live around Gurúè. Instead of the traditional exchange of gifts (lobola – bride price or dowry) to seal an engagement, an exchange of services is often required – anything from repairing a fence to building a house – so that the man is able to prove he can work. Another tradition stemming from the matrilineal culture is that after marriage, the groom sets up his house near that of his mother-in-law.

(also known as Cha Sambique), which you can see in the distance to the north; ask locals to point out the way and allow about 45 minutes on foot. From UP4, it's another 1½ hours on foot through overgrown tea plantations and forest to the falls, which will be to your right. En route are several detours offering beautiful views back down towards Gurúè. Swimming is possible in the pools above the falls. There are said to be some wild horses from colonial days in the surrounding hills, as well as herds of cattle. As the falls are situated in the middle of tea plantations, you will need permission to visit. This is free and can be obtained from the Gulamo company at their UP6 warehouse, a complex of white buildings several kilometres out of town off the Quelimane road; ask for Senhor Rafiq. At UP6 you may also be able to arrange to tour one of the tea factories, which still have much of their original equipment, including an old steam engine.

In the hills about 12km northeast of town is **Casa dos Noivos** – originally a honeymoon spot (hence its name, 'House of the Newlyweds'). It's well past its prime, but makes a good spot for watching the sunset. The house itself consists of a single room, with several other smaller houses on the property, presumably used to accommodate the accompanying entourage.

MT NAMÚLI

Rising up from the hills about 15km northeast of Gurúè are the mist-shrouded slopes of Mt Namúli (2419m), from which flow the Licungo (Lugela) and Malema Rivers. If you find yourself in the area with time to spare, it makes a scenic but challenging climb for which you'll need a good level of fitness and lack of a fear of heights (as there are several near-vertical spots where you'll need to clamber on all fours). The mountain is considered sacred by the local Makua people, so while climbing is permitted, you'll need to observe the local traditions. Guides – essential, as the route isn't straightforward and it's easy to get lost – can be arranged in Gurúè through Pensão Gurúè (opposite) or Pensão Monte Verde (opposite), but allow several extra days to sort out the logistics. The going rate for a guide is from about Mtc300.

Before setting out, buy some farinha de mapira (sorghum flour), rice and sugar at the market in Gurúè (it shouldn't cost more than Mtc50 for everything), to be used to appease both the spirits and the local régulo (chief). Also set aside an additional Mtc300 per person for further appeasement of the chief, and pack along some water purification tablets for yourself.

The climb begins about 6km outside Gurúè near UP5, an old tea factory. To reach here, head south out of Gurúè along the Quelimane road. Go left after about 2km and continue several kilometres further to UP5. With a vehicle, you can drive to the factory and park there. With a 4WD it's also possible to drive further up the mountain's slopes to Mugunha Sede, about 40km from Gurúè by road and the last village below the summit. There's no public transport.

Shortly before reaching UP5 you'll see a narrow but obvious track branching left. Follow this as it winds through unrehabilitated tea plantations and stands of bamboo and forest, until it ends in a high, almost alpine, valley about 800m below the summit of Mt Namúli. The views en route are superb. On the edge of this valley is Mugunha Sede, where you should seek out the chief, request permission to climb further and request a local guide for the remainder of the way. If you don't speak Portuguese, bring someone along with you who knows either Portuguese or the local language, Makua. If you've come this far with a 4WD, you'll need to arrange to leave it here. The sorghum flour that you bought in Gurúè should be presented to the chief as a gift, who may save some to make traditional beer and scatter the remainder on the ground to appease the ancestors. The chief will then assign someone to accompany you to the top of the mountain, where another short ceremony may be performed for the ancestors.

About two-thirds of the way from the village is a spring where you can refill your water bottle, although it's considered a sacred spot and it may take some convincing to persuade your guide to show you where it is. Just after the spring, the climb steepens, with some crumbling rock and places where you'll need to use your hands to clamber up. Once near the summit, the path evens out and then gradually ascends for another 1.5km to the mountain's highest point. The top of Namúli is often shrouded in clouds, so you may have better views during the climb than from the summit itself. After descending the mountain, present the rice that you bought at the Gurúè market to the chief as thanks.

Overnight Options

It's theoretically possible to do the climb in a long day from Gurúè if you get an early start and drive as far as Mugunha Sede, from where it's about three hours on foot to the summit. However in practice, this often doesn't work out, as you need to allow time to track down and talk with the chief; it's better to plan on at least an overnight.

To do the entire climb on foot from Gurúè, allow three days, walking the first day as far as Mugunha Sede (about seven to eight hours from Gurúè), where the *régulo* will show you a spot to camp or arrange basic accommodation in a local house. The second day, head up to the summit and back, sleeping again in Mugunha Sede and returning the next day to Gurúè. With an early start and good fitness levels, it's possible to combine the second and third stages into one long day. If you have an extra day available, there's a longer detour route possible via the UP4 warehouse and a beautiful waterfall. Camping on the summit isn't permitted (and isn't a good idea anyway because of rapidly and often dramatically changing weather conditions). At any time of year, be prepared for rain and cold during the climb. Also, if it's raining, the guide will definitely want an extra incentive to continue up to the summit.

Sleeping & Eating

Catholic Mission (Artes e Ofício; r with half-board Mtc400) Located on the edge of town, this place is clean, tranquil and good value, and provides tasty meals and hot water. The gates close at 9pm.

Pensão Monte Verde (Avenida da República; s/d Mtc500/550) This place on the main street near Millennium BIM has simple rooms with bathrooms and is worth checking out if Pensão Gurúè is full.

Pensão Gurúè (☎ 24-910050, s/d Mtc500/600) On the main street near Pensão Monte Verde, this is the best of the local-style guesthouses. Rooms have bathrooms, and meals can be arranged with lots of advance notice, as can guides for climbing Mt Namúli.

For meals, other than what you can arrange at the hotels, try Café Domino, just up from Pensão Gurúè, or Restaurante Zamzam. There's also inexpensive food in the large concrete building behind the market. The owners of Greenside Café are planning to open a supermarket soon. Meanwhile, for self-catering, try Aquíl Comercial near Restaurante Namúli.

Getting There & Away

From Nampula, take the Mecula bus to Alto Molócuè (Mtc150), where you can then get a waiting chapa on to Gurúè (Mtc200). Going in the other direction, you'll need to depart Gurúè by 5am at the latest for Nampevo junction to get a connection on to Nampula.

For connections to/from Quelimane, there's a daily direct chapa departing at 4.30am (Mtc300, six hours); buy tickets the day before. Otherwise there are several vehicles daily to Mocuba (Mtc200, 3½ to four hours), from where you can continue to Quelimane.

It's also possible to take the train from either Nampula or Cuamba to Mutuali, where you'll find a waiting open-backed pick-up truck on to Gurúè (Mtc150, four to five hours). This works best coming from Cuamba; coming from Nampula, most of the journey to Gurúè will be at night. There's also usually one vehicle daily between Cuamba and Gurúè (Mtc250 to Mtc300, five hours). To Milange, it's fastest to go via Mocuba.

Transport in Gurúè departs from near the market.

ALTO MOLÓCUÈ

This agreeable town is a refuelling point between Mocuba and Nampula.

Pensão Santo António (d Mtc450) on the main square has clean doubles and meals. Several vehicles daily go to/from Nampula (3½ hours) and Mocuba (four hours).

Northern Mozambique

If southern Mozambique's lures are the accessible beaches and relaxing resorts, in the north it's the paradisal coastal panoramas, the sense of space and the sheer adventure of travel. This is one of Africa's last frontiers – wild, beautiful and untamed. Inland are vast expanses of bush where enough lions and elephants still roam to be the stuff of local lore and wreak havoc on villages. Along the coast is an almost endless succession of unspoiled beaches and islands, plus Mozambique Island – one of southern Africa's most alluring destinations.

In many respects, the north – the provinces of Nampula, Niassa and Cabo Delgado – might as well be a separate country. It's divided from the rest of Mozambique by several major rivers and hundreds of kilometres of road. And, although home to one-third of Mozambique's population, it accounts for only one-fifth of the gross national product, has the lowest adult literacy rates and often seems to drop out of sight for the southern-oriented government.

Culturally, northern Mozambique is intriguing as the home of many matrilineal tribes, in contrast with the strictly patrilineal south. Islamic influences are also stronger here, with centuries-old ties to the ancient Swahili trading networks. The north is also the birthplace of Mozambique's independence struggle. It was here, in the bush, that the Frelimo cadres did their training, and it was here – in the unlikely village of Chai – that the first shots of war were fired.

In the main destinations – Nampula, Mozambique Island, Pemba, the Quirimbas Archipelago and Lichinga – there is enough infrastructure to travel as comfortably as you like. Elsewhere, most journeys are rough and rugged.

HIGHLIGHTS

- Wander at dawn through the streets of **Mozambique Island** (p133), taking in the surreal, time-warp atmosphere
- Go island hopping by dhow or chill out on your private slice of paradise in the **Quirimbas Archipelago** (p155)
- Revel in the rugged remoteness of the **Lake Niassa** (p144) shoreline and spend a night or three at **Nkwichi Lodge** (p146)
- Set off on one of the wildest safaris of your life in the **Niassa Reserve** (p147)
- Take a ride through the heart of rural Africa on the **Nampula–Cuamba train** (p141)

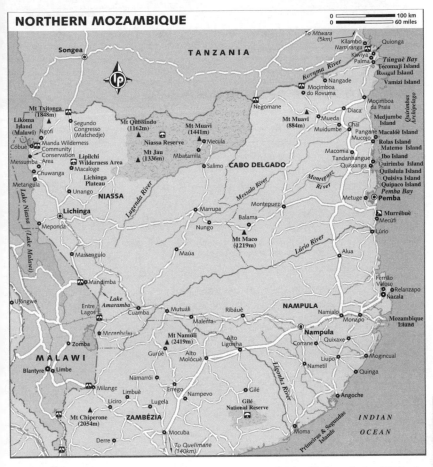

NORTHERN MOZAMBIQUE

Climate

In theory, the rainy season starts somewhat earlier in Mozambique's far north – from late December until March – although in recent years the rains have held off until later, around February, and have continued through to April. There's less rainfall along the coastal areas and more in inland areas at altitude.

Getting There & Away

There are straightforward air and road connections linking northern Mozambique with Tanzania and Malawi. If this is your focus, it's often less expensive and more time-efficient to enter from one of these neighbours than via Maputo. Once in Mozambique, there

are good north–south air links. While the north–south road situation is improving (it's mostly tarmac the whole way, following main routes), it's still a long journey; allow ample time for overland travel.

NAMPULA

Nampula – Mozambique's third-largest metropolis – is a crowded city with a hard edge. As the jumping-off point for visiting Mozambique Island, it's also an inevitable stop for many travellers. While there are few tourist attractions, Nampula's negatives are redeemed somewhat by its good facilities, broad avenues and its main plaza, graced by an imposing white cathedral and rimmed by flowering trees.

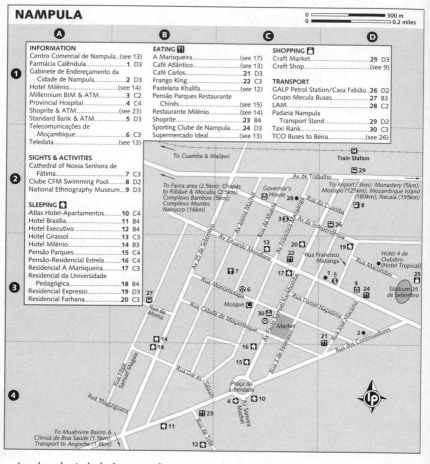

NAMPULA

INFORMATION	
Centro Comercial de Nampula..(see 13)	
Farmácia Calêndula....................**1** D3	
Gabinete de Endereçamento da	
Cidade de Nampula.................**2** D3	
Hotel Milénio.........................(see 14)	
Millennium BIM & ATM...........**3** C2	
Provincial Hospital.................**4** C4	
Shoprite & ATM......................(see 23)	
Standard Bank & ATM.............**5** D3	
Telecomunicações de	
Moçambique.........................**6** C3	
Teledata................................(see 13)	

SIGHTS & ACTIVITIES
Cathedral of Nossa Senhora de
Fátima...................................**7** C3
Clube CFM Swimming Pool.......**8** D2
National Ethnography Museum...**9** D3

SLEEPING
Atlas Hotel-Apartamentos.........**10** C4
Hotel Brasília...........................**11** B4
Hotel Executivo........................**12** C4
Hotel Girassol..........................**13** C3
Hotel Milénio...........................**14** B3
Pensão Parques........................**15** C4
Pensão-Residencial Estrela........**16** C4
Residencial A Marisqueira..........**17** C3
Residencial da Universidade
Pedagógica............................**18** B4
Residencial Expresso.................**19** D3
Residencial Farhana..................**20** C3

EATING
A Marisqueira...........................(see 17)
Café Atlântico..........................(see 13)
Café Carlos...............................**21** D3
Frango King..............................**22** C3
Pastelaria Khalifa......................(see 12)
Pensão Parques Restaurante
Chinês................................(see 15)
Restaurante Milénio..................(see 14)
Shoprite...................................**23** B4
Sporting Clube de Nampula.......**24** D3
Supermercado Ideal...................(see 13)

SHOPPING
Craft Market.............................**25** D3
Craft Shop................................(see 9)

TRANSPORT
GALP Petrol Station/Casa Fabião..**26** D2
Grupo Mecula Buses..................**27** B3
LAM..**28** C2
Padaria Nampula
Transport Stand......................**29** D2
Taxi Rank.................................**30** C3
TCO Buses to Beira....................(see 26)

Another plus is the lush surrounding countryside dotted with enormous inselbergs – large masses of smooth volcanic granite which intruded into the earth's crust aeons ago and were then exposed over the millennia by the erosion of the softer surrounding rock. Some soar close to 1000m into the air. For any technical climbing, you'll need to get permission from the local district administrator.

History
It's only recently that Nampula has come into its own, having spent much of the 19th century languishing in the shadow of nearby Mozambique Island. The construction of a rail link from the coast in the 1930s and the expansion of the city's port in the late 1940s boosted Nampula's growth as a rail junction and administrative centre. Today, it's the capital of Nampula province (Mozambique's second most populous province after Zambézia) and the commercial centre of the north.

Orientation
The train station and main transport stand are at the northern edge of town. About 10 minutes on foot southwest of here is the cathedral, a major landmark. Once at the cathedral, internet cafes, ATMs and several hotels are within easy reach, scattered around within about a 1km radius.

The best map, if you can manage to find one – check in local stationery shops or at **Gabinete de Endereçamento da Cidade de Nampula** (256 Rua

Daniel Napatima) – is *Planta de Endereçamento da Cidade de Nampula.*

Information
INTERNET ACCESS
There's wi-fi access in the lobby of Hotel Milénio.

Teledata (Centro Comercial de Nampula, Avenida Eduardo Mondlane; per hr Mtc80; ☺ 8am-noon & 2-8pm Mon-Fri, 9am-1pm & 3-7pm Sat) Internet access.

MEDICAL SERVICES
Clínica de Boa Saude (☎ 26-215092; Rua dos Viveiros, Bairro Muahivire) Missionary-run and one of the better bets if you're ill. Just off Avenida das FPLM.

Farmácia Calêndula (Avenida Eduardo Mondlane; ☺ 8am-8pm Mon-Sat, 9am-1pm Sun) One block up from the museum.

Provincial Hospital (Praça da Liberdade) Malaria testing.

MONEY
Centro Comercial de Nampula (Avenida Eduardo Mondlane) ATM inside; same location as Hotel Girassol.

Millennium BIM (cnr Avenidas da Independência & Francisco Manyanga) ATM.

Shoprite (Rua dos Continuadores) ATM at entrance.

Standard Bank (Avenida Eduardo Mondlane) ATM; just up from the museum.

TELEPHONE
Telecomunicações de Moçambique (Rua Monomotapa) Telephone calls; near the cathedral.

Sights & Activities
The **National Ethnography Museum** (Museu Nacional de Etnografia; Avenida Eduardo Mondlane; admission Mtc100; ☺ 9am-5pm Tue-Fri, 2-5pm Sat & Sun) is worth a visit, with a collection documenting various aspects of local life and culture, and explanations in English and Portuguese.

Nampula doesn't have as much to offer architecturally as Maputo and Beira, but there are a few intriguing buildings. The main one is the imposing **Cathedral of Nossa Senhora de Fátima**, in a large plaza flanked at one end by the governor's house.

The public **swimming pool** (Clube CFM; Rua 3 de Fevereiro; entry Mtc70) is a decent spot to cool off. The **pool** (Riháué Rd; adult/child Mtc100/50) at Complexo Bamboo is smaller and cleaner, and the surrounding greenery is pleasant.

About 5km north of town is a **monastery** run by a contemplative women's order, with an interesting church that is periodically open to the public. Follow the airport road

out of town past the roundabout to the first major fork; take the first left and watch for the small signpost.

Sleeping
BUDGET
Pensão Parques (Avenida Paulo Samuel Kankhomba; r without bathroom & with fan/air-con Mtc600/800) Rooms here are very basic, noisy and on the grungy side, but they are among Nampula's least expensive. Downstairs is a reasonably priced Chinese restaurant.

Hotel Brasília (☎ 26-212127; 26 Rua dos Continuadores; s/d/tw Mtc700/750/960; ☒) Hotel Brasília has clean rooms that are among the better-value choices in the budget category. All come with bathroom, and there's a small restaurant. It's close to Shoprite, but a 20-minute hike from the bus and train depots.

Residencial da Universidade Pedagógica (840 Avenida 25 de Setembro; s/tw Mtc800/1000) This university housing is in a quiet area next to Hotel Milénio, with simple, clean, secure, good-value rooms and breakfast. Overall, a good choice.

Residencial A Marisqueira (☎ 26-213611; cnr Avenidas Paulo Samuel Kankhomba & Eduardo Mondlane; s/d/tw Mtc800/850/1010; ☒) Residencial A Marisqueira has no-frills rooms (ask for one of the 'newer' ones), all with TV, plus a convenient (albeit busy) central location and a restaurant downstairs serving inexpensive local meals. There's no hot water, and the hallways and common areas seem to be permanently under construction.

Residencial Farhana (☎ 26-212527; Avenida Paulo Kankhomba; s/d/tw Mtc800/850/1010; ☒) Formerly Pensão Marques, this large, rather dingy edifice has a row of straightforward rooms – the doubles come with a rattling air-conditioner and musty private bathroom – plus hot water and TV. There's no food. Rooms to the front have small balconies, but they get the street noise; those to the back are quieter, but ventilation isn't as good.

Pensão-Residencial Estrela (☎ 26-214902; Avenida Paulo Samuel Kankhomba; tw without/with bathroom Mtc1190/1390) Proudly displaying its single star (only about half of which is actually merited), this shoestring establishment has overpriced twin-bedded rooms with fan – some with TV and minifridge – a tolerable shared bathroom, and a central but noisy and rather seedy location one block downhill from the post office. There's no food.

MIDRANGE & TOP END

Atlas Hotel-Apartamentos (☎ 26-218222; fax 26-218233; Avenida Samora Machel; s/d Mtc1300/1560; ☒) Spacious (though the bedroom itself is small-ish) and rather heavily furnished self-catering apartments with sitting room, kitchenette and fridge. It's at the southern edge of town near the hospital.

Residencial Expresso (☎ 26-218808/9; Avenida da Independência; s/d from Mtc1450/1750; P ☒) Six large, spotless, modern rooms with fridge and TV. Breakfast is included and meals can be arranged.

Complexo Bamboo (☎ 26-217838; www.teledata.mz /bamboo; Ribáuè Rd; s Mtc1500, d & tw Mtc2000; P ☒ ☒) Pleasant, well-maintained rooms (the twins are nicer than the doubles) in expansive grounds with a children's playground make this a good choice for families. All rooms have TV and minifridge and there's a popular restaurant. It's about 5km out of town – follow Avenida do Trabalho west from the train station, then right onto the Ribáuè Rd; Bamboo is 1.5km down on the left.

Hotel Executivo (☎ 26-219001/2; hotelexecutivo@tdm .co.mz; 370 Rua de Tete; s Mtc1990, d & tw Mtc2250; ☒ ☎) An efficient, newish place about two blocks down from Shoprite. All rooms have a view to the pool (which was closed at the time of research) and come with full buffet breakfast. There's also a restaurant.

Hotel Milénio (☎ 26-218877, 26-218989; hotel milenio@teledata.mz; 842 Avenida 25 de Setembro; tw/d/ste Mtc1950/1850/2500; ☒ ⬚ ☎) Another newish place with large rooms and a restaurant downstairs. Wi-fi is in the lobby only.

Hotel Girassol (☎ 26-216000; www.girassolhoteis .co.mz; 326 Avenida Eduardo Mondlane; s/d from Mtc2400/2750; P ☒) Upstairs in the Centro Comercial de Nampula high-rise, this four-star place has Nampula's priciest rooms – with TV and minifridge – although the price difference with the other options in this category isn't justified. Ask for a room with views over the cathedral and town.

Complexo Montes Nairucco (☎ 26-240081, 26-215297; idalecio@teledata.mz; Ribáuè Rd; campsite per person Mtc100, s US$50, d & tw US$65, day visit per person Mtc50) This Portuguese-run working farm is nestled under the towering Monte Nairucco about 16km west of town, and dotted with mango and orange groves. It makes a peaceful weekend retreat or day trip (open 6am to 10pm), with a reservoir where you can swim, a restaurant, a bar and a braai (bar-becue) area, plus walks in the vicinity. The camping ground overlooks the reservoir and gets high marks from overlanders. Taxis from town charge about Mtc350. If you're driving, follow the Ribáuè Rd for about 15km to the signpost, from where it's 1km further down a small lane.

Eating

Café Atlântico (Centro Comercial de Nampula, Avenida Eduardo Mondlane; snacks & meals from Mtc50; ☾ 6am-9pm; ☒) Burgers, pizzas and other light meals.

Pastelaria Khalifa (Rua de Tete; snacks from Mtc55) Coffees, sandwiches, snacks and milkshakes. It's next to Hotel Executivo.

Frango King (Avenida Eduardo Mondlane; half/whole chicken Mtc75/150; ☾ 7.30am-4am) Head here for grilled chicken to go, at almost any hour.

Pensão Parques Restaurante Chinês (Avenida Paulo Samuel Kankhomba; meals Mtc100-180) Reasonably priced Chinese food in a rather busy, unappealing location downstairs at Pensão Parques.

A Marisqueira (☎ 26-213611; cnr Avenidas Paulo Kankhomba & Eduardo Mondlane; meals Mtc150) Reasonably priced plates of the day.

Sporting Clube de Nampula (Avenida Eduardo Mondlane; meals from Mtc170; ☾ 8am-10pm) Next to the National Ethnography Museum, this long-standing watering hole features the usual chicken and fish grills, plus *feijoada* (a bean-and-sausage dish). There's inside and outdoor seating.

Café Carlos (☎ 26-217960; Rua José Macamo; meals from Mtc170; ☾ closed Sun) Just off Rua dos Continuadores in a small, walled courtyard, with reasonable meat and seafood grills, and a pizza oven.

Restaurante Milénio (Avenida 25 de Setembro; meals Mtc175-250, Sun buffet Mtc400; ☾ 6am-10pm; ☒) This hotel restaurant is short on ambience, but the food – Indian vegetarian dishes, piz-zas, Chinese and Portuguese – is good, and the English menu translation provides hu-mour while you wait. (Try Jab of Shrimp Pizza of Daisy, Beef in the Track Brag or Grilled Thread.)

Complexo Bamboo (☎ 26-216595; www.teledat .mz/bamboo; Ribáué Rd; meals from Mtc200; ☒) The outdoor restaurant at this hotel serves tasty versions of all the usual dishes in pleasant leafy surroundings.

Self-caterers can try **Shoprite** (Rua dos Continuadores; ☾ 9am-8pm Mon-Sat, to 3pm Sun) or

Supermercado Ideal (326 Avenida Eduardo Mondlane), in the Hotel Girassol building.

Shopping

The best place for crafts is the Sunday morning **craft market** (🕑 dawn-dusk) in the large stadium downhill from Hotel 4 de Outubro (the former Hotel Tropical). The best time to go is about 7am, before things get hot and crowded. Leave your bags at home, and watch out for pickpockets.

There's a small selection of ceramic Makonde pots, basketry and woodcarvings on sale behind the museum.

Getting There & Away

AIR

There are flights on **LAM** (☎ 26-213322, 26-212801; Avenida Francisco Manyanga; 🕑 7.30am-12.30pm & 2.30-5.30pm Mon-Fri) to Maputo (daily), Beira, Lichinga, Quelimane, Tete and Pemba (all several times weekly).

The airport is about 4km northeast of town (Mtc150 in a taxi).

BUS & CHAPA

Grupo Mecula buses go daily to Pemba (Mtc250, seven to eight hours) and Quelimane (Mtc350, 11 hours), all departing at 5am from the Grupo Mecula garage on Rua da Moma, just off Avenida 25 de Setembro and one block south of Rua Cidade de Moçambique in the area known as 'Roman'.

To Mozambique Island (Mtc120, three to four hours), chapas depart between 5am and 11am from the Padaria Nampula transport stand along Avenida do Trabalho east of the train station. Look for one that's going direct – many go only to Monapo, where you'll need to stand on the roadside and wait for another vehicle. The best connections are on one of the *tanzaniano* chapas, which depart Nampula between around 7am and 10am, depending on how early they arrive from Mozambique Island, and which continue more or less nonstop to the island. The Padaria Nampula transport stand is also the place to find chapas to Mossuril, Namapa, and other points north and east.

Vehicles to Angoche (Mtc120, three hours) – all go via Nametil – depart from about 5am from Muahvire bairro, along the extension of Avenida das FPLM. Go over the small bridge and continue all the way uphill to the start of the Angoche road.

TCO (☎ 82-509 2180, 84-601 6861) has twice-weekly bus service between Nampula and Beira (Mtc1600, 16 hours), departing at 4am in each direction, although the days vary. Departures in Nampula are from the GALP petrol station ('Casa Fabião') on Avenida da Independência, just east of Avenida Paulo Samuel Kankhomba.

Chapas to Mocuba leave from the 'Faina' area, about 2.5km west of the train station along Avenida do Trabalho near the Ribáuè road junction, but it's faster to take the Mecula bus to Quelimane and have them drop you.

It's also possible in theory to get transport from in the Faina area to Cuamba, although most people go via Gurúè or by train. If you do attempt this way (no public transport was running at the time of research), we've been told that there's accommodation en route at **Complexo Turístico Malaya** (☎ 26-340004; d about Mtc600; 🏊) in Malema, with small and surprisingly decent rondavels, and a restaurant.

TRAIN

A six-times weekly passenger train connects Nampula and Cuamba; see p141.

Getting Around

The main **taxi rank** (Avenida Paulo Samuel Kankhomba) is near the market. For car hire, the best bet is **Imperial** (☎ 26-216312, 82-300 5170; Imperialnampula@hotmail.com; airport).

ANGOCHE

Angoche, an old Muslim trading centre dating from at least the 15th century, was one of the earliest settlements in Mozambique. While little evidence of its long history remains, the area, and especially the nearby islands, are caught in an intriguing time warp, and you can still hear Arabic spoken in many areas.

For internet access, visit **Intra BroadBand** (Avenida Liberdade; per min Mtc1); head next door to Millennium BIM for an ATM.

History

Angoche (formerly António Ennes) initially gained prominence as a gold and ivory trading post. By the late-16th century, the town had been eclipsed by Quelimane as an entry port to the interior. However, it continued to play a role in coastal trade and was an important economic and political centre, with close ties to Mozambique Island. In the 19th century, Angoche became the focus of the clandestine slave trade, which continued until the 1860s when the town was attacked by the Portuguese. While effective Portuguese administration was not established until several decades later, the attack marked the beginning of Angoche's downfall and the town never regained its former status.

Sights & Activities
There's a small but lively afternoon **fish market** near the Catholic church. Go left and down towards the water after passing the church.

About 7km north of town is the long, wide and stunning **Praia Nova** (New Beach), with perhaps the whitest sand that you'll see anywhere. It has no shade or facilities. The start of the road to reach Praia Nova is a few blocks past the far (northern) end of the park (past O Pescador restaurant), from where it's 7.5km further – you'll need to walk or hitch. About 45km further on is the village of **Quinga**, near another beautiful stretch of sand for which you'll need your own 4WD transport.

Dhows or motorised boats to the nearby **islands** can be arranged at the *capitania* (maritime office), at the base of the main road near the Praça dos Heróis. Dhows also leave frequently from the fish market.

Stretching well south of Angoche towards Moma and on to Pebane are the archipelagos of the **Primeiras and Segundas Islands**, slated to be Mozambique's newest protected area. Several of the islands are favoured as nesting areas by local green turtles and many are encircled by coral reefs. Dugongs are also frequent visitors. There are no tourist facilities yet, although several projects are underway.

Sleeping & Eating
Pensão Mafamete (s/d/tw Mtc200/300/400) This very basic place is the best of the local *pensões* (inexpensive hotels), with a few clean rooms in a building that was under renovation when we visited. All have fan, but no nets (although the windows are screened), and all share bathrooms without water. There's no food available. When entering town, turn off the main road to the left at the first round marker in front of the Governo building. Go three blocks down – Mafamete is on your left, on the final block before reaching a small park.

Hesada Apartments (☎ 026-720327/8, 82-666 8880; hetulsacicant@gmail.com, www.hesadapartments.webs.com; d/apt Mtc500/1000; ✕) This group of rooms

and apartments is the best accommodation in Angoche. On offer are several rooms in the city centre, plus two self-catering apartments in a quiet area on the outskirts of town. All are clean and pleasant, and have en suite and reliable 24-hour water supply (a rarity in Angoche). The apartments – each with two rooms – also have well-equipped kitchens. The owner is very helpful with information about Angoche and the surrounding area, and also has a 4WD vehicle available for rent in the Angoche area.

Casa de Hospedes Inas (☎ 21-720612; self-catering house Mtc1300) If the Hesada Apartments are booked, this place – a three-room self-catering house that is only rented out in its entirety – is the next best bet. It's in the Mooxelele area behind the Catholic church, but to book or get the key you'll need to go first to the INAS ('Acção Social') office on the park, just around the corner from Pensão Mafamete.

Restaurante O Pescador (☎ 84-470 8481; meals from Mtc150; ☾ lunch & dinner Mon-Sat) O Pescador has good, well-prepared meals, a cool interior with checked tablecloths, and shaded parking. On Sunday, it's sometimes possible to arrange meals in advance with the proprietress. It's around the corner from Pensão Mafamete on the park – look for the blue-and-white parking awning.

Getting There & Away
Chapas go daily to/from Nampula (Mtc120, four hours), departing from the transport stand at the top entrance to town, about 1km from the central area. All go via Nametil. The route via Corrane (Nampula–Corrane–Liupo–Angoche) is possible with your own high-clearance 4WD, but not recommended, as the stretch from Corrane to Liupo is in poor condition and almost devoid of vehicle traffic – not optimal should you have a breakdown.

With your own transport (4WD), or with time and persistence on public transport, it's possible to travel between Angoche and Monapo (near Mozambique Island) via the sizeable settlement of Liupo. This route had just been graded when this book was researched, and was in good condition.

The beach at Quinga can be reached with your own vehicle from Angoche (going inland via Namaponda), or via Liupo, from where there's a daily chapa on to Quinga. There is no direct public transport between Quinga and Angoche. The owner of Hesada Apartments (see opposite) can also help with 4WD rental in and around Angoche.

MOZAMBIQUE ISLAND (ILHA DE MOÇAMBIQUE)

Tiny, crescent-shaped Mozambique Island (Ilha de Moçambique) measures only 3km in length and barely 500m in width at its widest section. Yet it has played a larger-than-life role in East African coastal life over the centuries, and today is one of the region's most fascinating destinations. Close your eyes for a minute and imagine the now-quiet streets echoing with the footsteps of Arab traders, ushered in on the monsoon winds. Or hear the crisp voice of the Portuguese governor-general barking orders from his plush quarters

in the Palácio de São Paulo. Or try to imagine the sweat, anger and despair of the Africans herded into the closed cells of the Fort of São Sebastião before being sold into slavery.

Today, Mozambique Island is an intriguing anomaly – part ghost town and part lively fishing community. It's also a picturesque and exceptionally pleasant place to wander around, with graceful praças rimmed by once-grand churches, colonnaded archways and stately colonial-era buildings lining the quiet, cobbled streets of the Stone Town. In Makuti Town, with its thatched-roof huts and crush of people, narrow alleyways echo with the sounds of children playing and chickens squawking, while fishermen sit on the sand repairing their long, brightly coloured nets.

MOZAMBIQUE ISLAND (ILHA DE MOÇAMBIQUE)

INFORMATION
BIM..1 B2
Capitania (Port Captain's Office).2 B2
Immigration Office.......................3 A2
Telecomunicações de
   Moçambique.............................4 A1

SIGHTS & ACTIVITIES
BIM Bank.................................(see 1)
Chapel of Nossa Senhora de
   Baluarte...................................5 D1
Church of Santo António.............6 B4
Church of the Misericórdia...........7 A1
Colonial Administration Offices...8 B3
Fort of São Sebastião..................9 D1
Hindu Temple............................10 B2
Maritime Museum...................(see 12)
Mosque.....................................11 A3
Museum of Sacred Art..............(see 7)
Palàce & Chapel of São Paulo...12 A1
Pool.......................................(see 21)

SLEEPING
Amakuthini (Casa de Luís).........13 A3
Casa Branca...............................14 A2
Casa das Ondas.........................15 C2
Casa de Dona Kero....................16 B2
Casa de Dona Shamu.................17 B2
Casa de Yasmin.........................18 C2
Hotel Omuhi'piti........................19 D1
Mooxeleliya..............................20 A1
O Escondidinho.........................21 B2
Patio dos Quintalinhos...............22 A3
Residencial Amy........................23 B2
Ruby Backpacker........................24 B2

EATING
Bar Flôr de Rosa........................25 B3
Bar-Restaurante Watólofu.........26 B2
Café-Bar Âncora d'Ouro.............27 A1
O Escondidinho.....................(see 21)
O Paladar..................................28 B2
Relíquias....................................29 A1
Shipping Container Shop............30 B2

TRANSPORT
Dhows to Cabaceira Grande......31 B2
Fish Market & Dhows across
   Mossuril Bay...........................32 A2
Transport Stand.........................33 A4

Since 1991, this cultural melting pot has been a Unesco World Heritage site and, while there are still many crumbling ruins, there's fresh paint and restoration work aplenty.

Interestingly, there are no wells on Mozambique Island; it was settled despite the lack of water sources because of its favourable location and natural harbour. To compensate, most houses in the early days had cisterns, as did the Fort of São Sebastião, which had three. Now, water is piped in from the mainland.

History

For most of its history, Mozambique Island has served as a meeting point of cultures and a hub of Indian Ocean trade. As early as the 15th century it was an important boat-building centre, and its history as a trading settlement – with ties to Madagascar, Persia, Arabia and elsewhere – dates back well before that. Vasco da Gama landed here in 1498 and in 1507 a permanent Portuguese settlement was established on the island. Unlike Sofala to the south, where the Portuguese also established a foothold at about the same time, Mozambique Island prospered as both a trading station and naval base, with connections to places as far away as Macau and Goa. In the late-16th century, the sprawling Fort of São Sebastião was constructed. The island soon became capital of Portuguese East Africa – a status that it held until the end of the 19th century when the government was transferred to Lourenço Marques (Maputo). As focus shifted southwards, Mozambique Island's star began to fade. The construction of a rail terminus at nearby Nacala in 1947 and the development of the Nacala port during the 1950s sealed the island's fate and sent it into an economic decline from which it never recovered.

Apart from its early strategic and economic importance, Mozambique Island also developed as a missionary centre. Beginning in the 17th century, numerous orders established churches here and Christians intermixed with the island's traditional Muslim population and Hindu community. Various small waves of immigration over the years – from places as diverse as East Africa, Goa and Macau – contributed to the ethnic and cultural mix and the resulting melange is one of the island's most intriguing aspects. Over the last century, as the Portuguese presence on the island has faded into obscurity, Muslim influence has reasserted itself and, together with local Makua culture, is now dominant.

Orientation

Mozambique Island's fusion of cultures is best seen in Stone Town, as the quiet, cobwebbed northern half of the island is known. Here, you'll find the majority of historic buildings, most constructed between the early-16th and late-19th centuries when the Portuguese occupied the island and most original residents were banished to the mainland. Makuti Town – the island's younger, more colourful southern half – reflects Mozambique Island's other face. It dates from the late-19th century, and is where most islanders now live with daily Makua life going on much as it has for centuries. The waterfront in between, along the island's eastern edge, is known as the *contracosta*.

Maps are available from vendors at the entrance to the governor's palace.

Information

BIM (Avenida Amilcar Cabral) Has an ATM, and changes cash (US dollars, euro and rand).

MUSIRO

All along the northern coast, and especially on Mozambique Island, you'll frequently see women with their faces painted white. The paste is known as *musiro* (also *n'siro* or *msiro*), and is used as a facial mask to beautify the skin, and sometimes as a sunscreen by women working in the fields, or as a medicinal treatment (though the medicinal paste usually has a yellowish tinge). *Musiro* was also traditionally applied in ways that conveyed messages – for example whether the wearer was married, or whether her husband was away – although most of the meanings have since been lost.

Musiro is made by grinding a branch of the *Olax dissitiflora* tree (known locally as *ximbuti* or *msiro*) against a stone with a bit of water. Local women usually leave the mask on for the day, and sometimes overnight. If you go walking in villages early in the morning and see women with white paste on their hands, chances are that they are in the midst of preparing *musiro*.

Immigration Office Diagonally opposite Mooxeleliya.
Telecomunicações de Moçambique (per min Mtc1;
⏱ 7.30am-8pm) Internet access and international calls;
near the Palace and Chapel of São Paulo.

Sights
PALACE & CHAPEL OF SÃO PAULO
This imposing **edifice** (Palácio de São Paulo; ☎ 26-610081; adult/child Mtc100/25; ⏱ 9am-4pm) – the former governor's residence and now a museum – dates from 1610 and is the island's historical showpiece. The interior has been renovated to give a remarkable glimpse into what upper-class life must have been like during the city's 18th-century heyday. In addition to an impressive collection of knick-knacks from Portugal, Arabia, India and China, there are many pieces of original furniture, including an important collection of heavily ornamented Indo-Portuguese pieces. In the chapel, don't miss the altar and the pulpit, the latter of which was made in the 17th century by Chinese artists in Goa. On the ground floor is the small **Maritime Museum** (Museu da Marinha, closed at the time of writing), with relics hauled up from the surrounding depths. Behind the palace are the **Church of the Misericórdia** (still in active use) and the **Museum of Sacred Art** (Museu de Arte Sacra), containing religious ornaments, paintings and carvings. The museum is housed in the former hospital of the Holy House of Mercy, a religious guild that assisted the poor and sick in several Portuguese colonies from the early 1500s onwards. The ticket price includes entry to all three museums.

FORT OF SÃO SEBASTIÃO
The island's northern end is dominated by the massive **Fort of São Sebastião** (⏱ 8am-5pm, closed for renovations at the time of writing), which is the oldest complete fort still standing in sub-Saharan Africa. Construction began in 1558, and about 50 years later the final stones were laid. Just beyond the fort, at the island's tip, and also inaccessible at the time of writing due to ongoing renovations, is the whitewashed **Chapel of Nossa Senhora de Baluarte**. Built in 1522, it's considered to be the oldest European building in the southern hemisphere and one of the best examples of Manueline vaulted architecture in Mozambique. At the southern tip of the island, keeping watch over the fishing port, is the impressive (and no longer used) **church of Santo António**. Nearby is a **cemetery** with Christian, Muslim and Hindu graves.

OTHER SIGHTS
Other places to watch for while wandering through Stone Town include the restored, ochre-toned **BIM bank** (Avenida Amilcar Cabral) and the ornate **colonial administration offices** overlooking the gardens east of the hospital. A few blocks north of the market is the recently restored **Hindu temple** and on the island's western edge a fairly modern **mosque** painted an unmissable shade of green.

Activities
While Mozambique Island has several small beaches – the cleanest of which is Nancaramo Beach, next to the fort – it's much better to head across Mossuril Bay to Chocas (p138) and Cabaceira Pequena, where there is beautiful, clean sand. Strong tidal flows make it dangerous to swim around the northern and southern ends of Mozambique Island. For cooling off, try the small **pool** (Avenida dos Heróis; adult/child Mtc50/25) at O Escondidinho. For excursions to the outlying islands, see p137.

Sleeping
There's a reasonably good range of accommodation on the island, but at the budget level, many of the rooms are small and poorly ventilated. If your funds permit, it's worth paying a modest amount more for one of the midrange places.

BUDGET
Casuarina Camping (☎ 82-446 9900; casuarina09@hotmail.com, helenaabelali@gmail.com; campsite per person Mtc150, r per person Mtc700) Casuarina is on the mainland opposite Mozambique Island, just a two minute walk from the bridge. On offer is a well-maintained camping ground on a small beach (where you can also swim), plus simple bungalow-style rooms, ablution blocks with bucket-style showers and meals. Entry costs Mtc120 for vehicles; day visitors pay Mtc25.

Otherwise, the cheapest options are in local homes, most with small, basic rooms in the family quarters. These include:

Amakuthini (Casa de Luís; ☎ 82-436 7570, 82-540 7622; dm Mtc300, s/d with shared bathroom Mtc350/700) Very basic, but tidy and welcoming, and the closest you can get to experiencing daily life in Makuti Town. It has an eight-bed dorm and several small, dark rooms with fan in a tiny garden behind the family house. All accommodation has nets, and the room price includes breakfast. There are also rustic cooking facilities, laundry service and a refrigerator. Meals can be arranged with advance notice. It's on the edge of Makuti Town: take the first left after passing the green mosque (to your right), and watch for the signpost.

Ruby Backpacker (☎ 84-398 5862; ruby@the mozambiqueisland.com; dm Mtc350, tw/d Mtc800/900) A new place with dorm beds, twin and double rooms, a self-catering kitchen, hot showers, a bar, rooftop terrace and tourist info. It's near the police post and the Palace and Chapel of São Paulo.

Casa de Dona Kero (☎ 26-610034; Contracosta; r Mtc400) A small house with small rooms, all with fans but no nets, and on the stuffy side, but the proprietors are friendly. Price includes continental breakfast. It's opposite Complexo Índico.

Residencial Amy (Avenida dos Heróis; d Mtc450) Near the park, with several basic, dark rooms – most lacking exterior windows – in the main house and a common area with TV.

Casa de Dona Shamu (Avenida dos Heróis; r Mtc500) Just down from Residencial Amy, and of similar standard.

Casa de Yasmin (☎ 26-610073; Rua dos Combatentes; r from Mtc500) Near the cinema at the island's northern end, with a handful of small rooms – some with bathroom and some being upgraded to have air-con – in an annex next to the family house. There's no food available.

MIDRANGE

Casa das Ondas (☎ 82-438 6400; r without/with bathroom Mtc600/750) Another good-value place, with three rooms (one with private bathroom), a sitting area, a kitchen and a bougainvillea-bedecked courtyard. It's just to the left of the cinema and unmarked – look for the arched windows.

Casa Branca (☎ 26-610076; flora204@hotmail.com; Rua dos Combatentes; r with shared bathroom Mtc750, with minifridge & bathroom Mtc1000) On the island's eastern side near the Camões statue, Casa Branca has three simple but spotless rooms with views of the turquoise sea just a few metres away and a shared kitchen. One room has its own bathroom, and the other two share. Rates include breakfast. Adjoining is a seaside garden/sitting area.

Mooxeleliya (☎ 26-610076, 82-454 3290; flora204@ hotmail.com, ia_petersson@hotmail.com; d without/with air-con Mtc750/1500, f Mtc1500) Under the same management as Casa Branca and also recommended – the Makua name translates roughly

as, 'Did you rest well?'. It has five simple but spacious high-ceilinged rooms upstairs and two darker, slightly musty three- to four-person family-style rooms downstairs. All rooms have their own bathroom, breakfast is included and there's a small cooking area with refrigerator and a communal TV/sitting area. It's just down from the Church of the Misericórdia.

Patio dos Quintalinhos (Casa de Gabriele; ☎ 26-610090; www.patiodosquintalinhos.com; Rua do Celeiro; s/d with shared bathroom US$20/25, d US$30, q & ste US$35; P) A cosy place opposite the green mosque, with a handful of comfortable, creatively designed rooms around a small courtyard, including one with a loft, and a suite with its own skylight and private rooftop balcony with views to the water. All have bathroom, except for two tiny rooms to the back. There's also a rooftop terrace and secure parking; breakfast is included and meals can sometimes be arranged, as can bicycle and vehicle rental and excursions to the outlying islands.

O Escondidinho (☎ 26-610078; ilhatur@teledata.mz; Avenida dos Heróis; r Mtc1000-1950;) This atmospheric place has spacious, high-ceilinged rooms, all with nets, ceiling fans and mosquito netting in the windows, plus a garden courtyard, and a good restaurant. A few rooms have private bathroom. It's near the public gardens.

Hotel Omuhi'piti (☎ 26-610101; h.omuhipiti@teledat .mz; s/d from Mtc1900/2200;) In a good setting at the island's northern tip, this three-star establishment has modern, quiet rooms, most with views over the water. Breakfast is included and there's a restaurant.

Eating

O Paladar (meals from Mtc100; lunch & dinner) At the eastern corner of the old market and unmarked, O Paladar is the place to go for local cuisine. Stop by in the morning and place your order with Dona Maria for lunchtime or evening meals.

Bar-Restaurante Watólofu (off Rua dos Combatentes; meals Mtc130-250; lunch & dinner) This quiet establishment is tucked into an unsignposted walled compound behind O Escondidinho. It serves tasty grilled chicken, squid, shrimp and other local dishes.

Café-Bar Áncora d'Ouro (☎ 26-610006; light meals from Mtc150; 8am-11pm Wed-Mon) A good bet, featuring muffins, pizzas, sandwiches, soups, homemade ice cream, waffles and other goodies, plus prompt service and airy seating. It's diagonally opposite the Church of the Misericórdia.

Relíquias (Avenida da República; meals Mtc160-230; ☺ 10am-10pm Tue-Sun) Another good spot, with well-prepared seafood and meat dishes, plus prawn curry, *matapa* (cooked cassava leaves with peanut sauce) and coconut rice. It's near the museum, and has seating indoors or outside overlooking the water.

Bar Flôr de Rosa (☎ 82-745 7380; snacks from Mtc50, meals from Mtc200; ☺ 5pm-midnight Wed-Mon; 🖳) This small, chic Italian-run place has delicious coffees and espressos, a selection of pastas, soups and snacks, and a rooftop terrace for sundowners. It's near the hospital.

O Escondidinho (☎ 26-610078; meals about Mtc350) The restaurant at this hotel has a changing daily menu featuring well-prepared shrimp, crayfish and other seafood dishes with French overtones and tables near the small garden.

For self-caterers, there's a well-stocked shipping-container shop next to the market.

Entertainment

Mozambique Island is a good place to see *tufo* dancing, although finding it can be a bit of a challenge. Try asking at your hotel, and checking with staff at the museum.

The best time to experience Mozambique Island's time-warp atmosphere is just before dawn, or on an evening when the power goes off, especially if there's a full moon.

Getting There & Away

AIR

There's an airstrip at Lumbo on the mainland for charter flights.

BUS & CHAPA

Mozambique Island is joined by a 3.5km bridge (built in 1967) to the mainland. Most chapas stop about 1km before the bridge in Lumbo, where you'll need to get into a smaller pick-up to cross over Mossuril Bay, due to vehicle weight restrictions on the bridge.

Leaving Mozambique Island, all transport departs from the bridge. The only direct cars to Nampula (Mtc120, three hours) are the *tanzaniano* minibuses, with at least one or two departing daily between 3am and 5am. The best thing to do is to ask at your hotel for help to get a message to a chapa driver to collect you. Alternatively, go the day before to the minibus stop in Lumbo and arrange with a driver to be picked up at your hotel. Currently only one (departing about 5am) goes nonstop to Nampula. After about 6am, the only option is open pick-up trucks to Monapo (Mtc40, one hour), where you can get transport on to Nampula or Nacala.

Once in Nampula, there are daily buses north to Pemba and south to Quelimane, though both leave early so you'll need to overnight in Nampula. To head direct to Pemba, take the 4am *tanzaniano* as far as Namialo, where – with luck – you can connect with the Mecula bus from Nampula, which passes Namialo about 6am.

Chapas to Lumbo cost Mtc5. If you're driving, wide vehicles won't pass over the bridge, and maximum weight is 1.5 tonnes. There's a Mtc10 toll per vehicle payable on arrival on the island. Chartering a vehicle from Nampula to Mozambique Island costs about Mtc3000 one way.

AROUND MOZAMBIQUE ISLAND
Goa Island

This tiny island (known locally as Watólofu) is about 5km east of Mozambique Island. It has a lighthouse that was built during the 1870s, and is today run by a lighthouse keeper and his family, who have lived on Goa for more than 20 years. The lighthouse is now solar powered, and according to the keeper, the batteries give out about 1am. You can climb to the top for some views.

The island's name comes from the its position on the sea route from Goa, India, which was the base for local Mozambican government between 1509 and 1662.

Before visiting, get permission at the *capitania* on Mozambique Island; it's free and can be arranged on the spot. You'll also need to hire a motorised dhow (about Mtc1500/2500 per five-/seven-person boat plus about Mtc750 for petrol), which can be done directly at the *capitania*, or through most hotels. Be prepared for choppy seas, and tidal limits on the length of time you can spend on the island. Allow about 40 minutes one way with favourable winds and currents; in unfavourable conditions, allow at least double this.

Sena Island

About 2km south of Goa Island is Sena Island (also known as the Island of Cobras). It takes its name from its location along the old sea

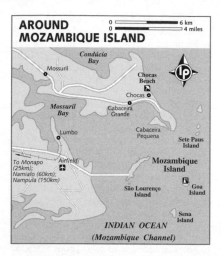

AROUND MOZAMBIQUE ISLAND

a restaurant serving Portuguese cuisine. It's signposted from the entrance to Chocas. Discounted midweek rates are available.

CABACEIRA PEQUENA
Continuing south from Chocas town along a sandy track roughly paralleling the beach takes you to **Cabaceira Pequena**, with a beautiful white-sand beach and views across the bay to Mozambique Island. Just inland are the ruins of an old Swahili-style mosque and the ruins of a cistern used as a watering spot by Portuguese sailors.

Carrusca Mar & Sol (☎ 82-516 0173, 26-213302; r.falcao@idppe.org; 4-/7-person bungalows Mtc1250/2750) is a good, relaxing accommodation choice, with a handful of large, spotless, nicely outfitted bungalows with terraces, all set on a rise between the mangroves and one of the best stretches of beach. There's also a restaurant featuring seafood, pasta and pizza (meals about Mtc260), a small children's playground and sunset views of Mozambique Island. It's about 2km south of Chocas town, en route to Cabaceira Pequena. Advance bookings are essential on weekends and holidays.

Varandas (campsite per person Mtc75; closed at the time of research) Camping (bring your own tent) under simple thatched shelters on the beach at Cabaceira Pequena, several kilometres past Carrusca Mar & Sol. Bring everything with you, and ask around in Chocas town or on Mozambique Island before coming to find out what the status is. Just next door, the upmarket **Coral Lodge 15.41** (www.corallodge1541.com) was under construction when we visited.

CABACEIRA GRANDE
Further along (northwest) from Cabaceira Pequena is **Cabaceira Grande**, with a small treasure-trove of ruins, including a well-preserved church (Nossa Senhora dos Remédios) dating from the late 16th-century and the ruins of the mid-19th-century governor-general's palace. You can carefully climb up the latter for superb views.

The Cabaceira Grande area is also notable as the site of Lisa St Aubin de Terán's (author of *Mozambique Mysteries*) Colégio de Turismo e Agricultura (Tourism Training School), housed in the restored naval academy.

Dois Coqueiros (meals from Mtc90), a small restaurant with inexpensive local-style meals, is next door to and under the same management as the Colégio de Turismo e Agricultura.

route aiming towards the trading centre of Sena, on the Zambezi River. It's rocky, and seldom visited. Permission from the *capitania* on Mozambique Island is necessary to visit, and details for getting here are the same as for Goa Island.

São Lourenço Island
Just off the southern tip of Mozambique Island is this tiny island, which is completely covered by an eponymous fort dating from 1695. You can walk across the channel at low tide (watch that you don't get stuck out there), but will need to clamber up over the walls, as the ladder into the fort is missing.

Lumbo
Sleepy Lumbo, on the mainland opposite Mozambique Island, was formerly the terminus of a railway line from the interior. Today it's of interest for its Commonwealth war cemetery; a once grand but now abandoned hotel; a few old Portuguese houses; and salt flats.

Chocas & Around
Just to the north of Mozambique Island and across Mossuril Bay is the old Portuguese holiday town of Chocas. It makes an agreeable day or overnight excursion, except during holiday weekends when it's completely overrun.

The busy **Complexo Turístico Namarralo** (☎ 26-660049; 2-/4-person bungalows Mtc1000/2000; 🅿) has straightforward stone bungalows in a large, fenced compound on the beach. All have bathroom and breakfast included and there's

MOSSURIL

Apart from Chocas, the closest major village in the area is Mossuril, which you'll pass en route when travelling to Chocas by road, and which hosts a lively Saturday market.

Pensão-Restaurant Sunset Boulevard (r Mtc500) is in the São João area of Mossuril, about 800m from the Mossuril Governo building, and a good half-hour walk from the main Mossuril village transport junction. It's a restored residence with surprisingly nice rooms (given its unlikely location on the road to nowhere) and meals, and lots of information on and help with organising exploration of the surrounding area. It's part of the Téran Foundation's tourism activities, designed to provide local tourism training, and is a fine chill-out spot if you're interested in seeing Mozambique well away from any sort of established route. Nearby is a small patch of beach. On Saturday evening, there are open-air 'boma dinners' with traditional dancing (per person Mtc450).

GETTING THERE & AWAY

Boat

There's at least one dhow daily connecting Mozambique Island with Cabaceira Grande and Mossuril, departing the island at about noon from the beach down from BIM bank, and departing Mossuril about 6am (Mtc20). For Sunset Boulevard, ask to be dropped off at 'São João', from where the *pensão* is just a short walk up from the beach. From Mossuril village, it's about 1½ hours on foot to Cabaceira Grande. If you want to return the same day, you'll need to charter a boat (about Mtc600 for a motorised dhow). Dhows across Mossuril Bay also depart from the fish market on Mozambique Island just down from the green mosque. Hotels on Mozambique Island can also organise Chocas/Cabaceira excursions. For all travel to/from the Cabaceiras, be prepared for lots of wading and walking.

Bus

There's one daily direct chapa between Nampula and Chocas, departing Nampula between 10am and noon, and departing Chocas about 4am (Mtc150, five hours). Otherwise, take any transport between Nampula or Monapo and Mozambique Island to the signposted Mossuril turn-off, 25km southeast of Monapo (Mtc100 from Nampula to the Mossuril turn-off). Sporadic

chapas go from here to Mossuril (20km), and on to Chocas (12km further, Mtc40), with no vehicles after about 3pm. From Chocas, it's a 30-minute walk at low tide to Cabaceira Pequena, and from one hour to 1½ hours to Cabaceira Grande.

NACALA

Nacala is set on an impressive natural harbour. Its port, developed in the mid-20th century, is northern northern Mozambique's busiest. The town itself has nothing of interest for travellers, but there's good diving and attractive beaches nearby. The most popular are **Fernão Veloso** (with a resident dive operator) to the north, and **Relanzapo** to the east.

Orientation

The first part of Nacala you'll enter is Nacala-Alta (the high town) which merits no more time than it takes to drive through. After several kilometres, you'll see the bay ahead of you, and the main street (Rua Principal) begins to head downhill to the train station and harbour in the baixa or Nacala-Porto (port) area. The market, transport stand, banks and most shops are along or just off Rua Principal during its route downhill. The best place to get off the bus is at the top, near Hotel Maiaia. The beaches are about 10km to 15km north and west of town, reached via a turn-off in Nacala-Alta.

Information

Barclays Bank (cnr Rua Principal & Rua 8) ATM.

BP Petrol Station (Nacala-Alta) ATM.

Farmácia Calêndula (Rua 8; ✷ 8am-6pm Mon-Fri, to noon Sat)

Telecomunicações de Moçambique (per min Mtc1; ✷ 8am-8pm Mon-Fri, to 1pm Sat) Internet access; diagonally opposite Hotel Maiaia.

Sleeping & Eating

NACALA TOWN

Residencial Bela Vista (☎ 26-520404; Nacala-Alta; s/d with shared bathroom from Mtc400/500, d Mtc900; ✵) This shoestring place in Nacala-Alta is only worth considering if you don't want to be by the beach, don't have the budget for Hotel Maiaia and don't have onward transport to anywhere better. Rooms are very basic – most share bathrooms – and there's a restaurant. Turn left off the main road at the town entrance in front of Mini-Bar Owannhoka. Chapas to the baixa pass nearby.

Hotel Maiaia (☎ 26-526842; inturhoteis@teledata.mz; Rua Principal; s/d from Mtc1855/2150; 🕮) The centrally located three-star Maiaia caters to business travellers, with simple rooms with TV (some also have a tiny balcony) and a restaurant. It's on the main street diagonally opposite the central market, where the road starts its final descent into the baixa. Visa cards are accepted.

AROUND NACALA

Libélula (☎ 82-304 2909, 82-306 6473; www.divelibelula .com; Fernão Veloso; campsite per person US$8, dm US$10, d with shared bathroom US$30, 2- to 4-person chalets US$45-60; 🕮) This place, in a fine setting on an escarpment overlooking the beach and the aqua waters of Nacala Bay, had just reopened under new ownership as this book was being written, and early reports are promising. On offer are rustic but comfortable reed-and-thatch chalets, dorm beds, campsites, a restaurant, snorkelling and fine diving (including, soon, diving instruction). It's all very relaxing, very tranquil and warmly recommended – many travellers come for a few days and wind up staying much longer. To get here, follow directions to Fernão Veloso (see right), and then follow the Libélula signs. Pick-ups can be arranged from Nacala town or Nampula.

Nuarro Lodge (www.nuarro.com; per person US$295) This new and promising place was set to open imminently at the time of research. It's 90km from Nacala on the Baixa do Pindo peninsula; transfers can be arranged from Nacala, Nampula and Pemba. Rates include accommodation, meals and some activities (drinks not included).

Getting There & Around

Grupo Mecula buses to Pemba (Mtc250, seven hours) depart Nacala every other day at 5am from the Mecula garage. Head down Rua Principal to the large roundabout, then follow the street going left and uphill next to Mozstar. Mecula is about 400m up on the left, behind an unmarked wall.

There are chapas each morning to Nampula (Mtc125), Namialo (Mtc75) and Monapo (Mtc60, one hour), departing from the big tree next to Telecomunicações de Moçambique. Once in Monapo (ask your hotel for help in timing the connection), there's onward transport to Mozambique Island and Namialo (the junction town for Pemba).

To get to Fernão Veloso: after entering Nacala, the road splits – follow the left fork, and continue for 2km to the unmarked airport and military base turn-off to the right. Go right here. After about 9km watch for the signposted Libélula left-hand turn-off opposite the base, from where it's another 1.5km.

Chapas run frequently from the port area past Hotel Maiaia and on to Nacala Alta (Mtc5) – the best place to catch these is from the blue container opposite Hotel Maiaia – and then from Nacala-Alta to Fernão Veloso (Mtc10).

Relanzapo is reached by taking the same turn-off for the airport and military base as for Fernão Veloso. Turn right on the dirt road immediately before the base and continue 15km east; there's no public transport.

CUAMBA

This lively rail and road junction was formerly known as Novo Freixo. With its dusty streets, flowering trees and large university student population, it is the economic centre of Niassa province and a convenient stop-off if you're travelling to/from Malawi. The surrounding area is known for its garnet gemstones and for its scenic panoramas, especially to the east around Mt Mitucué (Serra Mitucué).

Information

Millennium BIM (Avenida Eduardo Mondlane) ATM; near the post office.
Telecomunicações de Moçambique (Avenida Eduardo Mondlane; per min Mtc1.50; 🕮 9am-noon & 2-7pm Mon-Sat) Internet access and telephone calls; a few doors up from Millennium BIM.

Sleeping & Eating

Pensão São Miguel (☎ 271-62701; r with shared bathroom Mtc500, r with fan/air-con Mtc800/1000; 🕮) This long-standing, local-style guesthouse has small clean rooms crowded behind the restaurant-bar area. Each room has one small double bed, and some have been recently renovated. While it's not the most luxurious of establishments it's the best value-for-price option in the town centre, and located an easy 10-minute walk from the train station and bus stand. A good breakfast is included in the deal, and the restaurant also serves decent lunches and dinners. Staff can help arrange local bike rental.

Quinta Timbwa (☎ 82-692 0250, 82-300 0752; quint timbwa@yahoo.com.br; tw with shared bathroom Mtc500, d Mtc750, rondavel without/with air-con Mtc1000/1200

[X]) This newish place is set on a large estate about 2.5km from town, and signposted. It's tranquil and good value, with spotless, pleasant rooms – some in attached rows, some in small rondavels – surrounded by expansive grounds and a small lake. It's ideal for families, or for anyone with their own transport. There's also a restaurant.

Hotel Vision 2000 (☎ 271-62632; h-vision2000@ teledata.mz; cnr Avenidas Eduardo Mondlane & 25 de Junho; s/d US$50/75; [X]) Vision 2000, at the main intersection, is not the newest of hotels, as its name gives away, and rather down at the heel these days, although the shower-bidet combo in a few of the rooms might be an attraction for some. The attached restaurant has a small selection of meals, and visits to the nearby garnet mines (about 5km from town) can be arranged.

Supermercado Pera-Doce (town centre) Just down from Pensão Namaacha, this supermarket has a good selection of basics, and is convenient for stocking up before the train ride to Nampula.

Getting There & Away
BUS, CAR & CHAPA
Most transport leaves from Maçaniqueira market, at the southern edge of town and just south of the railway tracks. Chapas also come to meet arriving trains. The best times to find transport are between 5am and 6am, and again in the afternoon at the station, when the train from Nampula arrives.

To Gurúè, the best routing is via train to Mutuali, from where you can find waiting pickups on to Gurúè. This generally works best going from Cuamba to Gurúè; going in the other direction entails long waits and travel at night. There's also a direct pick-up most days to Gurúè (Mtc250 to Mtc300), departing Cuamba by about 6am. Once in Gurúè, you can connect to Mocuba (Mtc200 Gurúè to Mocuba) and Nampula (Mtc120 Mocuba to Nampula) the same day. At the time of research, there were no direct vehicles from Cuamba to Nampula. You'll need to take the train, or go via Gurúè (Mtc300 Gurúè to Nampula direct).

To Lichinga (Mtc350, eight to nine hours), there are several trucks daily via Mandimba (Mtc175), with the first departure at about 4am.

To Malawi, there is at least one pick-up daily from Cuamba to Entre Lagos (Mtc150, 1½ hours). Once at Entre Lagos, you'll need to walk across the border, where there's a weekly train on the Malawi side to Liwonde. For travel via Mandimba, see p143.

TRAIN
A train connects Cuamba with Nampula (Mtc332/132 for 2nd/3rd class, 10 to 12 hours), departing in each direction daily except Monday at 5am (and soon also to run on Monday). First class has been discontinued, as has the dining car (although this is scheduled to resume 'soon'), and 2nd class only runs in each direction on alternate days (currently from Cuamba on Wednesday, Friday and Sunday and from Nampula on Tuesday, Thursday and Saturday). It's well worth planning your travels to coincide with a day when 2nd class is running, as third class often fills up and is uncomfortable. Second-class tickets can be purchased between 2pm and 5pm on the day before travel (but not earlier), and should be purchased then, as they sometimes sell out if you wait until the day of travel. Third-class tickets are always available, up until the time of departure.

It's a great ride, with the train stopping at many villages along the way and offering a fine taste of rural Mozambican life.

Vendors sell food at every stop, but it's worth supplementing this by bringing some snacks along, and you should bring enough bottled water for the trip as well.

To transport your vehicle on the train (about US$90), you'll need to load it the night before and arrange a guard. During the journey you can ride with the car.

MANDIMBA
Mandimba is a small, bustling border town and transport junction. If you get stuck here, **Bar-Restaurante Ngame** (Senhor Liton's; d Mtc350), near the transport stop, has basic rooms looking out on a small courtyard, and meals with advance notice.

About 1km further along the road to Cuamba and on the opposite side is **Bar-Restaurante Massinga** (s without/with bathroom Mtc250/500, d with air-con Mtc1000), which has rather grubby singles in the restaurant compound, and better air-con double 'chalet' rondavels in a separate, pale pink, compound 500m further along the main road.

En route between Mandimba and Lichinga is the town of **Massangulo**, the site of the first Catholic mission in Niassa. Its church, about

LICHINGA

Approximate Scale

INFORMATION
Barclays Bank & ATM.................1 C2
BCI & ATM.................................2 B3
Lúrio Empreendimentos............3 C2
Meshi Internet Café...................4 C3
Millennium BIM & ATM..............5 C3
Sarifo's Net Café........................6 C3
Standard Bank & ATM................7 B2
Sycamore Services......................8 C3

SLEEPING
Hotel Girassol Lichinga..............9 C3
Ponto Final..............................10 D2
Pousada de Lichinga.................11 C3
Residencial 2+1........................12 C3

EATING
O Chambo................................13 D3
Padaria Mária...........................14 C3
Supermercado Socin.................15 A1

To Airport (4km);
Meponda (60km);
Metangula (104km)

Some Minor Roads Not Depicted

Military Barracks
Blue Mosque
Telecomunicações de Moçambique Satellite Office

Praça

Provincial Government Buildings
Palácio de Casamento

Cathedral

Petrol Station

Governor's Mansion
No Pedestrians Zone

Mcel

Provincial Tourism Directorate

Market

TRANSPORT
Bus Stand.................................16 D3
LAM..17 B1
Lúrio Empreendimentos......(see 3)
Transport to Tanzania...............18 D3

To Cuamba (300km)

2km off the main road, is worth a detour if you have your own vehicle.

Vehicles go daily to Lichinga (Mtc175) and Cuamba (Mtc175). For border information, see p184. Expect to pay Mtc30/50/100 for a bicycle/motorbike/taxi lift to cover the approximately 4km from Mandimba to the border, and Mtc30 to Mtc40 for a bicycle taxi across the 1500m of no-man's land to the Malawi border post.

LICHINGA

Niassa's capital is pretty, low-key Lichinga (formerly Vila Cabral), which sits at about 1300m altitude, with an invigorating, cool climate and quiet, jacaranda-lined streets. It's worth a day or two in its own right and is also the best jumping-off point for exploring the lake. The surrounding area – home mainly to Yao people, as well as smaller numbers of Nyanja and Makua people – is dotted with pine groves and ringed by distant hills.

Orientation

Lichinga is set out in a series of concentric circles, with a large plaza at the centre and

the main transport stand at its southeastern edge near the market. It's easy to cover on foot – nothing is more than about a 10-minute walk.

The section of road running past the governor's mansion on the northwestern edge of town is closed to vehicle traffic and the area immediately in front of the mansion is also closed to pedestrians.

Information

INTERNET ACCESS

Meshi Internet Café (Avenida Samora Machel; per hr Mtc60) Internet; next door to the Provincial Tourism Directorate.

Sarifo's Net Café (Avenida Samora Machel; per hr Mtc80) Internet; opposite Residencial 2+1 and Mcel.

Sycamore Services (Avenida Samora Machel; per hr Mtc100; ✆ 10am-6pm Mon-Fri, to noon Sat) Internet access.

MONEY

Barclays (main roundabout) ATM

BCI (Rua Filipe Samuel Magaia) ATM; in the Hotel Girassol complex, next to the hotel entrance.

NORTHERN MOZAMBIQUE

FIM DO MUNDO

Fim do mundo (the end of the world) is how many Mozambicans describe Niassa – the least populated of Mozambique's provinces – and as far as the rest of the country is concerned, it might as well be. The area is generally overlooked by the government and other locals and ignored by tourists. Yet if you're after adventure and time in the bush, it's an ideal destination. Apart from Niassa's scenic rugged terrain, the main attractions are the Lake Niassa coastline and the wild Niassa Reserve.

Millennium BIM (cnr Avenida Samora Machel & Rua Filipe Samuel Magaia) ATM.

Standard Bank (Rua Filipe Samuel Magaia) ATM.

TRAVEL AGENCIES

Lúrio Empreendimentos (☎ 271-21705, 82-492 3780, 84-308 4080; lempreendimentos@teledata.mz; main roundabout; ☻ 8am-noon & 2-5.30pm Mon-Fri, 9am-noon Sat), next to Barclays, is efficient, reliable and recommended. It's the best bet for car rentals, LAM bookings and for help organising travels anywhere in Niassa. This includes drop-offs and pick-ups in Cóbuè (for Nkwichi Lodge) and transport to/from and within the Niassa Reserve. It can also help with day visits to Meponda, southwest of Lichinga on the lakeshore, where it will soon be opening its own little lodge.

Sleeping

The owner of O Chambo (right) rents rooms (singles/doubles Mtc1100/1500) in her house; it's on the Cuamba road just after Socin supermarket.

Ponto Final (☎ 271-20912, 82-304 3632; Rua Filipe Samuel Magaia; s with shared bathroom Mtc650, d Mtc1000) At the northeastern edge of town, this longstanding place has clean, low-ceilinged rooms, a big, bright zebra painting in the courtyard and a popular restaurant-bar. Turn down the road at the small green-and-white Telecomunicações de Moçambique satellite office.

Pousada de Lichinga (☎ 271-20176/7; Rua Filipe Samuel Magaia; s/d with shared bathroom Mtc1000/1150, s/d Mtc1150/1250) The Pousada has a convenient central location, straightforward albeit rather rundown rooms and a restaurant. Prices include continental breakfast.

Residencial 2+1 (☎ 82-381 1070; Avenida Samora Machel; s/d Mtc1200/1500) Clean, efficient and central – within easy walking distance of the bus stand. Attached is a reasonably priced restaurant.

Hotel Girassol Lichinga (☎ 271 21280; www.girassol hoteis.co.mz; Rua Filipe Samuel Magaia; s/d with advance booking Mtc2000/2300; ☒ ▢ ☒) Hovering between three and four stars, this is Lichinga's most upmarket option, and one of the few places in the province catering to business travellers. It has satellite TV, huge rooms (most with large windows), a restaurant and tennis court. Book in advance for a discount – walk-in rates are higher.

Eating

In addition to the hotel restaurants, there are several other good options.

Padaria Mária (Avenida Samora Machel; snacks & light meals from Mtc50) Opposite Residencial 2+1, with a good selection of pastries, plus light meals and yoghurt.

O Chambo (☎ 271-21354, 84-319 8800; meals from Mtc120) A cosy place in the Feira Exposição Niassa (FEN) compound next to the market, with great soups and local meals. The owner also rents out rooms (see left).

Supermercado Socin (Cuamba road; ☻ 9am-1pm & 3-7pm Mon-Fri, 9am-noon Sat) For self-catering.

Entertainment

Lichinga has an active cultural scene. One of the highlights is Niassa province's renowned song and dance group, **Massukos** (www.massukos.org), which is based here and gives occasional performances.

Getting There & Away

AIR

LAM (☎ 271-20434, 271-20847; Rua da LAM), just off the airport road, operates four flights weekly to/from Maputo, going via Tete (weekly) or Nampula (three times weekly) and sometimes Beira. Flights out of Lichinga tend to be heavily booked, so reconfirm your reservation and show up early at the airport.

BUS & TRUCK

All transport departs from beside the market, with vehicles to most destinations leaving by around 6am. There are daily trucks to Cuamba (Mtc350, eight hours) via Mandimba (Mtc175), to Metangula (Mtc120, 2½ hours) and to Meponda (Mtc60, 1½ hours). The first vehicle to Cuamba departs between 3am and 4am. There's also at least one pick-up truck daily to Segundo Congresso/Matchedje and the Rovuma River (Mtc500, six hours), leaving anywhere between 7am and noon from the dusty street just before the transport stand – look for the blue *barracas* near Safi Comercial and enquire there. Once over the bridge, you can get transport to Songea for about US$5. In both directions, you'll need to have your visa in advance if using this crossing.

To Marrupa, there's a daily vehicle (Mtc350, three hours), but no public transport from there onwards, either to Niassa Reserve or to Montepuez.

If you're trying to hitch from Lichinga to Cuamba, the best place to wait for a lift is at the police checkpoint about 5km south of town at the beginning of the Mandimba/Cuamba road.

Getting Around
Lúrio Empreendimentos (p143) has a variety of 4WD vehicles for rent, with or without driver, at very fair rates. It can also help with booking taxi service within Lichinga.

AROUND LICHINGA
Lipilichi Wilderness Area
About 150km north of Lichinga, towards the Tanzanian border and edging the buffer zone of the Niassa Reserve, is the **Lipilichi Wilderness Area**, a wild and isolated tract of bush, and the site of the Chipanje Chetu community-oriented tourism initiative and wildlife conservation project. The area's status is currently somewhat controversial and in flux, although it is possible to visit during the hunting off-season (December through April) if you have your own 4WD transport and are willing to rough things. The area is home to wildlife including elephants, buffaloes, antelopes, wildebeests and zebras, although they are often difficult to spot. Better are the opportunities for bush walking and cultural interaction. Basic Yao and/or Swahili language skills are essential. Before heading up this way, contact the **Lipilichi Wilderness Area office** (☎ 271-21379, 271-21298; lipilichi@teledata.mz) at Hotel Girassol Lichinga (p143).

To get here, travel north from Lichinga to Unango (where the tarmac ends). Continue on for about 50km, past Macaloge village. About 4km before Nova Madeira, turn east and continue about 6km to a pricey hunting

lodge, which accepts tourists on a space-available basis. Advance bookings (through the Lipilichi Wilderness Area office in Lichinga) are essential. Camping in the area is also an option, although this also should be cleared in advance with the Lichinga office.

Via public transport, there's a daily chapa from Lichinga to Nova Madeira and on to the Rovuma River and the Tanzanian border, which can drop you at the Nova Madeira turn-off (Mtc150, five to six hours). For a negotiable extra fee, the driver may be willing to take you the additional 6km in to the hunting lodge. Note that if you will be continuing in to Tanzania, you need to arrange your Tanzania visa in advance.

LAKE NIASSA (LAKE MALAWI)
The Mozambican side of Lake Niassa (Lago Niassa) is beautiful and, in contrast to the Malawian side, almost completely undeveloped. It sees a small but steady stream of adventure travellers and is an excellent destination for anyone wanting to get off the beaten track.

The main area for exploring is the coast between Metangula and Cóbuè, with a succession of narrow beaches – some sandy, others gravel – backed by mountains and steep hills rising up directly from the lakeshore. Most local residents are Nyanja ('People of the Lake'), and their distinctively painted square, thatched dwellings dot the countryside. Fishing is the main source of livelihood, though it's mostly small scale. The only commercial fishing opera-

---

LAKE NIASSA FAST FACTS

- At more than 550km long, up to 75km wide, and 700m deep in parts, Lake Niassa is the third largest lake on the African continent after Lake Victoria and Lake Tanganyika.

- About 25% of the lake's area is in Mozambique.

- Within its deep blue waters are over 500 species of fish, including over 350 that are unique to the lake. Lake Niassa is also home to about one-third of the earth's known cichlid (freshwater fish) species, including the brightly coloured mbuna.

STAYING HEALTHY

In addition to being home to countless colourful fish, Lake Niassa also hosts healthy populations of the tiny snail that causes bilharzia. While there is less risk of bilharzia infestation on the Mozambique side of the lake, you should still use caution when swimming: don't swim anywhere with reeds and other shoreline growth, or in shallow, still water. If you swim anyway (and many people do, with no ill effects), get a bilharzia test once you return home. Keep in mind though that if you are infected, it won't show up for at least six weeks (and sometimes longer), and several tests may be necessary. One place where you can enjoy the lake without worrying about bilharzia is in the crystal clear waters around Nkwichi Lodge (p146).

Another water-related danger to watch out for is the crocodile. Locals say that they lurk in the river that joins Lake Niassa near Meponda and in other river mouths along the lakeshore.

If you do become ill while travelling in the area, ask locals to point you to 'Dr Peg', who is based in Cóbuè, although she is often away in outlying villages where she provides medical support – many times as the only medical resource for remote communities all along the Lake Niassa shoreline.

---

tion on the Mozambican side of the lake is at Metangula.

Allow plenty of time for getting around and be prepared to rough it. When venturing onto the lake, keep in mind that squalls can arise suddenly, often with strong winds.

Meponda

This small, lakeside village is completely undeveloped and a possibility for a day trip from Lichinga. The tiny harbour to the south of the main road as you enter Meponda is the hub of activity, with the town centre and market nearby. About 1km north of here is a small beach, which is ideal for picnicking and watching the fish eagles. Local fishermen will take you out on the lake for about Mtc50 per hour.

The small **Lúrio Lodge** (☎ 271-21705; lempreendi mentos@teledata.mz) on the lakeshore should soon be open. Contact Lúrio Empreendimentos in Lichinga (see p143) for details.

GETTING THERE & AWAY

Meponda is 60km southwest of Lichinga. A few chapas run between the two towns daily (Mtc70, 1½ hours). Schedules don't usually cooperate to make a day trip possible. However if you take a chapa out in the morning on the weekend, it's usually easy to find a lift back to Lichinga in the afternoons.

Meponda was formerly linked with Malawi's Senga Bay via the weekly MV *Mtendere*. It wasn't running when we visited, but ask around to see if ferry services have resumed.

Metangula

Bustling Metangula is the capital of Lake District, the largest Mozambican town along the lakeshore, and the site of a small naval base. The town is divided into two areas – the staid administrative quarters perched on a small escarpment with wide views over the lake, and the lower lying residential areas along the lake shore. Metangula itself has little for visitors. However about 8km north of town is the tiny village of **Chuwanga**, which is on an attractive beach, and is a popular weekend getaway from Lichinga. About 5km northeast of Chuwanga is **Messumba**, site of a well-known Anglican mission that traces its history back to the arrival of the first missionaries in the area in 1882.

Until being forced to close during the war, Messumba served as headquarters for Anglican missionary activity in northern Mozambique. It was renowned for its hospital and for the Colégio de São Felipe, where numerous notables studied, including several members of Frelimo's elite. Most of the mission buildings are now in disrepair, although you can still visit the impressive church and walk around the grounds. Today, the only secondary school in the district is in Metangula.

SLEEPING & EATING

Pensão Mari (s/tw with shared bathroom Mtc250/500, d Mtc400) This is the nicest option in town, with clean, no-frills rooms with nets in a good setting at the point near the water. Meals can sometimes be arranged with advance notice.

Cimel Guesthouse (s/tw with shared bathroom Mtc250/500, d Mtc400) Near the administration building in the centre of town, with some niceish rooms in the owner's personal living quarters (sharing the house bathroom), and some less nice, basic rooms (shared bathroom) in the adjoining compound.

Chuwanga Beach Hotel (Catawala's; Chuwanga Beach; campsite per person Mtc150, d Mtc400) Almost everyone heads out of town to this long-standing place on the beach at Chuwanga. It offers camping, and simple reed bungalows on the sand, with shared ablutions. Meals and drinks are available and there's a grill for cooking your own food.

Mbuna Bay (☎ 82-536 7782; www.mbunabay.ch; s/d with full-board in bush bungalow US$125/190, in beach chalet US$165/250) About 15km south of Metangula, Mbuna Bay is considerably upmarket, with lovely lakeshore bungalows, a restaurant and the chance to organise canoeing and other local excursions. Transfers from Lichinga can be arranged, and the *Dangilila* ferry (see opposite) stops here on request.

GETTING THERE & AWAY

Daily chapas connect Metangula and Lichinga (Mtc120, 2½ hours), most departing Lichinga early. There's also one chapa daily between Metangula and Cóbuè (Mtc150, four hours). Departures in Metangula are from the fork in the road just up from the market at Bar Triângulo – look for the yellow Mcel wall. The final 20km or so of the good tarmac road from Lichinga to Metangula are very scenic as they wind down to the lakeshore.

There are occasional chapas between Metangula and Chuwanga, and hitching is easy on the weekend. Otherwise, get a Cóbuè chapa to drop you at the Chuwanga turn-off, though it's probably just as fast to walk from Metangula. To get to Messumba, you'll need your own 4WD.

For information on the *Ilala* ferry between Metangula and Malawi, see p186. For more on the *Dangilila* ferry between Metangula and Cóbuè, see opposite. Both these boats depart Metangula from the small dhow port just down from Bar Triângulo and below the Catholic church.

Cóbuè

Tiny Cóbuè is the gateway into Mozambique if you're travelling from Malawi via Likoma Island, about 10km offshore. The island is surrounded by Mozambican waters, but belongs to Malawi.

In addition to its immigration post, Cóbuè's attractions include a lakeside setting dotted with mango trees, the remains of a school once used as a wartime base by Frelimo, and the ruins of an old Catholic church, with goats lying around in the shade. Cóbuè is also the jumping-off point to reach Nkwichi Lodge (see below).

SLEEPING & EATING

Rest House Mira Lago (Pensão Layla; r with shared bathroom Mtc200; **P**) Directly in the village centre, this place has solar-powered lighting and a row of no-frills, clean rooms. Each has a small double bed. Meals can sometimes be organised with advance notice.

Khango Beach (☎ in Malawi 88-856 7885, 99-962 0916, from Mozambique 00-265-856 7885; r with shared bathroom per person Mtc200; **P**) This rustic place, run by the affable, English-speaking Julius (a former employee of Nkwichi Lodge), has simple reed bungalows directly on the sand. All have nets and clean shared ablutions. Tasty, filling meals can be arranged with advance notice.

Mchenga Wede (per person about Mtc200) About 8km south of Nkwichi Lodge along the lakeshore, at Mbueca village, this place is also run by some enterprising staff from Nkwichi. It was temporarily closed when we passed through, though it's worth inquiring with Julius at Khango Beach in Cóbuè or with staff at Nkwichi Lodge to see if it has reopened. When operating, it has campsites, basic bungalows and meals, plus bush walks and canoe trips.

Nkwichi Lodge (www.mandawilderness.org; s/d with full-board in chalet US$375/580, in private house US$420/640) Apart from its convenient location as part of a larger southern Africa circuit linking Mozambique and Malawi, the main reason to come to Cóbuè is to get to this highly recommended lodge. It's one of the most appealing and genuinely community-integrated lodges we've seen in the region, and worth the splurge. It offers the chance to explore an area of southern Africa that is about as remote as it gets, while enjoying all the comforts and contributing to the local community and to the local environment. The lodge is linked with the Manda Wilderness Community Conservation Area – a privately initiated conservation area along the lakeshore that also promotes community development and responsible tourism. The surrounding bush is full of birds, with ospreys, palm nut vultures, Pell's fishing owls and fish eagles all regularly seen.

Accommodation is in six spacious handcrafted bungalows, with private outdoor baths and showers built into the bush, and several looking out onto their own whitesand coves. There are also two private houses – Makolo House and Songea House – each nestled on its own in the bush, with lake views, private chef, and lots of space and privacy; they're ideal for groups. The lake at Nkwichi is crystal clear and safe for swimming and, for all guests, there's a dhow for sails and sunset cruises. You can also arrange canoeing and multinight wilderness walking safaris, or visits to the lodge's demonstration farm.

Boat transfers from Cóbuè (US$45 per person one way, minimum US$65) take about one hour. It's also possible to arrange pick-ups from Likoma Island. Advance bookings are essential.

GETTING THERE & AWAY
Air
There's an airstrip in Cóbuè for charter flights. More common is to charter a flight from Lilongwe (Malawi) to Likoma Island (about US$300 per person one way, book through Nkwichi Lodge) and then arrange a boat transfer from there with the lodge.

Boat
The *Ilala* ferry (weekly, in theory) no longer stops at Cóbuè – you'll need to take it to either Metangula or Likoma Island and arrange transfers from there; see p186. It's possible to get a Mozambique visa in Cóbuè, and if you're travelling to/from Malawi, you'll need to go to Immigration (on the hill near the large antenna) to get your passport stamped.

The *Dangilila,* a local boat that plies the waters on the Mozambican side of the lakeshore between Metangula and Ngofi village (north of Cóbuè) stops almost everywhere on demand, including at Nkwichi Lodge, Cóbuè, Mbuna Bay and Mbueca village. It departs Metangula early Thursday morning, arriving in Cóbuè at about 2pm. Departures from Cóbuè are at about 3am on Saturday, arriving in Metangula about noon (Mtc150 between Metangula and Cóbuè). Buy your tickets when boarding.

Bus & Car
A daily chapa runs between Metangula and Cóbuè, departing Metangula about 7am and Cóbuè about 8am (Mtc150, four hours).

The road between Cóbuè and Metangula (75km) is unpaved but in good condition, and there's secure parking at Khango Beach and Rest House Mira Lago in Cóbuè. Walking between Cóbuè and Metangula takes about two days, going along the river via the villages of Ngoo and Chia.

NIASSA RESERVE
About 160km northeast of Lichinga on the Tanzanian border is the **Niassa Reserve** (Reserva do Niassa; www.niassa.com; adult/child/vehicle per day US$25/10/25, discounts for longer stays & for Mozambican & other SADC nationals), a vast tract of wilderness with the largest wildlife populations in Mozambique (although the animals can be difficult to spot). Wildlife includes elephants (estimated to number about 12,000), sable antelopes (over 9000), buffaloes and zebras. There are also duikers, elands, leopards, wildebeests, hippos and a population of the endangered African wild dog, as well as over 400 different types of birds.

The reserve is also notable for its ruggedly beautiful scenery – dense bush and woodlands laced with rivers and dotted with massive inselbergs. It's twice the size of South Africa's Kruger National Park, and was established in the early 1960s to protect local elephant and black rhino populations. However, because of inaccessibility, scarce finances and the onset of war it was never developed. Although wildlife populations here suffered during the 1980s from poaching and the effects of armed conflict, losses were far less than those in other protected areas further south. In more recent times, significant progress has been made in curbing poaching, and there has been a trend of increasing animal numbers.

In the late 1990s Niassa Reserve was given new life when a group of private investors, working in partnership with the Mozambican government, was granted a 10-year renewable lease on the area. The reserve's size was increased to about 42,000 sq km, and the boundaries now stretch from the Rovuma River in the north to the Lugenda River in the south and east.

An estimated 20,000 people live within the reserve's boundaries, which also encompass a 20,000 sq km buffer zone, and there are future plans for community-based tourism. You'll undoubtedly come in to contact with locals setting their fish traps, walking, or paddling in dugout canoes (for which a few words of Swahili or Yao will stand you in better stead than Portuguese).

Information

The reserve headquarters are about 40km southwest of Mecula at Mbatamila.

Wildlife in Niassa Reserve is spread relatively thinly over a vast area, with dense foliage and only a skeleton network of bush tracks. As a result, most tourism to date has been exclusively for the well-heeled, with the most feasible way to visit by charter plane from Pemba. With the opening of two safari camps and the gradual upgrading of road connections linking Cabo Delgado and Niassa provinces, this is beginning to change, although the reserve's main market is likely to remain top end for the foreseeable future.

For self-drivers it is possible in theory to do drive-in visits. However, given the lack of a developed network of tracks, this is only recommended for the adventure and the wilderness, rather than for the safari or 'Big Five' aspects. Note that Niassa's tsetse flies are very aggressive and very numerous. Any activity in a vehicle will need to be done with windows up.

At the time of research, fees were not being collected at the reserve entrance, but rather are payable in advance – in person or via cheque – through the Maputo office of the **Sociedade para a Gestão e Desinvolvimento da Reserva do Niassa** (SGN; ☎ 21-329807; sgdrn.map@tvcabo.co.mz; 1031 Avenida Mao Tse Tung) – the entity charged with managing the reserve. The receipt should then be presented when you reach the reserve. That said, the entire reserve infrastructure is still in very early stages, and we haven't heard of anyone being turned away at the gate for lack of a receipt.

Sleeping & Eating

At the time of writing, there was no official public camping ground, although there is a rudimentary area near Mbatamila headquarters where you can pitch a tent. Bring all food, drinking water and supplies with you.

Moja Safari Wilderness (www.mojasafariwilderness.com; s/d all-inclusive US$425/700) This recommended operator, which was about to commence operations as this book was

researched, offers multinight canoeing along the Lugenda River, hiking up an inselberg and the chance to explore the bush on foot and by boat under the expert guidance of the owner-managers Rob and Jos. The camp itself consists of one semi-permanent camp – about a five-hour drive from Mecula – together with a series of bush fly camps set up along the river.

Lugenda Bush Camp (☎ 21-301618; www.lugenda.com; per person US$450; ☻ Jun-Nov) This lovely place on the Lugenda River near the eastern edge of the park caters primarily to fly-in guests, and offers a unique safari experience that's likely to appeal to well-heeled safari connoisseurs seeking an 'unpackaged' experience with all the amenities. There's a set of maintained roads around the camp to facilitate wildlife tracking.

Getting There & Around

AIR

There are about 11 airstrips that can accommodate charter flights, including one at Mecula. The reserve sits roughly midway between Lake Niassa to the west and the Indian Ocean to the east, both about an hour's flight away via small plane. The easiest charter access is from Pemba (per person one way US$560), which can be arranged with Lugenda Bush Camp, Moja Safari Wilderness, or with Kaskazini (p151).

CAR

By road, it's possible to reach Mbatamila in the dry season via Montepuez, Balama and Marrupa, although the Balama–Marrupa section is in extremely poor condition. Allow up to two days from Pemba, and plan on bush camping en route. Better is approaching the reserve from Lichinga, where you have good tarmac as far as Marrupa. Once at Marrupa, the remaining stretch up to the Lugenda River and on into the reserve is dirt but in reasonable shape. The unpaved road from Cuamba to Marrupa is another doable option, especially during the dry season. Petrol is generally available on the roadside in Mecula, however this should not be relied upon, and plenty of extra supplies should be carried along from either Cuamba, Pemba or Lichinga.

Once across the Lugenda, you'll need to sign in at the reserve, before continuing on towards Mecula and Mbatamila park headquarters – set in the shadow of the 1441m-high Mt Mecula – where you can arrange a guide.

MONTEPUEZ

Montepuez, a busy district capital, previously rivalled Pemba as the largest town in Cabo Delgado. Today, it's known for its marble quarries, and as the start of the wild 'road' west across Niassa province towards Lichinga. It would also be the overland gateway to the Niassa Reserve, were it not for a 100-or-so kilometre stretch of road to the west from Balama to Marrupa that is usually impassable during the rains. The main road in town is Avenida Eduardo Mondlane; everywhere listed here is either on or just off it.

Residencial do Geptex (☎ 272-51114; Avenida Julius Nyerere; r Mtc400) has very basic rooms with double beds, bucket baths, fan and no nets. It's at the western end of town, two blocks north of the main road.

Vivenda Angelina (Avenida Julius Nyerere; r Mtc500) is considerably nicer, with clean, quiet rooms in a private house sharing a bathroom, and (often) running water. There's no food and no signpost. Coming from the main road, turn right at the Plexus signboard at the western end of town, go two short blocks, and then turn left onto Avenida Julius Nyerere. It's the second house on the left.

BIM Casa de Hospedes (r Mtc750, 3-bedroom house Mtc2150) Above Millennium BIM just off the main road near the entrance to town, on the corner of Eduardo Mondlane, this private, relatively plush (for Montepuez) furnished apartment can be rented in full or per room.

For meals, there's a **refrigerator** (☼ from 7am Mon-Sat) next to the bakery – which is on a side street one block before the bus stand – with juice, yoghurt and (sometimes) apples. Also try the small **café** (light meals from Mtc80) behind the park with the aeroplane.

Getting There & Away

The transport stand is about two blocks south of Avenida Eduardo Mondlane – turn down the street with Millennium BIM. Several chapas daily go between Pemba and Montepuez (Mtc150, three hours). Heading west, there's regular transport to Balama (Mtc150), but from there to Marrupa (for Niassa Reserve) there is no option other than hitching a lift with a tractor or a truck. If you're driving, the Balama–Marrupa stretch is only feasible in the dry season.

PEMBA

Pemba sprawls across a peninsula jutting into the enormous and magnificent Pemba Bay, one of the world's largest natural harbours. It was established in 1904 as administrative headquarters for the Niassa Company and for much of its early life was known as Porto Amelia. Today it's the capital of Cabo Delgado province, the main town in Mozambique's far north, and gateway to the Quirimbas Archipelago and an endless string of white-sand beaches. Although lacking the charm to be a destination in itself, the town makes for a relaxing and enjoyable stop, with almost perpetual sunshine and blue skies, a long beach nearby and a lazy, languid ambience.

Orientation

Pemba's baixa area is home to the low-lying port and old town, with a row of small shops and traders lining the main street. Steeply uphill from here, the busier and less atmospheric town centre is the place to get things done, with banks and offices, a few restaurants and hotels, and the main bus stand. About 5km east of the town centre is Wimbi (also spelled Wimbe) Beach, the main hub of tourist activity and the favoured destination of most visitors.

MAPS

The best map is *Planta de Endereçamento da Cidade de Pemba*, part of the series done by Coopération Française in cooperation with the local Conselho Municipal, usually on sale at Artes Maconde's main branch on Avenida 25 de Setembro. Kaskazini also has a free Pemba tourist map.

Information

IMMIGRATION

Immigration office (Rua 16 de Junho; ☼ 7.30-11am & 2-4pm Mon-Fri) Just off Rua Base de Moçambique.

INTERNET ACCESS

Sycamore Services (☎ 272-21999; 1282 Avenida 25 de Setembro; per hr Mtc100; ☼ 7am-9pm Mon-Sat, 8am-noon Sun) Internet connection; it's just after Mcel.

MEDICAL SERVICES

Clínica de Cabo Delgado (☎ 272-21462; Rua Modesta Neva 10) For medical treatment.
Farmácia São Carlos Lwanga (☼ 7am-6.30pm Mon-Fri, 8am-5pm Sat) Well-stocked pharmacy. It's one block back from Avenida 25 de Setembro, on the same street as the Mecula bus office.

lonelyplanet.com

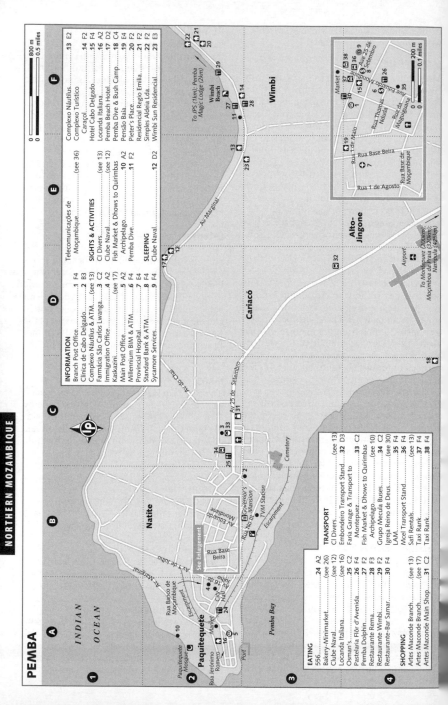

Provincial Hospital (cnr Ruas Base Beira & 1 de Maio) Malaria tests.

MONEY

There's an ATM in the lobby of Complexo Náutilus at Wimbi Beach.

Millennium BIM (Avenida Eduardo Mondlane) ATM.
Standard Bank (Avenida Eduardo Mondlane) ATM.

POST

Branch post office (Avenida 25 de Setembro)
Main post office (Rua No 1, Baixa) Poste restante.

TELEPHONE

Telecomunicações de Moçambique (cnr Avenidas Eduardo Mondlane & 25 de Setembro; 7am-6pm) Domestic and international telephone calls.

TOURIST INFORMATION

Kaskazini (272-20371, 82-309 6990; www.kaskazini .com; Pemba Beach Hotel, Avenida Marginal, Wimbi Beach; 8am-3pm Mon-Fri, 8.30am-noon Sat) Efficient, knowledgeable and an excellent first stop. It gives free information on Pemba and elsewhere in northern Mozambique, helps with accommodation and flight bookings, and can organise everything from dhow safaris to sunset cruises.

Sights

Almost everyone heads straight for **Wimbi Beach**, where you can swim or enjoy the sea breezes at one of the many waterside restaurants or bars.

On Pemba's outskirts are several colourful and vibrant *bairros* (neighbourhoods). The most intriguing is **Paquitequete**, which is on the southwestern edge of the peninsula and is Pemba's oldest settlement. In contrast with the other *bairros*, which are newer and more heterogeneous, the population here is almost exclusively Muslim, and predominantly Mwani and Makua. The atmosphere is at its best in the late afternoon just before sunset. At Paquitequete's northern edge is a small **fish market**. The nearby beach buzzes with activity in the early morning as *makuti* dried palm fronds used for constructing roofs), bamboo and other building materials are unloaded and readied for market.

Up on the hill behind the governor's mansion is a large **cemetery**, with fragrant frangipani trees shading the Christian and Muslim graves. Close to the sea is a section containing Commonwealth war graves.

Beginning about 10km south of town is a string of tranquil, attractive beaches, includ-

ing **Murrébuè** (p155), ideal for kite surfing, and **Mecúfi**.

Activities

Families can use the pool and small playground at Clube Naval (see p153) for free if a meal is ordered.

DIVING

There's rewarding diving around Pemba; see p53. Pemba Beach Hotel has resident dive instructors available for its guests.

CI Divers (272-20102; www.cidivers.com; Complexo Náutilus, Avenida Marginal, Wimbi Beach) The main operator, offering PADI open-water certification, equipment rental and boat charters.

Pemba Dive (82-661 1530; www.pembadivecamp .com) Further down Wimbi Beach, opposite Complexo Turístico Caraçol. Offers equipment hire and dives (though no instruction).

CI Divers and Pemba Dive can also help arrange excursions to the Quirimbas Archipelago, and with jet ski, fishing boat, sailboard, windsurfing and bicycle rental.

DHOW SAFARIS & SAILING

Kaskazini (left) can arrange day trips around Pemba Bay or overnight dhow safaris to Quirimbas Archipelago (from about US$150 per boat, up to six people). Together with Pemba Beach Hotel, it also offers an upscale sunset cruise. Pemba Beach Hotel's private luxury yacht can be chartered for sails.

Sleeping

TOWN CENTRE

Central Pemba has slim accommodation offerings. With the exception of Locanda Italiana, all are budget – at least in standard, if not in price. For most travellers, it's only worth considering staying in town if you can't find anything at Wimbi Beach or if you have an early morning bus.

Pensão Baía (cnr Rua 1 de Maio & Rua Base de Beira; d with shared bathroom & fan Mtc500, d with air-con Mtc600) Spartan budget rooms, and breakfast on request. It's brightish, cleanish and a good local-style place.

Hotel Cabo Delgado (272-21552; cnr Avenidas 25 de Setembro & Eduardo Mondlane; s/d/tw/ste Mtc550/800/850/1200) This ageing hotel on the main street is well past its prime, although the central location (diagonally opposite the Mcel

---

CABO DELGADO

Although remote geographically and otherwise from Maputo, Cabo Delgado province has played a disproportionately important role in recent Mozambican history. It's known in particular as the birthplace of the independence struggle, which began here supported from bases in nearby Tanzania. Cabo Delgado is also where some of the most protracted fighting took place during the 1980s. At the height of the war, it could take up to a month to travel – convoy-style, and moving only at night – between Pemba and Moçimboa da Praia, which makes the seven-hour bus ride today seem like a stroll in the park. Another legacy of the war years is that most district capitals in the north have airstrips, including some large enough to accommodate jets.

As in neighbouring Niassa province, large tracts of Cabo Delgado are wild and trackless and local lore is full of tales about the dangers of lions and the like.

Major ethnic groups include the Makonde, the Makua and, along the coast, the Mwani.

---

transport stop) is convenient. The faded rooms come with bathroom (though not always with water), fan (though not always with electricity) and, with luck, continental breakfast.

Locanda Italiana (☎ 272-20672, 82-688 9050; locanda italiana@tdm.co.mz; 487 Rua Gerónimo Romero; r Mtc2900-3500; 🔀 🛜) This cosy boutique and business travellers hotel, in an impeccably restored building in the baixa, has six spacious, quiet and very well-appointed rooms, including one with a sunken bathtub built around a spreading fig tree. Everything is spotless, service is good and there is a restaurant with delicious meals.

OUTSIDE THE TOWN CENTRE

Pemba Dive & Bushcamp (Nacole Jardim; ☎ 82-661 1530; www.pembadivecamp.com; campsite per person US$10, dm US$20, d/q chalet US$100/140) Tranquil, and with a good camping ground for families. There are also dorm beds, several screened-in chalets, a beachside bar and braai area, and botanical walking tours on request. It's about 10 minutes from town (Mtc200 in a taxi), behind the airport on the bay, and about 3km off the main road down an unpaved track. It's under the same management as Pemba Dive.

WIMBI BEACH

Almost everyone stays at the beach. Book in advance if travelling during the December/January and South African Easter school holidays.

Budget

Pemba Magic Lodge ('Russell's Place'; ☎ 82-686 2730, 82-527 7048; www.pembamagic.com; campsite per person US$8, dm US$15, rental tents per person US$15, d & q chalet US$60; 🛜) About 3.5km beyond Complexo Náutilus along the beach road extension, this

long-standing and recently renovated lodge has campsites with ablutions (although no self-catering), a handful of rustic but new and comfortable chalets with fan and bathroom, some tents for rent and (soon) both a dorm and a pool. There's also a bar-restaurant with a large menu (including pizzas), plus free wi-fi and an upstairs lounge. The beach is just a few minutes' walk away (high-tide swimming only). Staff is also very helpful with travel information for overlanders.

Complexo Turístico Caraçol (☎ 272-20147; sulemane @teledata.mz; Avenida Marginal; r Mtc1000, 1-/2-room apt Mtc1500/1700; 🔀) This place is well-located – on the inland side of the beach road just beyond Complexo Náutilus. It's nothing fancy, but reasonable value for money. The slightly musty rooms – all set in a row of apartment blocks – are straightforward, and have either fan or air-con. The apartments have hot plate and minifridge and some have views to the water.

Midrange

Wimbi Sun Residencial (☎ 82-318 1300; wimbisun@ teledata.mz; 7472 Avenida Marginal; r/ste Mtc1250/1600, 🔀) Clean, modern rooms (the best are the spacious 'suites') none with nets, and all with bathrooms. It's at the start of the Wimbi Beach strip, diagonally opposite Complexo Náutilus on the inland side of the road. Breakfast costs Mtc150 extra.

Pieter's Place (☎ 272-20102; cidivers@teledata.mz; Avenida Marginal; d about US$70) Along the extension of the Wimbi beach road with two small airy rooms in the shaded grounds of a private residence, and dorm rooms planned. There's no food, although a restaurant is also planned. Just outside is a huge baobab tree, with a sitting area built into its upper branches.

Simples Aldeia Lda (SAL; ☎ 272-20134; Avenida Marginal; s/d from Mtc1500/2000; 2-room cottage s/d Mtc2850/3750; ☒) This self-catering place, about 1.5km beyond Caraçol, and on the opposite side of the road, has simple, rather faded rooms in three small cottages, all with twin beds, TV, screens, fridge and hotplate.

OUR PICK Residencial Regio Emilia (☎ 272-21297, 82-928 5510; residencial.reggio.emilia@gmail.com; www.wix.com/akeelz/Residencial-Reggio-Emilia; 8696 Avenida Marginal; r US$80, per r in self-catering chalets US$80; P ☒ ☎) A lovely spot next door to Pieter's Place with spacious, spotless rooms – all with hot water, air-con, DSTV and minifridge – and a few self-catering chalets in quiet grounds. All are nicely decorated with locally-sourced materials such as Palma mats, and all have mosquito screens on the windows. Breakfast costs extra. A restaurant is planned. The owners are very knowledgeable about Cabo Delgado and it may be possible to arrange cultural tours in various languages.

Complexo Náutilus (☎ 272-21520; nautilus@teledata.mz; Avenida Marginal; s/d/q bungalows Mtc2500/3000/3500; ☒ ☎) A good setting directly on the beach, marred only by indifferent service and management. Accommodation is in closely spaced beachside bungalows of varying sizes, all with TV and minifridge, and there's a restaurant. Ask for one of the 'newer' front bungalows. Rates include breakfast.

Top End

Pemba Beach Hotel (☎ 272-21770; www.pembabeachresort.com; Avenida Marginal; s/d from US$165/330; P ☒ ☐ ☎) This five-star establishment has expansive grounds overlooking the water, well-equipped rooms, a restaurant (closed at the time of research) and a yacht for charters round the Quirimbas Archipelago. Package deals from Johannesburg are available that also include sister lodges in the Quirimbas and Bazaruto archipelagos.

Clube Naval (☎ 272-21770; www.pembabeachresort.com; Avenida Marginal; 4- to 6-person self-catering apt from 55410) Next door to Pemba Beach Hotel and under the same management, Club Naval has upmarket self-catering apartments accommodating four adults and two children. There's also a restaurant.

Eating

DOWN CENTRE

Pastelaria Flôr d'Avenida (☎ 272-20514; Avenida Eduardo Mondlane; meals from Mtc100) A long-standing

and informal eatery, with outdoor tables on a small, street-side plaza, and a selection of standards and pastries.

Restaurante-Bar Samar (☎ 272-20415; Avenida 25 de Setembro; meals from Mtc150; ☾ 9am-10pm Sun-Fri) Tucked away in the car park of the Igreja Reino de Deus, this place features hearty Portuguese cuisine served on a shaded porch.

556 (☎ 272-21487; Rua No 1; meals Mtc180-400; ☾ 10am-10pm Mon-Sat; ☒) On the hill overlooking the port and the bay, with South African meats, plus chicken grills, pizzas, hamburgers, grilled prawns, squid, pub food and ice cream.

Locanda Italiana (☎ 272-20672; 487 Rua Gerónimo Romero; meals about Mtc250; ☾ from 5pm Mon-Sat) Delicious and reasonably priced Italian cuisine served in a quiet courtyard in the baixa. It makes a calming retreat from the heat and bustle of town.

For self-catering try **Osman's** (Avenida 25 de Setembro), about 1.5km east of the main junction, or the **bakery-minimarket** (Avenida Eduardo Mondlane) next to Pastelaria Flôr d'Avenida.

WIMBI BEACH

Restaurante Rema (Avenida Marginal; meals from Mtc120) A good spot for local meals and vibes. It's just opposite Pemba Dolphin.

JPS (Avenida Marginal extension; half chicken & chips Mtc150; ☾ lunch & dinner Tue-Sun) A local haunt on the inland side of the road just beyond SAL, with grilled chicken, *matapa* (cooked cassava leaves with peanut sauce) and other local dishes, and screened-in eating areas. Service isn't speedy, but the price is right and the food is good.

Restaurante Wimbi (Avenida Marginal; meals from Mtc150) A local place featuring seating on the beach, seafood grills and good service.

Pemba Dolphin (Avenida Marginal; seafood grills from Mtc180) Directly on the beach, with music and a beach-bar ambience, plus seafood grills.

Clube Naval (☎ 272-21770; Avenida Marginal; meals from Mtc250; ☾ 10am-midnight) A waterside restaurant-bar with a breezy setting directly on the beach and a large menu featuring salads, seafood, chicken, ribs, pizzas and desserts. There's a volleyball area on the sand, plus a children's playground.

Getting There & Away

AIR

LAM (Avenida Eduardo Mondlane; ☾ 7am-4.30pm Mon-Fri, 9.30-11.30am Sat) flies daily to/from Maputo

NORTHERN MOZAMBIQUE

CRAFT SHOPPING

Even if you don't think you want to buy crafts, it's worth stopping in at the excellent **Artes Maconde** (☎ /fax 272-21099; artesmaconde@tdm.co.mz; town centre Avenida 25 de Setembro; Wimbi Beach Pemba Beach Hotel; Wimbi Beach CI Divers), especially its main shop in the town centre, which is packed with a wide range of quality carvings, crafts and textiles sourced from throughout Mozambique, as well as from elsewhere in the region. It's one of the best craft shops in the country, as far as quality of the artistry and uniqueness of the art are concerned, and craftsmen come from outlying villages throughout Cabo Delgado and as far away as the DR Congo (Zaïre) to deliver their wares. It does international air and sea shipping, and also takes orders.

(via Nampula and/or Beira), and three times weekly to/from Dar es Salaam (Tanzania). **SAAirlink** (☎ 272-21700; www.saairlink.co.za; airport) flies twice weekly between Johannesburg and Pemba.

For charters to the Quirimbas Archipelago or Lake Niassa, contact Kaskazini (p151). For the Quirimbas, also see the boxed text, p157.

BUS & CHAPA
Grupo Mecula (☎ 272-20821) has daily buses to Nampula (Mtc250, seven hours), Moçimboa da Praia (Mtc250, 7½ hours) and Mueda (Mtc250, 10 hours) – with the same bus going first to Moçimboa da Praia and then on to Mueda. There's a direct bus every other day to Nacala (Mtc250, seven hours); otherwise take the Nampula bus to Namialo junction and wait there for onward transport. For Mozambique Island, the best bet is to continue to Nampula, and then get onward transport from there the next day. You can also try your luck getting out at Namialo junction and looking for onward transport from there, but the timing often doesn't work out, and Namialo is unappealing as an overnight spot. All Pemba departures are at 4.45am from the Grupo Mecula office, just off the main road and about 1.5km from the centre on a small side street behind Osman's supermarket. All buses also pass by the Mcel office (corner of Avenidas 25 de Setembro and Eduardo Mondlane) before departing town by around 5am.

Otherwise, try your luck with other transport at Mcel, or head to Embondeiro transport stand, 3km from the centre (Mtc75 in a taxi). Alternatively, *tanzaniano* chapas depart in all directions from Igreja Reino de Deus from 4am, with high speeds and prices only marginally cheaper than those of the Mecula buses.

To Montepuez (Mtc130, two hours), mini-buses depart from Faria garage, on Avenida 25 de Setembro opposite the Catholic church from around 4.30am.

Getting Around
BICYCLE
CI Divers (p151) rents bicycles for about US$5 per hour.

BUS & TAXI
There are taxi ranks on Avenida Eduardo Mondlane just down from Mcel and at the same junction along Avenida 25 de Setembro. Town to Wimbi Beach costs from Mtc150. There's also a public bus that runs between 6am and 7pm from town to Wimbi Beach and beyond (Mtc10).

RENTAL CAR
Safi Rentals (☎ 82-380 8630, 82-684 7770; www.pemba rentacar.com) comes highly recommended, offering reliable car rentals for very reasonable prices. Rates include unlimited kilometres and open the door to many attractions in the north that would be otherwise inaccessible for budget and midrange travellers. It was based at Complexo Náutilus at the time of research, but if you don't find it there, make a call, send an email, or send a message through Artes Maconde.

It's also possible to arrange car rental through Kaskazini (p151).

AROUND PEMBA
Within about a 2½- to three-hour drive from Pemba are several camps and lodges, all of which offer visitors a chance to experience part of Cabo Delgado's wild, untamed bush and possibly see an elephant or two.

Beautifully set on the northern side of Pemba Bay, **Londo Lodge** (www.londolodge.com; per person full-board from US$545; 🏊) has beach-facing villas overlooking the bay, a restaurant and range of water sports. Short bushwalks ca also be arranged, and sunset dhow cruises are included in the price.

Taratibu (Veka; ☎ 82-327 0654; www.taratibulodge.com; per person full-board incl bush walks US$155) is a rustic bush camp set in a wilderness tract about 160km northwest of Pemba in Ancuabe district in a wild area known for its elephants. There are a handful of pleasant double bungalows, and the chance for bush walks and vehicle safaris. Advance bookings are essential.

About 12km south of Pemba is **Murrébuè**, a lovely stretch of sand known for its optimal kite surfing conditions. **Il Pirata** (www.murrebue.com; d US$80-110) is the hub of activity. It also has some lovely bungalows and delicious Italian meals. Airport transfers cost a very reasonable US$30 return.

Just down from Il Pirata is **Isanja Beach Cottages** (☎ 82-8198890; ganddwilliamson@gmail.com; 6-person cottage US$100), consisting of two cottages overlooking the sea, each with two double bedrooms, a large living room that can sleep an additional person or two, and self-catering and braai facilities. Meals can also be arranged with advance notice, as can airport transfers.

The government is pushing development of the Murrébuè area, so changes here are likely.

QUIRIMBAS ARCHIPELAGO

The Quirimbas Archipelago consists of about two dozen islands and islets strewn among the turquoise waters along the 400km stretch of coastline between Pemba and the Rovuma River. Some are waterless and uninhabited, while others have histories as long as the archipelago itself.

Throughout, the archipelago's natural beauty is astounding, with searingly white patches of soft sand surrounded by brilliant turquoise and azure waters alternating with greener and vegetated islands and extensive stands of mangroves. Dense mangrove forests also link many of the islands with each other and with the coast, with only skilled dhow captains able to navigate among the intricate channels that were cut during Portuguese times.

Today, many of the southern islands, including Ibo, Quirimba, Matemo and Rolas, are part of the **Quirimbas National Park** (Parque Nacional das Quirimbas; adult/child Mtc200/100), which also includes large inland areas on the fringing coastline. Fees are collected by hotels within the park area, although this is likely to change.

There are also various other park fees, including Mtc100 per person per day for camping, but their enforcement status is still in flux.

In addition to its pristine natural beauty, the archipelago is known for its diving, which is considered to be especially good around Quilaluia, Vamizi and Rongui (see p53), and for its birdwatching. Local bird guides are being trained within the framework of a community-based initiative, and can be booked through the tourist information office on Ibo.

History

Ibo and Quirimba, the two main islands in the archipelago, were already important Muslim trading posts when the Portuguese arrived in the 15th century. The islands were renowned in particular for their production of silks, cottons and maluane cloth – on some old maps, they are shown as the Maluane Islands. Ivory, ambergris and turtle shell were also important items in local commerce, and trade extended south as far as Sofala, Zambézia and north to Malindi, off the Kenyan coast.

By the early-17th century the Portuguese had established a mission on Quirimba and a fortified settlement on Ibo. They also built cisterns to store rainwater, which encouraged the development of agriculture, and the islands began to supply food to Mozambique Island. Beginning in the mid-18th century, the archipelago – particularly Ibo Island – served as a base for the clandestine slave trade, attracting boats from as far away as Zanzibar and Kilwa in present-day Tanzania. In the late-19th century, as the slave trade came to an end and colonial attention shifted to the mainland, trade in the archipelago began to decline. Today Quirimba, with its coconut and sisal plantations, is probably the most economically active of the islands, though all are quiet – largely ignored until recently and caught in a fascinating time warp.

Information

A combined Quirimbas National Park office and tourist information office has just opened on Ibo Island opposite the church and near the dhow port, where you can get information and arrange guides, and pay park entry fees. Various community-based tourism activities are also planned, including dhow excursions, traditional dancing and guided tours. Once the program is up and going, you can

NORTHERN MOZAMBIQUE

arrange these here as well. Meanwhile, the hotels should be able to help.

Ibo Island

Ibo, the best-known of the Quirimbas islands, is an enchanting place. Its quiet streets are lined with dilapidated villas and crumbling, moss-covered buildings, and echo with the silent, hollow footsteps of bygone centuries. Architecturally it is more open than Mozambique Island, although its ambience is more insulated and its pace more subdued. The best time to visit is during a clear, moonlit night, when the old colonial houses take on a haunting, almost surreal aspect.

Ibo was fortified as early as 1609 and by the late-18th century had become the most important town in Mozambique after Mozambique Island. During this era, the island was a major export point in the slave trade, with demand spurred by French sugar plantation owners on Mauritius and elsewhere. In the late-19th century, it served briefly as headquarters for the Niassa Company. However, in 1904, the headquarters were relocated to Pemba (then Porto Amelia) to take advantage of Pemba's better sea access routes and harbour, and Ibo faded into oblivion.

At the island's northern end is the star-shaped **Fort of São João**, which was built in 1791 and designed to accommodate up to 300 people. In the days when Ibo was linked into the slave trade, the fort's dark, cramped lower chambers were used as slave holding points. Today it's known for the **silver artisans** who have set up shop near the entrance. Much of the silver used is made from melted-down coins and is often of inferior quality, but the distinctive and refined Swahili artisanship is among the best in the region.

There are two other forts on the island, neither well preserved. The **Fort of São José** to the southwest dates from 1760, but ceased to have any military use once the larger fort of São João was built. The **Fort of Santo António** near the market was built around 1830. Other places of interest include a large church near the fort of São José, and the island's three cemeteries, including an old Hindu crematorium along the road running northwest from the port.

Traditional religious practices are alive and well on Ibo and if you spend some time on the island, you'll undoubtedly come into contact with them. One of the best times to see dancing is in late June, when the feast of São João is celebrated with numerous festivities.

Ibo doesn't have many beaches, but as compensation there are magical sunset views over the mud flats just north of the tiny port. With some time, you can also take day excursions to a nearby sandbank, or to a lovely patch of beach on the other side of the island.

If you speak Portuguese or have a translator, don't miss visiting **Senhor João Baptista** – Ibo's official historian, and a wealth of information of the island. His house – marked by a signpost ('Conselheiro e Historiador do Ilha do Ibo') – is along the shaded path leading from town to the fort of São João.

Those interested in doing some volunteer work can contact the **Ibo Eco-School** (www .iboecoschool.be) and Montessori Kindergarten Project. The project, founded by Belgian couple Winnie de Roover and Jorick Vandaele, aims to help counter low educational levels on the island by giving Ibo's children a solid educational start. It's still in its early stages, but kindergarten classes are up and running, and work is underway to make the project sustainable, and expand it into a network of satellite schools on nearby islands.

SLEEPING & EATING

The accommodation situation on Ibo is rapidly changing, with new places planned, so it's well worth stopping by Kaskazini (p151) in Pemba for an update before heading out this way.

It's possible to arrange **homestays** (☎ 82-551 1919; r Mtc250) with local families. Contact Ibraimo Assane directly at this booking number, or arrange through Kaskazini in Pemba. You'll get a taste for how locals live and get to sample local meals. Be prepared for extremely basic conditions.

A three-bedroom self-catering house with adjoining garden was being rehabilitated as part of community-based tourism initiatives on Ibo when we visited. Once finished it will be able to be rented by room or in its entirety. It's near the small St António fort and the antenna. Check with the tourist information office on Ibo or in Pemba for an update.

Campsite do Janine (campsite per person Mtc150) This simple campsite is just up from Ibo Island Lodge and the dhow port. Check with Kaskazini (p151) in Pemba first to confirm it's still operating.

ISLAND HOPPING

If you've ever dreamed of sailing around tropical islands surrounded by turquoise waters and past deserted white sandbanks, the Quirimbas Archipelago is the place to come.

Fim do Mundo Safaris (☎ 82-511 6925, 82-304 2908; www.fimdomundosafaris.com) offers live-aboard trips departing from Ibo Island on its handcrafted 42ft wooden sailing and motorised dhow (which takes from two to six guests). Apart from sailing, days are spent snorkelling, diving (certified divers only), kayaking and exploring deserted beaches and islands. Prices are US$120 per person per day including meals, and the sailing calendar is posted on its website. The owners are long-time Mozambique residents and divers and very knowledgeable on the area, and the ambience is laid-back and convivial.

If you're in a group or aren't feeling up to the rigours of public transport to reach Ibo, or are simply wondering how to reach the other islands, there's a private **transfer service** (☎ 82-724 4437; jorickv@gmail.com) based out of Ibo. It costs US$200 to charter a vehicle (up to six passengers) for a one-way transfer in either direction between Pemba and Tandanhangue or US$30 per person to hitch a lift if the vehicle is going anyway between the two towns. The same operator also offers transfers in a motorised boat between Tandanhangue and Ibo (US$30 one way), as well as island hopping services from Ibo to Matemo or Pangane (US$60, 1½ hours Ibo–Matemo, US$90, 2½ hours Ibo–Pangane). Alternatively, for a US$10 organising fee it can help you sort out a reliable local nonmotorised dhow to any of these destinations or other spots in the archipelago. Expect to pay Mtc1000/2000 per boat from Ibo to Matemo/Pangane.

Another option is a private **dhow charter** to cruise around the Quirimbas. Stephane has a six-sleeper cabin dhow for charter anywhere in the archipelago, and also runs regular trips from Pemba to Ibo with an overnight stop at Mefunvo island, where you rough camp on the beach (per person US$80 for the entire trip with three meals). Dimitri has motorised and nonmotorised boats available for dive charters or transfers. Both of these can be contacted through the private transfer service listed above, through Miti Miwiri hotel (below) on Ibo Island, or through Kaskazini (p151) in Pemba.

Tikidiri (airfield road; tw Mtc300) This community-run place, about 2km from the dhow port opposite the old cemetery along the path leading to the airfield, has basic but clean stone-and-thatch bungalows, all with nets and private bucket baths. There's no electricity and no breakfast, but good local meals can be arranged, as can guides for exploring the island and elsewhere in the archipelago.

Telecomunicações de Moçambique Casa de Hospedes (s/d with shared bathroom from Mtc400/700, ste Mtc900) About 500m east of the port near the telecom building, this guesthouse has spacious, cleanish no-frills rooms with fan, nets, occasional electricity and a TV in the common area, plus clean bucket showers. It's a decent enough deal if other budget places are full. The only problem is that there's not always someone around to open it up for you, and when there is, it's often filled with official guests. It's just around the corner from Miti Miwiri, at the start of the road leading to the airfield.

Miti Miwiri (☎ 26-960530, 82-543 5864; www.mitimiwiri.com; dm US$20, d US$50-80; ☒) A lovely, atmospheric place in a restored house with a handful of spacious, en suite good-value rooms with fan, including one 'dorm' room with two double beds. There's a large, walled garden with two large swings, a bar and sheesha lounge, and a restaurant with good meals (including vegetarian selections). Staff can also help with tourist information and excursions, flight bookings to/from Pemba and international telephone calls. It's in the heart of the town, and about 10 minutes on foot from the dhow port – ask any of the children who come to meet the boat to show you the way. Continental/full breakfast costs Mtc100/150 extra.

Cinco Portas (www.cincoportas.com; s US$35-60, d US$60-100, 8-person house US$240; ☒) This is another atmospheric, good-value place in a restored mansion with a lovely garden. It's just up the road from Miti Miwiri in a fine location overlooking the bay, and has a variety of rooms, some with sea-facing verandahs, and a restaurant (breakfast costs extra). It's also possible to rent out the main house.

Ibo Island Lodge (www.iboisland.co.za; s/d with half-board from US$435/670; ☒) This nine-room luxury boutique hotel the most upmarket accommodation on Ibo – is housed in two restored mansions in a prime setting overlooking the water near the dhow port. Relax on the sea-facing verandahs, enjoy a sundowner overlooking the water, or luxuriate in the comforts of the rooms.

Quirimba Island

Quirimba, just south of Ibo, is the most economically active island of the archipelago, with large coconut plantations, a sizeable sisal factory and an airstrip. While it is more bustling than Ibo, it is far less interesting from an architectural and historical perspective and not nearly as scenic as the little patches of paradise further north. It is possible to walk between Quirimba and Ibo at low tide, but the route is through dense mangrove swamps, and you'll need a guide.

Historically, Quirimba was an important Muslim trading centre well before the arrival of the Portuguese. In 1522 it was raided by the Portuguese and the town was destroyed, although it was later rebuilt. In the 16th century Quirimba served as a centre for missionary work.

There is no accommodation on the island, though this is likely to soon change.

Quilaluia

Until recently, tiny Quilaluia was inhabited only by seasonal fishing communities. Now, it's a protected marine sanctuary and home to **Quilálea**, a luxurious private resort with nine sea-facing villas that was closed at the time of research due to owner and management changes. Once it reopens, it is likely to be for exclusive bookings only. The surrounding waters offer prime diving and snorkelling immediately offshore.

Medjumbe & Matemo

Idyllic Medjumbe is a narrow sliver of island draped with white coral sand and home to **Medjumbe Island Resort** (www.medjumberesort .com; per person with full-board from US$515; 🔀 🔝). Accommodation is in 13 thatched wooden chalets set directly on the sand. Diving and fishing are available just offshore.

Unlike Medjumbe, which is unpopulated except for the resort, the much larger island of Matemo, north of Ibo, has been inhabited for generations, and was an important centre for cloth manufacture into the 17th century. Today villages dot much of the north

and interior of the island. **Matemo Community Campsite** (campsite per person about Mtc100) was just getting started as this book was researched. It's on the southern coast of Matemo island near Muanancombo village, with four no-frills A-frame bungalows and a camping area, all with shared ablutions and communal cooking facilities. An informal 'restaurant' (meals cooked by local women) and a small shop selling some basics are planned. Also on Matemo is the very upmarket **Matemo Island Resort** (www .matemoresort.com; per person with full-board from US$460; 🔀 🔝), currently the largest of the island developments, with 24 chalets – all with sliding glass doors opening onto the beach, indoor and outdoor showers and Moorish overtones in the common areas.

Both Medjumbe Island Resort and Matemo Island Resort are run by Rani Africa, which also runs the Pemba Beach Hotel in Pemba and Lugenda Safari Camp in the Niassa Reserve, and island/mainland packages are available.

Vamizi, Rongui & Macalóè

These three islands are part of the currently stalled **Maluane Project** (www.maluane.com) – a privately funded, community based conservation project. Ultimately plans are for it to encompass not only the islands, but also an adjoining coastal strip and a 33,000 hectare inland area, where wildlife safari/tropical island combinations will be possible. For now, only Vamizi has accommodation, with lodges on Rongui and Macalóè and an inland luxury bush lodge still very much in the developmental stages.

Historically, the most important of the three islands was Vamizi – a narrow, paradisal crescent about midway between Moçimboa da Praia and Palma at the northernmost end of the archipelago. It was long a Portuguese and Arabic trading post and there are ruins of an old Portuguese fort at its western end, plus a large village and several stunning beaches to the north and east. All three islands are important seasonal fishing bases.

Vamizi Island Lodge (www.vamizi.com; per person with full-board & activities US$770) is a 24-bed luxury getaway on a long arc of spectacular white sand draped along Vamizi's northern edge, and one of the most beautiful places to relax along the northern Mozambican coast. The 10 spacious beach chalets have large, open sitting areas and private verandahs, plus all the comforts you could want, presented in a tasteful and low-key way. There's diving and snorkelling offshore. Deep-sea fishing, walks – including to some hawksbill and green turtle nesting areas – and birdwatching can be arranged.

Other Islands

Tiny **Quipaco**, about midway between Pemba and Quissanga and the first island in the Quirimbas string, is notable for its birdlife and mangrove ecosystems. The surrounding waters, especially at the nearby Ponto do Diablo, are considered prime fishing areas and the island is tranquil, although it lacks the tropical backdrop of some of the other islands.

Further north is small **Quisiva**, which has no infrastructure, although you can still see some old Portuguese plantation houses. The tiny and densely vegetated **Rolas** is uninhabited except for some seasonal fishing settlements and a fascinating population of coconut crabs. The island is part of the Quirimbas National Park area; there's no accommodation.

Getting There & Away

AIR

Several of the islands, including Ibo, Quirimba and Matemo, have airstrips for charter flights. Book directly through the island lodges or through Kaskazini (p151) in Pemba. Individual seats are often available; Pemba to Ibo costs US$110 per person one way.

BOAT

For boat transport information, see the boxed text, p157.

If none of those options suit: to reach Ibo or Quirimba on your own steam, you'll need to go first to Quissanga, on the coast north of Pemba, and from there to the village of Tandanhangue, where you can get a dhow to the islands. A direct chapa departs Pemba from the fish market (Map p150) behind the mosque in Paquitequete bairro (Mtc200,

four to five hours) at about 4am daily. Once in Quissanga, most vehicles continue on to Tandanhangue village (Mtc200 from Pemba), 5km further, which is the departure point for dhows to Ibo (Mtc100) and Quirimba islands. In a private car, the trip to Quissanga and Tandanhangue takes about 3½ hours. In the dry season, it's sometimes possible to find a vehicle from Pemba going via Metuge (Mtc150), which saves a bit on time.

For drivers (4WD), there's secure parking at Gringo's Place next to the Tandanhangue dhow port for Mtc50 per day, and at Casa de Isufo (signposted 2km before the Tandanhangue port) for Mtc70 per day. The latter is a bit of a walk, but useful if you're visiting when rains or high water make the intervening stretch of mud flats impassable for a vehicle. (A bridge is planned over the flats.)

Dhows leave Tandanhangue only at high tide (with a window of about two hours on either side of the high-tide point), and non-motorised boats take from one to six hours to Ibo (about 45 minutes with motor). There's no accommodation in Tandanhangue, but if you get stuck waiting, Isufo (at Casa de Isufo) can help you find a meal (allow plenty of time), and has an enclosed area where you can sleep on the ground or set up a tent. Chartering a motorised boat for yourself to Ibo will cost about Mtc800 to Mtc1000 one way.

For speedboat charters from Pemba direct to the islands, contact the upmarket lodges or Kaskazini (p151). For those with plenty of time, there's a dhow (nonmotorised) that sails with some regularity from Paquitequete in Pemba to Ibo (Mtc100, about 12 hours). To hire a Paquitequete-Ibo dhow for yourself, expect to pay about Mtc2500.

MACOMIA

The small district capital of Macomia is the turn-off point for the beach at Pangane and the end of the good tarmac if you're heading north. If you find yourself stuck here on a weekend, chances are good that you'll be able to see some *mapiko* dancing. Football (soccer) is also popular and there are frequent matches pitting local teams against those from Pemba and elsewhere in the area.

Pensão-Residencial Caminho do Norte (r Mtc350), on the main road just north of the junction, has no-frills rooms. **Bar Chung** (at the junction) has a few very basic rooms in the family compound to rent, and can help with meals.

COCONUT CRABS

Rolas Island is known for its giant coconut eating land crabs. These nocturnal creatures, considered to be the largest arthropods in the world, sometimes grow up to 1m long. They get their name from their proclivity for climbing coconut palms, shaking down the nuts, and then prying the cracked shells open to scoop out the flesh.

Several vehicles daily go to Mucojo, sometimes continuing on to Pangane. Hitching is possible but very slow. If you're stranded, a good place to ask for a lift is at Bar Chung, at Macomia's main intersection.

To continue southwards to Pemba, the Mecula buses from Moçimboa da Praia and Mueda pass Macomia from about 9am. Going northwards, you'll often need to wait until around 9am or 10am for a vehicle to pass through.

CHAI

It was in the large village of Chai that Frelimo's military campaign against colonial rule began in 1964. There's a small monument near the main road and every year on 25 September (Revolution Day), national attention turns here as the independence struggle is remembered with visits by high-ranking officials and re-enactments of historical events.

Chai is about 40km north of Macomia along the main road between Pemba and Moçimboa da Praia. Take any vehicle heading to/from Pemba and ask to be dropped off, but do it early enough in the day so that you have a chance of onward transport, as there's no accommodation.

PANGANE

Pangane is a large village on a long, lovely palm-fringed beach about 10km north of Mucojo, and 50km off the main north–south road. Many seasonal fishermen come up from Nacala and other places in the south, so the sand isn't always the cleanest, but the setting is beautiful, just on the edge of paradise. Just offshore is Macalóè Island, part of the Maluane project (p158), and beyond that the St Lazarus Bank, renowned for their diving and fishing.

Sleeping & Eating

Hashim's Camp (campsite per person Mtc200, bungalow s/d with shared bathroom Mtc400/600) Run by the helpful Hashim and his family, this place is set at Pangane's breezy point on the nicest stretch of sand and is ideal for sitting back for a few days. Staff will prepare local-style grilled fish meals and otherwise take care of you and while everything's very basic, it's clean and relaxed. Sleeping is in reed bungalows on the sand, with mattresses and decent ablutions.

Guludo (☎ in UK 01323-766 655; www.guludo.com; r per person with full-board from US$285) This upmarket fair-traded camp – set against a backdrop of palm groves, white sands and turquoise seas – makes a fine base if you want to get a taste of northern Mozambique's coastal paradise while learning about and supporting local community development initiatives. Accommodation is in well-appointed safaristyle tents or more upmarket 'adobe bandas'. There's also a spacious family banda, and the chance for island excursions, diving and even

MAPIKO DANCING

If you hear drumming in the late afternoons while travelling around Cabo Delgado, it likely means *mapiko* – the famed masked dancing of the Makonde.

The dancer – always a man – wears a special wooden *lipiko* (mask, plural: *mapiko*), decorated with exaggerated features, hair (often real) and facial etchings. After being carved, the masks are kept in the bush in a special place known as the *mpolo*, where only men are permitted to enter. Traditionally, they cannot be viewed by women or by uncircumcised boys unless they are being worn by a dancer.

Before *mapiko* begins, the dancer's body is completely covered with large pieces of cloth wrapped around the legs, arms and body so that nothing can be seen other than the fingers and toes. All evidence that there is a person inside is supposed to remain hidden. The idea is that the dancer represents the spirit of a dead person who has come to do harm to the women and children, from which only the men of the village can protect them. While boys learn the secret of the dance during their initiation rites, women are never supposed to discover it and remain in fear of the *mapiko*. (*Mapiko* supposedly grew out of male attempts to limit the power of women in matrilineal Makonde society.)

Once the dancer is ready, distinctive rhythms are beaten on special *mapiko* drums. The dance is usually performed on weekend afternoons, and must be finished by sunset. The best places to see *mapiko* dancing are in and around Mueda and in Macomia. To take a mask home, look in craft shops in Pemba and Nampula.

THE MAKONDE

The Mueda Plateau around Mueda is home to the Makonde people, who are renowned throughout Africa for their amazing woodcarvings. Like many tribes in the north, the Makonde are matrilineal. Children and inheritances normally belong to the woman and it's common for a husband to move to the village of his wife after marriage, setting up house near his mother-in-law. Settlements are widely scattered – possibly a remnant of the days when the Makonde sought to evade slave raids – and there is no tradition of a unified political system. Each village is governed by a hereditary chief and a council of elders.

Due to their isolated location, the Makonde remained largely insulated from colonial and postcolonial influences. Even today, many Makonde still adhere to traditional religions, with the complex spirit world given its fullest expression in their carvings.

Traditionally, the Makonde practised body scarring and, while it's seldom done today, you may see older people with markings on their faces and bodies. It's also fairly common to see elderly Makonde women wearing a wooden plug in their upper lip, or to see this depicted in Makonde artwork.

---

elephant tracking. Staff can also arrange walks to see the village school and other community initiatives. It's about 15km south of Mucojo junction; transfers can be arranged from Pemba and Macomia.

Getting There & Away

Pangane is 50km off the main north–south road (the turn-off is at Macomia), and 9km north of Mucojo – a tiny junction village on the coast. There is at least one daily chapa between Macomia (where fuel is sometimes available) and Pangane (Mtc100), departing Pangane at about 5am. Departures from Macomia are at about 9am – the chapa waits until the Pemba–Moçimboa da Praia and Moçimboa da Praia–Pemba through buses arrive. There are also several chapas daily from Macomia to Mucojo, from where you can usually find a pick-up on to Pangane. Dhows to the Quirimbas islands can be arranged at Hashim's Camp (opposite) and Guludo (opposite); for dhows from Ibo or the other islands to Pangane, see p157.

There's an airstrip at Mucojo for charter planes.

MUEDA

Mueda – the main town on the Makonde Plateau and the centre of Mozambique's Makonde people – is rather lacking in charm. However this is compensated for by a wonderfully cool climate, a rustic, highland feel and an attractive setting, with views down from the escarpment along the southern and western edges of town. The surrounding area holds the potential for some good hiking, but

it was heavily mined during the war, so stick to well-trodden paths. The plateau itself lies at about 800m altitude, with water available only on its slopes and at its base.

Sights & Activities

Mueda was originally built as an army barracks during the colonial era. In 1960 it was the site of the infamous massacre of Mueda (see p23). There's a statue commemorating Mueda's role in Mozambican independence and a mass grave for the 'martyrs of Mueda' at the western end of town. Maria José Chipande – wife of Alberto Chipande, who was a well-known Makonde guerrilla commander during the independence struggle, one of the founding members of Frelimo and a former minister of defence – is also buried here. Just behind this monument is a ravine (known locally as *xiudi*) over which countless more Mozambicans were hurled to their deaths.

The outlying villages are good places to see Makonde woodcarvings.

About 50km northwest of Mueda on the edge of the Makonde Plateau is the outpost town of **Moçimboa do Rovuma**, which offers views down to the Rovuma River, although it's inaccessible unless you have your own vehicle.

Sleeping & Eating

Pensão Takatuka (Rua 1 de Maio; r Mtc200, in annexe Mtc250) Takatuka has reasonably clean but very basic rooms in the main building or in an annexe out back, all with shared bucket bath. Food can be arranged, but order well in advance. It's on the tarmac road in the town centre.

Motel Sanzala (Rua 1 de Maio; r Mtc250) Currently Mueda's best accommodation, with basic rooms sharing bathrooms, and no running water. Meals can be arranged. It's just down the road from Pensão Takatuka.

Getting There & Away

Grupo Mecula has a daily bus between Pemba and Mueda via Moçimboa da Praia (Mtc250, 10 hours), departing at 5am. Several vehicles go each morning between Mueda and Moçimboa da Praia (Mtc120, two hours). All transport leaves from the main road opposite the market, and it all leaves early. After about 10am, it's difficult to find vehicles to any destination.

If you're driving, there are two roads connecting Mueda with the main north–south road. Most traffic uses the good road via Diaca (50km). The alternate route via Muidumbe (about 30km south of Diaca) is scenic, winding through hills and forests, but rougher. Near Muidumbe is **Nangololo**, a mission station and an important base during the independence struggle, with an old airstrip large enough to take jets.

Expect changes to the roads (and probably also an increase of accommodation in Mueda) with the opening of the Unity Bridge between Mozambique and Tanzania.

MOÇIMBOA DA PRAIA

This bustling outpost is the last major town before the Rovuma River and the Tanzanian border. Most local residents are Mwani ('People of the Sea') – a Swahili and hence Muslim people known for their textiles and silver craftsmanship, as well as for their rich song and dance traditions. Moçimboa da Praia does a brisk trade with Tanzania, both legal and illegal, and from here northwards, a few words of Swahili will often get you further than Portuguese.

The town itself is long – stretched over several kilometres between the main road and the sea. In the upper-lying section is a small market, several *pensões*, a petrol station and the transport stand. About 2km east near the water are a few more places to stay, police and immigration, a lively fish market and the colourful dhow port.

Information

If you're travelling by dhow and enter or leave Mozambique here, have your passport stamped at the immigration office near Complexo Miramar. An immigration officer meets arriving charter flights.

Barclays Bank (Avenida 7 de Março) Has an ATM which takes Visa card and changes US dollars cash; out of hours, try changing with some of the Indian shop owners.

Telecomunicações de Moçambique (Avenida 7 de Março; per min Mtc1) Internet access.

Sights & Activities

Moçimboa da Praia makes an amenable base for exploring: Mueda is an easy day trip with private transport and also a possibility with

---

THE STORY OF THE NÁVILO

Once upon a time, the Yao and the Makonde, two of the largest tribes in northern Mozambique, were great enemies. This enmity arose in bygone days when Mataka was the most powerful Yao chief, and M'Bavale was an important leader among the Makonde. In those days the Yao (most of whom live in present-day Niassa province) earned their livelihood from hunting, fishing and trading. However the Makonde, who are at home in northern Cabo Delgado province, were farmers. As links between the coast and the interior grew, the Yao began to cross through the territory of the Makonde in order to trade with Arab coastal merchants. This intrusion on their territory angered the Makonde, and led to many battles. Before long, the Yao and the Makonde were sworn enemies, enmeshed in what seemed to be an intractable conflict.

Weeks, months and years passed. Finally, Mataka and M'Bavale reached an agreement that their people would stop fighting against each other. Not only that, but they would also embody this truce in a special relationship, known as the *návilo*. Under the *návilo*, the Yao and the Makonde would meet each other in peace. They would also each be bound to go to any length necessary to meet the needs of the other, and in turn would have full liberties with the property of the other. A Yao would thus always be welcome into the home of a Makonde and treated as a royal visitor, and a Makonde would receive the same treatment from a Yao. The demands made by each side would be tempered by the knowledge that the other party could request the same of them. According to many Yao and Makonde, this special relationship between the two groups endures to this day.

COASTAL LIFE – 1

Life along much of the northern Mozambican coast centres around fishing and dhow building, often using centuries-old methods and equipment. Dhows are often constructed without nails, using only wooden pegs and tightly fitted wooden slats, which are sealed and waterproofed with a mixture of natural gum and resin.

One of the main catches in Palma and other areas of the far north is octopus. Fishermen head out to sea armed only with a snorkel, mask and a spear or handmade spear gun. Once well offshore, they leave their boats and swim to locate the octopus, which they then target between the eyes.

At night, look out to sea and you'll see little lanterns – rigged on dhows to lure fish into large nets spread out in the surrounding waters – bobbing up and down on the waves. Sometimes, groups of fishermen will pull trawl nets – some up to 100m long – through shoreline waters in search of fish that feed on sea-grass meadows in the shallows. In delta areas and around mangrove creeks, you may see traps – some up to 50m long – made from mangrove poles. Smaller reed traps and baskets are often used in the southern part of the country and in inland lakes. A common sight at low tide is women in their brightly coloured *capulanas* (sarongs) and head scarves wading into the sand flats to harvest clams, oysters and other shellfish.

---

public transport, if you get lucky with timing the vehicles, and Palma is straightforward to visit for the day with public transport. Watching all the activity at the fish market, especially early morning or late afternoon, is fascinating. It's also possible to arrange a dhow to visit some of the outlying islands, or to visit the attractive swimming beach near Ncamangano – ask at the petrol station near the immigration office.

Sleeping & Eating

Pensão Leeta, at the town entrance opposite the transport stand, was rented out in its entirety when this book was researched, but you may still be able to pitch a tent in its grounds.

Pensão-Residencial Magid (☎ 272-81099; Avenida Samora Machel; r Mtc350) A short walk downhill from the transport stand and convenient to the Grupo Mecula bus 'garage', with basic rooms sharing facilities.

Bungalow (r Mtc350) This unsignposted place is about 100m further towards the fish market from Complexo de Contentores de Ilha Vumba, with a couple of small, straightforward rondavels on a large lawn.

Complexo Miramar (Complexo Natasha or Dona Bebé; ☎ 272-81135/6; r Mtc1000) Directly on the water at the lower end of town, with three very basic, darkish rondavels, although there is usually a trickle of running water and the sound of the water is relaxing. Meals are available with advance notice. Follow the main road – Avenida Samora Machel – downhill

to the water (about a 10-minute walk from the transport stand).

Complexo de Contentores de Ilha Vumba (☎ 82-311 4750; r small/large Mtc1170/2340; 🖳) This place – temporary housing for oil and tourism project workers – may not be there by the time you reach Moçimboa da Praia, but it's worth checking just in case. On offer are clean, air-con rooms in trailers. It's along the road paralleling the beach, and just up from Complexo Miramar when heading towards the fish market.

Hotel Chez Natalie (☎ 272-81092, 82-439 6080; natalie.bockel@gmail.com; campsite per person Mtc300, 4-person chalets Mtc1800) The best bet in town if you have your own transport, with large grounds overlooking the estuary, camping, and a handful of spacious family-style four-person chalets with running water and mosquito nets, and a grill. Very tranquil. Breakfast and other meals are available with advance arrangement only. It's 2.5km from the town centre; watch for the barely signposted left-hand turn-off from Avenida Samora Machel onto Avenida Eduardo Mondlane just after passing Clubé de Moçimboa. Continue along Avenida Eduardo Mondlane past the small Praça do Paz on your left for 400m. Turn left next to a large tree onto a small dirt path, and continue about 1km past a row of local-style houses to Chez Natalie. With advance notice, mapiko dancing can be arranged.

Restaurante Estrelha (Avenida Samora Machel) is opposite the police station and on the right, just before the park. There's outdoor seating

---

COASTAL LIFE – 2

I grew up along the coast near Quiterajo, north of Pangane. All the boys of my age learned the ways of a fisherman. The same man who taught us the Quran would also bring us in small groups down to the sea in the afternoon after our lessons. There, he would show us how to fish and teach us the ways of the sea. I speak Mwani – my mother was Mwani – as well as Swahili, Portuguese, some English and a bit of Yao. I now make my home in Lichinga, as there are more opportunities here for work. But, I return to the coast whenever possible to visit my family, who still lives there.

Here in Lichinga, as in so many parts of the country, the schools are too full. It can happen that up to 70 students are in a classroom, so almost no learning takes place. Together with a group of other parents who live in my neighbourhood, we have hired a tutor for our children. There are eight of us, and we each put in money each month for the tutor. He comes to a courtyard in our neighbourhood and gives the children additional instruction after they return from school in the afternoons. I think it is a good use of the money. Otherwise they would get through school and not be able to read.

Iusuf, age 36, Lichinga

---

and – with luck – a choice of grilled chicken or fish. Otherwise, try the cheap and reliable **Take Away** (Avenida Samora Machel), just down from and opposite Clube de Moçimboa.

Getting There & Away
AIR
There's an airstrip outside town for charter flights.

BUS & PICK-UP
The transport stand is near the market at the entrance to town, and near the large tree. Two pick-ups go daily to/from the Rovuma ('Namoto') via Palma (Mtc300, four hours), leaving Moçimboa da Praia between 2.30am and 3.30am or 4am latest; arrange with the driver the afternoon before to be collected from your hotel. Allow two to three hours between Moçimboa da Praia and Palma, and another 1½ to two hours to the border. If all goes smoothly, you can do the entire journey to Mtwara (Tanzania) in half a day in the dry season; see p185. During the rainy season, it takes much longer and sometimes, depending on river levels, isn't possible at all. Coming from Tanzania, the last vehicle to Moçimboa da Praia leaves the Rovuma by about noon.

To Pemba, the Mecula bus departs daily at 4.30am sharp (Mtc250, seven hours). The best place to get it is at the 'garage' where it's kept during the night, about midway between Complexo Miramar and the bus stand. Alternatively, catch it at the main transport stand. A few pickups also do the journey, departing by 7am from the main road in front of the market.

The not-so-nice Maningue Nice bus goes between Moçimboa da Praia and Nampula several times weekly, and several vehicles go daily to/from Mueda (Mtc120, two hours).

PALMA
The large fishing village of Palma is nestled among the coconut groves about 45km south of the Tanzania border. It's a centre for basketry and mat weaving – though most of this is done in the outlying villages – and for boat making, and it is fascinating to watch craftspeople using centuries-old techniques. The area is also a melting pot of languages, with Makwe, Makonde, Mwani, Swahili and Portuguese all spoken.

Palma has an upper, administrative section of town with immigration, the post office, a guesthouse and a small market, and a lower section, about 2km downhill along the water, with the main market and many local houses. There's nowhere to change money, although changing meticais and Tanzanian shillings at the markets is no problem.

Sights & Activities
About 15km offshore across Túnguè Bay is idyllic **Tecomaji Island**, which is usually deserted except for some local fishermen who use it for drying octopus. Dhows can be arranged from the small harbour at the base of town; allow about three hours with good winds, and bring water and everything else with you. Just south of Tecomaji is Rongui Island (p158), followed by Vamizi Island (p158), both of which are privately owned. Beaches in town are not clean enough for swimming.

About 20km north of Palma is tiny Kiwiya junction, where a sandy track branches about 17km seawards to **Cabo Delgado** – the point of land from which Cabo Delgado province takes its name – and a lighthouse.

Sleeping & Eating

Casa do Antigo Administrador (Casa de Mahmud, r Mtc500) This place, opposite the church at the town entrance, is the place to stay, with very basic albeit clean accommodation and meals with advance notice.

Getting There & Away

All transport leaves from the Boa Viagem roundabout at the entrance to town. Some drivers continue down to the market, or will at least be willing to drop you at the top of the hill. For travel between Palma and Tanzania, see p185.

Chapas from Moçimboa da Praia en route to the Rovuma River pass Palma between about 6am and 8am and charge Mtc200 from Palma. Transport from the Rovuma south to Moçimboa da Praia passes through Palma between 11am and 2pm, and there's usually a car from Palma to Moçimboa da Praia each morning (Mtc150, 2½ hours).

Dhows to the islands can be arranged from the harbour in the lower part of town, about 3km from the Boa Viagem roundabout; bring shade, food and water with you.

Directory

DIRECTORY

CONTENTS

ACCOMMODATION

Accommodation in Mozambique ranges from the most basic rooms to five-star luxury and upmarket island lodges. There's a wide choice in major cities and tourist destinations. Elsewhere, selection is more limited. Throughout the country, accommodation tends to be more expensive than elsewhere in the southern Africa region, though a few good deals are available.

Accommodation along the coast, and especially in the south, fills up around Christmas and during the South African school holidays (see p173); book in advance if you'll be travelling at that time. Discounts are often available during the low season, and sometimes also midweek – always ask. Almost all places offer children's discounts, and extra beds can usually be arranged for about Mtc300 to Mtc500. When quoting prices, many establishments distinguish between a *duplo* (a room with two twin beds) and a *casal* (double bed). Half-board rates include breakfast and dinner.

Sleeping listings in this book are divided into budget, midrange and top-end categories. See the inside front cover for approximate price ranges. Many places quote their rates in US dollars or South African rand, and payment can almost always be made in meticais, US dollars or rand.

Backpackers Lodges
There are several backpacker lodges ('backpackers') in Mozambique, especially in the south. Most offer a choice of dorm beds or private rooms, plus cooking facilities and sometimes campsites. They're always worth hunting down and are usually the best-value budget accommodation. The price of a dorm bed averages Mtc300.

Camping
There are plenty of camping grounds along the southern coast, plus enough others scattered around the country that it's well worth carrying a tent if you're trying to save money (and essential if you're cycling or spending significant time in rural areas). Per person prices range from Mtc100 to Mtc250 per night. Camping avoids grubby *pensões* (cheap, local hotels), and some of the beachside camping grounds are wonderful, with the surf just over the dunes

BOOK YOUR STAY ONLINE

For more accommodation reviews and recommendations by Lonely Planet authors, check out the online booking service at www.lonelyplanet.com/hotels. You'll find the true, insider low-down on the best places to stay. Reviews are thorough and independent. Best of all, you can book online.

Officially, camping is permitted only in designated areas. Free camping isn't wise due to wildlife and general security risks. In rural parts of the country, or wherever there is no established campsite, ask the local *régulo* (chief) for permission; you'll invariably be welcomed and well taken care of, and should reciprocate with a modest token of thanks. (Generally what you would pay at an official camping ground or a bit less should be fine.)

Hotels & Pensões

The cheapest hotels (*pensão,* singular, or *pensões,* plural) are about Mtc300 per room. For this price you can expect a tiny, non-ventilated box of a room with a communal toilet and bucket bath. There may or may not be electricity.

For midrange, with a private bathroom, hot running water, electricity, air-conditioning (sometimes) and a restaurant on the premises, expect to pay from about Mtc1500 per room.

Top-end hotels offer all the amenities you would expect from around Mtc3000 per room.

Self-Catering & Rentals

Along the coast, many places offer self-catering options – with sleeping facilities plus a kitchenette or braai (barbecue) area – and there are a number of places geared exclusively to self-caterers (ie they don't offer meals or other hotel services, so you'll need to bring all your food with you, although most places at least have a bar). Most self-catering places have kitchen utensils and plug points. Some supply bed linens, mosquito nets and towels, while for others you'll need to bring these yourself. It's also possible in some coastal areas to rent private beach houses.

ACTIVITIES
Birdwatching

Mozambique is an excellent birdwatching destination. Prime birdwatching areas include the Bazaruto Archipelago, Gorongosa National Park and nearby Mt Gorongosa, the Chimanimani Mountains, Mt Namúli, the southern coastal wetlands, the Maputo Special Reserve and the area around Catapu, near Caia.

Over a decade ago, the Mozambique Bird Atlas Project was initiated – a massive undertaking aimed at charting the distribution and abundance of all bird species in the country, beginning in the south and moving northwards. For the final report and associated publications, see the website of the South Africa–based **Avian Demography Unit** (http://web.uct.ac.za/depts/stats/adu/p_mozat.htm).

Other recommended contacts for bird lists and birdwatching trips include the Pretoria-based **Indicator Birding** (www.birding .co.za), **Southern African Birding** (www.sabirding.co.za) and the **African Bird Club** (www.africanbirdclub.org). A free, downloadable field guide to the birds of Gorongosa National Park is available from **Images du Mozambique** (www.imagesdumozambique .com, click on Books).

Dhow Safaris, Boating & Kayaking

The best places for arranging dhow safaris are Ibo (for sailing around the Quirimbas Islands, see p157) and Vilankulo (to the islands of the Bazaruto Archipelago, see p93).

In Pemba, Kaskazini (p151) can arrange upmarket yacht charters, as can Guludo (p160) near Pangane, and any of the upmarket lodges in the Bazaruto Archipelago. In Maputo contact Mozambique Charters (p72) or enquire at Clube Naval (p153).

In these places, and in Moçimboa da Praia and elsewhere along the coast, it's also easy enough to organise things on your own, though always ask at your hotel for recommendations of reliable captains, travel with the prevailing winds and see the boxed text, p188.

Sea kayaking is in its infancy, which means that for any major jaunts you'll need to bring boats and all other equipment with you. However, several resort areas, including Inhaca Island and the dive shops at Wimbi Beach in Pemba, rent small sea kayaks suitable for short paddles close to shore. Nkwichi Lodge (p146) can arrange kayaking and canoeing along the Lake Niassa shoreline for its guests.

Diving & Snorkelling

There are excellent diving and snorkelling opportunities; see the Diving chapter (p49), and individual town listings.

Fishing

The waters off the Mozambican coast have long been legendary among anglers, particularly in the south between Ponta d'Ouro and Inhassoro, and in the far north around Pemba, which is within easy reach of the famed St Lazarus Bank, east of Quilaluia in the Quirimbas Archipelago. Saltwater fly-fishing is also increasingly popular. Inland, the most popular fishing areas are Lake Cahora Bassa near Tete, and Chicamba Real Dam near Chimoio. Contacts include Ugezi Tiger Lodge (p117) for Lake Cahora Bassa; Mozambique Charters (p72, for Maputo and Inhaca area); Benguerra Lodge (p98) or the other Bazaruto lodges; Pomene Lodge (p92); BD Lodge (p99); and Pensão Inhassoro (p99).

Many people bring their own boats and equipment from South Africa. Fishing charters can also be arranged through most of the coastal resorts and upmarket hotels. If you're signed up with a charter, all the necessary paperwork should be already covered. If you are bringing your own boat to Mozambique, you will need a sport-fishing license (from about Mtc450 per month), as well as a Form ORI/IIP (Registration Form for Captured Sports Fish). Launching is allowed from designated beach-access roads with a permit (from about Mtc500, depending on the type of boat). These are available from the local *capitania* (maritime office) found in major coastal towns. Both fishing licenses and launch permits can usually also be sorted out with coastal resorts.

Species you are likely to encounter include marlin, kingfish, tuna and sailfish. Marlin season is from October/November to February/March. For sailfish, it is generally year-round. Tag and release is encouraged at many resorts. Officially, no more than 6kg of any one type of catch from sport- and deep-sea fishing can be taken out of the country.

Hiking

For almost all hiking in Mozambique you'll be on your own, as hiking outfitters are few and infrastructure remains a low priority.

Mountain climbs that are straightforward to arrange include Mt Gorongosa (p107) and Mt Namúli (p124). For hiking, head to the Chimanimani Mountains (p113), which also include Mt Binga, Mozambique's highest peak. The hills around Gurúè offer good walking.

Surfing

The best waves are at Ponta d'Ouro (see p75) in the far south of the country and (for skilled surfers) at Tofinho (see p88) – Mozambique's unofficial surfing capital. Boards can be rented at both places.

For kite surfing, contact Pirate Kites (www .murrebue.com) at Murrébuè (p155), or Moya Kite/Surf based at Dolphin Encountour (p75) at Ponta d'Ouro.

Wildlife Watching

Some of the best wildlife watching is underwater; see the Diving chapter (p49). Another highlight is whale watching (see p53).

On the terrestrial side, wildlife watching in Mozambique is very much for those with an adventurous bent who are seeking an alternative to southern and East Africa's established safari circuits. Unlike in some neighbouring countries, where the herds practically come to you, in Mozambique you'll need to spend considerable time, effort and, in some cases, money to seek them out, and the country shouldn't be considered a 'Big Five' destination. However the chance for a genuine bush adventure and the beautiful wilderness terrain compensate for the sometimes-challenging sightings. Prime wildlife-watching destinations include, first and foremost, Gorongosa National Park, as well as Niassa Reserve, Maputo Special Reserve and Limpopo National Park.

BUSINESS HOURS

For business hours, see the inside front cover; exceptions are noted in individual listings. Most *casas de câmbio* (foreign exchange bureaus) are open from about 8.30am to 5pm Monday to Friday, and on Saturday until about noon. Many shops and offices close for an hour or two between noon and 2pm. In northern Cabo Delgado province, where dawn comes early, many places open by 7am or 7.30am, and close by about 5pm or 5.30pm, particularly in towns without good electricity supplies.

CHILDREN

Mozambicans are generally very friendly and helpful towards children. The main considerations for travel here will likely be the scarcity of decent medical facilities, the length and discomfort involved in many road journeys, the challenge of maintaining a balanced diet outside the major towns, and the difficulty of finding clean bathrooms outside of midrange and top-end hotels.

The southern beach resorts – many of which have a swimming pool, in addition to the beach – are ideal for visiting with young children, and most offer children's discounts. Cots and spare beds are easily arranged.

Powdered full-cream milk is available in almost all midsized and larger towns, as is bottled water. Nappies (diapers) are available in Maputo, Beira, Chimoio and Nampula, as is prepared baby food. (Shoprite branches and well-stocked pharmacies are the best places to find baby supplies in all these towns.) It's a good idea to travel with a *capulana* (sarong) or blanket to spread out and use as a makeshift nappy-changing area. Useful items to bring from home include a supply of wet wipes (though these are usually available in major cities), an eye bath and antibiotic eardrops.

If you will be travelling with an infant, strollers (pushchairs) are not practical. Much better is some sort of harness or cloth that allows you to carry the baby on your back, Mozambican style, or in front of you. For long journeys, always take extra food and drink along (for the baby and for yourself).

In beach areas, be aware of the risk of hookworm infestation in populated areas, as well as the risk of bilharzia in lakes. Other things to watch out for are sea urchins at the beach – beach shoes are a good idea for children and adults – and thorns and the like in the bush.

For malaria protection, it's essential to bring nets from home for your children and ensure that they sleep under them. Also bring mosquito repellent from home, and check with your doctor regarding the use of prophylactics. Long-sleeved shirts and trousers are the best protection at dawn and dusk.

Maputo-based car-hire agencies can arrange child seats with advance notice, and upmarket hotel restaurants sometimes have child seats. Breastfeeding in public is a non-issue in Mozambique, as women do it everywhere. Child care is easy to arrange informally through your hotel.

Lonely Planet's *Travel with Children* is full of tips for keeping children and parents happy while on the road.

CLIMATE

Southern Mozambique becomes unpleasantly hot for only a short period between late December and February, when temperatures can climb to over 30°C at noon, and can get unpleasantly wet between January/February and late March/April. For the rest of the year, there is an abundance of clear, blue sky and sunny days, with temperatures averaging around 24°C. From June through to August the weather can get chilly at night, so bring a light jacket.

Heading north along the coast, temperatures and humidity levels rise, though conditions are moderated by sea breezes. At the height of the rainy season during February and March, be prepared for washed out roads in more remote areas, and flooding in parts of the south and centre.

The hottest areas of the country are in the dry west around Tete city and along the humid Zambezi River Valley, where the mercury frequently exceeds 30°C. The coolest areas – where a light jacket is essential in the winter months from June through August – are elevated parts of Nampula, Niassa and Manica provinces, and northern Tete province.

Rainfall averages 750mm annually in Maputo, and between 800mm and 900mm along the northern coast. In the rainiest parts of the country – such as around

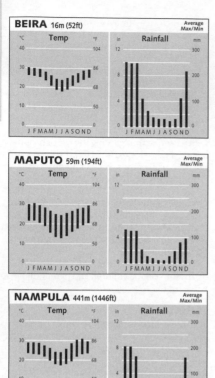

BEIRA 16m (52ft) — Average Max/Min — Temp — Rainfall

MAPUTO 59m (194ft) — Average Max/Min — Temp — Rainfall

NAMPULA 441m (1446ft) — Average Max/Min — Temp — Rainfall

Gurúè, southeast of Milange, and along the Zimbabwe border near Mt Binga – annual rainfall can be as high as 1800mm to 2200mm. Mozambique's zones of lowest precipitation are in the southwest, including parts of northwestern Gaza and western Inhambane provinces.

COURSES

There are several Portuguese language schools in Maputo (see p63). Elsewhere, private tutors can be easily arranged for lessons in Portuguese and local languages, although don't expect books or formalised instruction.

To arrange music (especially drumming) or dance instruction, try one of the provincial *casas de cultura* (cultural centres). In Maputo a good initial contact is the National Company of Song & Dance (Companhia Nacional de Canto e Dança; p68).

Diving-certification courses are available all along the coast.

CUSTOMS

It's illegal to export any endangered species or their products, including anything made from ivory or tortoiseshell. If you bring a bicycle, computer, video camera, generator, or major camping and fishing equipment into Mozambique, you'll need to fill out a temporary import permit. You'll then be given a receipt, which you'll need to present again (with the item/s declared) when leaving the country.

You're also supposed to declare imported cash in excess of US$5000 or the equivalent. You'll need to show the form again when leaving to justify any amounts over this. Local currency cannot be exported.

Importation of food and consumables is limited to a maximum value of US$50 per person.

'Reasonable' quantities of souvenirs for personal (rather than commercial) purposes can be exported without declaration.

Firearms of any type, including sporting firearms, aren't permitted to be brought into Mozambique unless you have a permit.

DANGERS & ANNOYANCES

Mozambique is a relatively safe place and most travellers shouldn't have any difficulties. That said, there are a few areas where a bit of caution is warranted.

Crime

Petty theft and robbery are the main risks: watch your pockets or bag in markets; don't leave personal belongings unguarded on the beach or elsewhere; and minimise (or eliminate) trappings such as jewellery, watches, headsets and external money pouches. If you leave your vehicle unguarded, don't be surprised if windscreen wipers and other accessories are gone when you return. Don't leave anything inside a parked vehicle. When at stoplights or slowed in traffic, keep your windows up and doors locked, and don't leave anything on the seat next to you where it could be snatched.

In Maputo and southern Mozambique – due to the proximity of South African organised-crime rings – carjackings and more violent robberies do occur, although most incidents can be avoided by taking the usual precautions: avoid driving at night; keep the passenger windows up and the doors locked if you are in a vehicle (including taxis) at any time during the day or night; don't wander around isolated or dark streets; avoid walking – alone or in a group – at dusk or at night,

---

BEACH BITS

Mozambique's beaches are idyllic, but there are some things to watch out for.

Crime Don't tempt someone by leaving your belongings unguarded on the beach, and avoid isolated areas.

Currents The strong pulls that often accompany tidal ebbs and flows make swimming risky in some areas; check with locals first before plunging in.

Jellyfish Bluebottles and other creatures with stinging tentacles are common in some seasons and areas. Most are painful rather than seriously harmful, but ask around locally if you see them on the beach.

Seashells, sea urchins & worms Sharp shells, sea urchins and the like inflict painful cuts that heal slowly in the tropics, so sandals or other footwear are a good idea if you'll be wading. They're also a good idea for beach walking, as more than one visitor has become infected with creeping eruption (also called cutaneous larva migrans or migrating larvae). This ailment is spread through the faeces of humans, dogs and other animals.

Tides Keep an eye on water levels if you're travelling by dhow. For swimming, the water goes far out at low tide and many beaches are only good for swimming at high tide.

---

particularly in isolated areas or on isolated stretches of beach; and avoid isolating situations in general. At all times of day, try to stick to busier areas of town, especially if you are alone, and don't walk alone along the beach away from hotel areas. If you're driving and your car is hijacked, hand over the keys immediately. The flashier the car, the higher the risk, with new 4WDs the main target.

When riding on chapas or buses, keep your valuables well inside your clothes to avoid falling victim to unscrupulous entrepreneurs who take advantage of overcrowded conditions to pick their fellow passengers' pockets.

All this said, don't let these warnings deter you, simply be a savvy traveller. The vast majority of visitors travel through this beautiful country without incident.

Hassles & Bribes

More likely than violent crime are simple hassles with underpaid authorities in search of a bribe. If you do get stopped you should not have any problem as long as your papers are in order. Being friendly, respectful and patient helps (and you won't get anywhere otherwise), as does trying to give the impression that you know what you're doing and aren't new in the country. Sometimes the opposite tack is also helpful – feigning complete ignorance if you're told that you've violated some regulation, and apologising profusely. If you are asked to pay a *multa* (fine) for a trumped-up charge, playing the game a bit (asking to speak to the supervisor or *chefe*, and requesting a receipt) helps to counteract some of the more blatant attempts, as does insisting on going to the nearest *esquadrão* (police station) – you should always do these things anyway.

Landmines

Thanks to a massive demining effort, many of the unexploded landmines littering Mozambique – a legacy of the country's long war – have been eliminated. The northern provinces of Niassa, Cabo Delgado, Nampula and Zambézia have officially been declared free of known mined areas. However, mines are still a risk in some areas. To be on the safe side, stick to well-used paths – including on roadsides in rural areas – and don't free camp or go wandering off into the bush without first seeking local advice. In areas where mine-removal work is still ongoing, you may see trucks or red-and-white markings in areas where mines have been identified for removal. Areas that should always be avoided include the bases of bridges, old schools or abandoned buildings, and water tanks or other structures.

EMBASSIES & CONSULATES

Countries with diplomatic representations in Maputo include the following. Most are open from about 8.30am to 3pm, often with a midday break. The closest Australian representation is in South Africa.

Canada (Map pp58–9; ☎ 21-492623; www.canada international.gc.ca/mozambique/index.aspx; 1138 Avenida Kenneth Kaunda)

France (Map pp58–9; ☎ 21-484600; www.ambafrance -mz.org; 2361 Avenida Julius Nyerere)

Germany (Map pp58–9; ☎ 21-482700; www.maputo .diplo.de; 506 Rua Damião de Gois)

Ireland (Map pp58–9; ☎ 21-483524/5; 3332 Avenida Julius Nyerere)

Malawi (Map pp58–9; ☎ 21-492676; 75 Avenida Kenneth Kaunda)

Netherlands (Map pp58–9; ☎ 21-484200; www.holland inmozambique.org; 324 Avenida Kwame Nkrumah)

TRAVEL ADVISORIES

Government travel advisories are good sources of updated security information, though read between the lines as some tend towards paranoia:

- Australia – www.smarttraveller.gov.au
- Canada – www.dfait-maeci.gc.ca
- UK – www.fco.gov.uk
- US – www.travel.state.gov/travel

Portugal (Map pp58-9; ☎ 21-490316; embaixada@embpormaputo.org.mz; 720 Avenida Julius Nyerere)
South Africa (Map pp58-9; ☎ 21-490059, 21-491614; consular@tropical.co.mz, sahc_cs@satcom.co.mz; 41 Avenida Eduardo Mondlane)
Swaziland (Map pp58-9; ☎ 21-491601; swazimoz@teledata.mz; Rua Luís Pasteur) Behind Netherlands embassy.
Tanzania (Map pp58-9; ☎ 21-491051; Avenida Mártires de Machava) Near corner of Avenida Eduardo Mondlane.
UK (Map pp58-9; ☎ 21-356000; http://ukinmozambique.fco.gov.uk; 310 Avenida Vladimir Lenine)
USA (Map pp58-9; ☎ 21-492797; http://maputo.usembassy.gov; 193 Avenida Kenneth Kaunda)
Zambia (Map pp58-9; ☎ 21-492452; 1286 Avenida Kenneth Kaunda)
Zimbabwe (Map pp58-9; ☎ 21-490404, 21-486499; 1657 Avenida Mártires de Machava)

EMERGENCIES

Meagre salaries, poor organisational infrastructure and low morale mean that Mozambique's police are often not particularly useful in an emergency. To facilitate things, always carry a copy of your insurance information (including contact telephone numbers) with you. Before beginning your travels, also make copies of all other important documents, including passport, travellers cheque purchase receipts, credit cards, air tickets, drivers licence and international health card. Leave one copy with someone at home and keep another with you, separate from the originals.

If you'll be travelling upcountry for an extended period, try to register with your embassy in Maputo, and carry a copy of its telephone number with you as well (although remember that there are limits on what the embassy can do). It's a good idea to have emergency dollars hidden somewhere in case you should need them. If you have had items stolen and need a police statement for insurance purposes, you'll need to go to the police station responsible for the section of town where the robbery occurred. The procedure is generally straightforward enough, although time consuming.

FESTIVALS & EVENTS

Apart from national holidays – most of which are celebrated with parades, and song and dance performances – Mozambique has few countrywide festivals. Smaller events abound though, most with no advertising. For concerts and larger happenings, watch for posters around town, and announcements in *Notícias*, and check with the Centro Cultural Franco-Moçambicano (p56).

Baluarte Festival Held in June on Mozambique Island to celebrate local Makua culture, and to promote cultural links between Mozambique and its French-speaking Indian Ocean neighbours; dates vary.
Cedarte National Art & Crafts Fair (www.cedarte.org.mz) A celebration of artisanry of all types; held annually in December.
Dockanema (www.dockanema.org) A festival of documentary films, showcasing especially films from the southern Africa region and from other Lusophone countries. Held annually in Maputo in September.
Gwaza Muthini Marracuene's commemoration of the Battle of Marracuene and the start of the *ukanhi* season; dates vary, usually early February; see boxed text, p73.
Maputo International Music Festival (www.maputomusic.com) A celebration of all types of music, from classical to jazz to experimental; dates vary.
Marrabenta Festival (www.ccfmoz.com) Marrabenta music at its best; celebrated in various localities between Maputo and Marracuene; timing coincides with Marracuene's Gwaza Muthini commemoration.
Mozambique Jazz Festival (www.mozjazzfest.com) Held around April in Maputo.
Music Crossroads Southern Africa (www.jmi.net) A showcase for young musical talent from Mozambique, Malawi, Tanzania, Zambia and Zimbabwe; dates and locations vary.
Timbilas Festival The famed *timbila* festival of the Chopi held around August in Quissico; see the boxed text, p83.

FOOD

Eating listings are ordered by budgets; see inside the front cover for price ranges. For more on dining in Mozambique, see p37.

GAY & LESBIAN TRAVELLERS

Mozambique tends to be more tolerant than some of its neighbours, although gay sexual relationships are for the most part culturally taboo. The country's small gay scene, centred in Maputo, has traditionally been quite discrete, but things are starting to open up. From an official viewpoint male homosexuality is illegal in Mozambique, although this statute is rarely enforced and gay travellers should anticipate no particular difficulties.

There is very little tourism information available that is Mozambique-specific. Probably the easiest way to get information is to contact gay establishments in neighbouring South Africa. A good place to start is the **International Gay & Lesbian Travel Association** (www.iglta.org), which can link you up with gay-friendly travel agents in the southern Africa region. Also check out www.mask.org.za, following links to articles (including those in the archive) on Mozambique.

HOLIDAYS

Most Mozambican public holidays are celebrated with parades, and song and dance performances.

New Year's Day 1 January
Mozambican Heroes' Day 3 February – commemorating the country's revolutionary heroes
Women's Day 7 April
International Workers' Day 1 May
Independence Day 25 June – Mozambique's independence from the Portuguese colonial government in 1975
Lusaka Agreement/Victory Day 7 September – the signing of the independence treaty
Revolution Day 25 September – the initiation of Mozambique's independence struggle in Chai, Cabo Delgado province
Christmas/Family Day 25 December

Each city and town also has a 'city/town day' commemorating its founding. Maputo Day is 10 November.

The main holidays affecting accommodation availability, especially in the south, are South African school holidays, particularly the December-January holiday break, and around Easter. For exact dates, see www.saschools.co.za/calendar.htm.

INSURANCE

A travel-insurance policy to cover theft, loss and medical problems is essential. Before choosing a policy spend time shopping around, as those designed for short package tours in Europe won't be suitable for Mozambique. Also be sure to read the fine print, as some policies specifically exclude 'dangerous activities', which can include scuba diving, motorcycling and more. At a minimum, check that

the policy covers emergency medical evacuation to Johannesburg and/or an emergency flight home. Also see p193 and p189.

INTERNET ACCESS

Internet access is easy and fast in Maputo, where there are numerous internet cafes. Elsewhere, there are internet cafes in most provincial capitals and some larger towns – often at the local Telecomunicações de Moçambique (TDM) office – although connections are often slow. Rates average Mtc1 per minute. Broadband connections are cropping up in the most unlikely places (eg Angoche and Gurúè), and many midrange and upmarket hotels and eateries have wireless.

LEGAL MATTERS

The use or possession of recreational drugs is illegal in Mozambique. However, marijuana and other drugs are readily available in several places along the coast where an influx of travellers has created demand. If you're offered anything, it is often part of a set up, usually involving the police, and if you're caught, penalties are very stiff. At the least, expect to pay a large bribe to avoid arrest or imprisonment (which is a very real risk).

If you're arrested for more 'legitimate' reasons, you have the right to talk with someone from your embassy, as well as a lawyer, though don't expect this to help you out of your situation with any rapidity. Driving on the beach, driving without a seatbelt (for all vehicle occupants), exceeding speed limits, driving while using your mobile phone, turning without using your indicator lights and driving without two red hazard triangles in the boot and without a reflective vest are all illegal, and are common ways of attracting police attention and demands for a bribe or *multa* (fine). For more on what to do if you're stopped by the police, see p171.

MAPS

The detailed *Reise Know-How Mosambik & Malawi* map (1:1,200,000) shows altitude gradients and many obscure roads and villages (in addition to major destinations), and is readily available outside Mozambique. The *Globetrotter Mozambique* map (1:2,300,000) is less detailed, but readily available in Maputo, and also includes city inserts. If you'll be self-drive touring off main roads, check out www.tracks4africa.co.za for downloads of GPS maps.

Coastal and maritime maps (cartas náuticas) are available from the **Instituto Nacional de Hidrografia e Navegação** (Inahina; Map pp58-9; ☎ 21-429240, 21-429108; Rua Marques de Pombal) in Maputo for a negotiable Mtc300 apiece. Inahina is at the capitania, behind the white Safmar building near the port. Inahina also sells a tabela de marés (tide table) for the country.

For detailed topographical maps, contact the **Direcção Nacional de Geografia e Cadastro** (Dinageca; ☎ 21-302555; 537 Avenida Josina Machel, Maputo).

There is an excellent series of city maps for several of Mozambique's provincial capitals put out by Coopération Française together with the local municipal councils. They cover Maputo, Beira, Quelimane, Nampula and Pemba, but can be difficult to find – check at bookstores and hotel bookshops, or at the local municipal council.

MONEY

Mozambique's currency is the metical (plural meticais, pronounced 'meticaish') nova família, abbreviated Mtc. Note denominations include Mtc20, Mtc50, Mtc100, Mtc200, Mtc500 and Mtc1000, and coins include Mtc1, Mtc2, Mtc5 and Mtc10. One metical is equivalent to 100 centavos (Ct), and there are also coins of Ct1, Ct5, Ct10, Ct20 and Ct50, plus a few old metical coins floating around. For sample exchange rates, see the inside front cover of this guide.

Under the old (pre-2006) metical system, a unit of (old) Mtc1000 was called a conto or, occasionally in street slang, a pão. This terminology is still sometimes heard. A metical nova família price of Mtc5 is occasionally still quoted as cinco contos, or sometimes cinco pão.

Outside of Maputo, the best way to travel is with a good supply of cash in a mixture of US dollars (or South African rand, especially in the south) and meticais (including a good supply of small denomination notes, as nobody ever has change). Supplement this with a Visa card for withdrawing meticais at ATMs (the best way of accessing money); and a supply of travellers cheques for emergencies (although they are difficult to change). Away from major towns and ATMs, cash is the only option.

ATMs

All larger and many smaller towns have ATMs for accessing cash meticais. Most accept Visa card only, although some also take MasterCard. Useful ones include Millennium

BIM (Visa, MasterCard), Standard Bank (Visa, MasterCard), Barclays (Visa) and BCI (Visa). Many machines have a limit of Mtc3000 (US\$120) per transaction. Standard Bank's limit is Mtc10,000 (US\$400) per transaction.

Black Market

There's essentially no black market. You may be offered 5% or 10% more than bank or bureau rates by shady looking characters on the street, but the risks are much higher than any potential gain and you can assume it's a set up.

Cash

US dollars are easily exchanged everywhere, and – together with South African rand (which are especially useful in southern Mozambique) – are the best currency to carry. Only new-design US dollar bills will be accepted. Euros are easy to change in major cities, but elsewhere you're likely to get a poor exchange rate. Other major currencies can be changed in Maputo.

Most banks don't charge commission for changing cash, and together with foreign exchange bureaus, these are the best places to change money, although some banks (including most Millennium BIM branches) will let you change cash only if you have an account.

In Maputo and other larger cities there are casas de câmbio (foreign exchange bureaus), which usually give a rate equivalent to or slightly higher than the banks, and are open longer hours. Shops selling imported goods will often change cash US dollars or South African rand into meticais at a rate about 5% higher than the bank rate and can be helpful outside of banking hours. Changing money on the street isn't safe anywhere and is illegal – asking shopkeepers is a much better bet.

Credit Cards

Credit cards are accepted at most top-end hotels, a few midrange places and at some car-hire agencies, but otherwise are of only limited use in Mozambique. Visa is by far the most useful, and is also the main (often only) card for accessing money from ATMs.

International Transfers

With time (allow at least several days) and patience, it's possible to organise international bank transfers in Maputo and sometimes you may have the choice of getting your money in dollars or rand rather than meticais. If you do request a transfer, arrange for the forwarding bank to send separate confirmation with full details. In the event of problems, you can then go into the local bank with the proof that your money has been sent. For all transfers, you'll need details of your home bank account, including account number, branch and routing numbers, address and telephone number.

Security

Because of the lack of ATMs outside of major centres and the near impossibility of changing travellers cheques upcountry, you may find yourself needing to carry a fair amount of cash. It's well worth taking the time to divide this into several stashes and sew a few inner pockets into your clothes – in addition to an internal money belt – to hide it away. We know several travellers who have been saved by a 'decoy' wallet that is easily accessible and can be handed over if you have the bad luck to be robbed, while the main part of your funds and passport remain safely hidden. Decoy wallet or not, it's also a good idea to keep a small amount of cash handy and separate from your other money so that you do not need to pull out a large wad of bills for making purchases.

Wear loose-fitting clothing so your internal money belt isn't visible. Wearing an external money pouch is just asking for trouble, as is keeping money in your back pocket.

Safes are available at top-end hotels and at some midrange establishments. However, many hotels in Mozambique don't offer this service. Leaving your valuables in your room is risky, though depending on the circumstances, it may be less risky than carrying them with you on the street.

Tipping & Bargaining

In low-budget bars and restaurants tipping is generally not expected, and locals usually don't tip unless they're out to impress. At anywhere upmarket or catering to tourists, tipping is customary. About 10% to 15% is usually appropriate, assuming service has been good. Tips are also warranted, and always appreciated, if someone has gone out of their way to do something for you.

Bargaining over prices is part of everyday life in Mozambique. However, apart from craft markets and other tourist-oriented places – where initial prices will almost always be wildly exaggerated – don't assume that every price quoted is inflated. In markets, especially in smaller towns, the first price is often the 'real' price (the same price locals pay). A bit of good-natured negotiating is never out of place, but if the seller refuses to budge, you can assume that their initial price was at a level they feel is fair. If you've just arrived in Mozambique, take time to become familiar with standard prices for basic items, keeping in mind that prices can vary depending on location and season: fruit and vegetables are generally more expensive in cities, whereas tinned goods cost more in remote areas, as transport costs must be paid.

Travellers Cheques

Regulations on travellers cheques change frequently, but when this book was researched only Standard Bank changed travellers cheques, with a minimum US$40 commission per transaction, and also require the original purchase receipts and lots of time. We've heard from some travellers who had luck with BCI, so it may be worth enquiring there. Only a small handful of hotels accept travellers cheques as direct payment, and then usually with a 5% surcharge to cover their banking costs. The bottom line: while it's OK to bring some cheques along as an emergency standby, they shouldn't be relied on as a ready source of funds in Mozambique.

PHOTOGRAPHY & VIDEO
Film & Equipment

Maputo has the best selection of camera equipment, although it's best to bring what you need with you, including extra memory cards.

There are several fairly reliable processing shops in Maputo for print and slide film, but not elsewhere. An increasing number of internet cafes and speciality shops in major cities can help with transferring digital images to CDs or other storage. It's a good idea to carry a USB converter for memory cards if you want to burn your photos onto CD or DVD, as many internet cafes and other shops don't have card-reader slots.

For film, ASA100 is good for most situations and lighting conditions in Mozambique. For shots of birds and wildlife, try a lens between 210mm and 300mm, or a 70mm to 300mm zoom. Zoom lenses are good as you can frame your shot easily to get the best composition; a 200mm lens is the minimum you will need to get good close-up shots. Telephoto (fixed focal-length) lenses give better results than zoom lenses, though you will be limited by having to carry separate lenses for various focal lengths. For photographing people, a 50mm lens should be fine. If you are using zoom or telephoto lenses, bring some ASA200 or ASA400 film with you from home.

Whatever equipment you take, carry it in a bag that will protect it from dust and knocks, and that ideally is waterproof. Also make sure your travel-insurance policy covers your camera. For more tips, look for a copy of Lonely Planet's *Guide to Travel Photography*.

Restrictions
Photographing government buildings, ports, airports, or anything connected with the police or military – including parades and other official gatherings – is not permitted. If you try anyway, it may result in your film being confiscated.

Technical Tips
The best times to take photographs are early in the morning and late in the afternoon, when the rising and setting sun optimally illuminates the country's rich panorama of colour. Mornings also have the advantage that the streets are not as busy, and there tends to be less dust in the air. To avoid underexposure in shots of people and animals, take light readings on the subject rather than on the background.

POST
International mail from Maputo takes about 10 days to Europe and costs Mtc34 per letter. Domestic mail is more sporadic, with letters taking between one week and one month to reach their destination.

Major post offices have poste restante. Letters are generally held for one month, sometimes longer, and cost Mtc5 to receive.

SHOPPING
Mozambique is known for its highly stylised woodcarvings and turned wood items, as well as for its paintings, pottery and basketware. Other crafts include jewellery (particularly silverwork), leatherwork and textiles.

For Makonde woodcarvings, Pemba, Nampula and Maputo are the best places to start your search. The widest selection of san-

dalwood carvings is in Maputo. Inhambane province is known for its baskets, and Cabo Delgado for its attractive woven mats. The etched clay pots made by Makonde women and sold in Nampula, Pemba and Maputo make beautiful but heavy souvenirs. Some of the best silver artisanship in the region comes from Ibo Island in the Quirimbas Archipelago. While the silver itself is often not of high quality, the craftsmanship is highly refined. The colourful *capulanas* worn by women around their waist can be found at markets everywhere and make practical souvenirs – useful as tablecloths, wraps, wall hangings and more. *Capulanas* are more colourful in the north, where shades of yellow and orange dominate.

When buying woodcarvings, remember that many of the pieces marketed as ebony may be simply blackened with shoe polish or dye. Rubbing the piece with a wet finger, or smelling it, should tip you off. Higher-quality pieces are those where more attention has been given to detail and craftsmanship.

If you're using this book as an armchair reader, and won't have the chance to get to Mozambique, you can contact Artes Maconde (see p154), which takes orders for local carvings and crafts, and will mail or ship internationally. Finely crafted wood products are also available online at www.allanschwarz.com.

SOLO TRAVELLERS
While you may be a minor curiosity in rural areas (especially solo women travellers), there are no particular problems with travelling alone in Mozambique, whether you're male or female. Times when it is advantageous to join a group are for car hire, dhow safaris and organised excursions (when teaming up can be a cost-saver); when going out at night (travelling solo can be limiting on the nightlife); and if you're interested in hiking (it's always wise to travel at least in pairs in the bush). If you do go out alone at night, take taxis and use extra caution, especially in urban and tourist areas. Also, it's generally assumed that everyone in bars – male and female – is looking to pick up or be picked up, unless you already have an escort.

Whatever the time of day or location, avoid isolating situations, including isolated stretches of beach. Women, especially, shouldn't hitch alone. For bus journeys, get to the bus stand early to try to get a seat up front, and if you're getting dropped off at a bus stand in the predawn hours, arrange for your taxi to wait with you until you can board the bus or until other people are around. If you are driving, avoid night travel.

TELEPHONE

The cheapest international dialling is with the Telecomunicações de Moçambique (TDM) Bla-Bla Fixo card, sold at all TDM branches. It's a prepaid card for fixed lines (including those at TDM offices), and is cheaper than dialling internationally from TDM directly.

Domestic calls cost about Mtc3 per impulse; most short calls won't use more than two or three impulses. Calls to Europe, the USA and Australia cost from about Mtc130 for the first three minutes (minimum), plus Mtc50 for each additional minute. Regional calls cost about Mtc100 for the first three minutes. Rates are slightly cheaper on weekends and evenings.

All landline telephone numbers have eight digits, including provincial area codes, which must always be dialled (even when calling a number in the same city). Codes are included with all telephone numbers in this book. No initial zero is required (and the call won't go through if you use one). If you are looking for a number, the Mozambique telephone directory (*Lista Telefónica*) is available online (www.tdm.mz and www.paginasamarelas.co.mz).

Mobile Phones

Mobile phones (GSM900 system) are widely used. Mobile phone numbers are seven digits, preceded by ☎ 82 for **Mcel** (www.mcel.co.mz) or ☎ 84 for **Vodacom** (www.vm.co.mz). No initial zero is required. Seven-digit mobile numbers listed with zero at the outset are in South Africa, and must be preceded by the South Africa country code (☎ 27) when dialling. Check the Mcel and Vodacom websites for *cobertura* (coverage) maps. Both companies have outlets in all major towns where you can buy Sim-card starter packs (under Mtc50) and top-up cards.

Telephone Codes

When calling Mozambique from abroad, dial the international access number (☎ 09 from South Africa), then the international code for Mozambique (☎ 258), followed by the provincial or city code (no zero) and the number. For mobile numbers, dial the international access number, followed by the international code, the mobile prefix (no zero) and the seven-digit number.

TIME

Time in Mozambique is GMT/UTC plus two hours. There is no daylight savings. Because the country is so large, and parts of it so far east in relation to other countries in this time zone, it gets light very early in some areas, with daybreak at about 4am in parts of Cabo Delgado province.

TOILETS

Toilets in Mozambique are either sit-down style with a toilet bowl and (sometimes) a seat, or squat style, with a hole in the ground, often rimmed by a tile frame with rests for the feet. For the uninitiated, the key to success with a squat toilet is to position your feet well, and ensure that odds and ends from your pockets don't fall down into the hole.

Running water is a luxury in many areas. With public toilets, if you have a choice, go for a squat-style toilet, as these usually come equipped with a bucket of water and tend to be more sanitary than flush toilets, which are often clogged. Public toilets almost never have toilet paper. For those that do, the custom is to dispose of the paper in the nearby basket, rather than into the toilet itself.

Bidets are a ubiquitous feature of many bathrooms in Mozambique, left over from colonial days, though most don't have running water, except those in upscale hotels.

TRAVELLERS WITH DISABILITIES

While there are few facilities specifically for the disabled, Mozambicans tend to be very accommodating and helpful to disabled people. Those who are mobility impaired are especially likely to meet with understanding, as there are hundreds, if not thousands, of amputees throughout the country – victims of landmines set during the war.

The most accessible and easily negotiable area of the country is Maputo. Many of the upscale hotels have wheelchair access and/or lifts, and taxis and hire cars are readily available (though taxis don't have wheelchair access, and most are small). While most footpaths have kerbs, often fairly high, the road network is tarmac and in good condition.

For travel upcountry, getting around on public transport usually means lots of crowds, heat and jostling. Travelling by hired car is the best option, though expensive. Along the coast you'll rarely need to deal with long flights of steps – just soft, deep sand – although chalets at some resorts are built on stilts.

The squat-style toilet facilities, common throughout Mozambique outside tourist hotels, can put a strain on anyone's knees, no matter what their physical condition. Except at top-end hotels in Maputo, there are never hand grips on the walls, and few bathrooms are large enough for manoeuvring a wheelchair. As far as we know, there are no facilities anywhere in the country specifically catering for deaf or blind visitors.

Organisations that disseminate information on travel for the mobility impaired include the following:

Accessible Journeys (www.disabilitytravel.com)

Access-Able Travel Source (www.access-able.com)

Endeavour Safaris (www.endeavour-safaris.com) Focuses on South Africa and other areas of the region, and may be able to help with Mozambique itineraries as well.

Epic-Enabled (www.epic-enabled.com) More of the same.

Holiday Care (www.holidaycare.org.uk)

Mobility International (www.miusa.org)

National Information Communication Awareness Network (www.nican.com.au)

VISAS

Visas are required by all visitors except citizens of South Africa, Swaziland, Zambia, Tanzania, Botswana, Malawi, Mauritius and Zimbabwe. Single-entry visas (only) are available at most major land and air entry points – but not anywhere along the Tanzania border – for US$25 for one month.

To avoid sometimes long visa lines at busy borders, or for a multiple entry visa, you'll need to arrange your visa in advance. If you're arriving in Maputo via bus from Johannesburg it's recommended (though not essential) to get your visa in advance; see p184.

Fees vary according to where you buy your visa and how quickly you need it, and range from US$20 to US$70 for a one-month single-entry tourist visa outside Africa. (The maximum initial length of stay available is three months.) Within the region, fees are cheaper, although you'll need to pay about double for express service (usually anything faster than one week). Same-day visa service is available at several places including Johannesburg and Nelspruit (South Africa). Note that for getting a visa in Johannesburg, you'll need to go first to a branch of Nedbank and make a cash deposit of the visa fee. Then, take the deposit slip with you to the embassy and make your visa application. Call the embassy for bank account details.

No matter where you get your visa, your passport must be valid for at least six months from the dates of intended travel, and have at least three blank pages.

For South Africans and citizens of other countries not requiring visas, visits are limited to 30 days from the date of entry, after which you'll need to exit Mozambique and re-enter. Note that the length of each stay for multiple-entry visas is determined when the visa is issued, and varies from embassy to embassy; only single-entry and transit visas are available at Mozambique's borders.

While in Mozambique, you may hear talk of a 'univisa' – initially planned to be implemented by 2010 by Mozambique and the other Southern African Development Community (SADC) countries, although now somewhat delayed. Once in effect, the same visa will be good for Mozambique and many of its neighbours.

Visa Extensions

Visas can be extended at the *migração* (immigration office) in all provincial capitals provided you haven't exceeded the three-month maximum stay. Processing takes from one to three days and is usually fairly straightforward. Don't wait until the visa has expired as hefty fines (US$100 per day) are levied for overstays.

VOLUNTEERING

Most volunteer work is in teaching or health care, and school construction. Initial contacts include **InterAction** (www.interaction.org), whose subscriber newsletter advertises both paid and volunteer positions internationally, including in Mozambique. A useful place to start is the Mozambique page of **Volunteer Abroad** (www.volunteerabroad.com/Mozambique.cfm), along with **Voluntary Service Overseas** (VSO; www.vso.org.uk), which provides placements for young professionals, and the similar US-based **Peace Corps** (www.peacecorps.gov), and **Frontier** (www.frontier.ac.uk).

There are also several volunteer holiday opportunities included in the Mozambique listings of **ResponsibleTravel.com** (www.responsibl

DOCUMENTS

All foreigners are required to carry a copy of their passport when out and about. Rather than carrying the original, it's much better to carry a notarised copy of the name and visa pages, as well as notarised copies of your drivers license and other essential documents. If you're stopped on the street or at a checkpoint and asked for any of these, always hand over the notarised copy, rather than parting with the original. Notary facilities are available in Maputo and other major cities; ask at your hotel for a recommendation. Some Mozambique embassies will also provide this service before you travel. The notarised copies will also be helpful in getting replacements, should your originals get stolen: bring the copies with you to the police station, where you will then be given a temporary travel document that should get you through the remainder of your travels.

travel.com). Also check out **Idealist.org** (www.idealist .org) and **Travel Tree** (www.traveltree.co.uk). Smaller Mozambique entities that accept volunteers include the **Téran Foundation** (http://teranfoundation org.blogspot.com), **Ibo Eco School** (www.iboecoschool .be) and **DolphinCare-Africa** (www.dolphincare.org).

There is extensive missionary work in Mozambique, so another possibility would be to make enquiries through your local church.

WOMEN TRAVELLERS

It's rare to find a Mozambican woman travelling alone for no apparent purpose and lone foreign women seen to be idly wandering around the country may be viewed as something of a curiosity, especially in remote areas. Apart from this, attitudes in Mozambique towards foreign women travelling alone tend to be fairly liberal. Although you'll still get questions about what you are doing, and where your husband and children are, reactions are usually matter-of-fact. In tourist areas, if you're backpacking, locals may assume you are a Peace Corps volunteer, and if you're in a vehicle, the assumption will be that you're either a South African on holidays, or one of Mozambique's large brigade of aid workers.

It's a great help both in explaining yourself, and in getting to know local women, if you are able to surmount the language barrier – either by learning Portuguese or by working with a translator.

Sexual hassles rarely go beyond the verbal. However, to avoid problems getting started, things such as dressing conservatively, wearing a ring, and having a husband or boyfriend (fictitious or not) somewhere nearby all seem to help, as do heeding the precautions outlined, right. Going to a bar on your own is seen as an open invitation.

For more on the role and status of local women in Mozambique, see p32.

Safety

As far as safety is concerned, the best maxim is 'an ounce of prevention is worth a pound of cure'.

Common-sense precautions are well worth heeding: don't wander around alone anywhere at night, and during the daytime avoid anywhere that's isolated, including streets, beaches and parks. A few extra meticais spent on a taxi are well worth it. Be cautious about opening your door to a knock if you're alone in your hotel room/house, and never let anyone unknown in with you. Especially away from the coastal resorts, dress modestly, and ideally with clothing that's not skin tight. Be wary of anyone who tries to draw you into an isolated situation. Also be wary of accepting certain invitations and of the signals your behaviour may be giving off. Avoid hitching alone and if you do hitch, avoid getting in cars with only men.

Many budget hotels double as brothels and are best avoided if you're travelling solo.

WORK

It isn't permitted to work in Mozambique if you enter on a tourist visa. In order to get the required residency (*Documento de Identificação e Residência para Estrangeiros* or DIRE) and work permits, you need an offer of employment. Your employer will also be required to pay various fees, including one equalling a month or two of your salary.

Apart from tourism-related establishments and resorts (where there are the occasional jobs with dive operators), the majority of positions are with international aid organisations. However, as most of these hire through their headquarter offices, it's better to start your research before leaving home.

Transport

CONTENTS

GETTING THERE & AWAY

ENTERING THE COUNTRY

Mozambique is straightforward to enter, although you may encounter the occasional bureaucratic hassle. For popular border posts such as South Africa and Swaziland, there may also be long lines at the visa counter during peak periods – a good reason to arrange your visa in advance.

A valid passport and visa are required to enter, plus the necessary vehicle paperwork if you are driving (see p189), and a yellow fever vaccination certificate if coming from an infected area (see p199).

THINGS CHANGE...

The information in this chapter is particularly vulnerable to change. Check directly with the airline or a travel agent to make sure you understand how a fare (and ticket you may buy) works and be aware of the security requirements for international travel. Shop carefully. The details given in this chapter should be regarded as pointers and are not a substitute for your own careful, up-to-date research.

AIR

Airports

Maputo International (MPM; ☎ 21-465827/8) is the main airport, with a modest collection of souvenir shops, an ATM (Visa cards only), post office, telephone booth, a branch of **Linhas Aéreas de Moçambique** (LAM; ☽ 6am-10.30pm) and **Cotacambios** (foreign exchange bureau, cash only; ☽ open for international flights).

Airports with regularly scheduled regional flights include **Vilankulo** (VNX; ☎ 223-82207), **Beira** (BEW; ☎ 23-301071/2), **Nampula** (APL; ☎ 26-213100/33) and **Pemba** (POL; ☎ 272-20312).

Airlines

Mozambique's national carrier is **Linhas Aéreas de Moçambique** (LAM; code TM; ☎ 21-468 0000, 21-490590; www.lam.co.mz; hub Maputo International). In addition to its domestic network, LAM flights connect Johannesburg with Maputo (daily), Vilankulo (four times weekly) and Beira (five weekly); Dar es Salaam with Pemba (six weekly); and Lisbon (Portugal) with Maputo (five weekly). Other airlines flying into Mozambique include the following:

Air Travelmax (☎ in South Africa 011-701 3222; www.airtravelmax) Several times weekly from Johannesburg's Lanseria to both Inhambane and Vilankulo.

Kenya Airways (code KQ; ☎ 21-320337/8; www.kenya-airways.com; hub Jomo Kenyatta International, Nairobi) Twice weekly between Maputo and Nairobi.

Pelican Air Services (code 7V; ☎ in South Africa 011-973 3649; www.pelicanair.co.za; hub OR Tambo International, Johannesburg) Daily between Johannesburg and Vilankulo via Kruger Mpumalanga International Airport.

SAAirlink (code SA; ☎ 21-495483/4; www.saairlink.co.za; hub OR Tambo International, Johannesburg) Five times weekly between Beira and Johannesburg, and between Maputo and Durban; twice weekly between Johannesburg and Pemba.

South African Airways (SAA; code SA; ☎ 21-488970, 84-389 9287, 21-465625; www.flysaa.com; hub OR Tambo International, Johannesburg) Daily between Maputo and Johannesburg.

TAP Air Portugal (code TP; ☎ 21-303927/8, 21-431006/7; www.flytap.com; hub Lisbon) Five flights weekly between Maputo and Lisbon.

CLIMATE CHANGE & TRAVEL

Climate change is a serious threat to the ecosystems that humans rely upon, and air travel is the fastest-growing contributor to the problem. Lonely Planet regards travel, overall, as a global benefit, but believes we all have a responsibility to limit our personal impact on global warming.

Flying & Climate Change

Pretty much every form of motor travel generates CO_2 (the main cause of human-induced climate change) but planes are far and away the worst offenders, not just because of the sheer distances they allow us to travel, but because they release greenhouse gases high into the atmosphere. The statistics are frightening: two people taking a return flight between Europe and the US will contribute as much to climate change as an average household's gas and electricity consumption over a whole year.

Carbon Offset Schemes

Climatecare.org and other websites use 'carbon calculators' that allow jetsetters to offset the greenhouse gases they are responsible for with contributions to energy-saving projects and other climate-friendly initiatives in the developing world – including projects in India, Honduras, Kazakhstan and Uganda.

Lonely Planet, together with Rough Guides and other concerned partners in the travel industry, supports the carbon offset scheme run by climatecare.org. Lonely Planet offsets all of its staff and author travel.

For more information check out our website: lonelyplanet.com.

Tickets

LAM and TAP Air Portugal run occasional specials between Lisbon and Maputo. SAA has good deals on intercontinental tickets; if you fly with them intercontinentally to Johannesburg, it's often only marginally more expensive to connect on to Maputo.

Otherwise, the best way to save money on your Mozambique ticket is to look for good deals on fares into Johannesburg or other regional capitals, and then travel overland or get an onward ticket from there. Also check fares into Nairobi, from where you can connect on Kenya Airways direct to Maputo. For northern Mozambique, look at fares into Dar es Salaam, with connections from there to Pemba.

Online ticket sellers include the following:
Cheapflights (www.cheapflights.co.uk)
Cheap Tickets (www.cheaptickets.com)
Expedia (www.expedia.com)
Flight Centre (www.flightcentre.com)
Kayak (www.kayak.com)
LowestFare.com (www.lowestfare.com)
OneTravel.com (www.onetravel.com)
Orbitz (www.orbitz.com)
STA Travel (www.statravel.com)
Travelocity (www.travelocity.com)

Africa

For regional connections, see Airlines (opposite) and Indian Ocean Islands (p182).

Several Maputo hotels, notably Hotel Polana (p66) and Hotel Pestana Rovuma (p66), offer package deals between Johannesburg and Maputo that also include airfare. Package deals are also offered out of Johannesburg by most of the lodges on the Bazaruto Archipelago, and by the beach resorts at Barra (p89) and south of Inhambane (p86).

Ticket discounters include **Rennies Travel** (www.renniestravel.com) and **STA Travel** (www.statravel.co.za), with offices throughout southern Africa. **Flight Centre** (☎ 0860 400 727, 011-778 1720; www.flightcentre.co.za) has offices in Johannesburg, Cape Town and several other cities.

Asia

Most routes go via Johannesburg. Possibilities include direct from Singapore on **Singapore Airlines** (www.singaporeair.com), from Hong Kong on **Cathay Pacific** (www.cathaypacific.com) and from Kuala Lumpur on **Malaysia Airlines** (www.malaysiaairlines.com). From Mumbai (Bombay) you can fly to Nairobi or Dar es Salaam, and connect to Pemba or Maputo, or alternatively go via Mauritius and Johannesburg on **Air Mauritius** (www.airmauritius.com).

Discounters include **STA Travel** Bangkok (☎ 02-236 0262; www.statravel.co.th); Singapore (☎ 6737 7188; www.statravel.com.sg); Hong Kong (www.hkst.com); Japan (☎ 03 5391 2922; www.statravel.co.jp).

In Japan also try **No 1 Travel** (☎ 03 3205 6073; www.no1-travel.com); in Hong Kong try **Four Seas Tours** (☎ 2200 7760; www.fourseastravel.com/english).

STIC Travels (www.stictravel.com) has offices in many Indian cities, including Delhi (☎ 11-233 57 468) and Mumbai (☎ 22-221 81 431).

Australia & New Zealand

There are direct flights to Johannesburg (with connections to Maputo) from Sydney and Perth on **Qantas** (www.qantas.com.au), and from Perth on SAA. Alternatively, connect to Johannesburg on Air Mauritius from Perth, or via Singapore, Hong Kong or Mumbai.

STA Travel (☎ 1300 733 035; statravel.com.au) and **Flight Centre** (☎ 133 133; www.flightcentre.com.au) have offices throughout Australia. For online bookings, try www.travel.com.au.

From New Zealand, the best options are via Australia, Singapore, Hong Kong or Malaysia to Johannesburg and on to Maputo. Another option is **Emirates** (www.emirates.com) via Dubai, with connections to Dar es Salaam, and then on LAM to Pemba or Maputo.

Both **Flight Centre** (☎ 0800 243 544; www.flightcentre.co.nz) and **STA Travel** (☎ 0508 782 872; www.statravel.co.nz) have branches throughout the country. Try www.travelonline.co.nz for online bookings.

Continental Europe

LAM and TAP Air Portugal fly between Lisbon and Maputo. From other European capitals the best routes are via Johannesburg, or via Nairobi on Kenya Airways. Hubs include Paris, Amsterdam, Frankfurt, Munich and Zurich.

For northern Mozambique, try looking for a good fare to Nairobi, Blantyre or Dar es Salaam, and then continue overland or via air from there. Ticket agencies include the following:

Airfair (☎ 020 620 5121; www.airfair.nl) Netherlands.
Barcelo Viajes (☎ 902 116 226; www.barceloviajes.com) Spain.
CTS Viaggi (☎ 06 462 0431; www.cts.it) Italy.
Expedia (www.expedia.de) Germany.
Lastminute (☎ 01805 284 366; www.lastminute.de) Germany.
Nouvelles Frontières (☎ 0825 000 747; www.nouvelles-frontieres.fr) France.

STA Travel (☎ 01805 456 422; www.statravel.de) Germany; for travellers under the age of 26.
Voyageurs du Monde (☎ 01 40 15 11 15; www.vdm.com) France.

Indian Ocean Islands

From Madagascar, connections are via Johannesburg or Nairobi on **Air Madagascar** (www.airmadagascar.mg), or via Johannesburg on SAA and SAAirlink. **Air Tanzania** (www.airtanzania.com) flies between Moroni (Comoros) and Dar es Salaam, from where you can connect to Pemba.

Mauritius is something of a hub, with connections from Asia (Singapore, Hong Kong and Mumbai) on Air Mauritius, and then to Johannesburg, Nairobi or Dar es Salaam and on to Mozambique.

For the Seychelles, connect via Johannesburg or Mauritius on **Air Seychelles** (www.airseychelles.com) or via Nairobi on Air Kenya.

Middle East

The best connections are from Cairo to Nairobi and on to Maputo on Kenya Airways or from Dubai to Dar es Salaam on Emirates, connecting to Pemba.

Agencies to try include **Al-Rais Travels** (www.alrais.com) in Dubai; **Egypt Panorama Tours** (☎ 2-2359 0200; www.eptours.com) in Cairo; **Israel Student Travel Association** (www.issta.co.il) in Jerusalem; and **Orion-Tour** (www.oriontour.com.tr) in Istanbul.

South America

SAA links São Paulo and Johannesburg. Malaysia Airlines flies between Buenos Aires, Cape Town and Johannesburg. Discounters include **ASATEJ** (☎ 54-011 4114-7528; www.asatej.com) in Argentina; the **Student Travel Bureau** (☎ 3038 1555; www.stb.com.br) in Brazil; and **IVI Tours** (www.ivivenezuela.com) in Venezuela.

UK & Ireland

Airlines flying between London and southern Africa include **British Airways** (www.britishairways.com), **Virgin Atlantic** (www.virgin-atlantic.com) and SAA, all to Johannesburg. Otherwise, hunt for a cheap fare to Nairobi or Dar es Salaam, and continue from there to Mozambique. Kenya Airways does the London to Maputo route via Nairobi. From Ireland, connect via London or a continental European capital.

Advertisements for many discounters appear in the travel pages of the weekend broadsheet newspapers, in *Time Out*, the *Evening Standard*, in the free online magazine

TNT (www.tntonline.co.uk) and in the **South African Times** (www.southafricantimes.co.uk), which is aimed at South Africans in the UK and sometimes advertises good deals to the region.

Recommended agencies include the following:

Flight Centre (☎ 0870 890 8099, flightcentre.co.uk)

Flightbookers (☎ 0870 814 4001; www.ebookers.com)

North-South Travel (☎ 01245 608 291; www.northsouthtravel.co.uk)

Quest Travel (☎ 0870 442 3542; www.questtravel.com)

STA Travel (☎ 0870 160 0599; www.statravel.co.uk) For travellers under the age of 26.

Trailfinders (www.trailfinders.co.uk)

Travel Bag (☎ 0870 890 1456; www.travelbag.co.uk)

USA & Canada

The only direct flights from North America are on SAA from New York or Washington, DC via Johannesburg to Maputo. Another option is flying to London on a discounted transatlantic ticket, where you can then purchase a separate ticket to Johannesburg or Nairobi, then to Maputo. Alternatively, watch for specials to Lisbon, with direct connections on to Maputo. Other options include Ethiopian Airways from New York to East Africa via Rome and Addis Ababa, and Kenya Airways together with **Virgin Atlantic** (www.virgin-atlantic.com) from New York to Nairobi and Dar es Salaam via London. From East Africa, you can then connect on to Mozambique.

From the US west coast, Malaysia Airlines flies from Los Angeles to Kuala Lumpur, from where you can connect to Johannesburg and on to Maputo.

For online bookings, see the agencies listed under Tickets, p181. In Canada, also try **Travel Cuts** (☎ 800-667-2887; www.travelcuts.com), Canada's national student travel agency.

LAND

Everyone entering Mozambique overland needs to pay an immigration tax of US$2 or the equivalent in meticais, rand or the local currency of the country from which they're arriving. Have exact change, and get a receipt. For additional fees for drivers, see p189.

Border Crossings

There are almost two dozen official land entry points into Mozambique. Except as noted, most border posts are open from 6am to 6pm.

MALAWI

The busiest crossing is Zóbuè, on the Tete Corridor route linking Blantyre (Malawi) and Harare (Zimbabwe). Others include at Dedza (85km southwest of Lilongwe), Milange (120km southeast of Blantyre), Entre Lagos (southwest of Cuamba), Mandimba (northwest of Cuamba), Vila Nova da Fronteira (at Malawi's southern tip), and Cóbuè and Metangula (both on Lake Niassa).

SOUTH AFRICA

The busiest crossing is at **Lebombo-Ressano Garcia** (☖ 6am-10pm), northwest of Maputo. Others include **Kosi Bay-Ponta d'Ouro** (☖ 8am-4pm), 11km south of Ponta d'Ouro; **Pafuri** (☖ 6am-5.30pm), in Kruger National Park's northeastern corner; and **Giriyondo** (☖ 8am-4pm Oct-Mar, to 3pm Apr-Sep), west of Massingir.

SWAZILAND

The main crossing is at **Lomahasha-Namaacha** (☖ 7am-8pm) in Swaziland's extreme northeastern corner, with another post at **Goba-Mhlumeni** (☖ 7am-6pm).

TANZANIA

The main crossing is at Kilambo (called Namiranga or Namoto on the Mozambique side), 130km north of Moçimboa da Praia. There are other crossings further west at Negomane and south of Songea (crossing to Segundo Congresso/Matchedje in Mozambique). On the coast, there are Mozambique border and customs officials at Palma and Moçimboa da Praia for those arriving in the country from Tanzania by dhow.

ZAMBIA

The main crossing is at **Cassacatiza** (☖ 7am-5pm), 290km northwest of Tete. There's another crossing at **Zumbo** (☖ 7am-5pm), at the western end of Lake Cahora Bassa.

ZIMBABWE

The main crossing points are at Nyamapanda on the Tete Corridor, linking Harare with Tete and Lilongwe (Malawi), and at Machipanda on the Beira Corridor linking Harare with the sea. Other crossings are at Espungabera, in the Chimanimani Mountains, and at **Mukumbura** (☖ 7am-5pm), west of Tete.

Malawi

TO/FROM BLANTYRE

The Zóbuè crossing – which is open until at least 9pm – has good roads and public transport connections on both sides. There are daily vehicles from Blantyre to the border via Mwanza. Once on the Mozambique side (the border posts are separated by about 5km of no man's land), there are daily chapas to Tete. Buses between Blantyre and Harare via Zóbuè can drop you at Tete.

The Vila Nova da Fronteira crossing sees a reasonable amount of traffic, although it's still an off-the-beaten-track journey on mostly unpaved but decent roads on the Mozambique side. There are daily minibuses from Blantyre to Nsanje and on to the border. Once across, you can find chapas along a reasonable road to Mutarara, from where you can make your way to Sena and on to Caia on the main north–south road.

The Milange border is convenient for Quelimane and Gurúè. There are regular buses from Blantyre via Mulanje to the border. Once across, there are several vehicles daily to Mocuba, and then frequent transport south to Quelimane and north to Nampevo junction (for Gurúè) and Nampula. On Sunday, passports aren't checked in either direction at the Milange border – good if you want to leave Mozambique and return the same day. If you are leaving for good though you'll need to ask for a stamp.

The crossing at Entre Lagos (for Cuamba and northern Mozambique) is possible with your own 4WD (allow about 1½ hours to cover the 80km from Entre Lagos to Cuamba), or by chapa (about 2½ hours) between the border and Cuamba, and is currently the preferred route for Cuamba residents, given the poor state of the road between Cuamba and Mandimba. On the Malawi side, there are minibuses from the border to Liwonde. Another option is to take the weekly Malawi train between the border and Liwonde – currently Thursday morning from Liwonde to Nayuchi on the border, and from Nayuchi back to Liwonde that same afternoon. There is basic accommodation at Entre Lagos if you get stuck.

At the Mandimba crossing, there's frequent transport on the Malawi side to Mangochi, from where you can get minibuses to Namwera, and on to the border at Chiponde. Once in Mozambique (bicycle taxis bridge the approximately 1.5km of no man's land for about Mtc30, and then vehicles take you on to Mandimba town), there are several vehicles daily from Mandimba to both Cuamba and Lichinga.

TO/FROM LILONGWE

The Dedza border is convenient for Lilongwe, and is linked with the N103 to/from Tete by a scenic tarmac road. From Tete, there's usually at least one chapa daily to Vila Ulongwé and on to Dedza. Otherwise, go in stages from Tete via Moatize and the junction about 15km southwest of Zóbuè. Once across the border, it's easy to find transport for the final 85km to Lilongwe. We've had several reports about travellers having difficulty getting a Mozambique visa at Dedza, so arrange one in advance.

South Africa

TO/FROM NELSPRUIT & JOHANNESBURG

Bus

The best option between Johannesburg and Maputo is one of the large 'luxury' buses that do the route daily (US$30 to US$35 one way, eight to nine hours), listed here. See p69 for Maputo location and contact details. All lines also service Pretoria. It's best to organise your Mozambique visa in advance. That said, some of the companies (eg Panthera Azul) will take you without a visa (especially if you don't advertise the fact that you don't have one). However, if you do this, and if lines at the border are long, the bus may not wait, in which case you'll need to take a chapa the remaining 85km to Maputo.

Greyhound (☎ in South Africa 083-915 9000; www .greyhound.co.za) Daily from Johannesburg's Park Station complex at 6.45am, and from Maputo at 7.30am.

Panthera Azul (☎ in South Africa 011-618 8811/2; panthera@tvcabo.co.mz) Daily from Johannesburg (Hotel Oribi, 24 Bezuidenhout Ave, Troyville) at 7.30am; from Maputo at 6.45am, though the schedule was being modified at the time of research, so check in advance. Mtc570/750 between Maputo and Nelspruit/Johannesburg.

Translux (☎ in South Africa 011-774 3333; www .translux.co.za) Daily from Johannesburg at 8.45am; from Maputo at 7.45am.

In addition to the Johannesburg services listed, which allow you to travel in each direction between Maputo and Nelspruit, but not between Nelspruit and Johannesburg, there is **Cheetah Express** (☎ 82-410 1213, 21-486 3222; cheetahexpress@tdm.co.mz), which goes daily between Maputo and Nelspruit (Mtc660 one way), departing Maputo at 7am from Avenida Eduardo Mondlane next to Mundo's (p66), and departing Nelspruit at about 4pm from Mediclinic, Crossings and Riverside Mall.

Car

There's a good road connecting Maputo with Johannesburg via Ressano Garcia, with tolls in Mozambique at Matola and Moamba, and in South Africa between Middelburg and Witbank, at Machadadorp, and west of Malelane.

TO/FROM KRUGER NATIONAL PARK

There are two border posts between Mozambique and South Africa's Kruger National Park: **Pafuri** (☻ 6am-5.30pm), 11km east of Kruger's Pafuri Camp; and **Giriyondo** (☻ 8am-4pm Oct-Mar, to 3pm Apr-Sep), 75km west of Massingir town and 95km from Kruger's Phalaborwa Gate. Neither is accessible via public transport. Visas are available on both sides of both borders. Officially, you're required to have a 4WD to cross both borders, and 4WD is essential for the Pafuri crossing, which involves an unbridged crossing of the Limpopo River near Mapai that's only possible during the dry season, and a rough bush track thereafter via Mabote and Mapinhane to Vilankulo. Allow two full days between Pafuri and Vilankulo; there's a **campsite** (per person US$5) with hot water showers near Mapai.

For those without their own transport, Dana Tours (p57) and several Maputo hotels offer day and overnight trips to Kruger (although using the Ressano Garcia border).

OTHER ROUTES

Between Durban and Maputo, **Panthera Azul** (☎ in Durban 031-309 7798) has buses via Namaacha and Big Bend in Swaziland (Mtc810, 8½ hours) departing Maputo at 6.30am Tuesday, Thursday and Saturday, and Durban at 6.30am Wednesday, Friday and Sunday.

For travel via the Kosi Bay border post, see p77.

Swaziland

BUS & CHAPA

Minibuses depart Maputo throughout the day for Namaacha (Mtc50, 1½ hours), with some continuing on to Manzini (3½ hours).

CAR

The road is fairly good tarmac the entire way and easily negotiated with 2WD. The Namaacha border is notoriously slow on holiday weekends; the quiet border at Goba (Goba Fronteira) – reached via a scenic, winding road on the Mozambique side – is a good alternative. The good road from Swaziland's Mananga border, connecting north to Lebombo–Ressano Garcia, is another option.

Tanzania

For all Mozambique–Tanzania posts, arrange your Mozambique (or Tanzania) visa in advance.

TO/FROM MTWARA

Pick-ups depart Mtwara (Tanzania) daily between 6.30am and 8am to the Kilambo border post (Tsh3000, one hour), and on to the Rovuma River, which is crossed – adventurously or dangerously, depending on your perspective and water levels – by dugout canoe (from Tsh2000, depending on your negotiating skills, 10 minutes to over an hour, depending on water levels). There is no longer a vehicle ferry. On the Mozambique side, there are usually two pick-ups daily to the Mozambique border post (4km further) and on to Palma (Mtc200) and Moçimboa da Praia (Mtc300, four hours). The last one leaves the Rovuma around noon, so it's worth getting an early start from Mtwara. Departures from Moçimboa da Praia to the Rovuma are daily between 2.30am and 3.30am. If you get stuck overnight at the Rovuma, camping on the river bank on the Mozambique side is the best of several rather bleak options.

The Rovuma crossing is notorious for pickpockets and for unscrupulous dugout canoe captains who can be extremely demanding when it comes to negotiating the crossing fare. Keep an eye on your belongings, especially when getting into and out of the boats, and keep up with the crowd when walking to/from the river bank.

Further west, the Unity Bridge (at Negomane, near the confluence of the Lugenda River), for vehicles, should be finished within the lifetime of this book, and possibly also some of the road work planned to link this with Mueda on the Mozambique side and Mtwara in Tanzania.

TRANSPORT

TO/FROM SONGEA

Still further west, there's a vehicle bridge and passport/customs posts at Segundo Congresso/Matchedje, with road links (and public transport) north to Songea and south to Lichinga. One or two chapas depart Lichinga daily from about 8am for the Rovuma (Mtc500, six hours). Once across, there's Tanzanian transport to Songea. No visas are issued on either side of this border, and drivers will have to complete vehicle formalities in either Lichinga or Songea (see p143).

Zambia

The roads on both sides of the Cassacatiza–Chanida border are reasonably good, but the crossing is seldom used as most travellers combining Mozambique and Zambia go via Malawi. Chapas go daily from Tete to Matema, from where there's sporadic transport to the border. On the other side, there are daily vehicles to Katete (Zambia), and then on to Lusaka or Chipata.

The rarely used crossing at Zumbo is difficult to access from Mozambique – the road route goes via Fíngoè – and is of interest primarily to anglers and birdwatchers heading to the western reaches of Lake Cahora Bassa.

Zimbabwe
TO/FROM HARARE

Both the Nyamapanda and Machipanda border crossings have reasonably good tarmac access roads, are heavily travelled by private vehicles, and are easy to cross using public transport or hitching.

From Tete there are frequent vehicles to Changara and on to the border at Nyamapanda, where you can get transport to Harare. Through buses between Blantyre and Harare are another option, though schedules have been erratic due to fuel shortages in Zimbabwe.

From Chimoio there is frequent transport to Manica and from there on to the border, from where you'll need to take a taxi onwards 12km to Mutare, and then get Zimbabwe transport to Harare.

The seldom-used route via the orderly little border town of Espungabera is slow and scenic, and an interesting dry-season alternative for those with a 4WD. Public transport on the Mozambique side is scarce.

Mukumbura, best done with a 4WD, is of interest mainly to anglers heading to Cahora

Bassa Dam. There is no public transport on the Mozambique side.

SEA & LAKE
Malawi

The *Ilala* ferry services several Mozambican ports (but no longer Cóbuè) on its way up and down Lake Niassa, departing Monkey Bay (Malawi) at 10am Friday, arriving in Metangula (via Chipoka and Nkhotakota in Malawi) early Saturday morning, then departing by about 9am or 10am and reaching Likoma Island (Malawi) about 3pm Saturday, and Nkhata Bay (Malawi) at around 1am Sunday. Southbound, departures are at 8pm Monday from Nkhata Bay and at 6.30am Tuesday from Likoma Island, reaching Metangula late Tuesday afternoon. The schedule changes frequently; get an update from **Malawi Lake Services** (ilala@malawi.net). Fares are about US$35/15 for a 1st-class cabin/economy class between Likoma Island and Metangula.

There are immigration posts in Metangula and Cóbuè (and on Likoma Island and in Nkhata Bay, for Malawi). You can get a Mozambique visa at Cóbuè, but not at Metangula. Slow sailing boats also go between Likoma Island, Cóbuè and Metangula; guests of Nkwichi Lodge (p146) can arrange boat transfers with the lodge.

Meponda was formerly linked with Malawi's Senga Bay via the weekly MV *Mtendere*. It wasn't running when we visited but it's worth asking around to see if services have resumed. Local boats travel frequently between Meponda and Senga Bay but the crossing is risky due to sudden squalls and is not recommended. The closest immigration office is in Lichinga.

South Africa

There are no regularly scheduled passenger ships between South African and Mozambican ports, other than luxury cruise liners. One to try is **Starlight Lines** (www.starlight.co.za), which runs luxury liners from Durban that call in at Maputo, Inhaca Island, Barra, the Bazaruto Archipelago and Mozambique Island. Otherwise, the best bet is to ask around at boating clubs in Durban to see whether any boats are looking for additional crew.

Cargo ships rarely take passengers, but if you want to try your luck, an initial contact is the **LBH Group** (www.lbh-group.com), which ha cargo ships between Durban and various Mozambican ports.

TOURS

All of the following companies organise travel to Mozambique, as well as in-country itineraries. Many top-end hotels and lodges in Maputo and Pemba also offer fly-in packages from Johannesburg. The Mozambique pages in the South African travel magazine **Getaway** (www.getawaytoafrica.com) are a good source of information on package tours and cruises.

Dana Tours (www.danatours.net) Long-established and highly reliable, Dana Tours covers most of Mozambique, plus Mozambique-South Africa combination itineraries, focusing particularly on midrange and upmarket.

Makomo Safaris (www.makomo.com) Combination itineraries for northern Mozambique, southern Tanzania and Malawi. Recommended for budget and adventure travellers, and for getting off the beaten track.

Mozaic Travel (www.mozaictravel.com) A long-standing and reliable operator catering to all budgets. It also has an office in Maputo.

Mozambique Collection (www.themozambique collection.com) A collection of environmentally conscious upmarket Mozambique lodges and experiences.

Mozambique Connection (www.mozambiqueconnect on.co.za) Covers most of the country and all price ranges.

Mozambique Tours (www.mozambiquetravel.co.za) Fly-in packages to the Bazaruto Archipelago and other southern Mozambique destinations.

Ocean Island Safaris (www.oceanislandsafari.com) Luxury itineraries to the Quirimbas and other Indian Ocean islands.

Tanzania Yachts (www.tanzaniayachts.com) Tanzania-Mozambique combination sailing itineraries.

GETTING AROUND

AIR
Airlines in Mozambique

The national airline is **Linhas Aéreas de Moçambique** (LAM; ☎ 800 147 000, 21-468000; linhad liente@lam.co.mz; www.lam.co.mz), which has flights linking Maputo with Inhambane, Vilankulo, Beira, Chimoio, Quelimane, Tete, Nampula, Lichinga and Pemba. Service has improved markedly in recent years, and flights are generally reliable, though overbooking on some routes is common and it's essential to reconfirm your ticket, and to check in well in advance. Flights can be paid for in local currency, dollars or rand, and in most offices also by Visa or MasterCard. Sample

one-way fares and flight frequencies include: Maputo to Pemba (US$382, daily), Maputo to Beira (US$222, daily), Maputo to Lichinga (US$358, four weekly) and Maputo to Vilankulo (US$222, four weekly).

Fares are expensive, especially last minute fares, although LAM offers occasional specials on domestic routes; always enquire before booking.

There are various small charter companies, including Rani Aviation (book through Kaskazini, p151) for getting around the Quirimbas Archipelago.

BICYCLE

Cycling is a good way to see the 'real' Mozambique, but you'll need plenty of time to cover the long distances. You'll also need to plan the legs of your trip fairly carefully and to carry almost everything with you, including all spares, as there are long stretches with little or nothing en route, including no water supplies. Avoid cycling in Maputo and along main roads whenever possible, as there's often no shoulder, traffic is fast and drivers have little respect for cyclists.

The most pleasant hours for cycling are between dawn and mid-morning to avoid the heat and the worst of the traffic, and to have plenty of time in the afternoon to relax on the beach. Carrying a tent is essential; always check in with the local *régulo* (chief) before pitching it. Bicycles can be transported on buses (Mtc50 to Mtc150, depending on the journey).

Rental & Purchase

Heavy, Chinese-made single-speeds can be easily rented for the day in most towns. Ask around by the market or at bicycle repair stands. In Maputo and other places with large numbers of expatriate residents, you can sometimes find decent mountain bikes for sale. Embassy noticeboards are a good place to start. A better option is to buy a bicycle in South Africa and then try to sell it in Mozambique before you leave, although the market can be limited. Spares for Western-made bicycles are not available in Mozambique. However, you may be able to pick up some useful parts from stolen bicycles at Maputo's Xipamanine Market (p69), and bicycle-repair stands everywhere are excellent at improvisation.

TRANSPORT

DHOW TRAVEL

Dhows (*barcos a vela* in Portuguese) have played a major role in Mozambican coastal life for centuries, and are still the main form of transport and means of livelihood for many coastal dwellers, especially in the north.

If the wind is with you and the water calm, a trip on a local dhow can be enjoyable, and will give you a better sense of the centuries of trade that shaped Mozambique's history. However, if you're becalmed miles from your destination, if seas turn rough, if the boat is leaking or over-loaded, if it's raining, or if the sun is strong, the experience will be much less pleasant.

The best way to try dhow travel is to arrange a dhow safari with the operators mentioned on p157 and on p167, all of which offer reliable boats and captains. If you decide to arrange things on your own, here are some things to keep in mind:

- Travel with the winds, which blow from south to north from approximately April/May to August/September and north to south from November/December through to February.

- Be prepared for rough conditions. There are no facilities on board local dhows, except possibly a toilet hanging off the stern. As sailings are wind and tide dependent, departures are often during the predawn hours.

- Journeys often take much longer than anticipated; bring plenty of extra water, food and sun protection plus waterproofing for your luggage and a rain jacket.

- Boats capsize and people die each year as a result. Avoid overloaded boats, and don't set sail in bad weather.

BOAT

There is no regular passenger service between major coastal towns. However, it's worth asking at ports and harbours, as there is frequent cargo traffic along the coast and captains are sometimes willing to take passengers. Chances improve the further north you go. Possibilities include small freighters running between Quelimane, Nacala and Pemba, and regular ferries between Beira and small towns along the Sofala coastline. On larger ships, once you find a captain willing to take you, the price generally includes meals and a cabin. On Lake Niassa there is passenger service between Metangula, Cóbuè and several villages further north.

If you've brought your own boat into Mozambique, beach launching requires a permit from the local maritime office (*administração marítima* or *capitania*). Most southern coastal resorts can also help you sort this out.

BUS

As long as you're fortified with nerves of steel (for the high speeds), plenty of patience (for the many stops en route) and lots of time (for the long distances), bus travel is the most straightforward and economical way to get around Mozambique. Direct services connect all major towns at least daily, although vehicle maintenance and driving standards leave much to be desired.

A large bus is called a *machibombo*, and sometimes also *autocarro*. The main companies are Grupo Mecula in the north and TCO in central Mozambique. Otherwise, most routes are served by freelancers/no-names. Ask staff at your hotel for recommendations about the best connections.

Most towns don't have central bus stations. Rather, transport usually leaves from the bus company garage, or from the start of the road towards the destination (which frequently involves a hike of 1km to 2km from the centre of town). Long-distance transport in general, and all transport in the north, leaves early – between 3am and 7am. Mozambican transport usually leaves quickly and close to the stated departure time. If a driver tells you they will be departing at 4.30am, get there by 4am at the latest. Sample journey fares and times Maputo to Inhambane (Mtc350, seven hours) Nampula to Pemba (Mtc250, seven hours) Maputo to Beira (Mtc1300, 16 hours).

Classes & Reservations

All buses have just one class. For some routes it's possible – but seldom essential – to buy a ticket a day in advance. Notable exceptions are TCO buses and buses from Vilankulo to Beira. Generally, showing up on the morning of travel (about an hour prior to departure for heavily travelled routes) is enough to ensure you get a place. If you are choosy about your seat (best is at the front, on the shady side), get to the departure point earlier. There tends to be a direct correlation between the amount of baggage on the roof and the degree of 'express' service offered by the bus.

CAR & MOTORCYCLE

If you have your own vehicle in the region, or can afford rental and fuel costs, Mozambique is an adventurous but highly satisfying destination to tour as self-drive. Road savvy helps, as does experience driving elsewhere in Africa.

Bringing Your Own Vehicle

In addition to a passport and driving licence, drivers need third-party insurance, a temporary import permit, the original vehicle registration papers and an authorisation document from the rental agency or registered vehicle owner, plus two red hazard triangles in the boot and a reflector vest. If you're towing a trailer or boat, a hazard triangle needs to be displayed on your front bumper and at the back of the trailer, and trailers also require reflective tape. You'll also need a sticker on the back of the vehicle (or at the end of the trailer) showing the country of registration (eg ZA for South Africa).

Temporary import permits (about US$2) and third-party insurance (about US$25 for 30 days, depending on vehicle size) are available at most land borders, or if not, then in the nearest large town. You'll be required to show the paperwork at all checkpoints (and will be fined if you can't produce it). Fees can be paid in meticais, US dollars or the local currency of the country you are leaving. As some smaller border posts don't always issue third-party insurance, it's worth arranging this in advance with your local automobile association if planning to enter Mozambique via an out-of-the-way route. If you find yourself in Mozambique without it, contact **Hollard Seguros** (☎ 21-313114; www.hollard.co.za) to help you sort it out.

Driving Licence

You'll need either a South African or international drivers licence to drive in Mozambique. Those staying longer than six months will need a Mozambique drivers licence.

Fuel & Spare Parts

Gasolina (petrol) is a scarce commodity off main roads, especially in the north. *Gasóleo* (diesel) supplies tend to be more reliable. Always carry an extra jerry can or two and tank up at every opportunity, as filling stations sometimes run out, especially in more remote areas. Or sometimes the fuel may be there but, if there's a power outage, it may not be accessible. In remote areas sometimes the only choice will be petrol sold from roadside *barracas* (stalls); watch out for petrol that has been mixed with water or kerosene. Fuel prices in Mozambique range from Mtc24 to Mtc34 per litre for petrol, and from Mtc29 to Mtc35 for diesel. At an increasing number of petrol stations in the south along the N1, it's possible to pay for your gas with Visa or MasterCard, but don't count on this.

A limited supply of spare parts is available in Maputo and in major towns. Otherwise, they'll need to be ordered from South Africa. In the south, Massinga (especially) and Vilankulo both have good repair facilities. A number of petrol stations don't have air for tyres, but in every major town you'll be able to find a tyre shop (look for old tyres stuck in the ground, usually under a large, shady tree) that can pump up your tyres or help with punctures.

Hire

There are rental agencies in Maputo, Beira, Nampula, Tete and Pemba, most of which take credit cards. Sticking with the major agencies (ie those listed in this book) is recommended. Elsewhere, you can usually arrange something with upmarket hotels. Rates start at US$100 per day for 4WD, excluding fuel. At the time of research only Europcar (p70) was offering unlimited kilometres. With the appropriate paperwork, rental cars from Mozambique can be taken into South Africa and Swaziland, but not into other neighbouring countries. Note, however, that most South African rental agencies don't permit their vehicles to enter Mozambique.

Insurance

All private vehicles entering Mozambique are required to purchase third-party insurance at the border (see left), which covers you to some degree in the event of hitting a pedestrian or another Mozambican vehicle. It's also advisable to take out good insurance coverage at home or (for rental vehicles) with the rental

ROAD DISTANCES (KM)

	Beira	Chimoio	Inhambane	Lichinga	Maputo	Nampula	Pemba	Ponta d'Ouro	Quelimane	Tete	Vilankulo
Chimoio	162										
Inhambane	707	664									
Lichinga	1184	1308	1938								
Maputo	1080	1037	406	2311							
Nampula	928	978	1608	688	1981						
Pemba	1355	1405	2035	746	2408	427					
Ponta d'Ouro	1190	1147	516	2421	110	2091	2518				
Quelimane	481	531	1161	814	1534	484	911	1644			
Tete	555	371	1035	560	1408	840	1267	1518	902		
Vilankulo	481	438	280	1712	620	1382	1809	730	935	809	
Xai-Xai	906	863	235	2137	174	1807	2234	284	1360	1234	449

agency to cover damage to the vehicle, yourself and your possessions. Car-rental agencies in Mozambique have wildly differing policies (some offer no insurance at all, those that do often have high deductibles and most won't cover off-road driving) so enquire before signing any agreements. If renting in South Africa, ask whether Mozambique is included in the coverage.

Purchase

High duties and associated costs, as well as problems with stolen cars, make it not really worth considering purchasing a vehicle in Mozambique for most travellers. If you will be in Mozambique for an extended period, embassy noticeboards are the best place to check for ads for used vehicles. As many of these will have been imported under the special tax provisions applicable to diplomats, check out the fees and taxes you'll need to pay in addition to the selling price.

Road Conditions

Mozambique's road network is steadily improving, and most southern coastal areas be-

tween Maputo and Vilankulo are reachable with 2WD, with the exception of some sandy resort-access roads. A 2WD vehicle is also fine for the roads connecting Nampula, Nacala, Mozambique Island and Pemba, for the Beira Corridor, and for the Tete Corridor between Harare (Zimbabwe) and Tete. For most other routes you'll need 4WD with high clearance. However, all it takes is a heavy rainstorm or some flooding to change the road map, so ask around to get the latest updates, and don't place too much reliance on what your map says. A bridge over the Zambezi River at Caia was set to be inaugurated as this book was researched, and the Unity Bridge over the Rovuma River between Mozambique and Tanzania should also be finished within the lifetime of this book.

A road distances chart is included (p190). However, it's usually senseless to calculate driving times based on distance without taking road conditions into account. A very rough average along the N1 and other main routes would be 50km to 70km per hour, and 30km per hour off main routes. A few examples: the 500km from Vilankulo to Beira (a combina-

TRANSPORT

NIGHT DRIVING

Night driving is particularly hazardous in Mozambique and should be avoided. Apart from road hazards (such as pedestrians, potholes and unmarked construction sites), many vehicles have no lights. Numerous accidents result when a broken-down vehicle is left on the roadway – without lights or other markers – and another vehicle slams into it in the dark.

Safety is also a concern, as there are long stretches of road with nothing along them – not ideal should you have a breakdown or otherwise need assistance. Armed robberies and carjackings are a risk in some areas, especially near the South African border. If you do need to drive at night, use appropriate speeds, watch for pedestrians and obstacles on the road and keep the doors locked and windows up.

The same applies to public transport; try to get an early enough start so that you reach your destination before nightfall and avoid night routes whenever possible.

---

tion of good and bad roads, and under construction at the time of writing) takes about nine hours by car and somewhat longer by bus, while the 300km between Lichinga and Cuamba takes about six hours. An exception is the excellent new highway between Inchope (west of Beira) and Caia.

Road Hazards

Drunk driving is common, as are excessive speeds, and there are many road accidents. Throughout the country, travel as early in the day as possible, and avoid driving at night (see the boxed text, above). If you are not used to driving in Africa, watch out for pedestrians, children and animals on the road or running onto the road. Many locals have not driven themselves, especially in rural areas, and are not aware of concepts such as necessary braking distances.

Tree branches on the road are the local version of flares or hazard lights, and mean there's a stopped vehicle, crater-sized pothole or similar calamity ahead. For public transport, where there's a choice, always take buses rather than chapas.

Road Rules

In theory, traffic in Mozambique drives on the left. At roundabouts, traffic in the roundabout has the right of way (again, in theory). There's a seatbelt requirement for the driver and all passengers. Other relevant provisions of Mozambique's traffic law (in effect since April 2009) include a prohibition on driving while using a mobile phone, a requirement to drive with the vehicle's insurance certificate, and a requirement to carry a reflector vest in addition to two hazard triangles. Speed limits (usually 100km/h on main roads, 80km/h

on approaches to towns and 60km/h or less when passing through towns) are enforced by radar, and should be strictly adhered to as controls are frequent, especially in the south. Fines for speeding and seatbelt and other traffic infringements vary, and should always be negotiated (in a polite, friendly way), keeping in mind that official speeding fines range from Mtc1000 up to Mtc24,000, depending on how much above the speed limit you are travelling and where the infringement occurs. In addition to avoiding fines, another reason to limit your speed is to escape axle-shattering potholes that can appear out of nowhere, or children or livestock running unexpectedly onto the road.

Although the rule is frequently violated, driving on the beach is illegal.

HITCHING

As anywhere in the world, hitching is never entirely safe, and we don't recommend it. Travellers who decide to hitch should understand that they are taking a small but potentially serious risk. This said, in parts of rural Mozambique, your only transport option will be hitching a lift. In general, hitching is not particularly difficult, though it's often slow off main routes. Going to/from beaches and resort areas is easiest on weekends. Payment for lifts is usually not expected, though it's best to clarify before getting in, and a small token of thanks, such as paying for a meal or making a contribution for petrol, is always appreciated. If you do need to pay, it is usually equivalent to what you would pay on a bus or chapa for the same journey. To flag a vehicle down, hold your hand out at about waist level and wave it up and down; the Western gesture of holding out the thumb is not used. The best place to wait is always outside town at the head of the road leading to your destination. Hitching in pairs is safer, and women should avoid hitching alone. In urban areas, hitching through less salubrious suburbs, especially at night, is asking for trouble. Throughout the country, the prevalence of drunk drivers makes it worth trying to assess the driver's condition before getting into a vehicle.

LOCAL TRANSPORT
Chapa
The main form of local transport is the chapa, the name given to any public transport that runs within a town or between towns, and isn't a bus or truck. On some longer routes, your only option will be a *camião* (truck). Many have open backs, and on long journeys the sun and dust can be brutal unless you get a seat up the front in the cab.

Chapas can be hailed down anywhere, and prices are fixed. Intra-city fares average Mtc5; long-haul fares are usually slightly higher than the bus fare for the same route. The most comfortable seat is up front with the driver, on the window side, though you'll have to make arrangements early and sometimes pay more.

Chapa drivers aren't known for their safe driving and there are many accidents. If you have a choice, bus is always a better option. Patience, combined with a sense of humour, also helps when taking local transport.

Like buses, chapas in Mozambique tend to depart early in the day and relatively promptly, although drivers will cruise for passengers before finally leaving town. City chapas run throughout the day, and can be hailed down almost anywhere.

Taxi
Maputo, Beira, Nampula, Pemba and several other towns have taxi services. Apart from airport arrivals, taxis don't cruise for business, so you'll need to seek them out. A few taxis have functioning meters, but usually you'll need to negotiate a price. Town trips cost from Mtc75.

TOURS
All of the tour companies listed on p187 can organise itineraries within Mozambique.

TRAIN
The only passenger train regularly used by tourists is the classic, slow line between Nampula and Cuamba (see p141). There are vendors at all the stations, but it's a good idea to bring along some food and drink to supplement what's available en route. Second class, when available, is not in the least plush, but is reasonably comfortable, and most cabins have windows that open. Third class is hot and extremely crowded. Bookings should be made the afternoon before travel. If you have the time, it's one of southern Africa's great journeys.

Health Dr Caroline Evans

A long as you stay up to date with your vaccinations and take basic preventive measures, you're unlikely to succumb to most of the health hazards covered in this chapter. While Mozambique has an impressive selection of tropical diseases on offer, it's more likely you'll get a bout of diarrhoea or a cold than a more exotic malady. The main exception to this is malaria, which is a real risk throughout the country.

BEFORE YOU GO

A little pre-departure planning will save you trouble later. Book a check-up with your dentist, and with your doctor if you have any regular medication or chronic illness (eg high blood pressure, asthma). You should also organise spare contact lenses and glasses (and take your optical prescription with you); get a first-aid and medical kit together; and arrange necessary vaccinations.

Travellers can register with the **International Association for Medical Assistance to Travellers** (IMAT; www.iamat.orq), which provides directories of certified doctors. If you'll be spending a lot of time in remote areas (ie anywhere away from Maputo), consider doing a first-aid course (contact the Red Cross or St John's Ambulance), or attending a remote-medicine first-aid course, such as that offered by the **Royal Geographical Society** (www.wildernessmedicaltraining .co.uk).

If you do need to bring some medications with you, be sure to carry them in their original (labelled) containers. A signed and dated letter from your physician describing all medical conditions and medications, including generic names, is also a good idea. If carrying syringes or needles, be sure to have a physician's letter documenting their medical necessity.

INSURANCE

Find out in advance whether your insurance plan will make payments directly to providers or will reimburse you later for overseas health expenditures. Most doctors and clinics in Mozambique expect up-front payment in cash. It's vital to ensure that your travel insurance will cover any emergency transport required to get you at least to Johannesburg (South Africa), or all the way home, by air and with a medical attendant if necessary.

If your policy requires you to pay first and claim later for medical treatment, be sure to keep all documentation. Some policies ask you to call back (reverse charges) to a centre in your home country where an immediate assessment of your problem is made. Since reverse-charge calls aren't possible in Mozambique (except to Portugal), contact the insurance company before setting off to confirm how best to contact them in an emergency.

RECOMMENDED VACCINATIONS

The **World Health Organization** (www.who.int/en/) recommends that all travellers be covered for diphtheria, tetanus, measles, mumps, rubella and polio, as well as for hepatitis B, regardless of their destination. The consequences of these diseases can be severe, and outbreaks do occur.

According to the **Centers for Disease Control & Prevention** (www.cdc.gov), the following vaccinations are recommended for Mozambique: hepatitis A, hepatitis B, rabies and typhoid, and boosters for tetanus, diphtheria and measles. While a yellow-fever vaccination certificate is not officially required to enter the country unless you are entering from a yellow-fever infected area, carrying one is advised, and is often requested; check with your doctor before travelling, and also see p199.

MEDICAL CHECKLIST

It's a good idea to carry a medical and first-aid kit with you, to help yourself in the case of minor illness or injury. Following is a list of items to consider packing.

- Acetazolamide (Diamox) for altitude sickness (prescription only)
- Antibiotics (prescription only), eg ciprofloxacin (Ciproxin) or norfloxacin (Utinor)
- Antidiarrhoeal drugs (eg loperamide)
- Acetaminophen (paracetamol) or aspirin
- Antibacterial ointment (eg Bactroban) for cuts and abrasions (prescription only)
- Antihistamines (for hayfever and allergic reactions)
- Anti-inflammatory drugs (eg ibuprofen)
- Antimalaria pills
- Bandages, gauze, gauze rolls and tape
- Insect repellent containing DEET for the skin
- Insect spray containing Permethrin for clothing, tents and bed nets
- Iodine tablets (for water purification)
- Oral rehydration salts
- Pocket knife
- Scissors, safety pins, tweezers
- Self-diagnostic kit that can identify malaria in the blood from a finger prick, and emergency treatment
- Sterile needles, syringes and fluids if travelling to remote areas
- Sun block

INTERNET RESOURCES

A good place to start is the Lonely Planet website at www.lonelyplanet.com. The World Health Organization publishes the helpful *International Travel and Health,* available free at www.who.int/ith/. Other useful websites include **MD Travel Health** (www.mdtravelhealth.com) and **Fit for Travel** (www.fitfortravel.scot.nhs.uk).

FURTHER READING

Good options for further reading include *Healthy Travel* by Jane Wilson-Howarth; *A Comprehensive Guide to Wilderness and Travel Medicine* by Eric A Weiss; *Africa: Healthy Travel* by Dr Isabelle Young and Dr Tony Gherardin; and *How to Stay Healthy Abroad* by Richard Dawood. Those travelling with children should get a copy of Lonely Planet's *Travel with Children*.

IN TRANSIT

DEEP VEIN THROMBOSIS (DVT)

Prolonged immobility during flights can cause deep vein thrombosis (DVT) – the formation of blood clots in the legs. The longer the flight, the greater the risk. Although most blood clots are reabsorbed uneventfully, some can break off and travel through the blood vessels to the lungs, where they can cause life-threatening complications.

The chief symptom is swelling or pain of the foot, ankle or calf, usually but not always on just one side. When a blood clot travels to the lungs, it may cause chest pain and breathing difficulty. Travellers with any of these symptoms should immediately seek medical attention. To prevent DVT, walk about the cabin, perform isometric compressions of the leg muscles (ie contract the leg muscles while sitting), drink plenty of fluids and avoid alcohol when flying.

JET LAG

If you're crossing more than five time zones you could suffer jet lag, resulting in insomnia, fatigue, malaise or nausea. To avoid jet lag try drinking plenty of fluids (non-alcoholic) and eating light meals. Upon arrival, get exposure to natural sunlight and readjust your schedule (for meals, sleep etc) as soon as possible.

IN MOZAMBIQUE

AVAILABILITY & COST OF HEALTH CARE

Maputo is the only place in the country with good emergency medical service, although for Western standards, expect to pay Western prices. Elsewhere, facilities range from limited to nonexistent. All provincial capitals have a hospital that can test for malaria. These tests are very cheap (usually about US$1) and well worth getting if you have even the slightest suspicion that you may have become infected. In smaller towns, the only facility will often be a local health post. If you become seriously ill, the best thing to do is to seek treatment in South Africa, return home or at least try to make your way to Maputo.

If you fall ill in an unfamiliar area, ask staff at a top-end hotel or resident expatriates where the best nearby medical facilities are, and in an emergency contact your embassy.

There are numerous well-stocked pharmacies in Maputo; upcountry, all provincial capitals have at least one or two. These will invariably carry chloroquine and sometimes Fansidar (both for malaria) and other basics, though it's best to bring whatever you think you may need from home. Malarone ranges from difficult to impossible to find in-country, except sometimes through a hospital with a doctor's prescription. Always check the expiry date before buying medications, especially in smaller towns. We've given some suggested dosages in this section, but they are for emergency use only. Correct diagnosis is vital.

There is a high risk of contracting HIV from infected blood transfusions. The **BloodCare Foundation** (www.bloodcare.org.uk) is a useful source of safe, screened blood, which can be transported to any part of the world within 24 hours.

INFECTIOUS DISEASES

Following are some of the diseases that are found in Mozambique, though with a few basic preventative measures, it's unlikely that you'll succumb to any.

Cholera

Cholera is usually only a problem during natural or artificial disasters (eg war, floods or earthquakes), although small outbreaks can possibly occur at other times. Travellers are rarely affected. Cholera is caused by a bacteria and spread via contaminated drinking water. The main symptom is profuse watery diarrhoea, which causes debilitation if fluids are not replaced quickly. An oral cholera vaccine is available in the USA, but it is not particularly effective. Most cases of cholera can be avoided by careful selection of good drinking water and by avoiding potentially contaminated food. Treatment is by fluid replacement (orally or via a drip), but sometimes antibiotics are needed. Self-treatment is not advised.

Dengue Fever (Break-bone Fever)

Dengue fever is spread through the bite of the mosquito. It causes a feverish illness with headache and muscle pains similar to those experienced with a bad, prolonged attack of influenza. There might be a rash. Self-treatment: paracetamol and rest.

Diphtheria

Diphtheria is spread through close respiratory contact. It usually causes a temperature and a severe sore throat. Sometimes a membrane forms across the throat and a tracheostomy is needed to prevent suffocation. Vaccination is recommended for those likely to be in close contact with the local population in infected areas. More important for long stays than for short-term trips. The vaccine is given as an injection alone or with tetanus and lasts 10 years.

Filariasis

Tiny worms migrating in the lymphatic system cause filariasis. The bite from an infected mosquito spreads the infection. Symptoms include localised itching and swelling of the legs and/or genitalia. Treatment is available.

Hepatitis A

Hepatitis A is spread through contaminated food (particularly shellfish) and water. It causes jaundice and, although it is rarely fatal, it can cause prolonged lethargy and delayed recovery. If you've had hepatitis A, you shouldn't drink alcohol for up to six months afterwards, but once you've recovered, there won't be any long-term problems. The first symptoms include dark urine and a yellow colour to the whites of the eyes. Sometimes a fever and abdominal pain might be present. Hepatitis A vaccine (Avaxim, VAQTA, Havrix)

HEALTH

is given as an injection: a single dose will give protection for up to a year, and a booster after a year gives protection for 10 years. Hepatitis A and typhoid vaccines can also be given as a single dose vaccine, hepatyrix or viatim.

Hepatitis B

Hepatitis B is spread through infected blood, contaminated needles and sexual intercourse. It can also be spread from an infected mother to the baby during childbirth. It affects the liver, causing jaundice and occasionally liver failure. Most people recover completely, but some people might be chronic carriers of the virus, which could lead eventually to cirrhosis or liver cancer. Those visiting high-risk areas for long periods or those with increased social or occupational risk should be immunised. Many countries now routinely give hepatitis B as part of the routine childhood vaccination. It is given singly or can be given at the same time as hepatitis A (hepatyrix).

A course will give protection for at least five years. It can be given over four weeks or six months.

HIV

Human immuno-deficiency virus (HIV), the virus that causes acquired immune deficiency syndrome (AIDS), is a major problem in Mozambique, with infection rates averaging about 12.5% nationwide, but much higher – well over 20% – in some areas. The virus is spread through infected blood and blood products, by sexual intercourse with an infected partner and from an infected mother to her baby during childbirth and breastfeeding. It can be spread through 'blood to blood' contacts, such as with contaminated instruments during medical, dental, acupuncture and other body-piercing procedures, and through sharing used intravenous needles. At present there is no cure; medication that might keep the disease under control is available, but these drugs are too expensive for the overwhelming majority of Mozambicans and are not readily available for travellers either. If you think you might have been infected with HIV, a blood test is necessary; a three-month gap after exposure and before testing is required to allow antibodies to appear in the blood.

Malaria

This is the most serious risk in Mozambique. There are thriving populations of malaria-carrying mosquitoes throughout the country, and taking prophylaxis or otherwise protecting yourself from bites is very important. Infection rates are higher during the rainy season, but the risk exists year-round and it is extremely important to take preventative measures, even if you will just be in the country for a short time.

Malaria is caused by a parasite in the bloodstream spread via the bite of the female Anopheles mosquito. There are several types of malaria, falciparum malaria being the most dangerous type and the predominant form in Mozambique. Infection rates vary with season and climate, so check out the situation before departure. Unlike most other diseases regularly encountered by travellers, there is no vaccination against malaria. However, several different drugs are used to prevent malaria and new ones are in the pipeline. Up-to-date advice from a travel-health clinic is essential as some medication is more suitable for some travellers than others. The pattern of drug-resistant malaria is changing rapidly, so what was advised several years ago might no longer be the case.

Malaria can present in several ways. The early stages include headaches, fevers, generalised aches and pains, and malaise, which could be mistaken for flu. Other symptoms can include abdominal pain, diarrhoea and a cough. Anyone who develops a fever in a malarial area should assume malarial infection until a blood test proves negative, even if you have been taking antimalarial medication. If not treated, the next stage could develop within 24 hours, particularly if falciparum malaria is the parasite: jaundice, then reduced consciousness and coma (also known as cerebral malaria) followed by death. Treatment in hospital is essential and the death rate might still be as high as 10% even in the best intensive-care facilities.

Many travellers are under the impression that malaria is a mild illness, that treatment is always easy and successful, and that taking antimalarial drugs causes more illness through side effects than actually getting malaria. In Mozambique and elsewhere in the region, this is unfortunately not true. Side effects of the medication depend on the drug being taken. Doxycycline can cause heartburn and indigestion; mefloquine (Larium) can cause anxiety attacks, insomnia and nightmares, and (rarely) severe psychiatric disorders; chloroquine can cause nausea and hair

---

ANTIMALARIAL A TO D

A Awareness of the risk. No medication is totally effective, but protection of up to 95% is achievable with most drugs, as long as other measures have been taken.

B Bites – avoid at all costs:

- Sleep in a screened room, use a mosquito spray or coils and sleep under a permethrin-impregnated net at night. Light-weight travel-style nets are not available in Mozambique, so buy one before leaving home.

- Cover up in the evenings and at night with long trousers and long sleeves, preferably with permethrin-treated clothing. Light-coloured clothing is best.

- Apply appropriate repellent to all areas of exposed skin in the evenings. While prolonged overuse of DEET-containing repellents may be harmful, especially to children, its use is considered preferable to being bitten by disease-transmitting mosquitoes.

- Avoid perfumes, aftershave and heavily scented soaps.

C Chemical prevention (ie antimalarial drugs) is usually needed in malarial areas. Expert advice is needed as resistance patterns can change, and new drugs are in development. Not all antimalarial drugs are suitable for everyone. Most antimalarial drugs need to be started at least a week in advance and continued for four weeks after the last possible exposure to malaria.

D Diagnosis. If you have a fever or flu-like illness within a year of travel to a malarial area, malaria is a possibility, and immediate medical attention is necessary.

---

loss; proguanil can cause mouth ulcers; and Malarone is very expensive. The side effects are not universal and can be minimised by taking medication correctly (eg with food). Also, some people should not take a particular antimalarial drug (eg people with epilepsy should avoid mefloquine, and doxycycline should not be taken by pregnant women or children younger than 12).

If you decide that you really do not wish to take antimalarial drugs, you must understand the risks and be obsessive about avoiding mosquito bites. Use nets and insect repellent, and report any fever or flu-like symptoms to a doctor as soon as possible. Some people advocate homeopathic preparations against malaria, such as Demal200, but as yet there is no conclusive evidence that this is effective and many homeopaths do not recommend their use.

People of all ages can contract malaria and falciparum causes the most severe illness. Repeated infections might result eventually in less serious illness. Malaria in pregnancy frequently results in miscarriage or premature labour. Adults who have survived childhood malaria have developed immunity and usually only develop mild cases of malaria; most Western travellers have no immunity at all. Immunity wanes after 18 months of non-exposure, so even if you have had malaria in the past and used to live in a malaria-prone area, you might no longer be immune.

If you will be away from major towns, it's worth considering taking standby treatment, although this should be seen as emergency treatment only and not as routine self-medication. It should be used only if you will be far from medical facilities and have been advised about the symptoms of malaria and how to use the medication. If you do resort to emergency self-treatment, medical advice should be sought as soon as possible to confirm whether the treatment has been successful. In particular you want to avoid contracting cerebral malaria, which can be fatal in 24 hours. Self-diagnostic kits, which can identify malaria in the blood from a finger prick, are available in the West and are a worthwhile investment.

The risks from malaria to both mother and foetus during pregnancy are considerable. Unless good medical care can be guaranteed, travel in Mozambique while pregnant should be discouraged unless essential.

Meningococcal Meningitis

Meningococcal infection is spread through close respiratory contact and is more likely in crowded situations, such as dormitories, buses and clubs. Infection is uncommon in travellers. Vaccination is recommended for long stays and is especially important towards the end of the dry season. Symptoms include a fever, severe headache, neck stiffness and a red rash. Immediate medical treatment is necessary.

The ACWY vaccine is recommended for all travellers in sub-Saharan Africa. This vaccine is different from the meningococcal meningitis C vaccine given to children and adolescents in some countries; it is safe to be given both types of vaccine.

Poliomyelitis

Generally spread through contaminated food and water. It is one of the vaccines given in childhood and should be boosted every 10 years, either orally (a drop on the tongue) or as an injection. Polio can be carried asymptomatically (ie showing no symptoms) and could cause a transient fever. In rare cases it causes weakness or paralysis of one or more muscles, which might be permanent.

Rabies

Rabies is spread by receiving the bites or licks of an infected animal on broken skin. It is always fatal once the clinical symptoms start (which might be up to several months after an infected bite), so postbite vaccination should be given as soon as possible. Postbite vaccination (whether or not you've been vaccinated before the bite) prevents the virus from spreading to the central nervous system. Animal handlers should be vaccinated, as should those travelling to remote areas where a reliable source of postbite vaccine is not available within 24 hours. Three preventive injections are needed over a month. If you are infected and have not been vaccinated, you will need a course of five injections starting 24 hours, or as soon as possible, after the injury. If you have been vaccinated, you will need fewer postbite injections and have more time to seek medical help.

Schistosomiasis (Bilharzia)

This disease is spread by flukes (minute worms) that are carried by a species of freshwater snail. The flukes are carried inside the snail, which then sheds them into slow-moving or still water. The parasites penetrate human skin during paddling or swimming and then migrate to the bladder or bowel. They are passed out via stool or urine and could con-

taminate fresh water, where the cycle starts again. Paddling or swimming in suspect freshwater lakes (including many parts of Lake Niassa) or slow-running rivers should be avoided. In some cases there may be no symptoms; in other cases, there might be a transient fever and rash, and advanced cases might have blood in the stool or urine. A blood test can detect antibodies if you might have been exposed and treatment is then possible in specialist travel or infectious-disease clinics. If not treated the infection can cause kidney failure or permanent bowel damage. It is not possible for you to directly infect others.

Trypanosomiasis (Sleeping Sickness)

Spread via the bite of the tsetse fly. It causes a headache, fever and eventually coma. There is an effective treatment.

Tuberculosis (TB)

Tuberculosis is spread through close respiratory contact and occasionally through infected milk or milk products. BCG vaccination is recommended for those likely to be mixing closely with the local population, although it gives only moderate protection against TB. It is more important for long stays than for short-term stays. Inoculation with the BCG vaccine is not available in all countries. It is given routinely to many children in developing countries. The vaccination causes a small permanent scar at the site of injection, and is usually given in a specialist chest clinic. It is a live vaccine and should not be given to pregnant women or immuno-compromised individuals.

TB can be asymptomatic, only being picked up on a routine chest X-ray. Alternatively, it can cause a cough, weight loss or fever, sometimes months or even years after exposure.

Typhoid

This is spread through food or water contaminated by infected human faeces. The first symptom is usually a fever or a pink rash on the abdomen. Sometimes septicaemia (blood poisoning) can occur. A typhoid vaccine (typhim Vi, typherix) will give protection for three years. In some countries, the oral vaccine Vivotif is also available. Antibiotics are usually given as treatment and death is rare unless septicaemia occurs.

Yellow Fever

Mozambique does not require you to carry a certificate of yellow-fever vaccination unless you're arriving from an infected area – a requirement which is vigilantly enforced, and which includes neighbouring Tanzania. However, it is still often requested at points of entry, and is recommended for almost all visitors by the **Centers for Disease Control & Prevention** (www.cdc.gov).

Yellow fever is spread by infected mosquitoes. Symptoms range from a flu-like illness to severe hepatitis (liver inflammation) jaundice and death. The yellow-fever vaccination must be given at a designated clinic and is valid for 10 years. It is a live vaccine and must not be given to immuno-compromised or pregnant travellers.

TRAVELLERS' DIARRHOEA

Although it's not inevitable that you will get diarrhoea while travelling in Mozambique, it's certainly very likely. Diarrhoea is the most common travel-related illness and sometimes can be triggered by simple dietary changes. To help prevent diarrhoea, avoid tap water, only eat fresh fruits and vegetables if cooked or peeled, and be wary of dairy products that might contain unpasteurised milk. The small plastic bags of water sold on street corners are best avoided. Also take care with fruit juice, particularly if water may have been added. Milk in many up-country restaurants is made from reconstituted milk powder, which is safe if it's been made with boiled or mineral water.

With its excellent fruits and fresh produce, and seafood-based cuisine, Mozambique can be quite healthy as far as diet is concerned. Yet while freshly cooked food can often be a safe option, plates or serving utensils might be dirty, so be selective when eating food from street vendors (make sure that cooked food is piping hot all the way through). If you develop diarrhoea, be sure to drink plenty of fluids, preferably an oral rehydration solution containing water (lots), and some salt and sugar. A few loose stools don't require treatment, but if you start having more than four or five stools a day, you should start taking an antibiotic (usually a quinoline drug, such as ciprofloxacin or norfloxacin) and an anti-diarrhoeal agent (such as loperamide) if you are not within easy reach of a toilet. If diarrhoea is bloody, persists for more than 72 hours or is accompanied by fever, shaking chills or severe abdominal pain, seek medical attention.

Amoebic Dysentery

Contracted by eating contaminated food and water, amoebic dysentery causes blood and mucus in the faeces. It can be relatively mild and tends to come on gradually, but seek medical advice if you think you have the illness as it won't clear up without treatment (which is with specific antibiotics).

Giardiasis

This, like amoebic dysentery, is caused by ingesting contaminated food or water. The illness usually appears a week or more after exposure to the offending parasite. It might cause only a short-lived bout of typical travellers' diarrhoea, but it can also cause persistent diarrhoea. Ideally, seek medical advice if you suspect you have giardiasis, but if you are in a remote area you could start a course of antibiotics.

ENVIRONMENTAL HAZARDS
Heat Exhaustion

This condition occurs following heavy sweating and excessive fluid loss with inadequate replacement of fluids and salt, and is particularly common in hot climates when taking unaccustomed exercise before full acclimatisation. Symptoms include headache, dizziness and tiredness. Dehydration is already happening by the time you feel thirsty – aim to drink sufficient water to produce pale, diluted urine. Self-treatment: fluid replacement with water and/or fruit juice, and cooling by cold water and fans. The treatment of the salt-loss component consists of consuming salty fluids as in soup and adding a little more table salt to foods than usual.

Heatstroke

Heat exhaustion is a precursor to the much more serious condition of heatstroke. In this case there is damage to the sweating mechanism resulting in an excessive rise in body temperature, irrational and hyperactive behaviour, and eventually loss of consciousness and death. Rapid cooling by spraying the body

TRADITIONAL MEDICINE   Mary Fitzpatrick

More than 80% of Mozambicans rely on traditional medicine, often because conventional Western-style medicine is too expensive, or because of prevailing cultural attitudes and beliefs. It might also be because there's no other choice: a World Health Organization survey found that although there was only one medical doctor for every 50,000 people in Mozambique, there was a *curandeiro* (traditional healer) for every 200 people.

Although some traditional remedies seem to work on malaria, sickle cell anaemia, high blood pressure and some AIDS symptoms, most healers learn their art by apprenticeship, so education (and consequently application of knowledge) is inconsistent and unregulated.

Rather than attempting to stamp out traditional practices, or simply pretend they aren't happening, a positive step has been an attempt to regulate traditional medicine by creating healers' associations, such as the Associação dos Médicos Tradicionais de Moçambique (Ametramo; see boxed text, p32). Among other things, Ametramo is working to obtain more formalised education for its members, and training them in HIV/AIDS prevention and treatment in ways that are compatible with Western medicine. Yet, in the short term, it remains unlikely that even a basic level of conventional Western-style medicine will be made available to all Mozambicans. Traditional medicine, on the other hand, will almost certainly continue to be widely practised.

with water and fanning is ideal. Emergency fluid and electrolyte replacement is usually also required by intravenous drip.

Insect Bites & Stings

Mosquitoes might not always carry malaria or dengue fever, but they (and other insects) can cause irritation and infected bites. To avoid these, take the same precautions as you would for avoiding malaria. Use DEET-based insect repellents. Excellent clothing treatments are also available; mosquitoes that land on treated clothing will die.

Bee and wasp stings cause real problems only to those who have a severe allergy to the stings (anaphylaxis). If you are one of these people, carry an 'epipen' – an adrenaline (epinephrine) injection, which you can give yourself. This could save your life.

Sandflies are found in some areas. They usually only cause a nasty itchy bite, but they can carry a rare skin disorder called cutaneous leishmaniasis. Prevention of bites with DEET-based repellents is sensible.

Bed bugs are often found in hostels and cheap hotels. They lead to very itchy, lumpy bites. Spraying the mattress with crawling-insect killer after changing bedding will get rid of them.

Scabies is also frequently found in cheap accommodation. These tiny mites live in the skin, particularly between the fingers. They cause an intensely itchy rash. The itch is easily treated with malathion and permethrin lotion from a pharmacy; other members of the household also need treating to avoid spreading scabies, even if they do not show any symptoms.

Snake & Scorpion Bites

Do not walk barefoot, or stick your hand into holes or cracks. However, 50% of people bitten by venomous snakes are not actually injected with poison (envenomed). If bitten by a snake, do not panic. Immobilise the bitten limb with a splint (such as a stick) and apply a bandage over the site, with firm pressure – similar to bandaging a sprain. Do not apply a tourniquet, or cut or suck the bite. Get medical help as soon as possible so antivenene can be given if needed.

Scorpions are frequently found in arid areas. They can cause a painful bite that is sometimes life-threatening. If bitten by a scorpion, take a painkiller. Medical treatment should be sought if collapse occurs.

Water

Avoid drinking tap water in Mozambique unless it has been boiled, filtered or chemically disinfected (such as with iodine tablets). Never drink from streams, rivers and lakes. It's also best to avoid drinking from pumps and wells – some do bring pure water to the surface, but the presence of animals can still contaminate supplies.

Language

CONTENTS

Portuguese is the official language of Mozambique. It is widely spoken in larger towns, less so in rural areas. Mozambique's numerous African languages, all of which belong to the Bantu family, can be divided into three groups: Makhuwa-Lomwe languages, spoken by more than 33% of the population, primarily in the north; Sena-Nyanja languages in the centre and near Lake Niassa; and Tsonga languages in the south. The exact number of languages spoken in Mozambique has not been established, but it is estimated that there are at least nine, and perhaps as many as 16. Outside southern resorts and the areas bordering Zimbabwe and Malawi, English is not widely spoken. In northern Cabo Delgado and Niassa provinces near the Tanzanian border, Swahili is frequently heard and is often more useful than Portuguese. See p202 for a few Swahili essentials. For a more in-depth language guide, check out Lonely Planet's *Portuguese* phrasebook. For a food and drink glossary, see p40.

PORTUGUESE

PRONUNCIATION

The sounds in Portuguese are quite similar to those found in English, and the pronunciation guides (explained in the lists on the

---

LOCAL GREETINGS

While learning some Portuguese will greatly facilitate your travels in Mozambique, learning a few words in one of the local languages is even better. Grammar books and the like are difficult to find. Bookshops in Maputo have the best selection, though even there the choice is limited. Your best bet is to arrange a tutor, but in the meantime a few greetings and basic phrases will be warmly received.

Changana (also called Tsonga) is one of the most useful languages in Maputo and southern Mozambique.

Good morning.	*lixile* (li·*shee*·le)
Good afternoon.	*lipelile*
Thank you.	*kanimambo*
Goodbye.	*salani*

In the far north near Lake Niassa, most people speak Nyanja.

Good morning.	*mwaka bwanji*
Good afternoon.	*mwalonqedza*
Thank you very much.	*zikomo kwambile*
Goodbye.	*ine de likupita*

The main languages in central Mozambique are Sena and Ndau. To greet someone in Sena, say *magerwa*. In Ndau, it's *mawata*. In and around Chimoio, you will also hear Manyika with the greeting *mangwanani*.

In much of Nampula and Cabo Delgado provinces, where major languages include Makonde and Makhuwa, the most useful greeting is *salaam'a*. In northern Cabo Delgado Swahili is useful (see p202).

---

following page) are included alongside the Portuguese phrases throughout this chapter. Read them as if you were reading English and you should have no problems being understood. Note that the stressed syllable within a word is indicated by italics.

A characteristic feature of Portuguese is the use of nasal vowel sounds. Pronounce them as if you're trying to make the sound through your nose rather than your mouth – the effect is similar to the silent '-ng' ending in English (eg in 'singing'). In our pronunciation guides, 'ng' after a vowel is used to indicate a nasal sound.

LANGUAGE

Vowels

a	among
aa	father
ai	aisle
ay	say
e	bet
ee	see
o	pot
oh	note
oo	zoo
ow	how
oy	toy

Consonants

ly	million
ng	sing (indicates that the preceding vowel is nasal)
ny	canyon
r	as in 'red' but rolled
rr	throaty, as in the French 'croissant'
sh	shot
zh	pleasure

GENDER

Portuguese nouns and adjectives have masculine and feminine forms. Their alternative endings appear in this language guide separated by a slash, with the masculine form given first (eg *obrigado/a*). Generally, a word that ends in **o** is masculine and a word ending in **a** is feminine.

ACCOMMODATION

Where's a ...?	Onde é ...?	ong·de e ...
camping ground	um parque de campismo	oong park de kang·peezh·moo
guesthouse	uma pensão	oo·ma peng·sowng
hotel	um hotel	oong oo·tel
room	um quarto	oong kwarr·too

I'd like a ... room.	Queria um quarto de ...	ke·ree·a oong kwarr·too de ...
double	casal	ka·zal
single	individual	ing·dee·vee·dwal
twin	duplo	doo·ploo

Is there ...?	Tem ...?	teng ...
a room with	um quartro com casa de	oong kwar·too kom ka·za de
a private bathroom	banho privativo	ba·nyoo pree·va·tee·voo
a safety deposit box	uma caixa de segurança	oo·ma ka·sha de se·goo·rang·sa

SWAHILI BASICS

A few basics in Swahili will be well received in northern Cabo Delgado.

Hello.	Jambo./Salama.
Welcome.	Karibu.
How are you?	Habari?
I'm fine, thanks.	Nzuri.
Goodbye.	Kwa heri.
Yes.	Ndiyo.
No.	Hapana.
Please.	Tafadhali.
Thanks (very much).	Asante (sana).

0	sifuri
1	moja
2	mbili
3	tatu
4	nne
5	tano
6	sita
7	saba
8	nane
9	tisa
10	kumi
11	kumi na moja

How much is it per ...?	Quanto custa por ...?	kwang·too koos·ta porr ...
night	uma noite	oo·ma noy·te
person	pessoa	pso·a
week	uma semana	oo·ma se·ma·na

Does it include breakfast?
Inclui pequeno almoço? — eeng·kloo·ee pee·ke·noo al·mo·soo

May I see it?
Posso ver? — po·soo verr

For (three) nights.
Para (três) noites. — pa·ra (trezh) noytsh

CONVERSATION & ESSENTIALS

Hello.	Bom dia.	bong dee·a
Hi.	Olá.	o·la
Good day.	Bom dia.	bong dee·a
Good evening.	Boa noite.	bo·a noy·te
See you later.	Até logo.	a·te lo·goo
Goodbye.	Adeus.	a·dyoos
Yes.	Sim.	seeng
No.	Não.	nowng
Please.	Por favor.	poor fa·vorr
Thank you (very much).	(Muito) Obrigado/a.	(mweeng·too) o·bree·ga·doo/a
You're welcome.	De nada.	de na·da

May I?	Da licensa.	da lee·seng·sa
Excuse me.	Com licença.	kong lee·seng·sa
Sorry.	Desculpe.	desh·kool·pe
What's your name?	Como se chama?	ko·moo se sha·ma
My name is ...	Chamo-me ...	sha·moo·me ...
How are you?	Como está?	ko·moo shta
Fine, and you?	Tudo bem, e tu?	too·doo beng e too
Pleased to meet you.	Prazer.	pra·zerr
Where are you from?	De onde é?	de ong·de e
I'm from ...	Sou (da/do/de) ...	soh (da/do/de) ...
May I take a photo (of you)?	Posso tirar(-lhe) uma foto?	po·soo tee·rarr(·lye) oo·ma fo·too

DIRECTIONS

Where's ...?
Onde fica ...?   ong·de fee·ka ...

Can you show me (on the map)?
Pode mostrar-me (no mapa)?   pod moos·trarr·me (noo ma·pa)

How far is it?
Qual a distância daqui?   kwal a dees·tan·see·a da·kee

How do I get there?
Como é que eu chego aí?   ko·moo e ke e·oo she·goo a·ee

Turn left/right.
Vire à esquerda/direita.   veer a skerr·da/dee·ray·ta

near ...	perto ...	perr·too ...
on the corner	na esquina	na shkee·na
straight ahead	em frente	eng frengt

north	norte	nort
south	sul	sool
east	este	esht
west	oeste	oo·esht

EATING OUT

I'm (a) vegetarian.
Eu sou vegetariano/a.   e·oo soh ve·zhe·ta·ree·a·noo/a

I don't eat meat.
Não como carne.   nowng ko·moo kaar·ne

I'll have a beer, please.
Vou tomar uma cerveja.   vo too·mar oo·ma ser·ve·zha

What would you recommend?
O que é que recomenda?   oo ke e ke rre·koo·meng·da

without/with chilli
sem/com piri-piri   seng/kong pee·ree pee·ree

That was delicious!
Isto estava delicioso!   eesh·too shtaa·va de·lee·see·o·zoo

The bill, please.
A conta, se faz favor.   a kong·ta se faz fa·vorr

EMERGENCIES

Help!
Socorro!   soo·ko·rroo

It's an emergency.
É uma emergência.   e oo·ma e·merr·zheng·sya

I'm lost.
Estou perdido/a.   shtoh perr·dee·doo/a

Where are the toilets?
Onde ficam os lavabos?   ong·de fee·kam oos la·va·boos

Go away!
Vai-te embora!   vai·te eng·bo·ra

Call a doctor!
Chame um médico!   sham oong me·dee·koo

Call an ambulance!
Chame uma ambulância!   sham oo·ma am·boo·lan·sya

Call the police!
Chame a polícia!   sham a poo·lee·see·a

I'd like (a/the) ..., please.	Queria ..., por favor.	ke·ree·a ... poor fa·vorr
local speciality	uma especialidade local	oo·ma shpe·see·a·lee·daa·de loo·kaal
menu (in English)	um menu (em inglês)	oong me·noo (enq eeng·lesh)

I'm allergic to ...	Eu sou alérgico/a ...	e·oo soh a·ler·zhee·koo/a a ...
nuts	oleaginosas	o·lee·a·zhee·no·zash
peanuts	amendoins	a·meng·doyngsh
seafood	marisco	ma·reesh·koo
shellfish	crustáceos	kroosh·taa·se·oosh

HEALTH

I'm ill.
Estou doente.   shtoh doo·eng·te

I've been vomiting.
Tenho estado a vomitar.   ta·nyoo shta·doo a voo·mee·tarr

I need a doctor (who speaks English).
Preciso de um médico (que fale inglês).   pre·see·zoo de oong me·dee·koo (ke fal eeng·glesh)

Where's the nearest ...?	Onde fica ... mais perto?	on·de fee·ka ... ma·ees perr·to
dentist	o dentista	oo deng·teesh·ta
doctor	o médico	oo me·dee·koo
hospital	o hospital	oo osh·pee·tal
medical centre	a clínica médica	a klee·nee·ka me·dee·ka

I feel ...	Estou com ...	shtoh kong ...
dizzy	tonturas	tong·too·ras
nauseous	naúseas	now·shas

antiseptic	antiséptico	an·tee·*sep*·tee·koo
asthma	asma	azh·ma
contraceptives	anticoncepcional	an·tee·kon·*sep*·syoo·nal
diarrhoea	diarréia	dee·a·*ray*·a
fever	febre	febr
malaria	malaria	ma·*la*·ree·a
pain	dores	dorsh
painkillers	analgésicos	a·nal·*zhe*·zee·koos

I'm allergic to ...	Sou alérgico/a à ...	soh a·lerr·*zhee*·koo/a a ...
antibiotics	antibióticos	ang·tee·*byo*·tee·koos
aspirin	aspirina	ash·pee·*ree*·na
bees	abelhas	a·*be*·lyas
peanuts	amendoins	a·meng·*doyngs*
penicillin	penicilina	pe·nee·see·*lee*·na

LANGUAGE DIFFICULTIES

Do you speak English?
Fala inglês?   fa·la eeng·*glesh*
Does anyone here speak English?
Alguém aqui fala inglês?   al·geng a·*kee* fa·la eeng·*glesh*
I (don't) understand.
(Não) Entendo.   (nowng) eng·*teng*·doo
Could you please write it down?
Pode por favor escrever num papel?   po·de porr fa·*vorr* es·kre·*verr* noom pa·*pel*

NUMBERS

1	um	oong
2	dois	doys
3	três	tresh
4	quatro	kwa·troo
5	cinco	seeng·koo
6	seis	saysh
7	sete	set
8	oito	oy·too
9	nove	nov
10	dez	desh
11	onze	ongz
12	doze	doz
13	treze	trez
14	quatorze	ka·torrz
15	quinze	keengz
16	dezesseis	dze·saysh
17	dezesete	dze·set
18	dezoito	dzoy·too
19	dezenove	dze·nov
20	vinte	veengt
21	vinte e um	veengt e oong
30	trinta	treeng·ta
40	quarenta	kwa·reng·ta
50	cinquenta	seeng·kweng·ta

60	sessenta	se·seng·ta
70	setenta	steng·ta
80	oitenta	oy·teng·ta
90	noventa	noo·veng·ta
100	cem	sang
200	duzentos	doo·zeng·toosh
1000	mil	meel

SHOPPING & SERVICES

What time does ... open?
A que horas abre ...?   a ke *o*·ras *a*·bre ...
I'd like to buy ...
Queria comprar ...   ke·*ree*·a kom·*prarr* ...
How much is it?
Quanto custa?   kwang·too *koosh*·ta
That's too expensive.
É muito caro.   e *mweeng*·too ka·roo

Where's a/the ...?	Onde fica ...?	ong·de *fee*·ka ...
bank	um banco	oom *ban*·koo
... embassy	a embaixada do/da ...	a eng·bai·*sha*·da doo/da ...
foreign-exchange office	uma loja de câmbio	oo·ma *lo*·zha de *kam*·byoo
market	um mercado	oom merr·*ka*·doo
pharmacy	uma farmácia	oo·ma far·*ma*·sya
police station	o posto de polícia	oo *pos*·too de poo·*lee*·see·a
post office	o correio	oo koo·*ray*·oo

Can I pay by ...?	Posso pagar com ...?	po·soo pa·*garr* kom ...
credit card	cartão de crédito	karr·*towng* de *kre*·dee·too
travellers cheque	traveler cheque	tra·ve·*ler* shek

I want to buy ...	Quero comprar ...	ke·roo kom·*prarr* ...
a phone card	um cartão telefónico	oong kar·*towng* te·le·*fo*·nee·koo
stamps	selos	se·loosh

Where can I ...?	Onde posso ...?	ong·de po·soo ...
change a travellers cheque	trocar traveler cheques	troo·*karr* tra·ve·*ler* she·kes
change money	trocar dinheiro	troo·kar dee·*nyay*·roo
check my email	ver o meu e-mail	ver oo me·oo ee·*mayl*
get internet access	aceder à internet	a·se·*der* a een·terr·*net*

TIME & DATES

What time is it?	*Que horas são?*	ke o·ras sowng
It's (ten) o'clock.	*São (dez) horas.*	sowng (desh) o·ras
yesterday	*ontem*	*ong*·teng
today	*hoje*	ozh
this morning	*esta manhã*	esh·ta ma·*nyang*
this afternoon	*esta tarde*	esh·ta tard
tonight	*esta noite*	esh·ta noyt
tomorrow	*amanhã*	a·ma·*nyang*
Monday	*segunda-feira*	sgoon·da·*fay*·ra
Tuesday	*terça-feira*	terr·sa·*fay*·ra
Wednesday	*quarta-feira*	kwarr·ta·*fay*·ra
Thursday	*quinta-feira*	keeng·ta·*fay*·ra
Friday	*sexta-feira*	saysh·ta·*fay*·ra
Saturday	*sábado*	sa·ba·doo
Sunday	*domingo*	doo·*meeng*·goo

TRANSPORT
Public Transport

Which ... goes	*Qual o ... que*	kwal oo ... ke
to (...)?	*vai para (...)?*	vai *pa*·ra (...)
(ferry) boat	*barco (de*	*barr*·koo (de
	travessia)	tra·*ve*·sya)
bus	*autocarro/*	ow·too·*kaa*·rroo/
	machibombu	ma·*shee*·bom·bu
train	*comboio*	kom·*boy*·oo
truck	*chapa(-cem)*	*sha*·pa(·seng)
When's the ...	*Quando sai o*	*kwang*·doo sai oo
(bus)?	*... (autocarro)?*	... (ow·too·*ka*·rroo)
first	*primeiro*	pree·*may*·roo
last	*último*	*ool*·tee·moo
next	*próximo*	*pro*·see·moo

What time does it get to ...?
Que horas chega a ...?   ke o·ras *she*·ga a ...

A ... ticket to (...).
Um bilhete para (...).   oong bee·*lyet pa*·ra (...)

Please take me to (this address).
Leve-me para (esta   *le*·ve·me *pa*·ra (esh·ta
morada), por favor.   moo·*ra*·da) porr fa·*vorr*

Private Transport

I'd like to hire	*Queria*	ke·*ree*·a
a/an ...	*alugar ...*	a·loo·*garr* ...
4WD	*um quatro*	oom *kwa*·troo
	por quatro	por *kwa* troo
bicycle	*uma*	*oo*·ma
	bicicleta	bee·see·*kle*·ta
car	*um carro*	oong *ka*·rroo
motorbike	*uma*	*oo*·ma
	motocicleta	mo·too·see·*kle*·ta

Is this the road to ...?
Esta é a estrada   esh·ta e a es·*tra*·da
para ...?   *pa*·ra ...

Where's a petrol/gas station?
Onde fica um posto   ong·de *fee*·ka oong *pos*·too
de gasolina?   de ga·zoo·*lee*·na

Please fill it up.
Enche o depósito,   *en*·she oo de·*po*·see·too
por favor.   porr fa·*vorr*

I'd like ... litres.
Meta ... litros.   *me*·ta ... *lee*·troosh

diesel	*diesel*	*dee*·sel
petrol	*combustível*	kom·boo·*stee*·vel
(unleaded)	*(sem chumbo)*	(seng *shoom*·boo)
a lift/ride	*uma boleia*	*oo*·ma bo·*lai*·a
avenue	*avenida*	a·ve·*nee*·da
beach	*praia*	*prai*·a
beach road	*marginal*	mar·zhee·*nal*
countryside	*mato*	*ma*·to
roadside stall	*barraca*	ba·*ra*·ka
street	*rua*	*roo*·a
track	*pista*	*pee*·sta

The car has broken down at ...
O carro avariou em ...   oo *ka*·rroo a·*va*·ryo eng ...

The car won't start.
O carro não pega.   oo *ka*·rroo nowng *pe*·ga

I need a mechanic.
Preciso de um   pre·*see*·soo de oong
mecânico.   me·*ka*·nee·koo

I have a puncture/flat tyre.
Tenho um furo no   *ta*·nyoo oong *foo*·roo noo
pneu.   pe·*ne*·oo

I've run out of petrol/gas.
Fiquei sem gasolina.   fee·*kay* seng ga·zoo·*lee*·na

I've had an accident.
Sofri um acidente.   soo·*free* oong a·see·*deng*·te

Also available from Lonely Planet:
Portuguese phrasebook

LANGUAGE

Glossary

See the food glossary on p40 for culinary terms.

ablutions block – a building containing a toilet, shower and washing facilities, found mainly in camping grounds and caravan parks
aldeamento – fortified village complex
ANC – African National Congress
assimilados – a colonial-era population classification, referring to Mozambicans who adopted Portuguese customs and ways

baía – bay
bairro – neighbourhood, area or section of town
baixa – the lower-lying area of a city or town; in coastal Mozambique this often means the part of the city near the port and the baixa is frequently synonymous with 'commercial district'
barraca – market stall or food stall; also a thatched shelter at camping grounds, often with plug points
BIM – Banco Internacional de Moçambique

camião, camiões – truck(s)
capitania – maritime office
capulana – sarong, colourful cloth worn by Mozambican women around their waists
casa de cultura – house of culture; cultural centre found in each provincial capital; the *casas de cultura* exist to promote traditional culture and are good a source of information about traditional music and dance performances in the area
casal – room with a double bed
cascata – waterfall
casita – bungalow
cerveja – beer
chapa – any public transport that is not a bus or truck; usually refers to converted minivans or pick-ups; derived from 'chapa cem' meaning 'tin 100', in reference to the original price for a ride (Mtc100) in the days of the old metical
correios – post office
curandeiro – traditional healer

dhow – traditional Swahili Arabic sailing boat
dia da cidade – city or town day; a holiday commemorating the town's founding, often celebrated with parades and song and dance performances
duplo – room with twin beds; see also *casal*

EN1 – Estrada Nacional 1; the main south–north highway; also often N1
EN6 – Estrada Nacional 6; the highway running from Beira west towards Chimoio and the Zimbabwe border; also often N6
estrada – road, highway

feira – trading fair
feticeiro – witch doctor
fortaleza – fort
Frelimo – Frente pela Libertação de Moçambique; Mozambique Liberation Front; current ruling political party

galabiyya – man's full-length robe

ilha – island
indígenas – indigenous people; refers to a colonial-era population classification
inselbergs – isolated rocky hills common to parts of southern Africa; literally means 'island mountains'

LAM – Linhas Aéreas de Moçambique; the national airline
lobola – bride price or dowry
lago – lake

machamba – small farm plot
machibombo – bus
makwaela – a type of dance popular in the south, characterised by a cappella singing accompanied by foot percussion
mapiko – a ritual dance of the Makonde in northern Mozambique; *mapiko* also refers to the wooden masks worn by the dancer
marginal – beach road
marrabenta – Mozambique's national music, with an upbeat style and distinctive beat
mbila – African marimba or xylophone used by the Chopi people, made from strips of resonant wood with various-sized gourds for sound boxes; plural *timbila*
mercado – market
metical, meticais – Mozambican currency
migração – immigration
minas de terra – landmines; usually simply called *minas*
monte(s) – mountain(s)

nyanga – panpipes; also the name of a dance in which the dancer plays the panpipes

parque nacional – national park
pastelaria – shop selling pastries, cakes and often light meals as well
pensão, pensões – inexpensive hotel(s)
piri-piri – hot pepper (a common addition to food in many parts of the country)
pousada – hotel or inn, usually a step up from a *pensão*
praça – square
praia – beach
prazeiro – *prazo* holder
prazo – privately owned agricultural estates allocated by the Portuguese crown; the *prazo* system was used by the Portuguese between the 17th and early 20th centuries in an attempt to strengthen control in Mozambique
profeta – spirit medium or diviner

refresco – soft drink, soda
régulo – chief, traditional leader
Renamo – Resistência Nacional Moçambicana; Mozambican National Resistance; the main opposition party
reserva – reserve
rondavel – round African-style huts or buildings
rua – street

TDM – Telecomunicações de Moçambique; the national telecommunications company
timbila – see *mbila*
tufo – a dance of Arabic origin, common on Mozambique Island and along the northern coast

xima – maize- or cassava-based staple, usually served with a sauce of beans, vegetables or fish; also known as *upshwa* in some areas

Behind the Scenes

THIS BOOK

This 3rd edition of Lonely Planet's *Mozambique* guidebook was researched and written by Mary Fitzpatrick. The previous two editions were also written by Mary Fitzpatrick. The Health chapter was written by Dr Caroline Evans. This guidebook was commissioned in Lonely Planet's Melbourne office, and produced by the following:

Commissioning Editors Sasha Baskett, Will Gourlay, Shawn Low

Coordinating Editors Martine Power, Dianne Schallmeiner

Coordinating Cartographer Alex Leung

Coordinating Layout Designer Cara Smith

Managing Editors Liz Heynes, Annelies Mertens

Managing Cartographers Adrian Persoglia, Amanda Sierp

Managing Layout Designers Sally Darmody, Laura Jane

Assisting Editor Justin Flynn

Assisting Cartographers Andras Bogdanovits, Xavier Di Toro, Diana Duggan

Cover Research Kate Slattery, lonelyplanetimages.com

Internal Image Research Sabrina Dalbesio, lonelyplanetimages.com

Project Managers Chris Girdler, Glenn van der Knijff

Language Content Branislava Vladisavljevic

Thanks to Lucy Birchley, Indra Kilfoyle, Lisa Knights, Wayne Murphy, Naomi Parker, Lyahna Spencer

THANKS
MARY FITZPATRICK

Many people helped me during the research and writing of this edition. In particular, I'd like to thank Sidney Bliss and David Ankers in Maputo; Vasco Galante at Gorongosa National Park; Jasper van Straaten, Lesley Sitch, Bart van Straaten and Rebecca Phillips Marques in Pemba; Juliana da Silva Soares in Quelimane; and Pamela and Riley Ganz in Ile. Special thanks also to Andrew Kingman and Stefaan Dondeyne in Chimoio for their assistance with the Chimanimani research; the staff at Imperial Tete for their patience, assistance and kindness; Lúrio Empreendimentos in Lichinga; and Bryan Pesti and all the other PCVs who so generously helped me out with time and information. Last but not least, a big thank you to Rick, Christopher and Dominic for their enthusiasm, support, patience, company, fun and good humour during the research and writing of this book.

CONTRIBUTING AUTHORS

Dr Caroline Evans wrote the Health chapter. Having studied medicine at the University of London, Caroline completed general-practice training in Cambridge. She is the medical adviser to Nomad Travel Clinic, a private travel-health

THE LONELY PLANET STORY

Fresh from an epic journey across Europe, Asia and Australia in 1972, Tony and Maureen Wheeler sat at their kitchen table stapling together notes. The first Lonely Planet guidebook, *Across Asia on the Cheap,* was born.

Travellers snapped up the guides. Inspired by their success, the Wheelers began publishing books to Southeast Asia, India and beyond. Demand was prodigious, and the Wheelers expanded the business rapidly to keep up. Over the years, Lonely Planet extended its coverage to every country and into the virtual world via lonelyplanet.com and the Thorn Tree message board.

As Lonely Planet became a globally loved brand, Tony and Maureen received several offers for the company. But it wasn't until 2007 that they found a partner whom they trusted to remain true to the company's principles of travelling widely, treading lightly and giving sustainably. In October of that year, BBC Worldwide acquired a 75% share in the company, pledging to uphold Lonely Planet's commitment to independent travel, trustworthy advice and editorial independence.

Today, Lonely Planet has offices in Melbourne, London and Oakland, with over 500 staff members and 300 authors. Tony and Maureen are still actively involved with Lonely Planet. They're travelling more often than ever, and they're devoting their spare time to charitable projects. And the company is still driven by the philosophy of *Across Asia on the Cheap*: 'All you've got to do is decide to go and the hardest part is over. So go!'

clinic in London, and is also a GP specialising in travel medicine. Caroline has acted as expedition doctor for Raleigh International and Coral Cay expeditions.

OUR READERS

Many thanks to the travellers who used the last edition and wrote to us with helpful hints, useful advice and interesting anecdotes:

Cindy Acutt, Thalia Arzoglou, Caroline Bell, Elizabeth Cohen, Paul Dobson, Neelke Doorn, Anna Gueorguieva, Simone Gunkel, Anna Jonkman, Susana Jose, Tamara Kahn, Daan Marcellis, Floor Oudshoorn, Rochelle Pincini, Marcelina Porsteinsson, Charlie Radclyffe, Christie Rowe, Johann Seeberg-Elverfeldt, Dan Taylor, Kimon Theodossis, Kim Verheul, Per Vilhelmsson

ACKNOWLEDGMENTS

Many thanks to the following for the use of their content:

Globe on title page ©Mountain High Maps 1993 Digital Wisdom, Inc.

LONELY PLANET AUTHORS

Why is our travel information the best in the world? It's simple: our authors are passionate, dedicated travellers. They don't take freebies in exchange for positive coverage so you can be sure the advice you're given is impartial. They travel widely to all the popular spots, and off the beaten track. They don't research using just the internet or phone. They discover new places not included in any other guidebook. They personally visit thousands of hotels, restaurants, palaces, trails, galleries, temples and more. They speak with dozens of locals every day to make sure you get the kind of insider knowledge only a local could tell you. They take pride in getting all the details right, and in telling it how it is. Think you can do it? Find out how at **lonelyplanet.com**.

SEND US YOUR FEEDBACK

We love to hear from travellers – your comments keep us on our toes and help make our books better. Our well-travelled team reads every word on what you loved or loathed about this book. Although we cannot reply individually to postal submissions, we always guarantee that your feedback goes straight to the appropriate authors, in time for the next edition. Each person who sends us information is thanked in the next edition and the most useful submissions are rewarded with a free book.

To send us your updates – and find out about Lonely Planet events, newsletters and travel news – visit our award-winning website: **lonelyplanet.com/contact**.

Note: we may edit, reproduce and incorporate your comments in Lonely Planet products such as guidebooks, websites and digital products, so let us know if you don't want your comments reproduced or your name acknowledged. For a copy of our privacy policy visit lonelyplanet.com/privacy.

Index

GREENDEX

The following attractions, tours and accommodation choices have been selected by the author because they demonstrate an active sustainable-tourism policy. Some are involved in environmental or wildlife protection, some foster authentic interaction and greater understanding between travellers and their local hosts, while others are community-owned or make a point of employing local people. If you think we've omitted someone who should be listed, or if you disagree with our choices, contact us via www.lonelyplanet.com/feedback. For more information, see www.lonelyplanet.com/responsibletravel.

MAP LEGEND

ROUTES

Tollway	Mall/Steps
Freeway	Tunnel
Primary	Pedestrian Overpass
Secondary	Walking Tour
Tertiary	Walking Tour Detour
Lane	Walking Trail
Under Construction	Walking Path
Unsealed Road	Track
One-Way Street	

TRANSPORT

Ferry	Rail
Bus Route	

HYDROGRAPHY

River, Creek	Canal
Intermittent River	Water
Swamp	Lake (Dry)
Mangrove	Lake (Salt)
Reef	

BOUNDARIES

International	Regional, Suburb
State, Provincial	Ancient Wall
Disputed	Cliff
Marine Park	

AREA FEATURES

Airport	Land
Area of Interest	Mall
Beach, Desert	Market
Building	Park
Campus	Reservation
Cemetery, Christian	Rocks
Cemetery, Other	Sports
Forest	Urban

POPULATION

◯ CAPITAL (NATIONAL)	◉ CAPITAL (STATE)
● Large City	◯ Medium City
● Small City	◯ Town, Village

SYMBOLS

Sights/Activities
- Beach
- Castle, Fortress
- Christian
- Diving, Snorkeling
- Islamic
- Monument
- Museum, Gallery
- Point of Interest
- Pool
- Ruin

Eating
- Eating

Drinking
- Drinking

Entertainment
- Entertainment

Shopping
- Shopping

Sleeping
- Sleeping
- Camping

Transport
- Airport, Airfield
- Border Crossing
- Bus Station
- Cycling, Bicycle Path
- General Transport
- Parking Area
- Petrol Station
- Taxi Rank

Information
- Bank, ATM
- Embassy/Consulate
- Hospital, Medical
- Information
- Internet Facilities
- Police Station
- Post Office, GPO
- Telephone
- Toilets

Geographic
- Lighthouse
- Lookout
- Mountain, Volcano
- National Park
- Shelter, Hut

LONELY PLANET OFFICES

Australia (Head Office)
Locked Bag 1, Footscray, Victoria 3011
☎ 03 8379 8000, fax 03 8379 8111
talk2us@lonelyplanet.com.au

USA
150 Linden St, Oakland, CA 94607
☎ 510 250 6400, toll free 800 275 8555
fax 510 893 8572
info@lonelyplanet.com

UK
2nd fl, 186 City Rd,
London EC1V 2NT
☎ 020 7106 2100, fax 020 7106 2101
go@lonelyplanet.co.uk

Published by Lonely Planet
ABN 36 005 607 983

© Lonely Planet 2010

© photographers as indicated 2010

Cover photograph: Dhow on the water on a picture-perfect morning, Pemba, Mozambique, Jaco Janse van Rensburg/Alamy. Many of the images in this guide are available for licensing from Lonely Planet Images: lonelyplanetimages.com.

Printed by Fabulous Printers Pte Ltd
Printed in Singapore

Mixed Sources
Product group from well-managed forests and other controlled sources
www.fsc.org Cert no. SGS-COC-005002
© 1996 Forest Stewardship Council
FSC

Although the authors and Lonely Planet have taken all reasonable care in preparing this book, we make no warranty about the accuracy or completeness of its content and, to the maximum extent permitted, disclaim all liability arising from its use.